EMOTIONAL HERITAGE

Visitor Engagement at Museums and Heritage Sites

Laurajane Smith

Routledge
Taylor & Francis Group

LONDON AND NEW YORK

First published 2021
by Routledge
2 Park Square, Milton Park, Abingdon, Oxon OX14 4RN

and by Routledge
52 Vanderbilt Avenue, New York, NY 10017

Routledge is an imprint of the Taylor & Francis Group, an informa business

© 2021 Laurajane Smith

The right of Laurajane Smith to be identified as author of this work has been asserted by them in accordance with sections 77 and 78 of the Copyright, Designs and Patents Act 1988.

All rights reserved. No part of this book may be reprinted or reproduced or utilised in any form or by any electronic, mechanical, or other means, now known or hereafter invented, including photocopying and recording, or in any information storage or retrieval system, without permission in writing from the publishers.

Trademark notice: Product or corporate names may be trademarks or registered trademarks, and are used only for identification and explanation without intent to infringe.

British Library Cataloguing-in-Publication Data
A catalogue record for this book is available from the British Library

Library of Congress Cataloging-in-Publication Data
Names: Smith, Laurajane, author.
Title: Emotional heritage : visitor engagement at museums and heritage sites / Laurajane Smith.
Other titles: Visitor engagement at museums and heritage sites
Description: Abingdon, Oxon ; New York, NY : Routledge, 2020. | Includes bibliographical references and index.
Identifiers: LCCN 2020010318 (print) | LCCN 2020010319 (ebook) | ISBN 9781138888647 (hbk) | ISBN 9781138888654 (pbk) | ISBN 9781315713274 (ebk)
Subjects: LCSH: Museums—Psychological aspects. | Cultural property—Psychological aspects. | Historic sites—Psychological aspects. | Museum visitors—Interviews. | Museums—Political aspects. | Cultural property—Political aspects. | Historic sites—Political aspects. | Museums—Social aspects. | Cultural property—Social aspects. | Historic sites—Social aspects.
Classification: LCC AM7 .S635 2020 (print) | LCC AM7 (ebook) | DDC 069—dc23
LC record available at https://lccn.loc.gov/2020010318
LC ebook record available at https://lccn.loc.gov/2020010319

ISBN: 978-1-138-88864-7 (hbk)
ISBN: 978-1-138-88865-4 (pbk)
ISBN: 978-1-315-71327-4 (ebk)

Typeset in Bembo
by Apex CoVantage, LLC

EMOTIONAL HERITAGE

Emotional Heritage brings the issues of affect and power in the theorisation of heritage to the fore, whilst also highlighting the affective and political consequences of heritage-making.

Drawing on interviews with visitors to museums and heritage sites in the United States, Australia and England, Smith argues that obtaining insights into how visitors use such sites enables us to understand the impact and consequences of professional heritage and museological practices. The concept of registers of engagement is introduced to assess variations in how visitors use museums and sites that address national or dissonant histories and the political consequences of their use. Visitors are revealed as agents in the roles cultural institutions play in maintaining or challenging the political and social status quo. Heritage is, Smith argues, about people and their social situatedness and the meaning they, alongside or in concert with cultural institutions, make and mobilise to help them address social problems and expressions of identity and sense of place in and for the present.

Academics, students and practitioners interested in theories of power and affect in museums and heritage sites will find *Emotional Heritage* to be an invaluable resource. Helping professionals to understand the potential impact of their practice, the book also provides insights into the role visitors play in the interplay between heritage and politics.

Laurajane Smith is Director of the Centre for Heritage and Museum Studies, at the Australian National University, Canberra. She is Founding President of the Association of Critical Heritage Studies, the editor of the *International Journal of Heritage Studies*, the cogeneral editor of Routledge's *Key Issues in Cultural Heritage* and is best known for her previous book *Uses of Heritage* (2006, Routledge).

ALISON DRAKE, MBE, MA
1950–2019

CONTENTS

List of figures ix
List of tables x
Acknowledgements xi
List of abbreviations xiii

    Introduction 1

PART I
Heritage, politics and emotion 17

  1 Critical realist heritage studies: agency, reflexivity and materiality 19

  2 Reconsidering heritage and identity: the politics of recognition and the affective practices of heritage 38

  3 Registers of engagement 62

PART II
Methods and quantitative findings 83

  4 Methods 85

  5 Overall findings and national comparisons 111

6 Genres of museums and heritage sites: comparisons 141

7 Demographic variables and visitor responses 161

PART III
Emotional heritage: themes and performances **175**

8 Reassessing learning: changing views and deepening understanding 177

9 Performing reinforcement and affirmation: 'it just reinforces a lot of the stuff I think' 196

10 Emotional banality and heritage-making: the banality of grandiloquence revisited 218

11 Intergenerational communication and connection 240

12 Heritage and the politics of recognition 259

13 Heritage, privilege and the politics of misrecogntion 285

Conclusion 304

References *311*
Index *331*

FIGURES

8.1	Visitors engaging with the interview interactive in the *Getting In* exhibition, Immigration Museum, Melbourne	190
9.1	Bronze statue of a stockman, titled 'The Ringer', with saddle over shoulder and bridle in hand outside of the Stockman's Hall of Fame, Longreach, Queensland	204
12.1	Montpelier train station, James Madison's Montpelier, restored to the period of segregation	277
13.1	James Madison's Montpelier, with the wooden frames of the slave quarters	291

TABLES

4.1	Sites in England: genre, numbers interviewed and year of interviews	88
4.2	Sites in Australia and the United States: genre, numbers interviewed and year of interviews	92
5.1	Visitor occupations per nation	113
5.2	Visitor ethnicity and overseas tourist frequencies per nation	114
5.3	Reasons for visiting	117
5.4	What does the word 'heritage' mean?	118
5.5	Whose history or heritage are you visiting here?	122
5.6	Are you part of the history represented here?	122
5.7	Is there any aspect of your personal identity to which this exhibition speaks to or links?	124
5.8	How does it make you feel to visit this place?	125
5.9	What experiences do you value on visiting this place?	128
5.10	What does being here mean to you?	129
5.11	Are there any messages about the heritage or history of Australia/America/England that you take away from this place?	131
5.12	What meaning, if any, does an exhibition like this have for contemporary Australia/America/England?	135
5.13	Is there anything you have read/seen/heard today that has changed your views on the past or the present?	136
6.1	Visitor ethnicity and overseas tourist frequencies per genre	143

ACKNOWLEDGEMENTS

There are literally thousands of people to thank. I am most grateful to all the 4,502 people who generously stopped and allowed one of the members of the various research teams or myself to interview them. I am also grateful to the directors of the 45 institutions (see Chapter 4) that allowed me to survey their visitors and to the staff who agreed to be interviewed. The Australian Research Council funded the Australian and American phase of the project (FT0992071); the Research School of Humanities and the Arts, the Australian National University, provided funding to transcribe interviews. The English data was variously funded by the Arts and Humanities Research Council, Knowledge Transfer Fellowship (1807 Commemorated), the British Academy and the University of York. I want to thank the members of the 1807 Commemorated project, in particular, Geoff Cubitt, Kalliopi Fouseki and Ross Wilson. The majority of the interview transcriptions was done by Pam Ward, although Kalliopi Fouseki and Ross Wilson transcribed the '1807 Commemorated' material.

Thank you also to those who read drafts of various chapters, in particular, Alexandra Dellios, Scott Poynting, Kate Bowan, Paul Pickering, Rachael Coghlan and Diana James, and of course, any errors are my responsibility. Drafts of many of the chapters have been delivered at numerous seminars and conferences around the globe, and I thank the audiences of these for their feedback. The long-suffering people at Routledge and, in particular, Heidi Lowther, Katie Wakelin and Molly Marler dealt so understandingly with the lengthy delays to this book. Thank you, Bruce Pennay, for your support and encouragement.

I am, as always, indebted to Gary Campbell. Gary has had input into this project from the very start, helping to develop the interview schedule, undertaking interviews and working as my coding companion in the various mammoth stages of coding and recoding of the data. He has critically read various drafts and discussed ideas and concepts with me. Without his support and input, this book would most certainly not have been written.

Finally, this book is dedicated to the memory of Alison Drake, teacher, activist, inspiration, a force of nature and friend.

ABBREVIATIONS

Abbreviations used as prefixes to visitor interviews:

AWM	Australian War Memorial, Canberra
BECM	*Breaking the Chains*, British Empire and Commonwealth Museum, Bristol
BC	Burton Constable, historic house, England
BH	Brodsworth Hall, England
BM	*Inhuman Traffic: The Business of the Slave Trade*, British Museum
BMAG	Birmingham Museum and Art Gallery
CH	Country House study, 2004
EI	Ellis Island, New York City
F	*The Star-Spangled Banner: The Flag That Inspired the National Anthem*, National Museum of American History
H	Hermitage, Tennessee
HH	Harewood House
IL	Youngstown Historical Center of Industry and Labour, Ohio
IMM	Immigration Museum, Melbourne
ISM	International Slavery Museum, Liverpool
JANM	Japanese American National History Museum in Los Angeles
JMM	James Madison's Montpellier, Virginia
LH	Lanyon Homestead, Australian Capital Territory
LR	Stockman's Hall of Fame & Outback Heritage Centre, Longreach, Queensland
MADE	Museum of Australian Democracy at Eureka
MK	Mt Kembla Heritage Centre
MLD	*London, Sugar and Slavery*, Museum of London Docklands
NCM	National Coal Mining Museum, Wakefield, England
NCRM	National Civil Rights Museum, Memphis, Tennessee

NCWHM	National Cowboy & Western Heritage Museum, Oklahoma City
NHM	Nordic Heritage Museum, Seattle
NMA	First Australians Gallery, National Museum of Australia
NMM	National Maritime Museum, Greenwich, London
OMG	Old Melbourne Gaol, Australia
PM	Mashantucket Pequot Museum, Connecticut
RH	Rouse Hill House and Farm, Sydney
RS	Rivers of Steel National Heritage Area, Pittsburgh
SJM	*Slavery at Jefferson's Monticello: Paradox of Liberty*, National Museum of American History
TM	The Lower East Side Tenement Museum, New York City
TN	Temple Newsam, historic house, England
TP	Tolpuddle Martyrs Museum, Dorchester
U	Uluṟu-Kata Tjuṯa National Park
VH	Vaucluse House, Sydney
W	*The Price of Freedom: Americans at War*, National Museum of American History
WC	Museum of Work and Culture, Woonsocket Rhode Island
WH	Wilberforce House
Y	Yellowstone National Park

Additional Abbreviations

AHD	Authorised Heritage Discourse
NMAH	National Museum of American History
RoE	Registers of Engagement

INTRODUCTION

The day following the American Independence Day, 5 July 2012, was blisteringly hot in New York City, and I was standing on the forecourt of the Ellis Island National Museum of Immigration watching visitors come and go. I watched as a woman, and who I assumed was her daughter, enter the museum to exit a short time later. The older woman sat on one of the benches overlooking New York Harbor, while her daughter returned to the museum. I approached the woman to ask if I could interview her. Having agreed, she told me she was 97 years old, that she had lived in New York City all her life, but that this was her very first visit to Ellis Island. She was not much interested in the museum displays, she explained; rather, she had chosen to sit looking out at the water because she was 'waiting for her father'. She went on to quickly state that I was not to think she was crazy, senile or anything, but that her father, whom she had loved and respected very much, had passed through Ellis Island in 1901, and the island had been a very important site for him. She had never been to the island, but now, despite the heat, thought it was time to come, as she repeated, to 'wait for her father'.

The interview finished, I was walking away to ponder approaching yet another visitor to interview when I realised that I was crying. I was having a strong emotional response to what I had just heard. During the thousands of interviews I have conducted with visitors to museums and other sites of heritage across three different countries, I have had many people break down and cry or become speechless with emotions too complex to voice, and this was the one interview that had reduced me to the same state.

My encounter with this woman highlights several central issues that I explore in this book. First, it illustrates that museums may be used in quite active and complex ways by visitors; indeed, it suggests that the people we call 'visitors' may use museums and other sites of heritage in diverse ways that escape those traditionally identified in the literature. Second, it hints that the fascination with education and learning underlying much of the literature and policy practices in heritage and museum studies may be missing a rather complex point about how the public uses such places. Third, it indicates that emotion may be a key aspect of visiting. While I, then age 50, was quite emotional in response to what the woman was saying to me and the issue of mortality that she obliquely raised, the woman herself at 97 was quite calm as she contemplated her mortality and remembered her father. She was concerned only that I understood what she was trying to communicate to me about what she was doing at Ellis Island and that I would not dismiss her as 'crazy'. The point for her, it seemed, was that she wanted to demonstrate to me, but perhaps also to herself, that through her contemplation of her father – waiting for him – she was calm. *Being* calm, as well as taking the opportunity to contemplate and remember, was central to the meaning of her visit.

Why do people visit museums and heritage sites? On the surface, this is a relatively simple question and is addressed as such in academic discussion, policy and practice. Two core assumptions have traditionally framed responses: people come to either learn or to recreate. Both assumptions tend to define visitors as relatively passive consumers of curatorial or interpretative messages, and they tend to foreclose the possibility that other things may be occurring during individual and collective visits to such places. This book seeks to move beyond those limitations and reports the findings of 4,502 interviews with visitors to 45 different history and culture museums and heritage sites in the United States, Australia and England. Sites for interview were chosen either because they offered narratives of national history or dealt with dissonant and contested histories, addressing what Simon (2011) referred to as 'difficult knowledge'. In the context of this book 'museums' and 'heritage sites' (buildings, archaeological sites, etc) are all theatres of memory and places of heritage-making, and I draw no real theoretical or analytical distinction between the two. However, for practical purposes 'museums' refer either to the individual institutions listed in Chapter 4 or, more generally, to those institutions who define themselves as such and collect and display artefacts associated with human history and culture (i.e. the research has not engaged with science museums). To be clear, I am not talking about all types of heritage sites or museums, but more specifically about those sites of heritage-making that deal with social history.

The research aimed to find out what sort of memory and identity work people undertook while visiting different genres of sites in the three different national contexts and whether there were national differences evident. The interview schedule was designed with a set of core open-ended questions that would allow people to raise organically issues that were important to, or made sense to them, rather than using predominantly closed questions that tested the researcher's assumptions. This has resulted in an extensive qualitative database. Mixed methods research, using both quantitative and qualitative analysis, has been undertaken to verify aspects of the findings and to provide depth and nuance. There is a long history of research within heritage and museum studies that examine how museums or other heritage sites construct a sense of the past and define its meaning for the present and social aspirations for the future. This study looks at how people undertaking the act of visiting, individually and collectively, engage in the same process. The focus is foremost on the visitor and how they are constructing the meaning of their visit, and less so on the museum, exhibition or site as such, though I do make a distinction between genres of sites. This is not to say that curatorial and interpretive content is not important, as the findings suggest particular genres of sites elicit certain responses, but rather to ask what does visiting do. My starting assumption was that people as visitors have agency and are not passive audiences for curatorial and interpretive messages. If visitors have agency, it follows that it might be useful to consider and explore the partnership in meaning-making between museums/heritage sites and their visitors. My focus is thus on the neglected side in this partnership of meaning-making. Museums and heritage sites do not have social impact without their audiences; there is an interrelationship between the work that museums and heritage sites do in constructing and telling stories and histories and how they are then understood and used by visitors. It is generally understood that not all visitors will necessarily take away the curatorial or interpretive message that staff intend, but what does this mean? What meaning is being taken away, and what social impact or consequence does that have?

These are the core issues that instigated the research; I wanted to know what heritage-making people, as visitors, were engaged in at different sites; how they used those sites in their heritage-making and what the social consequences of this might be. Thus, my focus was not to cover the well-trodden ground of analysing exhibition content and curatorial intent and their assumed impact on visitors, but rather, how people used whatever it was they understood themselves to be visiting. Many assumptions are made about what people do and do not do at sites. Research that has tended to focus on science museums has suggested it is largely learning (Falk and Dierking 1992, 2000), while research from the Smithsonian Institute has argued it is about reinforcing entrance narratives and expectations (Doering and Pekarik 1996; Pekarik et al. 1999; Pekarik and Schreiber 2012). There were two overall surprises for me arising from this research. The first was the degree to which visitors *chose* not to engage in learning and the second was the degree to which the visit was predicated on emotionally investing in the meanings people both brought with them to the site and then reinforced during the visit. While some visitors did indeed engage in learning, as Pekarik and Schreiber (2012: 495) found, "only visitors already attuned to seeking these experiences are likely to find them". Indeed, while learning was a particular discourse that visitors themselves used, often about groups other than the one with which the visitor themselves identified, it was not something with which most visitors chose to engage. Visitors often used the language of learning to lend authority to the heritage meanings they were themselves re-creating or performing by their visit, but these meanings were not learnt; rather, they were brought to the site they were visiting for validation. As Doering and Pekarik (1996) found, what they defined as a person's 'entrance narrative' was most frequently authenticated and reinforced by a visit. Similarly, this study has also found that people, as visitors, most frequently engaged in various performances of reinforcing their existing beliefs, feelings, knowledge and understanding – they were emotionally *investing* in their prior commitments. A range of strategies could also be deployed to maintain these narratives if they were challenged or otherwise jeopardised by curatorial or interpretive content.

I have noted that visitors, and indeed museums and heritage sites, are engaged in 'heritage-making'. This draws on the idea that I have previously developed, that heritage is a process, an act of using the past to help make sense of the present and resource aspirations for the future (Smith 2006). Heritage is something that is done rather than possessed; it is an action and an intent rather than a 'thing' or a 'site'. Macdonald (2013) has referred to this process as 'past presencing'. In the first part of this book, I develop my previous arguments to theorise heritage as an emotionally charged action, or what Wetherell (2012) defines as an 'affective practice', to performatively use the past to construct meaning in and for the present – in other words, to engage in heritage-making. I have also interchangeably referenced museums, individual exhibitions and places traditionally referred to as 'heritage sites' as 'sites'. I draw no real distinction between museums and heritage sites, as both are theatres of memory (Samuel 1994) and sites of heritage-making. I have also, problematically, used the word 'visitor', a term that tends to imply a fleeting or distanced encounter with items that many 'visitors' perceived as their heritage. I discuss this unsatisfactory term in Chapter 3, and although I continue to use it, I do so with an understanding that visitors make choices and are active participants in the social and political meanings that they cocreate with museums and heritage sites and that these performances have social consequences outside of the 'visit'.

In developing the idea of the performative nature of heritage, the study identifies several different heritage performances in which people engage. These performances were identified both through quantitative and qualitative analysis of the interview data. The quantitative analysis was important, as analytical attention can often be arrested by the complexity and affective qualities of some responses and uses of sites, such as the woman's use of Ellis Island. The quantitative analysis illustrated not only the breadth of responses but also the frequencies in which they occurred, illustrating what may be referred to as 'performances of reinforcement' to be most common. However, the qualitative analysis allowed not only for the identification of different forms of these performances but also an assessment of their consequences. The performances are elaborated in more detail ahead; however, each performance has its particular resonances and affective qualities. One of the key issues emerging from the data is that heritage sites and museums are places where people choose to go to feel and to be emotional and that these emotions are then used to justify, inform or sometimes challenge the meanings people bring with them and take away from their visit:

> I don't go to museums for education; I can read material on the internet and in books, I come for emotional reasons. Coming for education makes no sense.
>
> (NCRM61: male, 55–64, retired health care, African American)[1]

Understanding the emotional content of the visit reveals the complex ways in which visitors react to curatorial messages and the sites themselves. Part of my goal is also to attempt to untangle the suites of affective/emotional responses and to explore how they impede or facilitate visitor engagement and the role these responses play in framing the moments of heritage-making in which visitors were immersed. To facilitate this, I develop the idea of 'registers of engagement'. This concept attempts to identify the different modes, scales and intensities with which different visitors engage with museums and heritage sites. The educational and learning literature often stresses that deep engagement is more significant than shallow engagement, arguing that the deeper the engagement, the more likely it is that learning will occur, where learning is measured as some form of change or deepening of understanding (M. Smith 2018). However, at least in the context of museums and heritage sites, this interrelationship is not so straightforward as has been assumed. Visitor engagement can range between very shallow, to the point of banality, to the very deeply emotionally and cognitively engaged. However, shallow engagement can do as much important cultural and political work as deep engagement can, and while deep engagement can generate intense emotions, it does not necessarily follow, however, that this will lead to critical insight for the visitor. Chapter 3 develops the idea of registers of engagement, and the concept is offered as a heuristic device to help understand and measure the personal, social, emotional and ideological contexts and consequences of the performances of heritage-making that visitors undertake. It needs to be noted that the measurements of intensities and registers of engagement were not derived against an arbitrary scale, but were all measured *relatively* within the range of engagements found within the database. As such, the specific modes and intensities of engagement may be specific to the dataset; however, the concept offers a way of understanding how visitors interact with sites without either predetermining or dismissing that the interaction is framed by learning or leisure/recreation. In short, the aim is to broaden the conceptual map about not only what meanings visitors construct but also how they actively do so and what the social and political consequences of these practices might be.

Four overall heritage performances are identified in the data: these are performances of reinforcement, intergenerational communication, recognition and misrecognition. Additionally, practices or engagements with education and learning also occurred, although these instances were the least frequent, and I return to this issue. People could engage in single or multiple performances during any one visit; however, performances of reinforcement were dominant. Learning, when this occurred, did so alongside heritage-making performances, excepting that the performance of misrecognition worked to actively preclude learning, while performances of reinforcement were more passively antithetical to learning. It is important to note that the terms reinforcement, confirmation or their synonyms were not used in the interview schedule. However, these terms commonly occurred when people talked about the meaning of the visit or the messages they took away or how the site made them feel and so forth. This performance of reinforcement was found across all genres of sites in all three countries, and interviewees reported that their visit was often about reinforcing not only what they already knew, but more importantly, what they already *felt* about particular topics and issues and their contemporary relevance.

What was reinforced could be either progressive or conservative readings of the past and its meaning for the present; nonetheless, there was a range of complex nuances across different performances of reinforcement. Within the performance of reinforcement, a particular performance of affirmation can be singled out; this is a performance that tends to seek validation of progressive/liberal values and meanings and is far more emotionally complex than the kinds of performances that reinforce national identity and ideologically conservative heritage meanings that were frequently encountered at national museums and sites (Chapter 9). A point to stress here is that different performances tended to mobilise different registers of engagement. Further, different emotional registers or 'signatures' underlie different performances, and certain performances tended to dominate at particular genres of site. For example, at museums and heritage sites that discuss the histories of immigration or labour, the performances were often focused on intergenerational communication and displayed critically and emotionally engaged elements of the registers of engagement. At national sites, overall, the registers of engagement (as a relative measure across the entire database) were often deeply engaged celebrations of reinforcement of nation. Genres of national or dissonant sites also generated their emotional tenor and associated performances (Chapter 6). For instance, at house museums, engagement was often quite shallow and based on emotions of comfort that, overall, produced politically conservative acts of reinforcement. Conversely, sites commemorating war histories were often emotionally 'flat' and less intense than other national sites while reinforcing values and narratives of historical gratitude and nationhood. On the other hand, sites of Indigenous culture and history, for example, tended to see a higher frequency of emotionally and cognitively complex performances of recognition.

National comparisons between the United States, Australia and England identified some differences in performances or their specific meaning to a visitor. However, the similarities between the nations outweighed the differences (Chapter 5). Where differences were most notable was both across the different genres of site, not only between the categories 'national' and 'dissonant' sites but also across the specific genres of sites within these two categories. In short, sites of national story-making tended to be dominated by performances of reinforcement, or of misrecognition when curatorial or interpretive interventions challenged performances of reinforcement. Other performances of intergenerational communication and recognition could also occur. At sites of dissonant history, performances of intergenerational communication and recognition were notable, while misrecognition was far less frequent than at national sites. Reinforcement also occurred at dissonant sites, but more often as politically progressive 'affirmation'.

Important differences also emerged across visitor demographics. The visitor profiles recorded at most sites in the study tended to be dominated by visitors from politically dominant ethnic groups within the three countries (i.e. Caucasian American, Anglo-Australian, White British, to use the descriptors commonly employed in the three countries), with high educational attainment and holding 'higher' socially valued occupations (Chapter 5). Overall, and in particular, at sites of national narratives, domestic visitors from dominant ethnic identities tended to be relatively cognitively uncritical and emotionally invested in and engaged in reinforcement. Overseas tourists, less invested in national narratives, tended to be a little more critically engaged than domestic visitors from dominant ethnic backgrounds. Those from non-dominant ethnic backgrounds and, to a less clear extent, those from dominant ethnic backgrounds but with low educational attainment were, in general, on the register of engagement, undertaking even more emotionally and intellectually critical heritage work, which tended to (but was not confined to) emphasise politically progressive content. In effect, there are two additional underlying performances: a performance of privilege, which sometimes was conscious and self-critical, but on the whole was not and a performance undertaken in the context of marginalisation and misrecognition, which was innately more critical and self-conscious. These two performances underwrite and inform the four performances discussed previously, as performing privilege could underpin not only performances of reinforcement but also intergenerational communication and misrecognition (but, by definition, not recognition). While the performance based on experiences of social exclusion could underlie reinforcement (although this tended to underpin this performance as affirmation), it also informed intergenerational communication, recognition and, on occasion, misrecognition.

Janes argues that museums as institutions, to which we may add heritage sites sanctioned within the authorised heritage discourse (AHD), are keepers of the status quo. He notes that there is a persistent "tacit silence that surrounds" this role, which has yet to be successfully challenged by the cosmopolitan interventions of new museology (2016: 230). Scholars and practitioners within both new museology and the critical heritage studies movement have called for critical accountability in addressing the social and political consequence of museums and heritage sites. Any consideration of or attempts to challenge the regulatory role of museums/heritage sites in maintaining the status quo cannot, however, ignore how people, as visitors or audiences, use such sites. The interrelationship between heritage/museological professional and academic practices and the practices of people visiting work together to create heritage meanings that have material and social consequences. One of the significant performances that visitors undertook, especially at national museums, was the maintenance of and intergenerational inheritance of privilege (Chapter 11). This performance was casually and often unconsciously reinforced but was nonetheless actively defended when challenged (Chapter 13). It is also based on emotions of comfortable self-assurance and, most importantly, indifference. The affective state of indifference was reinforced to placate the fear of ambiguity and change that could occur when visitor self-assurance in their own social experience was jeopardised by cognitive dissonance toward curatorial and interpretative attempts to challenge the status quo.

As numerous studies identify, visitors to museums and heritage sites framed within the AHD consistently and overwhelmingly fall within socially privileged demographics (see Black 2012: 17f; Kinsley 2016; Chapter 5). The idea that visiting museums and other sites of heritage is an expression of Bourdieu's concept of acquiring and demonstrating cultural capital is well established in the literature, yet considering how visitors construct their sense of self and social place by their visits is often not given due consideration in assessing the regulatory role of museums. In part, this is because of the idea of Foucauldian governmentality that has framed much of the debate about the role of museums in regulating the conduct of citizens (see, in particular, Bennett 1995). The idea of governmentality, wherein particular technologies of government or forms of knowledge are used to regulate or govern conduct, establish those being governed as 'subjects' of regulation, which leaves little room for the agency of those subjects to either resist or acquiesce to such governance (Smith 2004). This is not to say that museums and heritage are not part of the processes of governing and regulating conduct and citizenship – simply that this conceptualisation tends to downplay the agency of those defined as the subjects of governance. The point to stress here, however, is that people as visitors do engage in the regulation and maintenance of the status quo – that is, they may acquiesce to or resist it. More importantly, they may even reassert it if they perceive the museum/heritage site is not living up to their expectations or fulfilling their role in the performance of reinforcement. The performance of privilege I am identifying can be situated in the historical development of museums as erudite national institutions and the development of authorised heritage as emblematic of national identity. These developments speak to particular forms of social experience and identities that tend to attract certain visitor demographics and not others. Thus, the performance of privilege is not surprising, given the dominant demographic of national museums and heritage sites framed by the AHD. It is a performance of preserving the status quo, which is continually reenacted by the interrelationship between museums/heritage sites and their communities of visitors.

The more critical performances, which push back at the regulatory role of museums/heritage sites, are found most consistently at sites of dissonance and from visitors from non-dominant ethnic backgrounds at either national or dissonant sites and are far more self-conscious and complex performances than the performance of privilege. It is these performances that have most to offer critical debates about the responsibility and critical role that museums and heritage sites could and can play. Overall, they illustrate the importance of engaging with a range of emotional responses to the past and their use in the present. There is often a hesitation to engage with emotions, and in particular, emotions that are defined as nostalgic, a hesitation that is particularly pronounced by the political left (Bonnett 2010). This hesitation misunderstands the role affect/emotions play in cognition (Ahmed 2004a; Wetherell 2012). Further, it also misunderstands the breadth and range of emotions such as nostalgia that, as Smith and Campbell (2017a) have argued, can take both progressive and reactionary forms. Rather than eschewing the emotional, the critical performances identified here, which are often but not uniformly informed by social exclusion, illustrate how particular affective states and empathetic and imaginative skills work to inform identity, make judgements and foster critical reflection on the present and the development of aspirations for the present and future. Importantly, they also illustrate that not all performances of reinforcement are about ensuring the status quo and that in affirming the history and experiences of social diversity, museums/heritage sites can play a vital role with visitors in imagining equitable and just presents and futures.

To illustrate the range of performances that visitors engaged in, and in this case, how critical performances can underpin the use of museums/heritage sites, it is useful to explore one quite complex visitor response to the question: 'Are there any messages about the heritage or history of America that you take away from this museum?' The visitor, a woman, visiting the National Civil Rights Museum, in Memphis, with her 12-year-old son, identified as a postal worker who was active in her union, and described herself, when I asked for her ethnic affiliation, as Black American. In her response, she references an exhibit that in 2012 was encountered early within the gallery titled 'Strategies for Change' and which contained, among other objects, a display case with a Klu Klux Klan hood and gown:

> It really is, just the history of it is so, to know – you know, [. . .].² And me being a union president and things, it puts me on focus. And being a parent, a parent of young kids, and a young parent, it just puts me on focus as to my kids. When I first brought my youngest son here, he'll be 13 next month, and we walked through [where] the Klu Klux Klan clothes were, I think he may have been about four. And when we came through my first thought was, 'What are white people doing in their head because they know what they did to us?' I mean, just honestly. And I'm looking around 'cos I'm astonished at that, and then, when my son walked upon the Klu Klux Klan he said, out loud, as kids do, 'Momma, whose pyjamas are those?' and everybody turned and looked at me, and I was like, 'Those aren't pyjamas.' I said, 'I'll tell you about them', and you know they're [white visitors] waiting for my answer, so we keep going, and I'm like reading this stuff to him, saying, 'And this is what they did to black people and this is what. . . ' and he burst out again, 'Who's black, mama?' And I said, 'Oh my God', and I looked at him, and you know I saw this [white] guy watching and I'm like [pause] 'You're black'. And he was like, 'No I'm not. I'm not black. I'm yellow.' And I said, 'Okay', and I remember what my pastor said: 'You don't know you're poor until you're told you're poor. You don't know you're black until you're told you're black.' He never knew he was black. So, you know, I'm like, Wow. So, when I bring him here, he learns more, and we come every year 'cos I have family down here.
>
> (NCRM53: *female, 45–54, postal worker, Black American*)

This visitor engaged in a range of performances. First, she was using the museum to remember and commemorate her own experiences in the civil rights movement, and with this remembering comes a reinforcement of her political and social values – this is a form of progressive self-conscious reinforcement, or affirmation, which was particularly strong at museums of labour, immigration and civil rights. At sites or exhibitions that represented consensus national narratives, what was remembered was often less personal, but still strongly held emotional commitments to master narratives of nation and citizenship. Nationalising narratives were frequently maintained and reinforced even in contexts where the curatorial message aimed at destabilising and challenging them.

This was her and her younger son's fourth visit to the museum, and she was using this and previous visits to pass on familial history and political values to her son. How museums were used as arenas for intergenerational communication and socialisation of children was significant. In this instance, the son was learning from his mother, supported by the museum, about familial history and values as well as about the history and relevance of the civil rights movement. Museums and heritage sites of all genres were used as cultural tools in the passing on of familial memory, knowledge and values. In some instances, the performance of visiting and where you visited was also something parents taught their children. For instance, visiting presidential houses or stately homes in all three countries was largely something people from a particular ethnic and socioeconomic background did and were engaged in passing on to their children – that is, the visit itself was a statement of belonging to a particular ethnic and class group. Further, children learned the appropriate affective state required for certain types of sites, such as reverence, pride, self-esteem, comfort and so forth. In many instances, what was also learned or communicated to children at national sites, dominated as they were by a particular demographic, was the overall performance of privilege. Thus, a nuance of intergenerational communication at certain sites was the communication or passing on of inherited privilege. Seeing people 'like yourself' at certain sites was part of, and integral to, performances of reinforcement and variants of intergenerational communication. Conversely, performances of recognition often relied on visiting sites where one might expect to encounter people unlike oneself.

The visitor had expressed, through the interview, discomfort at the presence of white visitors. In most cases, a desire to visit places where a visitor would see people like themselves was expressed by politically dominant ethnic groups such as Anglo-Australians, White British or Caucasian Americans. However, the reasons this visitor at the Civil Rights Museum is expressing distress at the presence of people unlike herself is more complex and tied to the politics of recognition. I draw, in Chapter 2, primarily on the work of Nancy Fraser to define the politics of recognition as part of pragmatic negotiations over not just social and cultural identity, but the redistribution of resources. Heritage, moreover, is implicated in the way claims for recognition and counter-assertions of misrecognition are made and legitimised or delegitimised. Performances of recognition and misrecognition occurred across all genres of site. Some visitors talked explicitly about their visit to heritage sites that were not their own as a statement or act of recognition. Other visitors cited self-respect and saw their visit to sites of their heritage as an assertion or claim for recognition. Sometimes visitors from hegemonic groups engage explicitly in recognition of themselves as the inheritors of privilege (this was particularly done at Indigenous sites) and in varying ways used their visit to certain sites to negotiate what that may mean both for themselves and other members of their society.

Others used museum displays as a form of 'social barometer' to assess the extent to which wider society was offering recognition or misrecognition of themselves and people like themselves.

The visitor, however, was engaged in a form of self-recognition. To understand her discomfort, we need to appreciate that she is passing on social and familial memories of not just discrimination, but of the civil rights movement's continuing struggles to overcome prejudice to her son, and thus, creating self-recognition of his place in US society. As Judith Butler notes, one of the problematic aspects of recognition is that it can "inscribe injury into identity and makes that a presupposition of political self-representation" and, as she goes on to warn, injury cannot then "be recast as an oppression to be overcome" (Butler and Athanasiou 2013: 87). The mother was reacting against this possibility; she was uncomfortable about the presence of whites in the museum because of the opportunity of misrecognition of self that their presence presented for her son. She did not want established ideas of recognition of African Americans to prevail; she did not want injury to be part of his self-recognition. As she noted earlier in the interview, being at the museum made her "feel good to know that there was a history for us to move forward" from (NCRM53). In effect, she is using this museum to offer self-recognition as a point from which to continue struggles for equity. However, the public arena of the museum opens up, for her at least, greater risks of misrecognition. One of the enduring ideas about museums is that they are safe places to explore complex topics (Gurian 1995, quoted in Cameron 2005: 214). For some, as this visitor illustrates, museums are not safe.

They can also be unsafe places for people who are confronted with a curatorial message that they find cognitively dissonant, and that challenges their entrance narrative, sense of self-assurance and privilege. Visitors used various emotional responses to render an unsafe or challenging museum/heritage site 'safe', to reaffirm indifference and thus continue to reinforce their entrance narrative and performance of privilege while making the concurrent choice not to learn. Several strategies were used by visitors to extricate themselves from the emotional impact of cognitive dissonance that ranged, on the register of engagement, from the passive to the very active. These registers tended to lead to performances of 'misrecognition' that actively facilitated the maintenance of privilege and indifference at the expense of acknowledging the validity of social justice claims.

But what of the issue of learning? To couch the visitor to the National Civil Rights Museum as a 'learner' and to say she was herself engaged in 'learning' is patronising. She was engaged in a range of performances: reinforcement that affirmed her commitment to the civil rights movement, "it put her on focus" as she noted as both an activist and as a parent; intergenerational communication, in this case, the passing on of values to her son; she was also asserting the validity of her self-esteem and recognition of identity as activist, mother and Black American. Yes, she used the museum as a tool for the education of her son, but to characterise her visit as about her 'learning' is to misunderstand the complexity and nuance of what she was doing. The dominant tendency both within the literature and public policy to identify what visitors do, or at least what they 'should' be doing, as learning simplifies the social and political work that visiting does.

The idea that visits should be a learning, or an educational experience, was, it must be stressed, often identified by visitors as a reason for their visit. However, when prompted to explain, the educational value tended to be largely discussed in relation to children or about groups of people other than that to which the visitor belonged, or as something that they felt they should be doing, even if they acknowledged that they were not. If learning is measured as a change of view or a deepening of understanding (Hooper-Greenhill 2007a: 31), the interview question 'Is there anything you have seen, heard or read here today that has changed your views about either the past or present?' aimed to get a sense of what it was visitors might have learned. However, only 18% of visitors said yes their views had changed, while the remainder said no, often nominating that the visit had reinforced their views. The frequency of those who said yes dropped to 10% at some national sites and increased to as much as 35% at certain dissonant sites. Of those who said yes, most were nominating they had gained more, but often minor information, rather than changing what they thought or felt. However, when a significant change or deepening of understanding occurred, learning was often triggered by intensely felt emotions combined with empathy that on the registers of engagement was both deep and entwined with imagination. Witcomb's (2015) arguments about a 'pedagogy of feeling' are important, as argued in Chapter 8, for addressing the educational mandates of museums/heritage sites and reviewing both the purpose and practices of their role in adult education. However, in addressing issues of social justice and diversity, museums/heritage sites must address and destabilise performances of misrecognition and conservative reinforcement. Acknowledging and engaging with the emotional repertoires that are invoked when histories and experiences of social privilege are challenged is vital in facilitating changes of views and understanding. So too is the role of empathy. This complex emotion and skill, measured as a register of engagement, could be shallowly experienced, which subsequently led to the maintenance of indifference, but as deeply experienced and entangled with imagination, sincerity and compassion played a vital role in helping visitors work through difficult knowledge and the negative emotions this triggered. Museums/heritage sites have the potential to be useful arenas to work through difficult emotional issues not only to inform or facilitate education but importantly to also engage in social debate. However, the emotive quality of debates about nation, citizenship, diversity and inequity require recognition and the engagement of strategies to acknowledge and constructively utilise and engage with emotional repertoires.

The study, it must be stressed, has its limitations. I am not making claims that the findings and performances identified here are universal. The research must be understood as having been undertaken at specifics sites, times and national contexts. For logistical reasons, it is confined to Anglophone and Western contexts (but see Zhang 2020). Additionally, if the reader is looking for a seamless research project with entirely like-to-like comparisons, you will be disappointed. The research was undertaken over a lengthy period, often responding to presented opportunities to undertake interviews, and there are some variations in the amount of data collected at some sites, and comparisons between the three nations and genres are by no means one-to-one. The comparisons have acknowledged limitations, and Chapter 4 details explicitly how and why the study was done so that its limitations, and how they may affect the findings, are made clear. Nonetheless, the study points to the diversity and consequences of how people undertaking the practice of visiting different types of heritage use and emotionally invest in the meaning of the past for the present.

The first part of the book outlines the theoretical framework and concepts that I use in the study. Chapter 1 outlines the idea of heritage as performance and responds to some of the dominant theoretical debates in critical heritage studies to clarify my position and conceptualisation of heritage and to stress the point that, fundamentally, heritage is about people and their social context. Chapter 2 deepens the argument about the performative nature of heritage by drawing explicitly on debates over the politics of recognition and debates over the nature of affect and emotion. I draw on the politics of recognition to extend my arguments about the political nature of heritage but also to inform the performances of both recognition and misrecognition discussed, respectively, in Chapters 12 and 13. Chapter 3 develops the idea of registers of engagement as well as defines some of the core terms, such as 'visitor', used in the study. Intensity, valence and conservative/progressive tendencies to interact with various modes of engaging, such as ideology, embodiment, remembering/forgetting, imagination, scope, time and so forth to produce registers of engagement that underpin and frame the various performances of heritage-making are elaborated.

Part II of the book details the history of the study, the sites at which interviews were undertaken and how and why the study was done (Chapter 4) as well as detailing the quantitative analysis. Chapter 5 describes the demographics of the interview population and details the descriptive statistics generated to describe the range of responses. Markers are identified that underpin or express the four specific heritage performances of reinforcement, intergenerational communication and recognition/misrecognition. The chapter also undertakes comparisons between the three countries. While there are differences between the three nations, most notably the deeper personal connections made by Americans to their heritage and the tendency of the English to be more overt in expressing their cognitive dissonance, there are far more similarities. Chapter 6 continues quantitative comparisons, cross-tabulating the categories of national and dissonant sites and specific genres within each of these categories to the descriptive statistics outlined in Chapter 5. While certain registers are not necessarily confined to specific genres, nonetheless there are registers of engagement that dominate at specific genres of site, and this tends to be consistent regardless of national contexts. This result underpins the identification of the types of performances of heritage-making that occur or dominate at different genres of site. Chapter 7 compares demographics to the results for each interview question and identifies the underpinning critical performances informed by social inequity/exclusion and the less reflexive performance of privilege and nation-making. What may be defined as a clinical variation in criticality and reflexivity emerges, as far as those from dominant ethnic backgrounds are over-represented at the banal and uncritical end of the spectrum. Overseas tourists overall and those of dominant ethnic backgrounds and low educational attainment at dissonant sites – that is, those less invested in nationalising narratives – tend to occupy the middle ground, while those from non-dominant ethnic backgrounds tend to occupy the more critical and reflexive end of the spectrum. In short, what Wertsch (2007, 2012) defines as conservative national narrative templates has the most power in framing the collective and individual remembering of those whose social and historical experience it most represents.

Part III of the book details the qualitative analysis of the four specific heritage performances. Chapter 8 address the issue of learning, identifying what the 'language of learning' does for both heritage professionals and visitors and how this counterintuitively works to facilitate conservative performances of reinforcement. The chapter, however, also enumerates the emotional repertoires that facilitated learning and the consequences of this for developing pedagogies of feeling. Chapter 9 details the range of performances of reinforcement, identifying both socially and politically conservative performances and those of progressive affirmation. The analysis is continued into Chapter 10 in a specific analysis of house museums to examine in depth the political consequences of these performances in each of the three national contexts. Chapter 11 analyses the range and diversity of performances of intergenerational communication. This performance has a range of variants and expressions from the 'imagined conversations' with absent family members to reflections on self-worth and family identity to the communication of values, identities and affective practices of visiting to younger generations. Chapter 12 develops the argument that heritage is implicated in the politics of recognition and outlines how different forms of recognition are played out at museums/ heritage sites. In particular, the idea of 'self-recognition', as either the inheritor of privilege or inequity, is argued to be foundational to the initiation and negotiation of claims and counterclaims for recognition and redistribution. Chapter 13, in detailing the performance of misrecognition, outlines the range of ways in which people attempted to preserve their entrance narratives and self-assurance in their social experiences. These performances tended to occur at national sites where specific curatorial or interpretive interventions had occurred to national narrative templates or entrance narratives (Doering and Pekarik 1996; Wertsch 2012). These were instances where visitors made active choices not to learn and to deny the advocacy and utility of the interpretive material before them. Performances of misrecognition were not a form of 'disengagement', however, but rather an active engagement and defence of performances of privilege and reinforcement.

Overall, those who visit museums/heritage sites are active agents in heritage-making, even when being quite passive on the registers of engagement. They are also agents in the roles cultural institutions have in maintaining or challenging the status quo. Heritage is about people and their social situatedness, and the meaning they, alongside or in concert with institutions such as museums, galleries, libraries, archives and heritage sites, make and bring forward to help them address social problems and expressions of identity and sense of place in and for the present. If heritage is to be understood as being more than artefacts or places, as being a performative process of making meaning for the present, then this book is a plea for scholarship and professional practice to address how people outside the heritage professions make and use heritage. If the agendas and debates for facilitating social change and activism in critical heritage studies and new museology are to be realised, engaging with how and why people use heritage – however defined – is vital. Certainly, in focusing on the materiality of heritage (as museum artefacts or collections, as sites, buildings etc), heritage meanings and social values appear easily definable and contained. Nonetheless, those meanings and values are themselves mobilised by people as they use the past to make sense of the present – this process is messy and complex – and recognising this is important for understanding the social and political phenomenon of heritage.

Notes

1 See Chapter 4 for an explanation of the descriptors, but note that occupation and ethnic identity are self-described by the interviewee and not attributed by the researcher.
2 Denotes material excised from the quote for brevity.

PART I
Heritage, politics and emotion

1
CRITICAL REALIST HERITAGE STUDIES

Agency, reflexivity and materiality

In *Uses of Heritage* (2006), I developed two core arguments. The first was that heritage was a discursive and social practice. I argued that heritage was something that was done rather than something that was possessed or 'saved', proposing that heritage was better conceptualised as a process, practice or performative activity. Ultimately, I suggested that there was no such 'thing' as heritage, but rather a set of practices tied up with the activities of remembering and commemoration that used the past to help make sense of the present. Heritage is a practice, not only in terms of professional practice but also in terms of how non-professionals practice it, which is fundamentally about negotiating the meaning and nature of social and cultural change and mediating social and cultural conflicts. My second argument stressed that heritage practices and performances were framed by particular heritage discourses, some of which were more politically powerful than others. I identified the Authorized Heritage Discourse (AHD), a hegemonic and professional discourse that stresses the nationalising values of material heritage and privileges the role of those possessing expert knowledge as stewards for all that is 'good' about the past. It has its roots in European nineteenth- and twentieth-century disciplinary debates and was both embedded in and continually authorised by national heritage agencies in Western European and other Western countries, and was internationally authorised by UNESCO and ICOMOS. I made no claims that this was the only heritage discourse nor that different versions or different authorised or dominant discourses did not exist; the primary utility of identifying this heuristic device was to question and challenge the hegemonic assumptions embedded in heritage management and conservation practices. Specifically, a central concern in identifying the AHD was to recognise other, less powerful and often ignored discourses that framed non-authorised or marginalised practices and understandings of heritage. Indeed, the tensions between subaltern heritage discourses and the AHD were a particular theme of that book. However, the tensions that underlie differing uses and meanings of heritage is developed here focussing on the performative practice of heritage-making that occurs as people visit heritage sites and museums. While the sites chosen for analysis in this book are all in many ways authorised sites, in that they have official and sanctioned status as 'heritage', my first aim is to explore the nuances and tensions that nonetheless exist as different people in different contexts 'use' such sites. My second related aim is to consider the social and political consequences and effects of these performances and practices.

Drawing on an extensive qualitative database, one of my aims is to expand on the idea that heritage is a performative practice. Two issues, which have been raised in my previous work, require further development and elaboration: affect/emotion and politics. Although *Uses of Heritage* addressed these issues, I am not satisfied that my analysis was adequately developed, nor am I entirely satisfied with how these concepts are dealt with in the wider heritage and museums literature. I believe that both concepts need to be more centrally positioned in the project of re-theorising heritage. Much is made of the observation in the heritage and museum studies literature that heritage is 'political', but what exactly is meant by that, and how can we understand the issues of power that make heritage 'political'? Additionally, the so-called affective turn in the wider humanities and social sciences has also influenced debates in heritage and museum studies in ways that, overall, I do not find particularly helpful or convincing, and that counterintuitively serves to reinforce the AHD. Thus, my aim in this and the following chapters in Part 1 of this book, is to develop my arguments about the performative nature of heritage by engaging specifically with affect/emotion and politics and, in doing so, identify what further insights they may offer in considering the phenomenon of heritage and in identifying what it is that heritage *does*.

A fundamental assumption of my work is that people matter. Finding out what people do with heritage, why they do it, and the consequences of their 'doing', should be central to critical heritage studies. A further aim in focusing on affect, emotion and politics is to centrally position people rather than things as central to heritage practice and theory. In drawing on a large body of qualitative data, my aim is to draw out what people do and say about the nature of their heritage performances while visiting heritage sites and objects. This can tell us not only about heritage as a social and political phenomenon but the work it does within society. The 'received knowledge' of the heritage sector is that 'visitors' to heritage sites are defined as learning from or being an 'audience' to, the work of heritage experts – such as curators, and those professionals involved in site interpretation and management. Following on from my aim to challenge the authority and underpinnings of the AHD, this book does not dismiss visitors/tourists by privileging material objects and sites as the first point of focus for analysis, but rather, takes visitors and tourists seriously and asks them what meanings are being made as they perform a particular type of heritage-making. Moreover, I also ask what implications particular forms of performances and practices have in wider social and political contexts. Given the importance I place on people and their experiences, it is useful at this stage to assess the heritage studies literature of the last decade and to establish why I have drawn on the particular theoretical and conceptual ideas that I do.

A critical realist heritage studies

My work has been incorrectly characterised as based on social constructivist epistemology (e.g. Albert 2013: 11; Harrison 2015: 27; Wells 2015: 252). This implies a relativist ontology, a characterisation that is, in part, a simple error of reading my work, but in some cases, a dismissive criticism. In the latter case, it tends to be linked to a sense of unease, often from archaeologists, over my attempts to disprivilege materiality (e.g. Pétursdóttir 2012; Harrison 2013, 2015). I find this an interesting critique from researchers who draw on Latour, who himself takes a Churchillian approach to social constructivism – that is, the only thing worse than social constructivism is not adopting social constructivism (Latour 2003). The argument that 'all heritage is intangible', in that heritage is a performative practice rather than simply a 'thing', has been a focus of critique. I will come back to this criticism ahead; however, it is important to re-emphasise that the ontological philosophical underlabourer of all my work is *critical realism* (Smith 2004: 60–62, 2006: 13–16). The misreading of my philosophical positioning is not an idle issue of semantics, as acknowledging the position I take is key to understanding not simply my argument but also the ethical imperatives and political agendas that drive the work. As Porpora (2015: 6) notes, critical realism is not a theory that attempts to explain anything, but rather a philosophical position that "establishes the boundaries between good and bad theorising". Being charged with being a 'constructivist' can hide and gloss over any number of suggested 'sins'. This is because what is meant by this charge is never clearly expressed or defined. The implication seems to be that I take a relativist stance, which assumes I am concerned *only* with the way social contexts influence the way heritage values and meanings are 'constructed', and that thus all readings or constructions are equally valid.

Situating my work within a critical realist ontology, a position associated with the earlier[1] work of Roy Bhaskar (1978, 1989) and more latterly with Margaret Archer (1995, 2000) and Andrew Sayer (2000), means accepting that the natural world, in this case, the material world, exists and that it exists independently of our knowledge of it. Critical realism may be seen as an attempt to bridge the claims of the relativist tendencies of extreme forms of social constructivism and various forms of realism in that it stipulates that the natural or material world may be understood in certain contexts and has implications for that understanding (Bhaskar 1978; see also Archer 1995: 19; Sayer 1992, 2000; Iosifides 2011). Relativism is rejected, and a distinction is made between ontology and epistemology so that, as Fairclough notes, a central concern is avoiding "the 'epistemic fallacy' of confusing the nature of reality with our knowledge of reality" (2005: 922). Crucially, as Fairclough goes on to argue, social research abstracts the concrete events of social life and "then 'forgets' the concrete"; however, critical realism must make the move back to the concrete (2005: 923). Thus, while critical realists may be concerned with understanding the way the social constructs knowledge and discourses, it does not forget the material or concrete; it understands that human agency has consequences. Moreover, it is understood that certain forms of knowledge and discourse have real causal powers that are continually in tension with the causal powers of social structures and practices (Fairclough, Jessop and Sayer 2002; Fairclough 2005; Elder-Vass 2010).

Critical realism underpins Critical Discourse Analysis (CDA), which in turn underpinned my arguments about the AHD (Smith 2006: 15). CDA, as a method, is explicitly concerned with identifying the links between discourse and practice and how particular discourses facilitate social change and/or maintain and legitimise ideologies and power relations (Fairclough 2003; Fairclough et al. 2004; Chouliaraki and Fairclough 2004; Fairclough and Fairclough 2013; Wetherell 2013a). CDA offers a range of techniques for analysing language and practice, and I use its underlying philosophical insights and positions to develop both the arguments about the AHD and the existence of oppositional and excluded discourses. In line with CDA, my concern with identifying the AHD was to challenge both it and the practices and power relations it frames. I have not, as is suggested by the 'constructivist' label, been interested in a Foucauldian sense of identifying and abstracting particular discourses or in pursuing solipsistic textual analysis. Rather, I am concerned with identifying and explaining the social and political context of knowledge about heritage and the ways this then sits in tensions with practices and social structures.

A particular issue for my current arguments is that of 'agency', and exploring this concept allows me to further unpack the philosophical and analytical utility of critical realism. Margaret Archer (1995, 2000, 2007) has developed important arguments about human agency and critical realist perspectives that I draw on here. In opposition to postmodernists, Archer, as with the proponents of CDA, does not "sever the relationship between language and the world"; discourse is thus never defined as 'closed' (2000: 3). Indeed, she argues that it is our interactions with the natural world, including material culture, which shape our individual sense of self and identity. Further, she argues that constructivism "impoverishes humanity" by defining us as nothing beyond what society makes us and neglects our embodied practices, as human agency is attributed only to discourse (2000: 4). This does not imply that the natural or material cultural world has its own innate 'agency' or that a sense of self exists that is "prior to, and primitive to, our society" (2000: 7). Nor does it imply that we can know the natural or material world in a value-free or theory-neutral way (Porpora 2015: 16). Rather, it explicitly acknowledges that meaning and self-consciousness is continually derived from embodied practices and interactions with the world. Archer, in reclaiming humanity from postmodern tendencies to render human action into "disembodied textualism" (2000: 2), argues that all human action is context-dependent and that humans are indeed social beings.

Further, she argues that humans "*are* simultaneously free and constrained" by the nature of social reality and that "we *also* have some awareness of it" because of human reflexivity (1995: 2, emphasis in original). Behaviour is thus not simply subject to Bourdieu's theory of *habitus*, and indeed Archer (2000) is critical of this idea, nor is behaviour simply subject to social structure, but also, and in some circumstances and contexts, attributed to conscious reflection (Elder-Vass 2010: 109–110). Change (what she calls morphogenesis) or stasis (morphostasis) in society and human behaviour is brought about by the interrelations between agency and circumstance – that is, between human actions and the real world (Archer 1995). As Porpora (2015: 118) summarises Archer's position:

> People act from social position related to other social positions and do so, although creatively, through the cultural milieu they inhabit. In the temporal process of acting, actors either reproduce or alter both or either their cultural and structural circumstances that originally bound them.

Structure, agency and culture must be separated ontologically and analytically so that how they interact may be identified (Archer 1995, 2000; Porpora 2015: 119). In disprivileging the idea of the materiality of heritage, I am specifically asking us to pay attention to the role of human agency and to the particular social contexts and material circumstances that may influence particular practices and understandings. That is, my aim both here and in *Uses of Heritage* is to understand human agency and the consequences of how heritage is used, while not conflating that agency with the material object itself, as tends to be done in the AHD.

Contra to Skrede and Hølleland (2018: 83–84), my disprivileging of heritage objects, sites and places, does not put me at odds with critical realism. I am not 'disinterested' in the material at all, as they claim, but concerned to theorise it in a meaningful way. There are two points to make here. First, in attempting to shift the theoretical gaze from the privileging of tangible heritage, I am simply asking us to reconsider how objects have been fetishised to the point that human agency and social relations become obscured within the AHD. The failure to engage explicitly with epistemology in considering how and why heritage matters to people will impede understanding of the material consequences heritage has for them. The second point to stress here is that within heritage studies and archaeology readings of critical realism are predisposed, due to their disciplinary ways of seeing, to equate 'real' with concrete materiality. In doing so, they ignore studies of social ontology informed by critical realism (e.g. Lawson 2012; Kaidesoja 2013), which offers, per Lawson (2012: 347): "an account whereby social reality is seen to be distinct from, and yet dependent upon, non-social material". In other words 'material' (objects, sites, places, etc) cannot be treated as ontologically privileged – that is, 'real' – in a way that social structures and relations are not. Within critical realism, social structures have always been ontologically 'real' and have causal consequences. Heritage performances have material consequences in lived experience, and concern with understanding these consequences, and how they may in turn feed back on heritage performances, is not at odds with critical realism.

A sense of humanism underpins critical realism (Porpora 2015: 131), which actively challenges the reduction or conflation of human action to culture (Archer 2000). To avoid such a conflation, Archer develops the idea of 'reflexivity'. Archer recognises that humans hold internal conversations with themselves and that this 'self-talk' or 'mulling things over' is not, and never has been, determined by habitual action (2007: 1–3). Indeed, she defines reflexivity as the ability to hold conscious and internal deliberations as we interact with the social and natural world (2007: 3–4) and sees reflexivity as "the process mediating the effects of our circumstances upon our actions" (2012: 6). She notes that the extent to which reflexivity is practised by social subjects will increase in proportion to the degree structural and cultural change, or morphogenesis, impinge upon those subjects (2012: 7). Conversely, the modality of reflexivity will also change in relation to morphostasis, or the reproduction of social contexts.

There are four points that emerge from explicating the critical realist underpinnings of the research. First, it explains that I am not *simply* interested in what particular individuals or collectives of people say, think or write about heritage. Rather, I am also explicitly concerned to identify and understand how this influences not only practice and the ways in which particular practices are reproduced or changed but also how it affects lived experiences. I believe that lived experience is central to understanding issues of power and politics and the way heritage is used and understood. Second, it explains my concern with interviewing people and asking them about the way they are thinking and engaging with heritage as they visit museums and heritage sites. As Archer states, "an ontology without a methodology is deaf and dumb; a methodology without an ontology is blind" (1995: 28). Thus, my ontological position drives the questions I ask and the methods I employ to address them. I am concerned with human agency and specifically with the reflexivity of particular users of heritage and the work their reflexivity then does in maintaining or challenging particular social practices and values. I will come back to Archer's ideas on reflexivity, particularly as they relate to issues of emotion and identity and as they offer additional analytical insights for this research. However, my third point is axiological and linked to a recognition of the political values that drive my research. Critical realist positions aim to not only identify the drivers of human experience but also to stress "the emancipatory potential of social scientific explanatory theorising" while rejecting the 'logic of immediacy' that tends to underlie both positivism and various versions of relativism (Iosifides 2011: 46). This is particularly important for understanding, finally, why ontologically and analytically the causal power of human agency is not conflated with or reduced to those of structure and culture. These last two points illustrate why I draw on particular theorists and not others and why I regard the so-called New Materialism or Post Humanist positions with deep suspicion.

Critical heritage studies

The idea of a 'critical' heritage studies has gained considerable traction in heritage and museum studies over the last decade (see Harrison 2010, 2013; Smith 2012a; Tunbridge, Ashworth and Graham 2012; Winter 2014). This process was facilitated by the development of the Association of Critical Heritage Studies in 2012, with its founding manifesto making an explicit call to arms for both practitioners and academics to engage in a "ruthless criticism" of the assumptions and ideas about the nature of heritage and the practices that surround the use of the past in the present (Campbell and Smith 2011). However, what constitutes 'critical'? In some cases, this has been taken as an exercise in criticising heritage professionals (Witcomb and Buckley 2013), leading to strange statements that such stances can be "anti-heritage" (Winter 2013: 533). From my point of view, critical heritage studies can benefit from considering a critical realist positioning to help understand and explain the social and political phenomena of heritage and identify what it *does* in society. That is, it is about being explicitly concerned with considering the consequences of the interplay between heritage theory and practice and how this, in turn, can facilitate policy debates about altering management and curatorial practices. It is a project of continual re-theorising and understanding the nature of heritage, and, as such, it may take a critical and reflexive framing to particular understandings and practices to understand what it is that these things *do*. It is not an approach that should be diluted to "addressing the *critical* issues that face the world today" (Winter 2013: 533, original emphasis); although this may be part of the project, it is not and should not be an end in itself. There has been an increasing tendency to see critical heritage studies as specifically 'issues' based, as witnessed by the increasing numbers of anthologies and readers within the field. This is not to say such approaches and synthesised overviews of specific issues relevant to academics and practitioners are not extremely useful, but the field cannot stop there. There have been calls for dialogue between heritage stakeholders (Campbell and Smith 2011; Witcomb and Buckley 2013; Winter 2013; Harrison 2013 among others); however, it needs to be asked: What should this dialogue be based on and to what purpose should it be directed? Jorma Kalela's (2012) arguments about history are important here, as he notes, history-making, for which we can substitute heritage-making, is an everyday practice, and people make use of their experiences in all sorts of ways. This simple observation needs to be the starting point of any dialogue, and to develop our understandings of such experiences, we need a deep ethnographic engagement that offers holistic attempts to understand people's experience as they interact with the social and political phenomena of heritage (see, for example, Cashman 2006; chapters in Sørensen and Carman 2009; Herzfeld 2016; Baird 2017). This aim lies at the heart of my attempts to re-theorise heritage as having elements of performance and practice.

Heritage as performance

The claim that all 'heritage is intangible' (Smith 2006: 56) is based on an argument that heritage is a performative practice. As a practice, it is the interaction of both actions and discourse that work to create or re-create heritage meanings that help validate the utility of the past for addressing the needs of the present. In short, 'heritage' is a continual embodied process of heritage-making. This argument finds common ground with previous arguments about heritage as performance. For example, Kirshenblatt-Gimblett (1998) argued that the curatorial practices of museum display are themselves a cultural production and performance of particular curatorial knowledge and meanings. Bella Dicks's (2000, 2003) argument that heritage is a communicative action or process across and between generations has similarities with my own arguments (Chapter 11). David Harvey (2001: 327) has also argued that heritage could be usefully understood as a process or "a verb, related to human action and agency". These arguments also find synergy with Sharon Macdonald's (2013) more recent arguments about 'past presencing' in which she argues that past historical narratives will be brought forward into the present to legitimise present-day aspirations and agendas. Heritage-making, moreover, is engaged in by the suite of institutions and practices that Macdonald calls 'memory complexes' (2013: 6–7) that work to legitimise certain readings of history and processes of remembering and forgetting. The idea of human agency is central to these theorisations of the concept of 'heritage', and all, to varying degrees, challenge the traditional professional preference for defining heritage as places or objects that are perceived to have often immutable and innate value. They also inevitably challenge the professional binary established by UNESCO between material and intangible heritage because those 'things', emphasised by the material heritage definition, become in James Wertsch's (2002; Wertsch and Billingsley 2011) terms 'cultural tools' in the processes of remembering and heritage-making and are not an end in and of themselves in this process. Indeed, drawing on Samuel's (1994) argument, that what are often called 'heritage sites' could be understood as theatres of memory, I defined those things traditionally demarcated as heritage places and objects as locations and props in practices that provided a sense of occasion or legitimacy to acts of remembering/forgetting and commemorating (Smith 2006: 66f).

In developing the idea that 'all heritage is intangible', I am explicitly stating that heritage is something that is *done* and that objects, places, sites, buildings and other 'stuff' are props that help us accomplish that 'doing'. In talking about heritage as a performance, I am drawing on a range of debates, and the tensions between them, about both practice and the related concepts of performance and performativity. In particular, I draw on Butler's (1990) idea of performativity in which the subject, in this instance, the gendered subject, is performativity constituted through acts that signify a particular gender. Drawing on the work of J. L. Austin and speech act theory, Butler (1997) examines the ability of speech acts to confer social existence. As Carlson (2017: 68) notes, Austin identified performatives as a particular type of utterance in which "someone does not simply make a statement . . . but performs an action, as for example, when one christens a ship or takes marriage vows". It is important, however, to stress that in Butler's (1990, 1996, 1997) work embodied acts must be repeated as social ritual, and in this process, the subject is not simply constituted but continually remade. This is similar to Bourdieu's notion of *habitus*: "those embodied rituals of everydayness by which a given culture produces and sustains belief in its own 'obviousness'" (Butler 1997: 152) and in which social action becomes a "scene of repetition, constraint and routine" (Wetherell 2012: 105) and therefore self-perpetuation (Schatzki 2008: 137). However, for Bourdieu *habitus* is "embodied history, internalised as a second nature and so forgotten as history" (1990: 56, quoted in Spatz 2015: 51), and thus, as Spatz identifies, distinct from personal agency. Indeed, the idea of *habitus* has been critiqued for developing an "'oversocialized' concept of the individual" (Lovell 2000: 15), insufficiently considering how habitual practices can become transformed and challenged (Archer 2007; Atkinson 2016). Butler's idea of performance and performativity explicitly accommodates the idea of resignification (1997: 163) and the possibility that a performance can fail to be effective (2010: 152). Embodied repetition is, thus, "not merely mechanical" and always involves both intended and unintended appropriations of normative and normalising acts (Jagger 2008: 14).

Further, while a subject is constituted via performativity, this act simultaneously calls into question the stability of that subject as well as the expressions and activities that formulated it (Butler 2010: 147). Performativity facilitates the identification of practices that reinforce hegemonic and normative identity constructions while also identifying the practices through which they are challenged. Butler (1997) argues that within the idea of *habitus*, social power becomes reducible to the social practices and the conditions they inform, and language is separated from the social; however, for Butler, as for Carlson (2017: 87), performance and performativity are "deeply involved both with the reinforcement and the dismantling of stable systems of meaning and representation".

While Butler's idea of performance and performativity informs the concepts of heritage performance that I use, I ground her more textually post-structuralist take on the more structuralist and critical reading of the concept of *habitus* and practice thinking. In developing Butler's ideas of performativity, I do not exclude the idea of practice; as Wetherell (2012: 23) states, practice thinking "is a way of conceptualising social action as constantly in motion while yet recognising too that the past, and what has been done before, constrains the present and the future". As noted, this does not mean that practice simply becomes unchangingly habitual; rather, notions of performance and performativity open the conceptual space for consciousness and reflection on social actions and practices (Carlson 2017: 87). The sense in which Butler is less concerned with the "activities of the thinking 'I'" (2015: 11, 2005) than with the conditions in which the subject is constructed may seem to be at odds, however, with the idea of self-narration and perspicuity developed by Archer (2000). The idea of reflexivity is central to my use of the concept of performance and plays an important role in identifying that human behaviour is not simply confined to habitual practice (Archer 2000). However, Butler's point that not all practices and actions are necessarily self-consciously aware or that "conditions of formation are not always recuperable and knowable" is also important (2005: 134). Further, intended actions may have unintentional or additional consequences to that intended, as Schatzki (2010: 117), drawing on Donald Davidson explains: for instance, turning on the lights in a house may be done to chase away the gloom but may also unwittingly notify a would-be prowler that someone is home.

Practices are, as Schatzki (2010: xv) argues, 'performed'. An action is what is performed or done, and in the event of the doing of that activity, the action exists through its performance, unless, as Schatzki (2010: xv) notes, that performance fails or is incomplete. It is through the performance of practice, through doing, that the 'patterns' of actions and their elements are produced and reproduced and become enduring entities (Shove et al. 2012: 7–8). However, it is also through the "moments of doing, when the elements of a practice come together" that such elements are potentially reconfigured in either subtle or significant ways, and thus, subsequent formulations are changed (Shove et al. 2012: 13). Practices and their performances are embodied; there is a body, a someone who performs physical, mental and cognitive actions (Schatzki 2008: 47). Drawing on Butler (1990, 1996), the performances of these embodied practices materialise the meanings and normative values that underwrite and are re/formulated in the performative nature of actions. In their materialisation, abstractions (such as identity, sense of place) are made material – that is, they have consequence in the doing world and the lived experiences of people. As this is an argument about 'heritage', it is important to stress that when I talk about the 'material' consequences of the doing of heritage, of the performative nature of heritage, I am talking about the consequences heritage has to individual and group experiences of such things as identity, wellbeing, sense of place and belonging. The implications of this are elaborated in Chapter 2, particularly to issues of identity, when I discuss how heritage may be understood, through its performance of identity-making, as a resource of power in negotiations over recognition and distribution. However, practices and their performances can (although not always) require the use of material things beyond the body. Material things, everyday objects – in particular, heritage objects – can be used to facilitate the performance of actions. Drawing on both Wertsch (2002) and Samuel (1994), I have argued that heritage artefacts, sites and places are important cultural tools and 'theatres of memory' that facilitate, mark as important and help authorise the heritage meanings, identities and values that are constituted through heritage performances (2006). The point here is that they *facilitate*, they are used as tools or locations that assist performances of remembering and other practices of heritage-making. They do not have, as Latour (2000: 113) argues, the ability "to construct, literally and not metaphorically, social order". It is worth pointing out that while Schatzki's work on practice thinking extends action, albeit with some caveats, to nonhuman entities (2002: 71, 2006: 3, 2010: 204), this is not a position I adopt. However, the tensions and synergies between ideas of practice and performance and the concept of performativity underpin my argument that heritage is something that is done. Heritage is an embodied performance of practices that affect heritage-making. That is, heritage performances, and the practices and actions that underpin them, constitute and formulate heritage meanings about the past that are brought to bear on the present to help us realise and negotiate present-day needs and aspirations. Heritage practices are performative in that they construct and express and continually *reconstruct* heritage meanings and values.

Heritage, as a performance, does not simply construct and materialise (or embody) abstractions such as identity, sense of place and so forth; heritage as performance may also be understood as embodying particular ways of knowing and understanding the world. Here, I also draw on Taylor's arguments that knowledge does not simply exist in texts or material culture, what she terms the *archive*, but also in the *repertoire* – that is, in ephemeral embodied practice (2003: 19). These embodied actions are neither ontologically separate from nor reducible to language (Butler 2015: 21) but are actions that transmit knowledge and memories or make political claims or express individual and group identity (Taylor 2003: 2). As Taylor argues, embodied practices do not happen without context; they are bound up with other cultural practices and ways of knowing and will be "intelligible in the framework of the immediate environment and issues surrounding them" (2003: 3). The recognition of the legitimacy of embodied knowledge is central to Taylor's work (2003: 18). As with Kirshenblatt-Gimblett (2004), Taylor (2003: 23–4) questions the utility of UNESCO's attempts to safeguard intangible heritage, suggesting that the 2003 *Convention for the Safeguarding of the Intangible Cultural Heritage* is an attempt to move the repertoire to the archive and, thus, to objectify and isolate embodied knowledge under the more governable term 'intangible heritage'. It is important to stress that the idea of performance developed here is not reducible to intangible heritage but rather refers to any performative action that contributes to the transmission and re/creation of knowledge, memory and/or identity.

The embodied practices of heritage and museum professionals, framed as they are by conventions and charters (which themselves are framed by the AHD), are particular performances of heritage-making. These performances occur in a range of different contexts and at different scales. As Graham et al. (2000) have pointed out, heritage sites or artefacts can function and have meaning at a variety of different scales (see also Harvey 2015; Lähdesmäki et al. 2019). Nationally and internationally, governments and intergovernmental agencies, such as UNESCO, are involved in heritage-making through the development and implementation of cultural and funding policies and activities, such as the amassing of lists of valued and protected heritage objects and intangible heritage practices. At this scale, the choices museum and heritage professionals make in amassing collections, developing exhibitions or not developing them, in conserving or preserving certain sites or buildings and not others and in the choices made to interpret them in certain ways are all performative heritage practices. National or international lists of valued material or intangible heritage are themselves a work of heritage, as they present and transmit certain messages, collective rememberings, forgettings and knowledge about what constitutes both the past and the present. The process of evaluating and articulating the 'heritage values' of specific heritage items that buttress any listing process is a procedure that identifies what social values in the present 'matter' or are seen as significant and worthy of validating through the accumulation of 'heritage'. If we accept that neither intangible nor material heritage have innate and immutable values but are rather valued because they are meaningful to people in the present, the activity of creating and maintaining lists is an act of meaning-making in and for the present. This process may bolster and help validate the aspirations people in the present have for the future (Holtorf and Högberg 2015; Harrison et al. 2016; Smith and Campbell 2017a). However, it is worth pointing out that heritage is not of necessity or primarily about the future, although future-making is important, but logically about negotiations over the legitimacy, or otherwise, of social meanings and values in the present. The validation or otherwise of social values and meanings may then be used to legitimate agendas and aspirations for an imagined future, but they will always be negotiations undertaken in the context of contemporary political and social needs and concerns. While the existence and development of lists are, as Taylor (2003) points out, part of the archive, the performative and repetitive action of nomination and getting sites and intangible heritage listed is, as ethnographers have documented, not only highly theatrical, they are also constitutively performative (in the case of UNESCO listings, see Hafstein 2009, 2018; Bendix et al. 2013; Brumann 2014; Meskell 2014; Meskell et al. 2015; Kuutma 2018). The World Heritage list is thus a work of heritage in its entirety – it re/creates and validates certain understandings about human history. A museum collection, in the same way, performs heritage-making. Sites and objects are not found, but rather they are identified as representative of the heritage stories that heritage and museum professionals wish to make (Kirshenblatt-Gimblett 1998). As Taylor (2003: 272) notes, the repertoire, as much as the archive, is mediated and authorised or rendered illegitimate depending on the context in which it occurs. In the case of national and professional heritage performances, this authorisation can occur both through the mere act of repetition of the repertoire but also in the way performances of embodied practices interact with and utilise the archive. While Taylor's (2003) arguments about performance work to identify the way knowledge is produced and transmitted outside the archive by often marginalised groups and individuals, her work also illustrates how particular professional forms of acting or performing also transmit and legitimise professional knowledge.

Another scale of the performance of heritage-making occurs within and between communities and other sub-national collectives. There is now a significant and growing body of literature that documents the way various communities, such as those defined by ethnic affiliations, local or regional neighbourhoods, class affiliations, or professional affiliations, define and use their heritage (Crooke 2008; Smith and Waterton 2009; Mydland and Grahn 2012; Little and Shackel 2016; Schmidt and Pikiray 2016; Johnston and Marwood 2017; Kiddey 2018; Kryder-Reid et al. 2018; Shackel 2018). These expressions are often, although not always nor inevitably, in opposition to nationalising forms of heritage that may be defined by various versions of the AHD. One of the key issues identified in much of the literature that documents community expressions of heritage is the degree to which certain communities draw attention to their absence in wider narratives of national or regional heritage commemorations (e.g. Hall 1999; Gregory 2015; Wilson 2015). A point Taylor (2003) raises is the issue of absence as performance. While she talks about this in the case of the missing of Argentina and the performative absence of the World Trade Centre in New York, a performance that draws attention to absence and disregard is a feature of much community heritage work. A third scale, however, and the one that is of central concern in this study, is that of the individual. Individual heritage performances can occur across the dining room table, as we glance through photo albums, talk to each other about familial histories and so on. They can also occur in the more formal, and indeed authorising, settings of museums and heritage sites. Institutions such as government heritage agencies and museums work to guide and influence the heritage-making of visitors to sites and museums by carefully designing and constructing exhibitions and interpretive material. It is, of course, hoped that such careful planning will ensure that their visitors take away the intended messages, although it is also acknowledged that the meaning that visitors take away cannot always be controlled (Falk and Dierking 1992, 2000; Falk 2005). Whether taking away the authorised or altogether unintended meanings, people, as visitors to such places or sites, are engaged in an embodied process of creating or rehearsing particular narratives of meaning and knowledge. As Archer (2007) reminds us, they are also, of course, engaged in reflexivity that facilitates the transition or rehearsing of a range of social values that validate the legitimacy of particular knowledge and social meanings.

In conceptualising heritage as an embodied act of meaning-making and knowledge transmission, there are three issues to elaborate. The first is to consider how material culture, or material heritage places and objects, what we may call the 'heritage archive', fit into this conceptualisation. This is worth drawing out not only because of the critiques of what has been incorrectly called 'the discursive turn' (Harrison 2013: 95f) in heritage studies but also to identify and acknowledge their contextual role in heritage performances. As the heritage archive, material things are given authority and legitimacy because of the historical power they have been afforded as 'evidence'. However, this leads us to the second issue, that of power. Different performative practices have clearly different consequences depending on the scale and authority of their practice. Those professional performances at national and international scales have the capacity to shape and reshape national or other large-scale collective identities and the social values that underwrite them. The power of these performances rests on the persuasive power of the AHD, which in turn, is continually given authority and legitimacy by the degree to which it is embedded in the practices and texts of state and intergovernmental agencies (Smith 2006: 87f; Waterton 2010: 38f). However, what is less clear is the nuances of how these national narratives and their consequences may be challenged or indeed become accepted and received at community or individual scales. In other words, what exactly is the power of heritage outside of state authorising institutions? Why do performances of absence matter? What power do objects of heritage have? To address this, I will turn to the debates surrounding the politics of recognition. The third issue is of affect/emotion; as I noted in *Uses of Heritage*, emotions play a role in the performances of heritage-making, but exactly how they work was not addressed in sufficient detail. However, before addressing the issues of politics and affect/emotion in the following chapter, it is important to clarify my position on materiality.

The problems with Post Humanism and New Materialism in heritage and museum studies

There has been something of a reaction against what Rodney Harrison (2013: 95f) misidentifies as the 'discursive turn' in heritage studies and the re-theorising of heritage as a form of action. I say misidentification, as those using discourse analysis in heritage studies do not engage in the 'exhorbitation of language' that Anderson (1983) identified and that I have also criticised (Smith 1994). However, driving this reaction is a concern that such theorising "does not always produce an account that adequately theorises the role of material 'things'" (Harrison 2013: 112; see also Solli 2011). Thus, Harrison is concerned to "bring the affective qualities of heritage 'things' more squarely back into the critical heritage studies arena" (2013: 112). Harrison notes that such a desire should not be viewed as "inconsistent with a consideration of the discourse of heritage and its knowledge/power effects", but is nonetheless concerned that heritage objects and places are "part of our 'being in the world'" (2013: 113) and thus need greater consideration. As argued, ontologically, material culture is indeed significant, but we must be careful not to conflate the material with the social meanings and values that are produced as people interact with such places and objects. Conflating what people do, and the meanings and knowledge this performs, with the material objects themselves obscures both the lived experiences of people and the politics of heritage. Such conflation, as Archer (2000) and Sayer (2011) warn, actively works to deny human agency, and is why Archer (1995) advises that ontologically materiality and the social be analytically identifiable.

Part of the theorising in *Uses of Heritage* was about identifying the various roles material objects and places played in legitimising and facilitating the heritage-making of individuals and groups. However, my intention of disprivileging materiality was precisely to illustrate the degree to which heritage studies and professional practice works to conflate the material with the human. Indeed, this is exactly what the AHD does, as in privileging the materiality of heritage, it reduces human values, concerns and aspirations to easily manageable issues over how to preserve certain objects, buildings or archaeological sites. For instance, struggles over Indigenous land rights and sovereignty become more tractable problems for policymakers if the issues can be reduced to how to manage particular heritage places (Smith 2004, 2007). Concerns over ensuring that the so-called innate aesthetic values of a stately home are preserved glosses over the maintenance of social and economic inequality (Deckha 2004; Gable 2009; Terry 2015). While, overall, the reproduction of received or consensus histories as heritage values works to exclude a range of social and cultural experiences (Hall 1999; Ashworth et al. 2007; Darian-Smith and Pascoe 2013; Grahn and Wilson 2018), traditional management practices that focus on the values that 'things' *have* will inevitably focus less on *how* these are valued (and thus by who). Indeed, there is a very real tendency to forget *why* these things matter and what effect valuing these things have on people. The AHD specifically identifies that things have a value, and indeed many of the internationally influential ICOMOS charters and UNESCO conventions talk about the values that things possess or simply 'have', and thus entirely misunderstand that things are *valued* – that valuing things is an activity and not a property of the thing being valued. In short, all 'heritage values' are associative and mutable and not inherent in an object.

The idea that materiality is a central concern of heritage studies and that such things have an inherent and immutable value is, contra to Pétursdóttir's (2012: 36–37) claim that this is not the case, still a majority position in heritage studies and museology. It remains a dominant international position that continues to be authorised by organisations such as UNESCO and ICOMOS. Despite this continued dominance, however, authorised ideas about materiality and its inherent values have been vigorously questioned, and there has been some movement in the discourse. The most significant example is, perhaps, UNESCO's own 2003 *Convention for the Safeguarding of the Intangible Cultural Heritage*. The push for this convention came from non-Western contexts, specifically from Asia, Africa and Indigenous peoples (Aikawa 2004; Aikawa-Faure 2009; Hafstein 2009, 2018; Akagawa 2014). Whether or not this convention, as Kirshenblatt-Gimblett (2004) warned, created just another heritage list, with all that implies about stultifying the creative practices of such heritage, it nonetheless has presented a considerable challenge to traditional Anglophone concepts that naturalised the materiality of heritage. The advent of international recognition of intangible heritage has also thrown up complex challenges for museums (Alivizatou 2012). This has occurred alongside long-term and continuing Indigenous and other stakeholder critiques of colonial practices of display and collection (Kreps 2003, 2009; Fouseki 2010; Golding and Modest 2013; Robinson 2017). The now extensive scrutiny of museums has seen an increase in moves by many such institutions to embrace broader civic and social functions (Conn 2010) and has witnessed explicit calls for museums to address social justice issues (Sandell and Nightingale 2012). It has also seen the development of organisations such as the Federation of International Human Rights Museums (Fleming 2012). This has led to ongoing questioning of the way objects are used and displayed in museums (Dudley 2010; Levitt 2015).

Indeed, all the challenges to received ideas of materiality within heritage studies and museology are politically and conceptually confronting, and it is not at all surprising that we may feel the field is drowning in a cacophony of 'critique'. All these challenges have occurred alongside a turn in the wider social sciences and humanities to the Post Human or New Materialism, which in many ways are reactions to the excesses of post-modernism and perceived neglect of materiality (Ahmed 2008). Within the stable of Post Human (PH) and New Materialism (NM), we can also locate Actor Network Theory (ANT) and Non-representational Theory (NRT), which have recently been taken up in heritage and museum studies (e.g. Harrison 2013, 2015; Waterton and Watson 2013, 2014; Harrison et al. 2013; Tolia-Kelly et al. 2017; Skrede et al. 2018).

Central to the new claims being made within New Materialism and Post Humanist positions is that the material world has been taken for granted and greater engagement with materialism is needed to understand the challenges people face in terms of ongoing changes to, amongst other things, the environment, global and local economies (Coole and Frost 2010: 3). Indeed, as Braidotti (2013: 194) points out, there is a certain sense of frustration with what she sees as the failures of the anthropocentric humanities to care about the natural world. A concern to understand human impact on what has been termed the 'Anthropocene' is key here. Linked to this is a concern that a post-modern or relativist emphasis on discourse limits and obscures the agency of the material world (Bauer and Kosiba 2016: 120). In identifying material, or what Latour refers to as the nonhuman, as having agency, neither object or subject can be treated as radically different, and indeed nonhumans are seen as foundational to the formation of human society (Sayes 2013: 136–7; see also Latour 2007). Nonhumans are understood as mediators and act to continually modify relations between human actors, but should not be understood as having the same agency as humans (Sayes 2013: 144). A key problem with NM, and ANT in particular, is that, as Fortun (2014: 312) notes, it misses the forest for the trees – that is, it actively turns away from questions of wider structural issues such as gender, class, ethnicity and so forth, as well as the political and economic, to a concern with the particular (see also Cresswell 2012). In doing so, matters of concrete social justice are sidestepped, and particular kinds of connections and disconnections remain unaddressed. Indeed, what Fortun identifies as a "gentlemen's engagement" emerges where issues of difference and the "way history weights the present and future" are discounted and "all attention is on what can be composed anew" (2014: 315).

An additional problem with much of NM and ANT is the problem of anthropomorphising, in which human agency is projected onto the material world (Zijek cited in Till 2015). While Sayes (2013: 139) challenges such critiques, arguing that nonhumans are not ascribed purpose and do not have a sense of justice or morality, the degree to which objects become conflated with human values is of concern. For instance, the theoretical process of constructing objects as agentic has led to claims that objects should be understood as having 'rights' (Pétursdóttir 2012: 43) or as "beings in the world alongside other beings such as humans, plants, and animals" (Olsen 2013: 9).

Extending the idea of rights to objects forcefully reminds me of an illustrative incident I experienced in my first job as a heritage professional. It was 1984, and I started a short-term job in Sydney, working for what was then the NSW National Parks and Wildlife Service, the agency that had the legal responsibility for managing Indigenous heritage in the Australian state of New South Wales. A colleague I had gone to university with earnestly took me aside when they understood I would be working with Indigenous activists to remind me that my first priority, as a professional, should be to look after "the rights of archaeological sites". They fervently believed that these material sites had particular and essential values as 'archaeological sites' that needed protection – although, the unspoken message was 'look after the interests of archaeologists in accessing their data' as they were ultimately seeking 'equitable' access to this material with Indigenous people. To invoke the idea of rights and the egalitarian treatment of objects with people or animals and to anthropomorphise material as 'beings' is simply invoking the rights of professionals to have access to the things that matter to *them*.

It is not easy to get to the heart of New Materialist and other Post Humanist writings simply because of the abstruse language that it tends to be written in. This is not a frivolous observation, as authors working in these areas adopt a tactic beloved of post-modernists before them of deploying dense language as an academic strategy. A strong emphasis is placed in the NM and PH position on identifying the emergence of flows and forces that interact and alter networks and assemblages of actants (Latour 2007). Social context disappears, and thus, for example, political action is seen as less a conscious result of individuals or collectives, but rather, as something that "emerges" through the allocation of "humans and things [with] similar capacities to act and make history" (Bauer and Kosiba 2016: 120). The stress on networks and assemblages and their 'self-organisation' emphasises what has been referred to as 'flat ontology', in that the organisation of entities is explained with reference to the interactions between particular and historically locatable entities (Pétursdóttir and Olsen 2018). Braidotti (2013: 35), for example, stressing the idea of a continuum between nature-culture rejects the binary opposition between the material world and the socially constructed and stresses the self-organisational force of all matter. In doing so, an ontology of "becoming" is sustained "that is the conceptual motor of posthuman nomadic thought" (Braidotti 2013: 170).

This ontological position privileges the idea of immanence as underlying the relations not only between humans, animals and the environment but also "between bodies and technological others" – that is, an acceptance that technologies have a biological impact in the world (Braidotti 2013: 90–91). This emphasis on immanence heavily informs Actor Network Theory. Latour (2007) advocates a semi-realist form of social construction in that nothing is presumed and processes are seen as organising themselves from the ground up rather than the top down. At one level, this may be seen as good methodology, but if based on a flat ontology with its focus on the local and the immediate – all of which is then imbued with creative energy – we lose the capacity to draw on explanations that engage social forces such as class, gender, power and so forth. Thus, much of the NM and PH work allows us to think of 'assemblages' of nonhuman actants and human subjects and the ways these work on the body and the environment but actively inhibit a consideration of 'power', or 'class', or 'gender' or 'exploitation', as these terms are held to presuppose too much.

In rejecting the discursive turn of post-modern constructivism and reasserting concern for the material, NM and PH writers recreate many of the problems they seek to address. Moreover, NM and PH theories, much like post-modernists before them, allow both a gesturing at the 'critical issues' that impact on human lives and yet maintain an intellectual distance from engaging in the contexts of both the creation and potential resolution of such issues. Within museum and heritage studies, it allows a gesturing at the engagement with the AHD but never really addresses the issues posed by the new emphasis on intangible heritage that demand us to explore new ways of knowing both the past and present. If we return our analytical gaze squarely back to objects by invoking the presumed agency of the material world, the anti-humanist assumption – shared by post-modernism and post-structuralism – that underlines this position must sideline human agency. These tendencies principally occur because the desire to disprivilege human agency and to focus on the emergent and immediate only facilitates an active forgetting of social contexts, which in turn, licences a range of contextless androcentric and Eurocentric assumptions about the essential nature of 'being' to be continually rehearsed and legitimised. Conceptualisations of the 'Anthropocene' and concern with attributing agentic properties to objects is, as Zizek (in Till 2015) argues, supremely and ironically anthropocentric. In criticising the NM and PH positions, I am not saying that objects, the environment and nonhuman animals do not matter or that human impact on these things is not of concern. Rather, I am stating that a flat ontology is not a useful position from which to start if we want to move away from the 'emergent moment' and engage with the material consequences and effects of human actions and understandings.

The usefulness of Harrison's (2013) observations that material culture matters is to remind us, as Hodder (2012) also identifies, that humans do become entangled with objects. Objects, while not possessing their own agency or performative abilities, nonetheless are used to facilitate heritage performances. Objects and sites, indeed, may be vital to certain forms of heritage performances, but their value, meaning and consequence to those performances are continually re/determined by the ways that they are used and constructed in and by those performances. Their meaning and values as heritage objects or places are as much constituted by the performances within which they are used as is the broader sense of identity, sense of place or belonging that are constructed in heritage performances. That objects and places become entangled within conceptualisations of identity, belonging, sense of place and so forth rests on the values and agencies *given* to these 'things' to stand in for, authorise and 'make real' abstract feelings and expressions.

Conclusion

This chapter has argued for human agency and has warned about past and current tendencies in heritage practices and theorising of conflating human agency with that of material objects. Under the AHD, New Materialist and Post Humanist positions, objects and sites become privileged over human values, knowledge and social experiences. This has happened, as critical realists have warned, because the nature of reality, in this case, heritage objects and places, have become conflated with the knowledge of that reality (Fairclough 2005: 922). As Archer (1995) notes, a critical realist ontology requires that materiality and the social be understood as analytically identifiable; this does not mean that they are considered separately, but only that by obscuring the social context we reduce our analytical power in understanding, and thus having an impact on, human lives and experiences. People interact with objects and can and do *give* objects and places the agency to do things for them, objects can and do 'speak' eloquently to individuals and collectives, they have meaning and are valued. The important point to stress, however, is that such agency is mutable, dependent on social context and discursively framed.

Building on arguments in *Uses of Heritage*, this chapter has argued for the performative and embodied nature of heritage, stressing the importance of human agency in how heritage is understood, valued and used. Heritage performances are performances of knowledge and meaning-making, in which material places and objects are reconceptualised as cultural tools, or *aide-mémoires*, that are used by people to facilitate the practices of remembering and forgetting. Adding, however, to this conceptualisation, I draw on Archer's notion of reflexivity, the idea that people hold conscious and internal dialogues with themselves as they interact, comprehend and respond to the social and natural world around them. In terms of heritage, those things, places or intangible events or elements identified as heritage, do not simply become the attention of such reflexivity but may also be conceptualised again as specific cultural tools that help us focus reflexive internal and externalised commentary about the meaning of the past for the present. One of the core meanings the past is assumed to have for the present centres on issues of identity and how the past informs a person's or a collective's sense of individual or shared identity and sense of place in the world.

The chapter has argued for the importance of considering social contexts, and it becomes useful to ask in what contexts, and why, do people utilise heritage objects and places? How are values and meaning given to material and intangible heritage? What does this process *do*? These questions are explored in the following chapter; however, in exploring these, I am not claiming, of course, to identify all the contexts and ways in which material and intangible heritage may be used. Nonetheless, I want to turn to a consideration of a mainstay assumption in heritage and museum studies that heritage is intimately linked to both the representation and embodiment of individual and collective identity. In considering the issue I ask, how may we better understand the consequences of this linkage? Why, and in what contexts, are heritage objects and intangible heritage events given such representational power that they can matter so much?

Note

1 As does Elder-Vass (2010: 11), I stress Bhaskar's earlier work, rejecting the spiritualist turn taken in his later work.

2
RECONSIDERING HERITAGE AND IDENTITY

The politics of recognition and the affective practices of heritage

In the last chapter, I developed an argument about the performative and embodied nature of heritage. In this argument, those things, places or intangible cultural elements that may be labelled 'heritage' are reconceptualised as cultural tools that are used by individuals and groups to facilitate the activities of remembering, forgetting and working through the meaning of the past for the present. How material or intangible heritage is used in heritage practices and performances, and the meanings subsequently constructed, will depend on the social contexts in which they are deployed. However, this process works in turn to give and re/create the values and meanings objects and places are often assumed to embody. That is, while I have argued against the idea of inherent object value and agency, I acknowledge that objects and places do take on and have very important meanings, particularly in terms of representing individual and collective identity. This chapter examines the representational power of material and intangible heritage and argues that it is the ability given to heritage to 'stand in for' and energise identity that underlies both its political and emotive nature. Drawing on debates over the 'politics of recognition', this chapter argues that heritage is drawn into how conflicts over recognition and misrecognition unfold. The conceptual framework offered by the politics of recognition helps explain why heritage can become entangled in conflicts ranging from the local to the international, which helps to reveal the political power of heritage and why heritage can matter so much and why, moreover, heritage objects and places sometimes can be presumed, dubiously, to have agency. In reconsidering the links between heritage and identity via the politics of recognition, the chapter also examines the emotional power that heritage can have and how emotion underpins the political and representational power of heritage. Heritage, linked as it is with identity, must stimulate emotive responses (Smith and Campbell 2016). This chapter also reviews how issues of affect and emotion have been dealt with in heritage studies and argues, drawing on the idea of affective practice developed by Margaret

Wetherell (2012), that heritage performances have affective energy that can be harnessed for a variety of purposes.

The politics of recognition

The tensions and conflicts that arise over the multiple meanings and valuations of intangible and material heritage, over who decides what is or is not heritage and how it should or should not be displayed for public consumption are, like Graham et al. (2000) note, foundational to defining 'heritage'. To mention 'politics' in relation to heritage or museums is to inevitably raise the issue of either 'identity politics' (Harrison 2010; Lowenthal 2015) or negotiations over the acceptance of cosmopolitan diversity (Mason 2013; Meskell 2016; Witcomb 2016). However, how does heritage become a resource of power; how is it 'political', how does it become embroiled in 'identity politics'? To answer these questions, I draw on debates over the politics of recognition and diversity and argue that this provides a useful conceptual framework for understanding why heritage matters and how it becomes a resource of power in political struggles. Moreover, the idea of heritage allows the concept of 'recognition', which has been criticised for being an abstraction yet to be substantiated in practical terms (McNay 2008), to be grounded in practical and everyday contexts.

The way in which 'politics' has been experienced by citizens in democracies has substantially changed since the 1960s (Thompson 2006: 2). As Thompson observes, the social democratic consensus has faced a number of challenges, not least of which is the rise of sub-national collectives and movements, such as the civil rights movement, the woman's movement, environmental movements and Indigenous movements, the latter of which specifically challenges both colonialism and the idea of the singular nation (2006: 2). We can also add to this the new politics of multiculturalism and diversity. More recently, the reinvention of right-wing populism has given weight to Mouffe's contention that thinking politically requires understanding that politics is by definition antagonistic, driven by attempts to impose or dispute hegemony, and energised by often passionate emotions (2013, 2019; see also Mishra 2017; Cossarini and Vallespin 2019; Slaby and von Scheve 2019; De Cesari and Kaya 2020). These developments have confronted assumptions about national identity and the idea that a monocultural national identity should correspond with political authority (Thompson 2006: 2). The idea of recognition, which incorporates a politics of identity, has been formulated to not only explain these changes but also as a response to them (Honneth in Fraser and Honneth 2003: 111).

There are a range of arguments about how to understand recognition in political philosophy, but there is a broad understanding that the politics of recognition can be characterised as a struggle in which a particular group demands acknowledgment and recognition from other groups in society of itself or aspects of its identity and, by extension, its particular historical and contemporary circumstance (Thompson 2006: 3). Other groups may resist these demands and thus work to exclude through the continuation of an absence of recognition or the maintenance or development of new forms of misrecognition of the group and its individuals (Tully 2000: 473). This interaction will then have implications for understanding the nature of justice and how society should be organised so that "everyone enjoys the recognition that is due them" (Thompson 2006: 9). How and why this unfolds, and most importantly, how the consequences of this are understood, is approached from a number of different positions in this debate. It is thus important to work through some of the nuances to tease out how I am applying the concept to heritage and institutions like museums and why, in particular, I favour the work of Nancy Fraser in this debate.

Both Charles Taylor (1992, 1994) and Axel Honneth (2005, 2008) define claims to recognition as a human and emotional need that involves a search for respect and esteem. Failure to gain respect, they argue, will do psychological harm to those who remain unacknowledged and/or for whom respect has been withheld (Taylor 1994; Honneth 2005). Taylor (1994) emphasises a politics of difference in which identity, for it to exist at all, requires unconditional recognition by others. The gaining of respect will be dependent on individual and group behaviour and achievements and will ensure access to what Taylor defines as the fundamental or universal rights of individuals (1994), while Honneth argues that receiving respect is central to individual and group self-respect and wellbeing (2008: 93–4, 2012: 41–42). Taylor, in particular, argues that lack of respect, itself a form of misrecognition, is an act of injustice that is separate from other forms of inequality or oppression (Young 2000: 105). Honneth (2005, 2012) also tends to see a search for respect as a key motive for recognition, although his argument about esteem adds another element to the politics of recognition. A search for esteem is about the negotiation of societal values, as part of the new politics of recognition; Honneth sees increasing pluralism in the values societies will accommodate or legitimise, and thus to be esteemed, is to have one's values recognised as contributing to ethical goals and cultural self-understanding (2005: 122). For Taylor and Honneth, the withholding of rights to a collective rests on the low valuation of respect and esteem given to this group (Thompson 2006: 60). For Nancy Fraser, however, a failure of individuals and collectives to be given respect and esteem, and indeed prestige, may be understood as part of the consequences of misrecognition and marginalisation and are in themselves insufficient to explain the drive for recognition (in Fraser and Honneth 2003: 14–15).

Moreover, she argues, "mortgaging normative claims to matters of psychological fact" renders claims to recognition "vulnerable to the vicissitudes of that theory" and denies the possibility of the subjectivity and plurality of what constitutes wellbeing and the human psyche (2003: 32). Fraser argues, recognition needs to be approached "in the spirit of [. . .] pragmatism" (2003: 45) and conceived as a remedy for social injustice that is explicitly linked to struggles over the distribution of resources. While a pragmatic response here is vital, Taylor and Honneth's emphasis on respect and esteem has been central to many conceptualisations of the politics of recognition. Their stress on the psychological aspects of seeking recognition is in and of itself insufficient to explain the experiences and consequences of recognition and misrecognition. However, it highlights the role that emotion and emotional judgements can have on the politics of recognition. I will return to this later.

Claims for the recognition of difference and identity are linked, as Fraser (2000) maintains, to demands and calls for restorative justice, social inclusion and greater equity in policy negotiations over the distribution of resources such as finance, welfare, housing, education. For Fraser (1995, 2008, 2010) redistribution and recognition are equally important and intertwined. Recognition cannot simply meet a human need or address an abstract sense of 'wellbeing'; it has, she argues, both a material motivation and consequence centred on restorative justice (2000, 2001, 2010). Central to her concern is the idea of 'parity of participation'. A lack of recognition or misrecognition denies parity of individuals and/or groups in participation in societal and policy negotiation over access to resources. The consequence of recognition should be equity in societal participation and in the distribution of resources and rights (2001: 27). Of course, it does not follow that recognition will easily or automatically lead to redistribution; those in privileged positions do not always surrender or share rights or resources easily. Thus, the politics of recognition offers both a means to understand the power and context of identity claims as demands for recognition as well as is a philosophical commitment to parity; as Fraser suggests, the slogan for such a commitment should be "no recognition without redistribution" (Fraser and Naples 2004: 1122).

For Fraser (2001), the best remedy to injustice will always depend on the particular circumstances of a case, and any remedy offered must not then result in the shift of injustice to another party or the creation of new injustices. Responses to recognition can equally result in the extension of rights to a marginalised group or to changing societal practices and/or the withholding to all groups of particular rights previously understood by Taylor as 'universal' (2003: 39–42). However, demands for recognition, as Fraser notes (1999: 35), do not always have to be met, particularly if meeting those demands creates new forms of injustice. For instance, any demand for recognition "cannot itself involve the misrecognition or non-recognition of others without committing a performative contradiction", and such one-sided demands are "unreasonable and should be ignored by the other members of the society" (Tully 2000: 474). Thus, the politics of recognition is conceived as a project of cosmopolitan governance, where the self-determination of self-identified peoples is the aim rather than a homogenisation of policy responses or responses that maintain or create new acts of inequity (Young 2000: 9). A politics of recognition must, by definition, accommodate diversity, and thus, assimilation of diversity into normative identities and values is not a resolution of claims to recognition.

Claims to recognition are usually "a means to undermining domination or wrongful deprivation" (Young 2000: 83) and as such may be separate from what is sometimes defined as 'identity politics'. Identity politics has often been dismissed or disparaged within heritage studies as the special pleadings of stakeholders or interest groups (e.g. Lowenthal 2006, 2009a). For Young (2000: 107), identity politics may be understood as an attempt to "cultivate mutual identification among those similarly situated". While these claims may generate conflict, they are differentiated from claims to recognition, as the latter are "rarely asserted for their own sake" and are part of claims for political inclusion and equal economic opportunity (Young 2000: 106). Identity politics, or a politics of difference, can form the basis of claims to recognition, but separating 'identity politics' out from a politics of recognition allows heritage professionals and academics to understand the wider political contexts in which some claims are made, and more importantly, the consequences of those claims for parity of participation.

A particular criticism of Fraser's approach is the lack of attention she pays to the state. As Thompson (2006: 126) notes, the state has a key role in limiting or facilitating parity of participation. In particular, the role of the colonial state in sanctioning or attributing particular identities has been a particular critique of Indigenous scholars. This criticism notes that struggles for recognition must go through state-sanctioned legal and policy frameworks, thus requiring Indigenous assimilation prior to recognition (Daigle 2016: 264; see also Chen 2018: 943–944). Additionally, state-sanctioned definitions and juxtapositions of race and class may also, as Reed and Chowkwanyun (2012: 169) argue, naturalise capitalist inequality and, in doing so, undermine the capacity to challenge exploitation. As Thompson, argues, not all inequality results from misrecognition or lack of recognition of the cultural value of particular groups and may rest, for instance, on changes in capital flows, but that misrecognition can and often does become a *post hoc* rationalisation for inequitable treatment (Thompson 2006: 60–61).

Additionally, as Chen (2018: 946), drawing on Fraser, argues, the naturalisation of state-sanctioned and devalued racial identities reinforces state authority and the unequal distribution of capital and social relations. The politics of recognition does not claim to address all forms of political negotiations nor does it seek to explain all forms of injustice; however, it offers a persuasive understanding of why identity has become such a central concern in social and political debates and how it may be utilised to develop rationalisations for new or ongoing injustice. The ability to see oneself reflected or not reflected in particular narratives of a nation has compelling consequences, as Stuart Hall has observed (1999: 4). Moreover, recognition, as Young (2000) argues, is also a necessary precondition for democracy and democratic representation (see also Thompson 2006: 129).

The relationship of recognition to democracy is circular, in that "democracy determines justice, but that justice is a necessary condition of democracy" (Thompson 2006: 131). However, this reveals another important aspect of the politics of recognition, that of the issue of 'struggle'. A sense of conflict and struggle lies under all characterisations of recognition (Thompson 2006: 160). In short, as individuals and groups attempt to gain recognition, that recognition may be resisted and denied, nor are claims for and the granting or withholding of recognition linear or closed processes (Fraser 2001, 2008). Tully (2000: 473–476) believes that in the search for recognition, equilibrium cannot be reached in democratic struggles over recognition, as any resolution will always contain non-consensus, injustice and compromise. As such, resolutions to claims for recognition will enviably be "open to further democratic dissent and renegotiation" (2000: 474). Nor is a struggle for recognition confined simply to two actors, the 'self and the other', as any group that makes a claim for recognition will affect other identities and the distribution of power within that group (2000: 474). Thus, Tully argues, struggles occur in "a complex, multilateral web of relations and their affects among actors of different types" (2000: 474). Further, demands will provoke other demands or be met with refusal and maintenance of the status quo; alternatively, they may be met with a willingness to negotiate or with counterdemands for recognition (2000: 247). As negotiations occur in what Tully refers to as 'real-time', there will be fluctuating constraints on negotiations, and importantly, the identities of those seeking recognition, as well as the identities of those from whom recognition is being sought, can change during, and as a consequence of, negotiations (2000: 476). In short, he suggests that:

> struggles over recognition, like struggles over distribution, are not amenable to definitive solutions beyond further democratic disagreement, dispute, negotiation, amendment, implementation, review, and further disagreement.
>
> *(2000: 477)*

Tully's account does not conflict with Fraser's conceptualisation of parity of participation but allows an appreciation that this will always be an ongoing struggle and part of the ongoing project of the democratic negotiation of justice (Young 2000; Fraser 2010).

Markell (2003: 10), in his critique of the politics of recognition, argues that there is too much focus on the issue of identity and suggests that in being concerned with seeking to recognise another's identity, there is a lack of acknowledgement of dominant identities, which is in itself a form of misrecognition (Thompson 2006: 13). The extent to which identity can become a fixed benchmark, used to arbitrate between recognition and misrecognition, Markell (2003: 12–13) argues, is problematic, as it fails to understand, as Tully (2000) also argues, that not only is identity fluid and mutable, but changes to identity may occur as part of the processes of recognition. Markell makes a case for the importance of acknowledgement and suggests that debates over recognition fail to consider how acknowledging "one's own basic ontological conditions" are implicated in aspirations for respect and sovereignty (2003: 10). Thus, a degree of what we might call 'self-acknowledgment', knowledge of one's own identity and 'self-recognition' of one's access, or lack of it, to privilege must underwrite a politics of recognition. That is, individuals and groups must be able to historically situate their social and cultural identity and experiences. Those seeking justice must first recognise themselves as the inheritors of particular marginalised identities and seek solidarity with those similarly positioned. In addition, those from whom recognition is sought must 'self-recognise' and historically situate themselves as the inheritors of privileges and rights denied to others. This is not to say that hegemonic groups have to take responsibility for past wrongs, only the contemporary legacies of those wrongs (Young 2000, 2011); however, the recognition of difference requires grounding in a reflexive recognition and acknowledgement of self. Moreover, any self-recognition must also acknowledge the power structures within which particular identities and groups are located. Failure to do so will mean that any offers of recognition will cultivate new misrecognitions and depravations (Markell 2003: 173; Butler and Athanasiou 2013: 76).

It is also useful to note that those from dominant groups may also seek recognition because they sincerely believe that they are discriminated against or as an active strategy to exclude the recognition of others. In either case, dominant groups will also enter into claims and counterclaims for recognition. However, the ability of dominant groups to engage in critical reflections to a level sufficient to acknowledge the need to recognise others, and in such a way that facilitates redistribution, requires extensive self-evaluation. It is at this point that I return to Honneth and Taylor's discussion about wellbeing and emotion.

Honneth argues that recognition meets a human need and that misrecognition or experiences of disrespect are always accompanied by affective sensations, which may compel individuals to act and make claims that attempt to generate self-esteem (1995: 136). While both Honneth and Taylor consider the emotional impact of non- or misrecognition, it is also useful to consider the requisite skills and consequences of also *offering* recognition. It is at this point that issues such as shame, pride, self-esteem and empathy need to be considered. Andrew Sayer (2005) notes that groups defined by class do not seek recognition in the same way as other groups. He argues they are not necessarily misrecognised, although stigmatisation and lack of respect for their identity can make their situation worse, and suggests that recognition may also take the form of "recognizing someone's moral worth as a person" (2005: 956). In developing his argument, he notes that:

> Sentiments such as pride, shame, envy, resentment, compassion and contempt are not just forms of 'affect' but are evaluative judgements of how people are being treated as regards what they value, that is things they consider to affect their well-being.
>
> *(2005: 948)*

These emotions may not only engender claims for recognition, as Honneth (2005: 135–6) argues but should be considered as central to the politics of recognition and distribution. For example, issues of shame can be used, as Sayer argues, to encourage social conformity in particular groups, which may then fail to make claims for recognition, or may compel others to seek recognition, although this "pursuit always carries the risk of failing and being shamed" (2005: 955, 2011: 167f). While emotions have consequences in how recognition may be pursued, they also remind us of the hazard of further undermining parity and equity (Butler and Athanasiou 2013: 86–91; Chen 2018: 946). As Eva Illouz argues, emotions, while not actions per se, nonetheless provide inner energy that "propels us towards an act" (2007: 2). This act may be to seek recognition, but equally, it can be about offering or withholding recognition. For instance, shame may work, as Sayer (2005: 955) argues, to motivate those offering recognition, and gives the example of anti-racists who may indeed be motivated by their shame of racism to extend recognition that facilitates redistribution. Also, as Laclau (2005) and Mouffe (2019) have argued in relation to agonistic politics, emotion is a crucial aspect of conflict. As argued in Chapter 13, negative emotions can play a role in withholding recognition as those from privileged positions shrink away from negative feelings such as guilt and shame. However, empathy, as illustrated in Chapter 12, is key to making evaluative judgements about the lack of equity and parity of participation needed for privileged groups to offer meaningful recognition. Empathy, as both an emotion and a skill, is central to the self-reflection and self-recognition needed by dominant or privileged groups to recognise themselves as needing to offer recognition and respect.

Empathy, however, is a difficult and contested concept, and it is important to define how I am employing the term in this book. Often criticised as a superficial emotion, empathy has been accused of allowing privileged groups to 'feel' for others, and once having 'felt' allows them to move on without gaining real insight into the inequitable experiences of others (Pedwell 2013). Others see empathy as simply mawkish and as so emotionally overcoming as to cripple those feeling it into inaction (Prinz 2011). Bloom (2016: 22–24), in his polemic book *Against Empathy* argues that it is the rational ability to see the structural and procedural issues in inequality, rather than overemotional empathising, that will ensure that useful moral judgements and actions are made and undertaken. Within heritage studies, empathy has certainly been treated with suspicion. For example, Cubitt (2011) has raised concerns about where the line between voyeurism and critical reflection may lie, while others, such as Lowenthal (2009b; see also Appleton 2007; Jenkins 2011), share Bloom's concern with privileging "cool logic and reasoning" (2016: 26). I am not here rejecting reason and rationality, but rather, taking the position that emotion and rationality are not inseparable (Sayer 2011). Neutrality and rationality, or affecting a 'cool logic', are all states of emotional being, and adopting such states has the same moral consequences as being 'empathetic'. As has been established in the social sciences, emotions, of whatever intensity, are integral to cognition and morality, and moral judgements are entangled with and facilitated by emotion (Ahmed 2004a; Sayer 2011; Wetherell 2012; Morton 2013).

Nevertheless, what of both Cubitt (2011) and Pedwell's (2013) concerns that experiencing empathy becomes an end itself rather than a prelude to understanding or action? More alarmingly, as Cubitt (2011) muses, can empathy be linked to or negated by voyeurism and the enjoyment of another's disadvantage? It is important to stress here that emotions and feelings do not exist in absolute or binary states; there are intensities or degrees of feelings. Clohesy (2013: 59), in his defence of empathy, states that "ambivalence to the suffering of others, or indeed our enjoyment of it, should not cause us to lose faith in our capacity to care" or to work toward understanding "the complex political, social and cultural dynamics that structure and inform our different responses" to inequality and suffering. As Berlant (2004: 6) notes in relation to 'compassion', a term Bloom (2016: 23) favours over empathy, compassion like empathy is conceived as a "simple emotion ideally, intending a clear program of amelioration or justice to follow", but in reality, there are scales of responses. Thus, it is not only the emotions an individual or group may bring to bear on particular problems that will influence how they are understood and resolved but also the scale or intensity of that emotion and the ways in which that emotion may be entangled with other emotions and indeed ideology. I will come back to the point about ideology in the following, but in defining how I am using empathy, I want first to acknowledge that empathy can do different things depending on its intensity and how it is linked to other factors. In particular, I draw on Sontag's (2004) idea of sincerity, and the importance of imagination that is raised in discussions over memory (Keightley and Pickering 2012), to argue for the utility of empathy in struggles over recognition and redistribution.

Insincere or shallow expressions of empathy or compassion will fail to extend recognition and may indeed only work to make those from dominant groups 'feel better' and more secure in their own identities. However, when empathy is combined with sincerity of intent and linked to imagination, it is vital in understanding difference and diversity (Clohesy 2013: 56) and to imagine "alternative futures and presents" where social justice is addressed (Johnson 2005: 42). If we accept that morality describes the desired state, rather than necessarily how the world is (Prinz 2007: 1), then the utility of imaginative empathy is evident. Imagination is also central "to the creative production of meaning about the past, present and future" (Keightley and Pickering 2012: 7). Debates over the nature of memory have established that memories change and shift and are only understood through a continual process of remembering and forgetting (Connerton 1991, 2008; Wertsch 2002). In this process, new meanings and understandings are created in the present (Landsberg 2004, 2009; Pickering and Keightley 2013). The idea of mnemonic imagination, developed by Keightley and Pickering (2012: 7), identifies the interplay that occurs as people reconstruct and negotiate the past in order to inform the present and future through performative acts of remembering that are animated by imagination.

Similarly, they argue that in the transmission from firsthand to secondhand experience, or to what Landsberg (2004) defines as the creation of 'prosthetic memory', imagination is central. In addition, however, emotions or skills, such as empathy, become integral first to an acknowledgment of difference and second to the imaginative leaps required for recognising the utility of prosthetic memories and their meanings being taken up in the present (Landsberg 2004: 135, 2009). Further, as Campbell (2006) and Morton (2002, 2013) argue, emotion is crucial to the processes of remembering and forgetting, as the degree to which emotions evoked by memories are considered 'accurate' or authentic work to help judge the utility or legitimacy of those memories (see also Bagnall 2003). However, for emotion to have a transformative effect on understanding the past and its meaning in the present, and specifically, to allow that understanding to extend to the possibility of recognition, it must engage emotional intelligence. Emotional intelligence is the skill to first recognise an emotional response and then to utilise that response in making judgements (Illouz 2007: 65; Mayer et al. 2008). Empathy, like the concept of heritage, has been dismissed as subjective, overly emotional and thus untrustworthy.

However, they are both occurrences that interact to have a consequence, in that they both have the facility to make and remake particular understandings that can have moral and political consequences. The discussion of emotion and heritage is expanded ahead; however, before turning to that, it is useful to summarise the implications the politics of recognition and redistribution have for heritage.

Heritage and recognition

Appeals to the past, or in Macdonalds' (2013) terms, making the past present, lend historical and cultural legitimacy to claims to difference and claims to identity. Heritage is implicated in the politics of recognition in numerous ways, but it may also allow us to add extra dimensions to the understanding of this struggle. There are seven points I would like to make about how heritage may be both understood within and may offer insight for the politics of recognition.

First, authority is given to the idea of heritage as a representation of identity. This assumption is played out daily and nationally and internationally authorised through various national legal and intergovernmental treaties. The highly performative and visible practices and activities associated with building and maintaining the World Heritage List and, more recently, the lists of intangible heritage, also afford authority and advertise the utility of heritage and its representational power for identity. One of the key developments in our understanding of the idea of 'heritage' arose in nineteenth-century debates within architecture, archaeology and art history. These debates, occurring simultaneously in these disciplines across Western Europe, led to the development of the AHD (Smith 2006). However, this discourse does more than legitimise and delegitimise particular understandings of heritage. Within this discourse the preservation of material heritage was stressed in terms of a desire to preserve the past in the face of two interlinked and increasing threats to first, a particular aesthetic sensibility, and second, and most importantly, an understanding of both the past and contemporary cultural and social experiences valued by a particular socioeconomic stratum of European society. Thus, we get the development of an understanding of heritage that becomes closely tied to developing concepts of nationalism, in particular, the political strategies used by social and economic elites to maintain political influence through an appeal to their historical and cultural significance as demonstrated by the then newly minted concept of national heritage. The important point here is that the AHD is explicitly linked to the justifications of professional and elite claims to control the past and its meaning for the present. At its inception, the modern European understanding of heritage was intimately linked to the identity politics being played out by European ruling and professional classes. This historical entanglement with 'identity politics' establishes the authority of heritage to not only represent but to also legitimate certain claims about the past in the present. As Derickson (2016: 825) observes, "knowledge production practices are themselves implicated in cultural marginalisation and misrecognition". That heritage became, during the twentieth century, an area of technical expertise and management does not negate its political implications, although this did work to naturalise many assumptions about the essential nature of heritage as evidential validation of identity claims.

The idea of the authority of heritage to represent identity is further reinforced by the institutional authority of museums. Museums and heritage sites, as Macdonald (2013) points out, are part of the memory complexes that facilitate expressions of identity. Various surveys in different national contexts have identified the degree of authority and legitimacy given to museums by their visitors and the wider public to 'accurately' portray history and culture (e.g. Cameron 2006; Ashton and Hamilton 2010; Bounia et al. 2012; Conrad et al. 2013). Moreover, as Bounia et al. (2012: 14) found, museums are charged with a particular responsibility by their audiences to provide an inclusive and representative sense of national identity. Thus, the authority of heritage and the institutional power of museums identifies heritage as an important resource in struggles over recognition. Additionally, as Kinsley (2016) argues, a critical understanding of the role of museums within the context of recognition *and* redistribution is required to achieve successful social inclusion outcomes.

The second implication is that individuals and groups may also be expected to seek validation or understanding of their own or another's identity and historical and contemporary social and economic experience. In this case, heritage sites and museums may directly or indirectly facilitate either the seeking or conferring of recognition, the maintenance of the status quo or offer more active strategies for denying recognition.

The third implication is that within the framework of the AHD, we could expect heritage representations to be used to overtly or covertly withhold or deny recognition and to offer resistance through misrecognition or lack of regard to claims by subaltern groups for recognition. How hegemonic groups construct understandings of both themselves and of 'the other' within the AHD are inevitably significant potential acts of misrecognition and exclusion.

A fourth implication is that those seeking recognition will tend to do so outside the confines of the AHD or risk assimilation into this discourse. Thus, how heritage is itself being used and defined by subaltern groups, and its subsequent legitimacy within professional contexts, must itself be addressed as a problem to be overcome within certain struggles for recognition. In effect, the challenging and legitimisation of heritage expressions may become part of the struggle for recognition and redistribution.

A fifth point relates to the re-theorisation of heritage as a cultural performance that rejects definitions of heritage as framed by the AHD. If we accept that heritage is not simply 'a thing, place or site', but is rather a negotiated and affective process and activity in which meaning and narrative are affirmed and remade, heritage becomes *directly* implicated in the politics of recognition. Indeed, heritage performances may be understood as a part of the process of asserting, negotiating and legitimising claims for recognition and redistribution as identities are themselves asserted, negotiated and re/constructed. Those sites and places normatively defined as heritage are important cultural tools in the processes of heritage-making. Such material things nonetheless can, as acknowledged in Chapter 1, be evocative and important arenas that facilitate the creation of heritage meaning. Heritage-making is a highly affective phenomenon, and sites and places are, as Poria et al. (2003) demonstrate, where people go to 'feel' and emotionally engage with their heritage; heritage has a particular power to compel action – and this may include to seek, offer or withhold recognition.

The sixth point is that heritage also highlights the importance of 'self-recognition' in the politics of recognition. One of the core findings discussed in the following chapters is the degree to which visitors to museums and heritage sites were engaged in a process of self-affirmation and reinforcement of knowledge, belief and identity. Chapter 9, in particular, illustrates the performance of affirmation of self that many visitors to heritage sites engaged in. The affirming authority of heritage to underpin self-confidence and self-esteem in one's identity is an important point from which individuals and collectives can launch claims for recognition, offer recognition to others or resolve to ignore and thus deny the claims of others.

Finally, it is worth stressing that the politics of recognition and redistribution provides a nuanced understanding of the consequences of the links between heritage and identity. It shows the power of heritage and why and how heritage is implicated in wider social and political struggles. Thus, I do not see heritage as something that, on occasion, may intersect with the politics of recognition, but rather, this association is part of the constitutive nature of heritage. While Chapters 12 and 13 illustrate the various ways that we might see recognition and misrecognition playing out in specific performative and affective practices of heritage-making, I also argue that the politics of recognition is indivisible from heritage. This is because whenever the idea that heritage constitutes identity is invoked, heritage immediately becomes implicated in struggles over recognition. These struggles may equally include the maintenance of dominant or received identities and the social and historical narratives that underpin them as much as they also challenge those identities and narratives and the instances of misrecognition they may maintain.

Heritage, affect and emotion: the affective practices of heritage

The preceding section noted the importance of emotion in relation to the ways in which heritage becomes a resource of power within the politics of recognition; this section offers a fuller consideration of the role of affect/emotion in the performance of heritage-making. Conceptualizing heritage as a performance opens up the possibility that heritage may be used by individuals and sub-national collectives or communities to create and recreate, either within or outside of the AHD, their own identities and narratives about the meaning of the past for the present. However, any engagement with ideas of performance also requires a consideration of the issue of embodiment (Chapter 1). This, in turn, allows considerations of knowledge production linked directly to the subjective ideas of emotion, imagination and memory. Issues of emotion and imagination have traditionally not been convincingly dealt with by rationalist forms of understanding, knowledge production and enquiry and are often dismissed as irrational (Ahmed 2004a).

As Smith and Campbell (2016) have argued, there has been a historical tendency within heritage and museum studies to treat emotion with suspicion and to either dismiss it altogether or to superficially reduce considerations to a concern with nationalistic celebrations or a critique of nostalgia (see, for example, Lowenthal 1985, 2009b; Wright 1985; Chase and Shaw 1989; Goulding 2001; Jenkins 2011). In these cases, emotion tended to be equated with either reactionary nationalising politics or with the commercialisation of heritage through tourism, itself often characterized as 'dumbing down' the meaning of the past (Smith and Campbell 2016: 448). This critique particularly focused on heritage tourism and tourists themselves who were often unfavourably defined as the perpetrators of mawkish romanticism or searching for mindless entertainment (Graburn and Barthel-Bourchier 2001; Ashworth 2009; Hall 2009; Watson 2010; Staiff 2014 for further critique). Indeed, emotion has often been identified as impeding a balanced understanding of the past and the role heritage can play in informing the present and educating tourists and other visitors to heritage sites and museums (Lowenthal 2009b; Jenkins 2011). The AHD itself assumes emotional neutrality through its stress on neutral, 'value-free', rational expert assessments of heritage values and the performance of professional practices. In privileging the assumed objectivity of expertise, those people who utilise and visit heritage sites and museums during their leisure times (i.e. tourists) are often dismissed as legitimate users of heritage, being irrationally emotional in their engagement with such places. This negativity is often coupled with the dominant assumption within the AHD that tourists epitomise a significant management 'problem'. That is, they are often conceived as constituting both a physical threat to sites by their mere presence and being the triggers for 'Disneyfication' or the 'dumbing down' of expert knowledge through entertaining appeals to emotionalism. Thus, any heritage-making that those identified as tourists may perform when visiting museums and heritage sites is often discounted and the irrational, non-expert visitor/tourist is relegated to the role of the receiver of expert and curatorial educational messages. The significance of this issue is discussed in Chapter 3; however, the simple point to stress here is that heritage is emotional. If we accept the assumption that heritage is linked in varying ways to the expression of identity, be it national, communal, familial or individual, we engage with an emotive concept. If heritage 'matters', then there is an emotional element in the way it matters.

The lack of regard for emotion in museum and heritage studies has, however, began to change alongside what has been called the 'affective turn' (Clough 2007) in the social sciences and humanities. The importation of these wider debates within heritage and museum studies, has, however, not always been productive. The importation, for example, of Non-representational Theory (NRT) and other positions that privilege the immediacy of affect as pre-social and pre-cognitive tend to reproduce some of the problematic issues discussed in Chapter 1 in relation to New Materialism and Post Humanism. This section offers an overview of some of the key debates on affect/emotion, drawing out issues and concepts relevant to heritage and museums, while arguing for a pragmatic approach to affect and emotion that defines both these terms as interrelated.

As Wetherell (2012: 2) states, the turn to affect primarily offers a provocation to broaden the scope of social investigation and "leads to a focus on embodiment". As she goes on to note, the significant advantage of affect is that it brings both the dramatic and the mundane back into social analysis, while adding "emotion to the inventory of social research topics" (Wetherell 2012: 2–3). Mouffe (2013) usefully suggests that emotion, in the same way that gender became an indispensable category in the social sciences, should become a central and unavoidable element of analysis. For Hoggett and Thompson (2012: 2) the turn to affect offers social science an opportunity to catch up with the feeling world around us. However, much of the literature on affect is also concerned, as with New Materialism, with what is perceived as an over privileging of discourse and configures affect as pre- or 'extra' discursive and is concerned with a desire to find new ways of articulating the biological and cultural (Massumi 2002; Thrift 2008; Anderson and Harrison 2010). Much of this latter approach builds on the philosophy of Gilles Deleuze (Crouch 2010; Wetherell 2013a), while the work of Thrift (2008) and Massumi (2002) have been influential in heritage and museum studies. As Wetherell (2013a: 350) notes, the work of these theorists intersects somewhat counterintuitively with the Post Human positions, where interest in and definitions of bodies encompass the biological and the technical. Here again, the emphasis is on the emergent and the immanent, that assemble within what Anderson (2009: 79) refers to as affective atmospheres, which are both "reducible to bodies affecting other bodies" while "exceeding the bodies they emerge from".

One of the core points of contention in the debates over affect and emotion is the conceptualisation of 'affect' and its relationship with 'emotion'. For key theorists such as Thrift (2004, 2008), Massumi (2002, 2015) and Anderson (2009), affect is separate from emotion; it is extra-discursive and pre-cognitive and unfettered by social context. For Thrift (2008), affect is located outside representational domains such as discourse and language; that is, it is more than representation (Lorimer 2005). The power of affect is identified as biologically based; it is intense and intuitive and is only mediated by social context after a momentary time lag (Massumi 2002, 2015). This formulation is based, as Leys (2011) and Wetherell (2012, 2013a) show in close detail, on a misreading of studies and debates in psychology and neuroscience that measured electrical activity in the brain. As Wetherell (2012: 61–62) points out, the debates are more complex than Massumi and Thrift allow and more typically tend to emphasise that affect is highly dynamic and interactive of bodily functions, such as sweating, trembling, blushing, and cognitive processes such as perception, memory and decision-making. Moreover, the interplay between biological responses and the social are often culturally and historically far more complex and nuanced than can be adequately addressed by neuroscience (Reddy 2001; Frevert 2011). Affect is inevitably and inescapably socially mediated (Clough 2007; Leys 2011; Wetherell 2012, 2013a).

However, in conceptualising affect as pre-social, those working within NRT or taking their theoretical cues more generally from Deleuze, Thrift or Massumi, highlight a number of epistemological and methodological problems. A core concern is that the conceptualisation of affect as pre-social has resulted in an analytical focus on emergent atmospheres – contextualisation of these being analytically irrelevant. Thrift (2008), drawing on a biological metaphor, sees these as spread contagiously, or as Brennan (2004) asserts, atmospheres are 'felt'. In such accounts, certain assumptions about the meaning of pre-social affect are allowed to exist unchallenged. As Cresswell (2012: 96) argues, these assumptions tend to reflect the social experiences of the researchers – that is, they tend to facilitate the perpetuation of androcentric and Eurocentric assumptions about what is 'felt' and the biological legitimacy of such 'feeling' (see also Thien 2005; Wetherall 2012). Contra to both Thrift's (2008) claims that such positioning allows greater attention to be given to different possibilities of knowing and engagement with intersubjectivity, logically the conceptualisation of pre-social and pre-cognitive affective responses belies the analytical possibility of engaging with contextual issues of class, race, gender and so forth. For example, recent research in this field in heritage studies has tended to employ auto-ethnographic methods to give accounts of the researcher's affective responses to heritage (e.g. Waterton 2014; Grewcock 2014; Arnold-de Simine 2019). This may tell us a lot about the privileged position of the researcher but fails to address how these experiences are contextually mediated. What we tend to get in this context is a range of case studies on affective responses, the accumulative weight of which work to reinforce and legitimise the innate affective agency of heritage sites and objects. What this inevitably adds to the heritage discourse is an understanding that heritage is affective, but along with those innate values defined by the AHD, its affective qualities tend to be reduced to the innate and immutable. As Wetherell (2013a) argues, the separation of affect from discourse, from its social context, creates a methodological and conceptual impasse.

The conceptualisation of affect within NRT and allied positions work to obscure human agency. Affect is presupposed as simply coming upon us unawares, that affective atmospheres seep into and confound us like rolling fogs. While, of course, we can be unexpectedly affected, caught off our guard and confronted by the unexpected affective moment (Ahmed 2004a; Thrift 2008), this does not mean that people do not exercise choice in being affected or in acknowledging and acting upon an affective experience. Affect can be anticipated; indeed, as Archer (2000: 202) argues, this is key to affect. If we did not anticipate as part of our inner conversations and reflections on events around us, any affective event would, as Archer observes, be reduced to the event itself. Acknowledging that one is being affected requires context, and Archer's (2000) notion of subjectivity is useful in this regard. Not everyone who encounters, for example, the sight of piled, discarded, used shoes will of necessity be affected – one has to know, for example, what these shoes may represent or be aware that one is encountering them in the context of the Holocaust Memorial Museum in Washington, DC. Standing on a vacant plot of land where you know a massacre has taken place can be immensely affective, but that affect does not 'just happen'; you need knowledge of the event. Walking over a grave can be distressing and disrespectful for some, while for others it is of no issue, as there are different ways to feel about and show respect to the dead. The point here is that to be affected by a heritage object or place requires two things. First, it requires knowledge of and valuation of that object or place; second, it requires you to *care* in particular ways.

Caring is influenced not simply by cultural or social context but also by ideology (Jost 2006): what a person chooses to care about, to be affected by, and how they are affected will be influenced by political beliefs and values. In dismissing social context, ideology becomes obscured. Rather than dismissing the idea that the political attitudes of individuals lack logical consistency and the coherence of organised ideology, Jost (2006: 651) argues that ideological positions help to frame the way an individual processes information. Political attitudes are argued to be linked to social and cognitive motives (Jost et al. 2003). The model of motivated social cognition illustrates, for example, that political conservativism may be embraced by individuals, in part, to alleviate fear, anxiety and uncertainty (Jost et al. 2003: 340). This motivated social cognition approach does not eschew individual reasoning but identifies that emotions and ideology are interrelated (Jost 2006: 655). The psychological motive to manage fear and uncertainty is pronounced in political conservatism (Jost et al. 2003: 351). Conservatives are identified as uncomfortable with social change, and that fear, and fear of ambiguity and change, in particular, is linked to politically conservative tendencies to resist social change and to justify and accept inequity to maintain the status quo (Jost et al. 2003: 351). Political conservatives are also more uncomfortable than those with progressive ideologies with dissonance-arousing situations and are thus far more likely to disengage from those situations (Nam et al. 2013).

Various studies in political science also indicate that, overall, individuals will process information in the context of their existing beliefs (Cobb and Kuklinski 1997; Taber and Lodge 2006; Nyhan and Reifler 2010). Additionally, this work also demonstrates that people are, in general, more likely than not to seek confirmation and reinforcement of what they already know and will do so even in the face of contradictory information. However, the desire for confirmation of one's beliefs and understandings, and the reliance on 'gut feelings', is particularly prevalent when the maintenance of a sense of personal stability and certainty is jeopardised (Jost and Krochik 2014). Those with conservative ideologies demonstrate a greater tendency to oversimplify and to be more selective in the information they process, often engaging in self-deception and relying heavily on intuitive thinking in the process, than progressives/liberals who, in being more comfortable with uncertainty, are more likely to possess skills in recognising and addressing argument quality and nuance (Jost and Krochik 2014). Ideologies and other belief systems, Jost (2006) argues, are linked to epistemic, existential and relational human needs and motivations. An important observation that emerges from identifying the influence of ideology on the skills, or lack of skills, to address and cognitively mediate particular emotional states is the recognition that individuals make choices and that there is human agency in the decisions made to exercise or not certain skills.

Both Archer's idea of reflexivity and the work on ideology, emotion and cognition, allows a recognition that people have agency in being, or not being, affected, and in managing and regulating the emotions that may, or may not, follow on from this (Mesquite and Albert 2007: 491). However, another issue to raise here is that stressing the emergent nature of affect also tends to lead us, as Berlant (2008: 7, 2011: 10) points out, to be concerned with the dramatic. For Massumi (2002), affect is excess, intense and 'wild', 'domesticated' and tamed only once it is turned into recognisable emotions that can be communicated and discussed with others (Wetherell 2013a: 354 for critique). In this process, the mundane, the gentler and calmer affective and emotional responses, are neglected. If we are to be concerned, as Ahmed (2004a) suggests, with understanding what emotions do, the everyday and the banal (Billig 1995) should become as analytically critical as the extraordinary and intense. As Berlant (2011) argues, trauma or crisis is worked through and made understandable in the ordinary and familiar.

Sara Ahmed (2004a, 2008), another significant theorist of affect/emotion, is concerned with understanding the social value of affect. She is quite clear that affect does not reside in an object, individual or sign, but rather, is produced in the circulation between these elements (2004b: 120). This circulation will see the accumulation of affective value over time, and thus, certain objects take on particular values as being affective (2008: 11). As she notes, particular 'affective communities' will value certain objects/circumstances that other communities do not, and so different communities will have different affective responses. Emotions do not reside but circulate, and in this process, they can 'stick' and adhere to certain objects and signs (2004a: 11). As Wetherell (2012: 158–159, 2015: 158) argues, this theorisation reduces emotion to a disembodied force, neither located in material things, signs nor individuals. In focusing on the circulation of emotion, we again end up considering the emergent, the points at which things stick or cease to stick. As Wetherell (2012: 160) states, focusing on the circulation of signs as Ahmed does is "to risk over-idealising affect and, paradoxically, [. . .] bodies completely disappear from the study of affect".

We have come to the impasse that Wetherell (2013a) identifies: How do we engage with affect that both deals with the body and the social? As Wetherell (2013a: 353) acknowledges, the overemphasis on discourse that concerns Thrift (2008) has indeed obscured embodiment. This does not mean, however, that discourse needs to be abandoned; rather, affect opens up questions about how the "speaking subject makes sense of and communicates affect" (Wetherell 2013a: 353). Wetherell (2012) has developed the idea of 'affective practice' to draw attention to how affect and emotion are bound up with social relations. This concept brings together emotion, discourse and practice and adds conceptual depth to arguments about the performative nature of heritage-making (Wetherell, Smith and Campbell 2018).

Affective practice

To address the "entanglements of embodiment and discourse", Wetherell's (2013a: 351) concept of 'affective practice' starts from the pragmatic position that affect/emotion has consequences for how people understand and experience the world. Underpinning this conceptualisation is the position that affect is not separate from emotion; rather, as Archer puts it, affect is "the signature tune of emotion" (2000: 201). In general, the term 'affect' tends to describe an embodied and initial registering of events; 'emotions' then refers to the processing of affect into cultural and linguistic categories such as joy, anger, fear and so on, while 'feeling' tends to be understood in a longer-term introspective and internalised quality (Williams 1977; Wierzbicka 1999; Wetherell 2015). However, as Wetherell argues, rather than there a being a sequencing of events where affect or the body comes first and emotions and meaning-making comes second, affect/emotion are always intertwined – both embodied and semiotic (Wetherell, Smith and Campbell 2018: 1). Practice, as Wetherell argues, as both noun and verb, is a way of conceptualising social action as "constantly in motion while yet recognising too that the past, and what has been done before, constrains the present and the future" (Wetherell 2012: 23). While practice can be about improvisation, it is also about repetition and training. Practice can be regulated and controlled, and, in drawing on the work of Nikolas Rose, she notes it can be a form of discipline and control (2012: 23). This sense of practice acknowledges Bourdieu's (1990) idea of social action as *habitus*, but also, as Wetherell (2012: 105) argues, that routine can be challenged through reflexive responses to new circumstances. Here, Wetherell draws on Archer's idea of reflexivity and the internal conversations in which people resist or conform to the patterns in their lives (2012: 105–106). As Archer observes, emotions are "among the main constituents of our inner lives" and fuel the inner conversation and are central to defining the things we care about and "to the act of caring itself" (Archer 2000: 194). Wetherell identifies what she calls 'canonical emotional styles' and 'affective repertoires' that "emerge in bodies, in minds, in individual lives, in relationships, in communities, across generations, and in social formations" (2015: 147). While these can feel uncontrollable and have an unbidden quality, and routine and habitual forms of affective practice may induce a sense of inevitable logic, they nonetheless need to be continually reworked according to situation and context (Wetherell 2015: 147). Alternatively, affective practices can be flexible and improvised, and different practices can intertwine and combine to create new forms of meaning (Wetherell 2013b: 232).

Thus, within the concept of affective practice, affect is relational and responsive to circumstances and situations. Emotions have a consequence not just for self, but occur in relation to culturally situated others, and it is this tension that ignites emotions with an 'energy' that motivates and underpins certain social actions and relationships (Archer 2000: 196; Illouz 2007). Sense is made of bodily responses by the emotions they provoke, as emotions become feelings; feelings, as Reddy (2001) and Mercer (2010) argue, are integral to thinking and understanding and mediating what we believe or disbelieve. How emotions, feelings and moods are expressed are not only regulated and moderated by discursive practices, they are also in a sense made 'real' by these practices. They are, of course, also influenced, intensified and rehearsed by the words used to communicate them (Reddy 2001: 104). As Wetherell, drawing on Burkitt, states:

> Feelings are not *expressed* in discourse so much as *completed* in discourse. That is, the emotion terms and narratives available in a culture, the conventional elements so thoroughly studied by social constructionist researchers, realise the affect and turn it for the moment into a particular kind of thing. What may start as inchoate can sometimes be turned into an articulation, mentally organised and publicly communicated, in ways that engage with and reproduce regimes and power relations.
>
> *(2012: 24, original emphasis)*

The idea of affective practices interlinks with ideas of practice and performance discussed in Chapter 1, in which embodied actions are defined as transmitting and/or constituting their own forms of knowledge and identity (Butler 1990; Taylor 2003). The affective qualities of performative practice influence the ways in which knowledge and identity are re/created and transmitted. Cognition and reason can no longer be separated from emotion (Barbalet 2001; Reddy 2001; Ahmed 2004a; Protevi 2009; Mercer 2010; Frevert 2011, among others). Indeed, emotions are central in making evaluative judgements and informing our moral lives (Sayer 2005; Mercer 2010; Morton 2013). They are also influenced and regulated by the particular context in which they occur. For instance, Berlant (2004: 450–451) discusses how research into particular publicly expressed feelings in the United States under the Bush administration motivated citizens to either turn out to vote or not vote (chapters in Thompson and Hoggett 2012). Emotions are often shared and collective and thus can help construct both personal and collective social meaning and narratives (Berlant 2004, 2011). The notion of 'affective communities' recognises the "sociability" of emotions (Ahmed 2008: 10–11; Walkerdine 2010), however; the point to stress here is that social structures such as class, gender, ethnicity and so forth, as well as social norms, mediate emotional expression and the work this emotion may then do (Archer 2000: 215; Sayer 2005; Illouz 2007: 73; Wingfield 2010; Wetherell 2013b;). There are 'structures of feeling' (Williams 1977), 'feeling rules' (Hochschild 1979) or 'affective repertoires' (Wetherell 2012, 2015) that are taken for granted and hegemonic and others that are subordinate and will both influence and regulate affective practices and the social or political legitimacy they are given. As Hochschild (1979, 1983) has argued, there are ways in which emotions are managed through latent social rules and 'conventions of feeling'. These conventions, where certain individuals may be identified as having 'a right' to or 'ought to' feel certain emotions in particular situations are controlled and regulated by class, gender, ethnicity and other social structures.

Reddy (2001: 104) and Wetherell (2012: 24) both note that particular emotional words or terms are speech acts, or performative utterances, that do things in the world. It is useful to consider that the term 'heritage' is itself an emotional utterance. Words and utterances that do things, what Reddy defines as 'emotives' (2001: 104), marshal the inner energy of emotion that propels us to act (Illouz 2007: 2), engage cognition and allow us to feel and believe (Mercer 2010) and facilitate and frame evaluative judgements (Sayer 2005) and help us to make sense of the word. Heritage becomes a performative process that is ultimately about expressing and negotiating an affective state of belonging and believing. This formulation adds a deeper nuance to my previous arguments about the processual and performative nature of heritage. It explicitly recognises heritage as a practice that is concerned with re/creating and negotiating the meaning of the past for the needs of the present. However, it also acknowledges that emotional investments may be made in the expression and justification of various social values and beliefs and the historical narratives they underpin.

An important point to stress here is that in relation to Reddy's (2001) idea of emotives, and at the risk of belabouring my point, emotions are not simply socially constructed by emotional labelling, but rather as Archer states, "are socially *constituted* properties which are emergent from the internal relations between the subject's concerns and society's normativity" (2000: 215, original emphasis). That is, emotions emerge and do 'work' for individuals and society in relation to a person's subject status in society, a society's moral order and the conjunction between personal concerns and social norms and values (Archer 2000: 215). It is through internal dialogue that emotions emerging from body/environmental relations are transformed into an emotional commentary on the practical world (Archer 2000: 221) and affective practices (Wetherell 2012: 106). There is not a singular affective practice, but rather, a range of practices. As these interrelate with social norms and values, some practices will be given more authority than others, and some will be admired or reviled by different social groups. Some practices will be habitual and routine, having worn as Wetherell describes it "grooves or ruts in people's bodies and minds" (Wetherell et al. 2018: 6), others more reactive and flexible (Wetherell 2013b).

Affective heritage practices

The idea of 'affective heritage practices' combines the arguments I have made in Chapter 1 about the performative nature of heritage with the idea of affective practices discussed previously and advocated by Wetherell (2012, 2013b, 2015). This section summarises the explicit way considering affect/emotion and informs and enriches the idea of heritage as a cultural process and performance so that we may move to the identification of 'affective heritage practices'. The focus of the performance of affective heritage practices will be the mediation of the meaning of the past in the present. However, there is not a singular and defining practice; rather, a range of performances are understood to exist, which will be expressed in many ways, some framed and informed by the AHD and others not. Some practices will be routine and mundane, others sporadic or special, some explicitly self-aware and others less so. Different practices will have different outcomes and re/create different heritage meanings and will have differing social and political implications and consequences.

However, elements that will be important in the performance of any affective heritage practice will include, but not be confined to, issues of memory, identity, sense of place, and contestation and dissonance, all issues discussed in *Uses of Heritage* as being central to heritage as a process of meaning-making. Remembering and the associated practices of forgetting are creative processes in which meaning and understandings about the past and its significance to the present are continually remade. Further, the process of remembering is explicitly undertaken to address the needs in the present, and the past is made and remade in the context of present-day aspirations (Wertsch 2002). As Macdonald (2013) argues, there are a range of 'memory complexes' that include museums, heritage sites, memorials and other institutions, and the events they sponsor, that frame, regulate and legitimise performances of remembrance and commemoration. The process of individual and collective remembering and forgetting will also be framed and influenced by what Wertsch (2008a) defines as schematic narrative templates, the agreed or authorised social and historical narratives that frame and organise the meanings created in the processes of remembering. However, this process is also energised and arbitrated by affect/emotion. Morton's (2002) concept of 'emotional truth' recognises that remembering and forgetting are both reflexive processes in which not only the strength of feeling but also the appropriateness of the emotional response is contextualised. The sense of 'accuracy' or 'authenticity' given to the emotions engendered by particular memories and processes of remembering imbue recollections with a dimension of legitimacy that is then used to negotiate the utility of the memory to present circumstances (Campbell 2006: 370).

The idea that emotions manage and frame the processing of 'memories' can be extended to the various ways in which the past is made useful and meaningful in the present. This process of emotional validation or invalidation subsequently impacts on the affective 'accuracy' of the narrative templates involved in the process of remembering. It will also impact on the sense of emotional authenticity and emotional links and boundaries people forge in constructing and experiencing a sense of place, identity and social and cultural wellbeing. As the discussion about the politics of recognition reveals, expressions and practices of identity-making do not simply address a human emotional need, but also have political, moral and ethical consequences (Sayer 2011). As a form of affective practice, the politics of recognition illustrates how emotions not only matter in concrete terms, but that considering human agency and choice in managing and expressing emotions is of analytical utility. Archer's (2000) idea of reflexivity is conceptually useful at facilitating how individuals mull over and make the links between their affective responses to certain situations and how they consider, mull over and pass judgements on social and historical issues.

Further, in my previous arguments about the performance of heritage-making, I argued that heritage was ultimately about the mediation of social change and dissonance (Smith 2006: 82). Dissonant heritage, or heritage that is contested and associated with uncomfortable and difficult histories, has tended to be defined as a particular 'type' of heritage; however, alongside Graham et al. (2000), I argue that dissonance is an integral aspect of heritage-making (see also Tunbridge and Ashworth 1996). *All* heritage is dissonant and contested by someone, and the idea that there can be 'universal' valuations of heritage is simply a rhetorical conceit of the AHD. If the working through and privileging or disprivileging of certain heritage claims, values and conflicts are emotionally entangled and implicated in the politics of recognition, then it is also ideologically consequential. Dissonance, as an integral aspect of affective heritage practices, becomes in this theorising more deeply significant and implicated in struggles over social change or social continuity. My position sits comfortably with that of Mouffe (2013) and Laclau (2005), who argue that democratic politics is agonistic – that is, typified by antagonisms, tensions over establishing hegemony and the mobilisation of intense emotions. The rhetorical appeals by conservative groups to maintain their 'heritage' in the face of demands to remove colonial statues as part of the Rhodes Must Fall campaign, or in response to ongoing civil rights debates over the symbols of the Southern Confederacy in the United States, are illustrative of the affective entanglement of heritage with ideology. The AHD has traditionally stressed social stasis and the continuity of heritage; in this discourse it is defined as 'non-renewable' and often critiqued as resulting in the management of heritage as something 'frozen' in time. It is energised by the fear of losing aspects of, or changing the meaning of the past, and in ensuring that heritage values are understood as immutable. Affective heritage practices framed within the AHD become easily entangled in certain ideological positions.

As argued, emotions do not simply come upon us; they are socially contextualised and mediated. The combined idea that emotions are used to validate or invalidate the meanings of the past and that they are themselves managed and regulated by social context, ideology and 'feeling rules' (Hochschild 1979) has two important consequences. First, it means that affect/emotion not only invigorates the legitimacy of the meanings of the past for the present that individuals and groups construct, it also secondly, actively frames and manages those heritage meanings and the social and political consequences they have. In short, context matters; social structures such as class, gender, ethnicity, race, age and so forth, as well as political beliefs, have consequences for the legitimacy and authenticity attributed to particular emotions and feelings and the affective practices they underwrite and inform. Additionally, this means that not only will certain emotions and affective heritage practices be given more validity than others, it reminds us that there are different intensities of emotions that invigorate different practices. Thus, the flat emotions of professional practice, where an 'objective emotional neutrality' may be striven for, are nonetheless as much of an affective practice as public memorialising and commemorating the grief and distress of historical atrocities. It also follows that analytical attention may usefully consider the flat, banal or 'everyday' or 'cool' emotions as much as the more intensely felt or 'hotter' emotions such as fear, anger, joy or grief.

Further, as the discussion over the politics of recognition and empathy reveals, particular emotions such as empathy, compassion, anger and indifference are not absolute and will be expressed at different scales or intensities (Barbalet 2001; Berlant 2004). Thus, a particular affective practice based on, for example, either empathy or fear does not assume particular understandings of the past nor the consequences that flow from that. In applying the idea of affect/emotion to the performances of heritage-making – that is, in developing the idea of affective heritage practices as part of my conceptualisation of heritage performances – it becomes useful to develop and assess ways of measuring and accounting for different types and intensities of emotion among other ways with which heritage is engaged. To that end, the idea of 'registers of engagement' that acknowledges that individuals and groups can engage differently to heritage sites has been developed (Smith 2011; Smith and Campbell 2016) and is explored in more detail in the following chapter.

Conclusion

Heritage is both political and emotive. In developing the theorisation of heritage as a performance of heritage-making, I have drawn on pragmatic theorisations that facilitate understanding the political and emotional power of heritage. In doing so, the representational role and influence of heritage have been both reconsidered and re-asserted. No claims are made that heritage is 'simply' discursive, but rather, that while heritage meanings and values may be discursively and contextually mediated, they also have material consequences. It is in considering these consequences that we get closer to understanding why heritage can matter so much in certain contexts.

Drawing on debates over the nature of the politics of recognition, heritage is theorised as both an explicit and implicit resource within struggles over recognition, social justice and redistribution. Heritage is often given the emotional and representational ability to 'stand in' for or express identity and, as such, it can be understood as a resource of power over which struggles and conflicts will occur and which, in turn, will have implications within wider conflicts over recognition. This is not to say that heritage is 'all powerful', only that it is one of the resources of power that stakeholders may draw on or use in struggles to assert their legitimacy or to deny the legitimacy of others, over equitable access to a range of resources.

Recognition will also address both a moral and emotional need for acknowledgement; heritage, as a particular 'emotive' (Reddy 2001), is imbricated in individual and collective expressions and claims for wellbeing, sense of place and belonging. Addressing the idea of emotion in heritage, the chapter reviewed the turn to affect in the social sciences, arguing that Wetherell's idea of affective practice usefully includes ideas of affect without doing violence to ideas of human agency and the social contexts that mediate the meaning and value of emotion and feeling. The idea of affective practice not only adds "emotion to the inventory" (Wetherell

2012: 2–3) of heritage research but also to ideas about the performance of heritage-making. The concept of heritage performance that I use in the following chapters incorporates the idea that practice and its performance is affective and discursively mediated.

Affective heritage practices will be performed in many forms; some will be framed by the AHD, and others will be performed outside of that dominant discourse and framed by competing and entirely different discursive contexts with differing aspirations. The politics of recognition may inform the goals and nature of the performance of certain affective heritage practices and the heritage-making they undertake but will be irrelevant to others. The issue now becomes this: How do we identify different affective heritage practices – that is, the ways in which emotion/affect frame and impel certain performances of heritage-making and their consequences?

It may be argued that differing affective/emotional resonances will inform and energise different performances; however, the observation that emotions will have different scales and intensities is important here. It is too simplistic to argue that empathy, for example, will engender a particular affective heritage practice and the consequent re/making of heritage meanings and values. Emotion is, of course, not the only energising factor in the performances of heritage-making; moreover, the different scales and intensities of affect/emotion will have different outcomes and consequences. Working through the entanglement of affective and emotional scales with the political and social aspirations and consequences of affective heritage-making is the subject of the following chapter.

3
REGISTERS OF ENGAGEMENT

The opportunity to interview visitors at the plantation site, the Hermitage, Tennessee, corresponded with a new exhibition on slavery that featured the history and lives of the enslaved at the plantation. The Hermitage had been the home of Andrew Jackson, the seventh president of the United States, a slave owner and the president responsible for the *Indian Removal Act*, 1830, and the subsequent Trail of Tears. Like all the sites at which I interviewed there were stand-out comments from visitors, those that left me either troubled or delighted. One such troubling response was by a young male student in answer to the question asking if his views had changed:

> How well the slaves were taken care of. I thought it was a little more of a rough existence. But I mean when they paint the whole picture, your family was here, you know. Your source of food was here. You had a day off. I thought that was pretty interesting. That was what I learned.
> *(H14 Male, 25–34, student, Argentinian American)*

The assertion that Jackson treated the enslaved 'well' was a theme repeated quite frequently by visitors to, it should be noted, the clear distress of the curatorial staff when I reported the findings of the interviews to them. While such reactionary responses were extremely concerning, I was also struck by an older man who sat with me for a while, ostensibly undertaking the interview to complain about the difficulty he had as a person with mobility issues moving about the site. He also took the time, however, to tell me the story of his family: how he and his son still lived on his family's land in South Carolina and that the family had owned slaves. I asked him if he thought the exhibition on enslavement was important, fearing his response, like so many others I had interviewed at the site, would be about how well the slaves had been treated or simply dismissed, as still others had done, as 'that was the way it was then':

> It's got to be there, you have to tell them as it was. You can sugar coat it and say it was just what they did at the time, and it was, but that's sugar coating. You have to know what you did wrong and what you did right and live with that as ordinary Americans. That's what my son and I are, we are just ordinary American guys.
> *(H34: male, 55–64, own business, American)*

While there was discomfort over his family's history, there is also ownership of it; his comment that he and his son are just 'ordinary guys' is a tacit acknowledgement that American identity encompasses complex historical tensions. The two marked comments I have provided here, however, stand in contrast to those that were simply prosaic in their banality and unimaginative response to either the house or to the accompanying exhibition on enslavement:

> They did a good job here of representing, not being biased towards Andrew Jackson. They showed his faults while showing off the good things as well.
> *(H18: male, 25–34, lawyer, American)*

> It makes me sad sometimes to think about how the slaves lived. That whole history fascinates me.
> *(H41: female, over 65, retired teacher, White American)*

Although I have used the example of the Hermitage, all the interview sites had visitors who expressed clear progressive or conservative views or engaged in alternatively imaginative or pedestrian responses. How do we make systematic sense of this apparent diversity of responses? What skill sets or modes of engaging or disengaging did people draw on to help them take meaning from the sites they visited, and how does this relate to the habitus of the visitors and the social and cultural 'work' they are 'doing' at the site? Moreover, if heritage is an embodied and affective performance, how do we make analytical sense of this?

In considering the performative nature of heritage, it is useful to consider ways of thinking about and assessing how heritage is performed and the ways in which heritage sites, objects and/or intangible heritage elements are used. This chapter develops the idea of 'registers of engagement' as a loose heuristic device to help understand and measure how people use museums and heritage objects and sites. The aim is to open the conceptual space to identify and measure the nuances and range of ways in which people interact with museum exhibitions and heritage objects and sites and to consider the consequences of the way they are used. In developing this concept, I am drawing both on my previous work (Smith 2006, 2011, 2017a, 2017b; Smith and Campbell 2016) and the ideas discussed in the previous chapters; in particular, I consider the ways in which affect and emotion frame and facilitate how heritage is used.

The elements that constitute 'registers of engagement' are outlined in this chapter, and it is important to stress that the concept is offering a way to describe and assess the nature and consequences of heritage performances. The way it is developed and used in this book specifically addresses how 'visitors' use and engage with museums and heritage sites. Further, in proposing the concept of 'registers of engagement', I do not presuppose that learning is the primary motivation or all that is done by visitors, nor do I assume that learning may not, indeed, be important. The analysis does not privilege the motivational aspects of 'visits', as has tended to be the case in most visitor study work within the museums and heritage literature (see, for example, Falk and Derking 2000; Falk 2006, 2009; and Black 2012: 31f for commentary), but rather explicitly focuses on what visitors are actually doing with their visit, and the consequences of the narratives they are re/constructing during and by their visits. Registers of engagement also explicitly considers not just the exceptional and outstanding aspects of the visitor experience but also the mundane and banal. Specifically, while affect is central to the idea of registers of engagement, spectacular or extraordinary affective responses are treated as being no more significant or important than the commonplace and routine. A consideration of ideology, scale and wider identity politics are also embedded in this concept.

However, the basic premises underlying registers of engagement are:

1   that there are socially regulated practices and performances of the creation (curation) and consumption (visiting) of heritage sites;
2   that there are a variety of practices and performances at heritage sites that relate to nation, genre of site and habitus/social position;
3   that despite there being regularised practices and performances at heritage sites and places, people actively commit to, question and qualify these practices, performances and narratives; and
4   that actively engaging with these sites to affirm or question 'what is important' displays a range of modes and registers of engagement, which mobilise intense and 'flat' affects and emotional responses, rhetorical claims to 'reason', elements of emotional repertoires, banal acceptance of received narrative templates, a range of intensities of response and tensions between 'progressive/liberal' and 'conservative' social and political positions.

In developing the concept of modes and registers of engagement, the chapter also discusses and defines the key terms 'visitors', 'tourists' and 'learning' and the assumptions and concepts that inform their use in this book. In developing this discussion, and the idea of registers of engagement, I am responding to a need, often signalled in both the museums and heritage literature (Janes 2007, 2016; Black 2012: 52; Witcomb 2013: 269; Carter 2016: 257), to understand museum and heritage site audiences. However, in doing so, my aim is to understand what these audiences or 'visitors' are doing in terms of their own actions, words, assumptions and reflections.

I explicitly and analytically treat visitors as independent beings, caught up in but not rigidly defined by performances and practices, whose heritage performances may, or may not, be informed or influenced by the interpretive or educational activities of the heritage and museum professionals at the sites with which they, the 'visitors', are 'visiting' or engaged. My focus is thus not *only* on how particular museums or heritage sites or curatorial or interpretive strategies have a particular impact or effect/affect, but rather, I aim to broaden the focus on what individually and collectively visitors are *doing* and how they emotionally invest in the meanings constructed by their visit. I am explicitly disprivileging the common focus on curatorial and interpretive staff practices/performances and how they display or exhibit specific objects or collections, though I do recognise that there are different genres of museums and heritage sites and that sites in genres may present themselves and be 'used' in different ways than in other genres. My focus is rather on how people who are not heritage or museum professionals engage in heritage practices and performances – in this case, not specific community groups who have often been the focus of such work, but the seemingly more nebulous group of museum/heritage site visitors.

There is an increasing emphasis within the heritage and museum literature to be more ethically and critically engaged with understanding how particular understandings and uses of the past impact on the present and imagined futures. As well, there are corresponding calls for museums and heritage professionals to engage more in public debates on a range of social and political issues. These professional aspirations are important but cannot be effective if such calls are framed, as they often are, as a need for professionals to do something to '*their* audiences' or to a vaguely defined 'public'. Registers of engagement aims to create a conceptual space to understand the agency of museum/heritage audiences and visitors. Understanding the range of ways and the extent of agency people display when they engage – or choose not to engage – with heritage is I believe a far more useful starting point to inform strategies for interventions into public debates that draw on heritage and its meaning in and for the present.

Defining registers of engagement

Registers of engagement (RoE) refers to a suite of ways of performing and practising contemporary and embodied interactions with what Macdonald (2013) calls 'memory complexes' – the range of sites, institutions, commemorations, memorials and rituals – that mediate people's mobilisation of the past in the present. It draws on ideas from the previous chapters and the visitor interviews discussed in this book to help sort through the complex personal, social and cultural forces at work in the performances and practices of visiting and engaging with museums and heritage sites and how they do concrete social and political work. Indeed, the starting point for laying out the concept of registers of engagement is that individuals, when engaging with historical and cultural museum exhibits and heritage sites, display, in the first instance, three important registers of engaging with and 'using' these sites.

First, the **intensity** of the engagement may vary from low, shallow or platitudinous to the intense, earnest and passionate, from the elaborately detailed to the terse and laconic. It is important to stress here that low intensity is significant but generally under-recognised as a form of emotional or reasoned response. It corresponds with what Gramsci refers to as common sense and Bordieu as doxa. The coding of the responses (see Chapter 4) often focussed on strong, neutral or weak levels of engagement. Strong or involved engagements could include combinations of emotional and cognitive intensity and extended attention to an issue or a complex consideration, or sometimes reconsideration, of an issue. Some respondents displayed quite strong emotions, which did not always mean a heightened level of engagement: for example, when demonstrating 'patriotic' sentiments at nationally important sites. Neutral and low-intensity engagement ranged from simply not registering what was going on to low-level avoidance and the use of platitudes and clichés to avoid uncomfortable issues or the ready acceptance of what was being displayed without the need to question the message or to be emotionally or otherwise engaged.

Second, its **valence**, that is, whether the site and engagement with it was experienced as affirming positive/good feelings and thoughts or was characterised by negative/bad emotions and thoughts, or neutral or ambivalent responses.

Third, and in conjunction with intensity and valence, the **tensions between conservative versus progressive/liberal social and political values**. This latter register is important for helping to identify and explore the consequences of the heritage performances that are enacted as people visit and engage with heritage places. In doing so, I kept in mind Jost's model of motivated social cognition and system justification theory, discussed in detail later, which addresses the two core elements of ideological conservatism: resistance to change and acceptance of inequality. While it is acknowledged that there can be exceptions to this, these two elements are nonetheless historically central to conservatism (Jost et al. 2003: 343). Specifically, motivating and facilitating these two core elements is a tendency for conservatives to be fearful, intolerant of ambiguity, to express dogmatism or to be closed-minded, to rely on 'gut feelings' and have a need for order and cognitive closure and will, on the whole, score higher on measures of subjective wellbeing (Jost et al. 2003; Jost 2019: 273–274).

Archer's (1995) emphasis on the agency and internal conversations of people as important in social morphogenesis (change) or morphostasis (stability/inertia) (see Chapter 1) also informs the idea of RoE in two ways. First, it suggests that what people say about their visits should be a focus of analysis. Second, it alerts the researcher to how visitors, *as they leave exhibits and sites*, are thinking *about* and mulling over their visits and the wider social consequences their visit may, or may not, have for them. The combination of intensity, valence and progressive/conservative values is a useful starting point for analysing the range of ways people react to heritage sites and places, especially those that emphasise social history. There are, however, a range of subsidiary modes of engagement that also underpin the concept of RoE.

Modes of engagement

Embodiment

Embodiment is a consideration of how important or unimportant either simply 'being there' or 'getting there' is to a person. For some heritage places, sites and/or museum exhibitions, the actual 'being there' was crucial; in others the 'getting there' was more meaningful. Physically being at sites was often expressed as enhancing understanding, of 'bringing' certain issues or understandings 'home' or of making more 'real' such things as collective familial memories or understanding the experiences of family members such as grandparents or of social or cultural groups to which the visitor did not belong. This recalls Samuel's (1994) characterisation of heritage as 'theatres of memory' and Landsberg's (2004: 135) argument that museums (and other heritage places) can be defined as 'transferal spaces' for the development of prosthetic memories, those memories that people take on and become affected by even though they themselves have not experienced the events being remembered.

Embodiment at times also references the significance attributed to getting to a particular site. This may, and at some sites in this study, was, expressed as a form of secular pilgrimage where the effort taken to get to a place was an embodiment of the level of importance a place had to an individual and the meanings and values that the place represented for them. The idea of secular pilgrimage incorporates the sense that the journey undertaken is "redolent with meaning" and is "more *real* and profoundly connected to identity than everyday existence" (Cusack and Digance 2009: 877, original emphasis). However, it should not be assumed that the importance of the physicality of being on site is a 'given'. For some visitors, the physical site was not important or not as important as other modes of engaging. Although visitors had travelled to sites, thus implying that the act of getting there might signal that the site was important in some way, this did not always translate into engagement with or a valuing of the physical nature of the site or exhibitions. For some visitors, it was the intangible elements of stories, memories, values or knowledge that were more important, while the space and time of 'being at' a particular site offered either a sense of occasion or opportunity to pay attention to the intangible.

Alternatively, those who admitted to being 'dragged' to a site by their companions sometimes professed a lack of physical connection, while for some who expressed cognitive dissonance with curatorial or interpretive messages, the physicality of being there was often discounted and devalued. Another aspect of embodiment, and this is particularly important for sites of national/ist commemoration is a rather unengaged sense of 'being there' as part of an exercise in dutifully visiting nationally important places because that is just 'what you do'. This underscores the importance of low intensity, neutral or positive valence, and often political conservatism, in the practices and performances of acts of social solidarity, which are hegemonic, common sense and unquestioned.

Affect, emotion and cognition – affirming, reaffirming or questioning what is important

The position I take is that affect and emotion are not separate but are associated physical and socially regulated processes and that affect/emotion and cognition are inextricably linked and essential to people being able to reflect on what is important to them. However, for analytical purposes, it is useful at times to distinguish between affect (the fleeting qualia of initial responses), emotion (longer duration) and cognition (assessing and comprehending knowledge). This is partly because these terms, or respondents' accounts of their engagement with heritage sites that reference the meaning of these concepts but not the terms themselves, feature in visitors' narratives about the sites they are visiting in significant ways. Some respondents would stress affect, emotions, feelings or moods to frame their engagement with the site. In doing so, they are, in the terms set out in Chapter 2, performing affective practices, drawing on emotional repertoires and accepting/rejecting/re-working feeling rules. Others would privilege a more formally cerebral approach, ostensibly free of emotive content, which stressed rationality, 'value-free' assessments, the study of formal history or the acquisition or exercise of cultural capital via education. To distinguish these latter responses, separating 'cognition' or 'reasoning' from the former, which use emotive terms, are best understood, as per the discussion in Chapter 2 and in the following, as examples of motivated cognition.

Despite these points, however, affect and emotional responses, combined in different intensities and valences, underlay all forms and registers of engagement. Affective and emotional responses in social history sites in particular draw on other-oriented emotions or empathic concern, which is "not a single, discrete emotion but includes a whole constellation. It includes feelings of sympathy, compassion, softheartedness, tenderness, sorrow, sadness, upset, distress, concern, and grief . . . empathic concern is other-oriented in the sense that it involves feeling *for* the other – feeling sympathy for, compassion for, sorry for, distressed for, concerned for, and so on" (Batson 2011: 4). Nor are they limited to the 'hot' or tumultuous emotions but also include the mild, gentle and understated. Further, flattened emotions or a strong belief that one is being non- or un-emotional are all affective states. Thus, while some people could be said to have adopted a style of 'Mr Spock' like cerebral distancing when talking about their visits, their engagement was no less affective than the more emotionally aware and impassioned, or what we may call the 'Captain Kirk' type, responses. Spock-like claims to emotional neutrality, or practices of emotional suppression, are themselves affective/emotional states and do their own work in negotiating heritage meanings and values. Such responses may exhibit low emotional intelligence, whereby emotional intelligence is defined as a skill that allows a person to recognise and actively use their emotional response to work through and think about the issues before them (Mayer et al. 2008). This does not mean, however, that impassioned 'Kirk like' responses are necessarily emotionally intelligent or that emotional intelligence equates with heightened emotions;

mild and calm as well as negative emotional responses could also be as explicitly and knowingly used by individuals like the more intense or positive emotions. It is also important to note here that emotional intelligence as a set of skills can be exercised. Alternatively, a person can choose not to exercise their emotional intelligence and can choose not to extend empathic concern, even in situations where it might be appropriate to do so when they see withholding empathy or withholding recognition as an appropriate response within a form of affective practice or motivated cognition.

The valence and authenticity, or what Morton (2002) refers to as the 'emotional truth', of the emotions experienced and expressed are, as discussed in Chapter 2, important in facilitating not only remembering and forgetting but the judgements, commitments and justifications that people make. Further, emotions and their intensities, will also, as discussed in Chapter 2, have implications for how recognition and misrecognition are negotiated and/or maintained. Feeling, as a form of believing (Mercer 2010), engages with cognition and reasoning to help people address, re-assess, avoid, qualify, explain away, prevaricate about or flat out ignore what makes them uncomfortable about the relevance of the past to the present.

Performing memory: remembering and forgetting

The interplay of affect, emotion, cognition and embodiment also impact on social memory. Memories are fluid and are maintained through the processes and practices of remembering (Wertsch 2002). Further, any act of remembering will also engage with corresponding acts of forgetting (Connerton 2008). While individuals may engage with personal, familial, collective and/or prosthetic memories, the mnemonic practices of remembering and forgetting will not only be influenced by the various modes of engagement outlined here but also through what Wertsch (2004, 2008a) refers to as schematic narrative templates. These abstract and historical narrative templates offer frameworks within which the practices and processes of both remembering and forgetting occur and are organised. For example, the US narrative of the 'quest for freedom' may be understood as a mnemonic cultural tool (Wertsch 2004: 58, 2008b) and tends not to be "readily available to conscious reflection" (2004: 57), often working to obscure or ignore conflicting understandings and experiences of the past (2008b).

Imagination and playfulness

Imagination, the opening or foreclosing of personal and social imagination, is, as noted in Chapter 2, important to how people participate in remembering and forgetting and address their affective responses to the world. The recognition of individual and social forms of imaginative practices and playfulness have gained increasing attention in heritage and museums studies (Bagnall 2003; Chronis 2005; Gregory and Witcomb 2007; Keightley and Pickering 2012; Lean et al. 2016). Individual and social imagination may at times be constrained by narrative templates and affective practices, but less constrained imaginative responses can also be vital for making creative leaps in reworking the meaning of the past in the present. Playful responses to heritage have been seen as important for allowing individuals and groups to challenge received narratives and their mnemonic authority (Rizzo 2010) or simply in working through and negotiating the meaning of the past (Wilson 2015). Playfulness, like imagination, will also inform affective and mnemonic practices.

Scale and scope

The various modes of engagement outlined previously also operate at different scales and scopes. Scale here refers to heritage presentations or experiences that reference objective categories such as geography (locality, city, region, nation, etc), social/cultural groups (ethnicity, class, gender, affinity group, organisations), the personal (the individual, family) or time (an historical period, the present, deep time, contemporary or historical events seen to be of historical significance). Scope, in the sense I am using it here, is a more active and subjective process of how respondents actively reached out to extend or narrow their engagement with the past to include and exclude issues, events, time or people.

A useful example of scoping is the issue of empathy and compassion – an element of emotional intelligence that almost all people have the capacity to exercise, if they so choose. The data for this study is replete with examples where people actively extended empathy and compassion to individuals or groups in their assessments of what they saw as important during their visits. The data also has many examples where empathy and compassion, in circumstances where the site interpretation or history lent itself to empathic and compassionate responses, was actively withheld. In addition, there were many respondents whose feelings of empathy or compassion were either held at low levels or in a rather passive way not seen as relevant. The suggestion here is that the presentation of heritage sites and responses to them range across geography, time, society and culture in terms of scale, but respondents could make active or sometimes unconscious choices about how to embrace, reject or ignore those scales; in other words, they could limit or expand the scope of what they would admit to being valid or relevant in the present.

Another example which is important to highlight in terms of scale and scope is time dilation. Time is one element of the scale of heritage sites, but there is a range of active and passive ways of 'scoping' time. For example, events that are either close or distant in time can be accorded positive valence, and recruited as being relevant to the present, or given a negative valence and rejected as being irrelevant. Perversely, many respondents managed to claim a positive connection to an event in the past, sometimes hundreds of years ago, at the same time as averring any relevance for something they were uncomfortable with which occurred at the same distance in time.

Ideology

Intensity, valence and progressive/conservative orientation were outlined to facilitate understading the heritage meanings and values the past has for the present. Identifying these meanings in terms of registers of political and social conservativism and progressive ideologies helps identify the ongoing consequences of heritage performances. Ideology may be defined as a mode of engagement that informs the conservative/progressive register. Further, ideology also facilitates understanding of how the interaction of particular modes of engagement can, on the one hand, inform and justify particular narratives and their reading of the meaning of the past for the present and, on the other hand, dismiss or ignore alternative narratives. It also helps one understand why 'reason' or an approach that focuses on traditional frameworks of 'learning' toward visitor engagement may not work or at least be inadequate to the task of influencing or intervening into the heritage performances of visitors and the heritage meanings they construct. To understand this process more firmly, I want to take a brief excursion into debates around system justification theory.

As touched on in Chapter 2, ideology has a consequence for how people care about certain issues and how they understand and process information (Jost et al. 2003; Jost 2006). The theory of political conservatism, as motivated social cognition, holds that ideologies, as socially shared but competing philosophies that interpret and describe the world and how it should be, express "different social, cognitive, and motivational styles or tendencies on the part of their adherents" (Jost et al. 2009: 309). Motivated social cognition is linked to system justification theory (van der Toorn et al. 2014), which developed out of the work of social psychologist John Jost and his concern to understand why people "blame victims of injustice and why victims of injustice sometimes blame themselves" (2017: 1). System justification argues that people are motivated, to varying degrees and in different contexts, to defend and justify aspects of the societal status quo (Jost 2017). Indeed, when motivation is heightened to justify the system, people are "more likely to embrace ideologies that emphasize the value of the status quo" (Thorisdottir et al. 2010: 10). Politically conservative or right-wing ideologies seek to resist change and view social and economic inequalities as both legitimate and desirable (Jost 2019: 286). Political conservatism, buttressed by fear of uncertainty and discomfort with social change (Jost et al. 2003: 340), also expresses a stronger attachment to the nation in defending and justifying the existing social system from criticism or attack than those who hold politically progressive opinions (van der Toorn et al. 2014). National narratives and the schematic narrative templates that frame them are, as Wertsch (2007) argues, also frequently politically conservative and highly resistant to challenge and change. Further, the tendencies for political conservatism to seek reinforcement or confirmation of knowledge that they already know, to rely on 'gut feelings' and to seek personal stability works to not only justify the status quo but also to bolster an individual's sense of security about their place in the world (Jost and Krochick 2014). Conversely, progressives/liberals are more likely to see injustice in inequalities and seek social change and will be more apt with dealing with emotional and informational ambiguity and dissonance (Nam et al. 2013).

I turned to the work by Jost and his colleagues in response to one of the main findings of the research, which was the degree to which visitors to museum and heritage sites talked about using their visits to reinforce or confirm what they already knew, felt or believed (Chapters 9 and 10). As I will argue in following chapters, the consequences of certain heritage performances are the maintenance of privilege and associated economic, cultural and political inequality through the justification and reinforcement of both social status quo and personal identity. Nonetheless, some performances also challenge the status quo and personal expressions of identity (Chapter 12). System justification theory does not argue that social change does not occur, but simply that protests against the status quo and achieving social change is difficult (Jost 2019: 265). While Jost acknowledges the possibility of change, he draws on Gramsci to elucidate the difficulties of obtaining that change: the "great mass of people hesitate and lose heart when they think of what a radical change might bring ... [and] only imagine the present being torn to pieces" (quoted in Jost 2019: 265). Further, as he notes, the defenders and challengers of the societal status quo are hardly on political, historical, economic or social equal footing.

However, change can occur through group justification of system improvements, although justification of the new or emerging status quo will occur quickly. Research in the United States on voting in the 2016 presidential election revealed nuances in the way system justification could occur and bring about political change. The research showed that general or diffuse system justification tended to correlate to a preference for Clinton over Trump (the 'mainstream' or 'status quo' candidate). However, economic and gender-specific system justification positively correlated to Trump supporters (Azevedo et al. 2017: 236–7; Jost 2019: 301). Rejecting the status quo of Democratic governance represented by President Obama and Hilary Clinton was facilitated by the system justification of existing economic and gender-based inequalities and perceived threats that both Obama and Clinton represented to mainstream cultural traditions. In addition, supporters of Trump, while frustrated by the consequences of the capitalist system in the United States, did not identify the system as the source of their frustration (Azevedo et al. 2017: 238).

System justification serves a palliative function by reducing uncertainty and increasing satisfaction with the status quo (Jost 2019), which has implications, as Jost (2019: 276–277) argues, for intergroup relations. Individuals from advantaged groups will engage in in-group justification and favouritism and seek to enhance collective and personal self-esteem and psychological wellbeing (Jost 2019: 276). The palliative aspect of system justification, however, does not mean that disadvantaged groups are more usually or typically likely to engage in justification than advantaged groups. Disadvantaged groups, as research reported on by Jost (2019: 277) shows, tend to be negatively associated with self-esteem, group favouritism and long-term wellbeing, although nonetheless, engagement in system justification tends to provide a long-term palliative role in reducing anxiety and depression in the disadvantaged. As Jost (2019: 277) states, "system justification is both a threat to the well-being of members of disadvantaged groups and a way of coping with that threat". The 'Belief in a Just World', the idea that people will 'get what they deserve', as Hafer and Choma (2010) argue, is one of the strong beliefs that legitimise the status quo. Jost (2018: 18–19) is, however, less convinced that system justification in disadvantaged groups is entirely based on optimistic views of the world, nor does it serve self-interest on the part of the disadvantaged, but rests on an ideological process that is analogous to Marxist notions of false consciousness and the internalisation of inferiority. The point to emphasise here is that political conservatism is not confined to groups that are advantaged or disadvantaged, but rather, that it informs cogitation and understandings of lived experiences, and that it will do so in some contexts against the economic or social self-interest of the individual or group. The corollary to this is that progressive or liberal ideologies will also influence understanding and cognition but will be more open to ambiguity and be more responsive to the quality and nuance of an argument (Jost and Krochik 2014).

Further, if people use emotion as a form of evidence to help them mediate what they believe or disbelieve (Sayer 2005; Mercer 2010), then the affective aspects of engagement will also be influenced by ideology. Conservatives tend to be more negatively responsive to feelings of fear or emotional contexts, such as appeals to empathy, which requires engagement with emotional ambiguity, uncertainty and discomfort (Jost et al. 2003). These propensities are reinforced by the tendency for conservatives to be far more likely to report greater happiness and personal satisfaction than progressives/liberals (Jost 2019: 273–274). This is not, as some have suggested, a result of conservatives being wealthier, as this negates the possibilities that economically disadvantaged individuals can embrace conservative ideologies. Jost (2019: 274) reports on research in Germany that found social justifications of economic inequality "mediated the relationship between conservatism and life satisfaction". In maintaining such satisfaction, positive emotions can not only be combined with but can also bolster conservative ideologies and play a significant role in certain heritage performances (Chapters 9 and 10). In turn, a facility for dealing constructively with negative emotions, such as guilt and shame, may tend to combine with progressive ideologies (Chapter 12). I am not suggesting that there is a definitive linkage or correlation here, just that valence can both inform and be influenced by ideology and further, that registers of particular emotions, such as nostalgia or empathy, may have an interlinked relationship with ideology. For instance, insincere or shallow empathy may have consequences for conservative readings of the past, while deep imaginative empathy that destabilises established states of identity will have consequences for progressive heritage performances. Mawkish nostalgia linked to the nation may reinforce conservative nationalising narratives, whereas other registers of nostalgia may inform more progressive readings (Smith and Campbell 2017a).

Jost (2019: 285–286) argues that the theory of system justification is a practical and useful way of understanding certain social phenomena and problems of exclusion, prejudice and scepticism about such things as climate change, among other issues. He argues for the utility of system justification motivations for understanding political behaviour and participation, or lack thereof, in collective action. System justification can also show how ideology, as motivated social cognition, works with valence, intensity and progressive/conservative orientations to frame people's engagement with heritage.

Registers of engagement

In summary, various modes of engagement interact with valence, intensity and conservative/progressive meaning to produce differing registers of engagement. In turn, registers of engagement will influence both the nature and consequence of heritage performances. These performances work to construct and reconstruct the meanings and narratives given to the past and the social and political values that are embedded in those narratives. Heritage performances also work to re/construct identity, a sense of individual and group social place in the world and will have an impact on individual and collective feelings of belonging, self-esteem and wellbeing. The meanings of the past and the legitimacy (or illegitimacy) of the meanings re/constructed in heritage performances are never engaged with and performed for their own sake but will be brought to bear on addressing present-day social problems and individual and group aspirations. They will have social and political consequences.

Understanding the heritage performances, and the modes and registers of engagement that underpin them is a useful way of examining what visitors do with their visits and what that, in turn, does in social life. It is a more useful way of understanding and analysing visitor interactions with heritage sites and museums than the dominant academic and professional tendency to frame understanding, and subsequent policy and professional practice, through the lens of 'education/learning'. Indeed, if we are to take seriously the calls of new museology and critical heritage studies to be more politically critical in the way we engage with heritage sites and museums (Vergo 1989; Janes 2009, 2016; Sandell 2007; Sandell and Nightingale 2012; Bennett et al. 2017, among others), then we need to move beyond a focus on the museum and heritage institutions and professionals and consider seriously what visitors are doing. A serious consideration of the social and cultural 'work' that visitors 'do' through the performativity of their visit is hampered by the assumption in both the museology and heritage interpretation field that what visitors do is 'learn'. I explore this assumption in the next section to argue for why 'learning' is in itself insufficient in providing a conceptual framework for understanding visitors as well as in defining both how I am using 'learning' and the equally problematic term 'visitor' in this study.

Not 'learners', 'visitors' nor 'tourists' – defining terms

Education, learning and 'learners'

The educational role of museums in both defining and regulating 'the good citizen' was foundational to their establishment (Bennett 1995). While the emphasis in museums and heritage interpretation has moved from a didactic sense of 'education' to the more open concept of 'learning', which encompasses both the ideas of lifelong learning and 'free-choice learning' (Falk and Dierking 2000; Falk 2005; Hooper-Greenhill 2007a; Gosselin and Livingstone 2016), the educational role of museums and heritage sites is often assumed as a given. This does not mean that the role, as Hein (2006) argues, has not been disputed, often in favour of the role of conservation, but that the educational aspects of museums and heritage sites are nonetheless generally held to be a central concern. Indeed, the educational role of museums, or their existence as learning resources, is a concern for the bodies that fund such institutions – a process that in itself works to reinforce the importance of education/learning (Hooper-Greenhill 2007a: 3).

The idea of learning is fundamental to museological practice and is equally embedded in the assumptions within heritage management practices. For example, the webpage of *Interpret Europe*, the European Association for Heritage Interpretation, states: "At its best, learning happens where people experience 'the real thing', in venues such as historic sites, nature parks, zoos or museums" (www.interpret-europe.net/feet/home/).[1] In both heritage management and museology, those who engage with sites and places, and who do so outside of the position of 'expert', are inevitably relegated to the role of 'learner'. Where this finds exception is in the literature and practices of community engagement or community participation where 'communities' may be defined as more active agencies in the cocuration or development and use of museological and heritage resources (Golding and Modest 2013; Onciul 2015; Haviland 2016; Kadoyama 2018; McGill 2018; Little 2019). Individual museum and heritage users are, however, configured as engaged in learning. This conceptualisation is very limiting and sets up a relationship between museum and heritage professionals and academics wherein 'the visitor' or 'the public' are relegated to a role as the receiver of curatorial and interpretive messages. This occurs even though it is acknowledged that visitors do not always take away from their visits the messages intended by curators and interpreters (Falk 2005; Hooper-Greenhill 2007a: 27) – a point, although often wryly acknowledged, that tends to be considered in terms of 'Why did they not learn and/or what can we do better?' or is met with the assumption that something else was learned (Hooper-Greenhill 2007a: 27), rather than tending to prompt 'What then are they doing?' The individual and collective agency of visitors as users of heritage tends to be neglected in the conceptualisation of 'learning', which allows both the literature and professional practice to assume a great deal not only about what visitors do and do not do but also what heritage and museums do and the consequences they have. As is argued in more detail in Chapter 8, the language and discourse of learning also lack the frameworks to assess what and why something may have been 'learned' (Biesta 2013).

As Bennett (1995) has argued, museums are concerned with the governance and regulation of citizenship. Heritage agencies and the legal and policy frameworks they work within are also implicated in the way national and sub-national identities are governed and regulated (Smith 2004). The impact of the regulatory authority of museums and heritage agencies, and the notion of heritage itself as framed with the AHD, has resulted in decades of sustained criticisms of museums and heritage agencies for the social, cultural and political impacts they have on various forms and expressions of national and sub-national identity. This criticism has not only come from academics and professionals working within museology and heritage studies but crucially also from a range of stakeholder and lobby groups from both the political right and left. Museums specifically have become embroiled in what has been termed the culture or history wars, particularly within Australia and North America (Kohn 1995; Engelhardt and Linethal 1996; Casey 2001; Trinca 2003). This history of critique has led to increasing arguments for the politicisation of museums and heritage sites, more generally. That museums and heritage agencies construct and convey subjective knowledge and messages through the work that they do in collecting, amassing heritage lists and registers and in exhibiting and interpreting the past for the present is understood and acknowledged (Macdonald 2002; Hooper-Greenhill 2007b; Harrison 2013; Message 2014). The knowledge and meaning constructed by this professional activity are also acknowledged as having authority and power and thus as being political (Littler and Naidoo 2004; Janes 2009; Macdonald 2009; Harrison 2010; Sandell and Nightingale 2012). However, the focus of much of this debate has been on what it is that museums and heritage agencies do or do not do. The assumption is that a primary impact of what they do is on the learning of their visitors; that is, that visitors overall take up or are in some way directly influenced by the messages and knowledge constructed by museums and heritage agencies and their staff. Indeed, as Carter (2016: 257) argues in the context of human rights museums, it is assumed visitors will demonstrate their "good citizenship by acting on what they have discovered". The definitions of learning mobilised in these debates and extolled within museological and interpretive practices are explicitly progressive. Claxton's assertion that learning "changes not just our knowing and our doing, but our being too" (1999, quoted in Hooper-Greenhill 2007a: 46) underpins definitions of learning that abound in museum and heritage studies. My concern is not with the progressive nature of this aim, but rather, that it simply does not adequately engage with the range of both progressive and conservative things that both visitors and museums and heritage sites do individually or collectively. Further, as Biesta (2013: 8) argues (Chapter 8), dominant ideas about learning may also re-create the regulation of the 'good' citizen identified by Bennett (1995).

Museums and heritage agencies do things in partnership with their audiences; how audiences or visitors engage or do not engage with the knowledge and messages of museums and heritage agencies adds its particular dimension to the critiques of museological and heritage management practices. Certainly, the meanings and knowledge that professionals and academics construct at museums and heritage sites have an important symbolic and authorising role in wider social and cultural debates about the meaning of the past for the present, as the role of museums and heritage sites within the culture and history wars demonstrates. However, the impact does not necessarily stop there; we cannot assume that the people who use heritage sites and museums as visitors are not in themselves doing their individual and collective social, cultural and political work and that the act of visiting does not have longer-term consequences both for the visitor and society. The act of visiting is a performative act – what are visitors performing and what consequence does their performance have?

This question cannot be adequately asked within a paradigm that assumes that what visitors do is primarily learn. Understanding visiting as learning constrains the conceptual space for engaging with the individual and collective agency of the people, whom we term visitors, who use museums and heritage sites and the consequences this has for society. This does not mean to say that learning does not or cannot occur, but framing our concern with museum and heritage site visitors as primarily about 'learning' limits the ability to consider not only what else visitors might be doing both individually and collectively but also what the longer-term and collective consequences of what the visit may be. The visit is a practice that, while it may – or may not – intersect with learning, has a longer-term consequence beyond the actual visit itself. I am not here necessarily referring to what the visitor may have learned during the visit, though longitudinal studies have demonstrated that any knowledge or sense of what may have been learned during visits is often not retained or remembered (Storksdieck et al. 2005: 358–359), or even that the exhibition they visited is recalled (Coghlan 2017). Rather, as a practice, visits construct and perform individual and collective knowledge and social meanings, depending on the heritage visited, about society, other cultures and the past and its significance for the present. Additionally, and perhaps more importantly, the practice of visiting performs and re/constructs social identities for and by the visitor. 'Learning' as the dominant framing assumption for understanding the practice of visiting, not only is conceptually constraining, it privileges the institutions of museums and heritage sites as locations of learning and thus as instrumental in social change. Moreover while, yes, museums and heritage sites, may indeed have such positive influence, this framing tends to forget that museums and heritage sites can as equally be sites instrumental in maintaining the status quo (Janes 2016: 230). This is particularly important to remember, as Kidd (2011: 244–245) argues, because museum cultures of institutional inertia lead to staff disempowerment and an aversion to challenging institutional norms. Indeed, this has been one of the main issues faced by museum professionals in developing educational agendas that challenged received histories and in implementing other aspects of new museology (Kidd 2011; McCall and Gray 2014; Janes 2016). The idea of museums as 'safe places for unsafe ideas' (Gurian 1995, quoted in Cameron 2005: 214) often works to contradict the ability of museums to challenge normative narratives because to do so makes museums 'unsafe' (Anderson and Gurian 2018).

Learning, also, quite simply, assumes a patronising relationship between the visitor and heritage professionals, as I argued when discussing the quite complex identity and memory work that the postal worker was doing at the National Civil Rights Museum. The emphasis on learning is framed by the AHD, which privileges and relegates expertise to the role of stewarding the management and meaning of the past as heritage, while those identified as non-experts are consigned to the position of learners or receivers of expert knowledge, and analysis is thus constrained. Within the AHD, and the more specific discourse of 'learning', a distance is established between those identified as members of 'the public' or as 'visitors' so that any links individuals or groups may have with heritage beyond that of a learner is obscured. Following decades of criticism from community groups, a wider acceptance has occurred within museum and heritage studies that communities have important and intimate cultural, social or historical links with certain heritage items or places and cannot, or should not, simply be defined as 'learners'. However, conceptually this understanding is yet to take firm hold when considering those who are often conceived of as visitors, audiences or 'the public'. The term 'visitor' has problematic connotations that I will turn to ahead; however, I need to unpack the issue of learning a bit more first.

In *Museum Basics*, Ambrose and Pain define learning as being "not just about facts – it also includes experiences and emotions. Leaning is something we *do*, and we all do it in different ways" (2018: 67, emphasis in original). In *The Museum Experience*, Falk and Dierking (1992) conceptually cemented the experiences of being at museums through their interactive experience model as intertwined with learning so that, conceptually and analytically, to simply *be* at a museum is to learn. In this model, the physical, social and personal contexts that impact on the museum experiences of visitors are discussed and identified as influencing the learning that visitors do (Falk and Dierking 1992). The assumption that what visitors are or should be doing is learning is clearly made throughout this and the latter influential work by these researchers (Falk 2005, 2009, 2011; Falk and Storksdieck 2005), and it is important to note that much of the research undertaken in developing these often useful learning engagement models was conducted at science museums and zoological parks. These assumptions were then imported into museums of history and culture as well as cultural heritage sites more generally where the issues being discussed and engaged with can be quite complex and contested. This is not to say that they are not at science museums – think for example about the tensions over climate change or evolution in some countries – but only that the social, cultural and historical stories and information presented at history and culture museums have their own nature and complexity relative to science museums. Further, as Hooper-Greenhill (2007a: 40) notes about the learning model constructed by Falk and Dierking, it assumes the purpose of learning is to "enable individuals to fit into pre-existing social arrangements", and this, as she argues, tends to constrain the model's ability to address the multiplicity of cultural perspectives that may influence the learning process. Indeed, criticism of Falk's (2009) work on 'museum identities' identifies the hesitancy of his learning model to engage with how issues of class, ethnicity, gender and other forms of social and cultural identities may influence learning (Bickford 2010; McCray 2010; Dawson and Jenson 2011). Nonetheless, learning has become *the* visitor experience for heritage and museums.

However, as Hooper-Greenhill (2007a: 31) notes, learning is a "slippery concept, with different meanings according to its context and use". Nonetheless, the learning discourse is linked to professional and academic responses to sustained critiques of museums and heritage sites that derive from both the political left and right. It is a significant aspect of the new museological arguments about the importance of museums as agents for social change (Sandell 2003, 2007; Witcomb 2003, 2013; Sandell and Nightingale 2012), and within heritage studies, it is part of the counterclaims of critiques that defined heritage as 'dumbing down' popular understandings of the past (Lowenthal 1985, 2009b; Wright 1985; Hewison 1987; Appleton 2007). The progressive/liberal cosmopolitanism intent of museum practice underpins the Museums, Libraries and Archives Council (MLA) definition, quoted by Hooper-Greenhill (2007a: 31):

> It may involve increase in or deepening of skills, knowledge, understanding, values, feelings, attitudes and the capacity to reflect. Effective learning leads to change, development and the desire to learn more.

In this definition, change is defined as central to learning. Indeed the idea of change is a pervasive view of learning more generally, as Mark Smith's (2018) review illustrates. The idea that some form of alteration of view or understanding will occur through learning in museum and heritage contexts is prevalent in the literature and thus informs the definition of learning used in this study. However, this definition does not engage with social and political conservatism and the issue of system maintenance, as discussed in the preceding section. An effective model of learning needs not only to acknowledge how individuals resist change but also the reality that both individuals and the institutions of museums and heritage agencies themselves are involved in system justification and the maintenance of the status quo. While a more effective learning model and definition may need to be developed that addresses the realities of conservative ideologies in institutions and their audiences (Chapter 13), it is not sufficient within the learning debate in museums and heritage studies to subsume all museum and heritage experiences under learning. Nonetheless, the definition of learning used in framing this study and that underpinned the visitor interview questions and coding that is discussed in the next chapter is that expressed by the MLA: that some form of deepening understanding and/or changing views will have occurred. Further, acknowledging the ways systems justification theory identifies why and how knowledge can be reinforced and affirmed means that the definition used in this study does not incorporate the idea that reinforcement or confirmation of ideas, knowledge and beliefs constitutes a form of learning. Learning/education, as it is applied in this book, incorporates a perception by the visitor that something changed, either new knowledge was gained (to a smaller or greater degree), understandings were deepened (again to a smaller or greater degree) or, more radically, that belief or behaviour was altered in some way. Change did not have to register as an epiphany, but could, and was recorded as mild or incremental.

Visitors, tourists, or?

I use the word 'visitor' throughout this book, and I am not happy about doing so. 'Visitor' connotes distance. It conjures up a sense that someone is simply passing through, engaging with something to which they stand at a distance or are gazing at that to which they are not in some way connected. Likewise, 'tourist' assumes distance, a temporary relationship with a place or people. Within the AHD, these terms establish an unequal relationship between the expert professional and the apparently 'non-expert' in both policy contexts and within a critical analysis. As 'visitor', those who use heritage as non-professionals tend to be treated as lacking agency. This is facilitated by the observation that most people visit heritage sites and museums as a leisure or recreational activity – that they are having 'a nice day out'. This observation has often led to debates over the utilisation of entertainment within learning contexts that are sometimes labelled 'edutainment' (Balloffet et al. 2014). While I have no problem with the need for education to be entertaining and enjoyable, it is the fact that the activity of visiting occurs in leisure time that tends to add another layer of assumption of passivity on the part of the visitor. Research from within leisure studies points to the complexity and agency of individuals in creating their own social and cultural meanings and sense of communal belonging in the process of recreating (Long et al. 2014; Mata-Codesal et al. 2015). Leisure activities may themselves be understood as embodied performances that demonstrate identity and "what we believe in" (Rojek 2000: 37).

Likewise, the term 'tourist' tends to encompass if not a passive engagement with heritage at least a focus on obtaining entertainment from a heritage visit. Within heritage studies tourists have tended to be defined as a particular 'problem' in the management and conservation of sites; tourists threaten the physical fabric of sites and have, it is argued, an impact on the cultural authenticity of heritage and, thus, need managing. Moreover, tourists tend to be characterised as naïve, banal and uncultured and thus in need of educating (Graburn and Barthel-Bouchier 2001; Hall 2009; Ashworth 2009). This concern to manage and educate has tended to dismiss 'the tourist' as inherently negative and lacking agency. Critical work within tourism and heritage studies has challenged these perceptions, arguing for how both tourism and tourists engage in cultural production (Kirshenblatt-Gimblett 1998; Urry and Larsen 2011; Staiff et al. 2013; Staiff 2014; Waterton and Watson 2014).

As with the concept of 'learning', the terms 'visitor' and 'tourist' tend to negate the possibility that the visitor is in fact in some way connected to the site being visited or used. These connections may include but are not confined to, the historical, cultural, social or political values or meanings represented by the site, or such links may not exist at all and the visitor is indeed 'visiting' another's heritage. Visitors and tourists, like communities and professionals, all use museums and heritage sites, the visit being a particular performative use. While I have not been able to substitute the terms 'visitor' or 'tourist' with more useful terms, and both are used in this book, they are used in quite specific ways. 'Visitor' identifies someone who is using a heritage site or museum in the practice of visiting. I start with the assumption that visitors have agency and that the heritage they are using and engaging with is something that they are actively doing even if the visitor perceives it as part of leisure or recreational activities. My use of the terms 'visitor' or 'tourist' also allows for the possibility that individuals may, but also may not, see themselves as linked or connected in some way with what they are visiting. That is it may have heritage values for them beyond that set by the meanings authorised by museums and heritage sites, or conversely, it may not. On a more pragmatic level, I use the term 'visitor' to identify anyone interviewed at a particular museum or heritage site, but who is not employed by that site or museum, and who comes from the country in which that site or museum is located. The term 'tourist' in this study is underpinned by the same assumptions as that of 'visitor' but is differentiated from other visitors as someone interviewed at a museum or heritage site in a country that they do not usually live in.

Conclusion

Registers of engagement, at its core, prosaically observes that different people respond differently to different museum and heritage contexts. The idea identifies that various modes of engagement will interact with intensity, valence and conservative/progressive tendencies that will influence the heritage meanings and values that in turn underpin heritage performances as discussed in Chapters 1 and 2. The performative practice of visiting museums and heritage sites does social and political work in society; it has its own consequences. These may reflect the consequences and impacts that the staff at museums and heritage sites themselves strive to make, or they have their own or additional consequences beyond which curatorial, educational or interpretive staff may intend. The concept of registers of engagement is offered as a way of both describing and measuring how visitors individually and collectively engage with heritage and as a way of analysing the impact of the meanings that are created and recreated through the practice of visiting.

Registers of engagement open up the conceptual room to move beyond the assumption that learning/education frames what visitors do, or should do. It does not assume that learning does not occur, but brings an analytical lens to the possibility that more is going on, that the individual and collective practices of visiting are performative and can have wider or more complex social consequences than the 'learning' framework allows. The politically progressive and cosmopolitan values that underlie much of the learning literature in heritage and museum studies are in part a response to the sustained criticism that both heritage and museum agencies have received for the roles they play in maintaining politically conservative readings of 'the good citizen' or indeed of offering challenges to those readings. To be effective, however, such cosmopolitan aims need to engage with an understanding of the role of museums and heritage sites that is defined within the AHD in upholding the status quo and the ways with which the agency of heritage audiences engage or entirely ignore those cosmopolitan aims.

The chapter has also defined the concepts of 'learning', 'visitor' and 'tourist' used in this study, noting that these terms are problematic and contested. In short, learning is defined as instilling some form or level of change, no matter how small, in a visitor/tourist's understanding. As used in this study, the terms 'visitor' and 'tourist' do not assume distance or lack of agency in how heritage meanings and values are constructed as individuals interact with museums, exhibitions and heritage sites. The overall aim of this chapter has been to define the assumptions I have incorporated into my use of these terms and that of registers of engagement and which in turn framed the study's aims, methods and analysis. The details of the study's methods are discussed in the following chapter and how the concept of registers of engagement was used in the coding and analysis of the visitor interviews is outlined.

Note

1 Website accessed 15 February 2019.

PART II
Methods and quantitative findings

4
METHODS

In 2010, I was interviewing at the National Museum of Australia's First Australians Gallery, a permanent exhibition on the Indigenous history of Australia. The exhibition featured a comprehensive account of the disastrous histories and legacies of the Australian colonial invasion and subsequent race relations, including the history and legacies of the Stolen Generations (Wilkie 1997; Read 2014). It also ran a film clip of Prime Minister Kevin Rudd delivering the 2008 'Apology to Australia's Indigenous Peoples' (Rudd 2008). I had just returned from nine years of living in England, and I was impressed with the degree to which visitors appeared to be giving me seemingly progressive and considered responses about this contentious history, especially as this gallery had been criticised by conservatives when the museum opened in 2001 (Casey 2001). I was pleased, and I expected that I wanted to be pleased that so many of my fellow Australians had become more critically engaged with this history during my absence overseas and following the Apology. However . . . I then coded the interviews.

In undertaking this coding, I found that, yes, there were indeed progressive responses, but not nearly so many as I had thought. Nor was this experience limited to this exhibition, as during coding I would remember being excited in the field by certain themes in visitors' responses, but then when coding realise that the themes I was excited by were not necessarily as dominant as I had thought, while other themes emerged as more prevalent than I had previously realised. Coding was used to 'quantitise' the qualitative aspects of the interviews (Collingridge 2013). It was used to check and verify the frequency of themes that emerged from the interview data and the impressions I had formed during fieldwork while also providing a broad analysis of the range and nature of the themes. In turn, qualitative data has been used to engage with the nuances and details of the themes that emerged. In short, this study is based on mixed methods research (MMR) strategies where qualitative and quantitative data are integrated not only to verify aspects of the data but also to provide breadth and depth of insight (Creswell 2014, 2016). This chapter outlines what I did and why I did it when collecting and analysing the interview data and defines and explains the MMR approach. It also discusses the philosophical underpinnings of my work, the specifics of the qualitative and quantitative methods used, how they were integrated and why I considered them useful in answering my research questions. The chapter also outlines the history of this lengthy project and provides overviews of the museums, exhibitions and heritage sites at which interviews were undertaken. A comprehensive account of the project's methods is given: first, as MMR is not frequently or explicitly used within heritage and museum studies; second, if people matter, then explicating methods for engaging both with people and how things matter to them is core to my argument; third, the detail is required so that the reader may understand the limitations of the study.

Aims: what I wanted to know

The overarching research aim was to find out how those people identified as 'visitors' or 'tourists' (see Chapter 3) to museums and heritage sites 'used' those sites and what the broader social consequences of this 'use' might be. More specifically, the research investigated what, if any, identity and memory work people were doing as they visited with different aspects or elements of heritage, to identify what stimulated and facilitated this 'work' and to find out what the visit might mean to people and what heritage meanings, if any, were constructed or activated by the visit. I also wanted to know if the meanings and how and why they were constructed varied across different types or genres of heritage sites and if they varied in different national contexts. In short, what does visiting do, and what meanings or messages do people take away from their visits to different types of heritage sites? As argued in the previous chapter, current debates about the political and social impacts of museums and heritage sites are predicated on assumptions that museums and heritage sites 'do things' and have an impact of some sort on their audiences. However, audiences are not passive and being part of a 'diffused audience' is a common and constitutive experience (Abercrombie and Longhurst 1998; Longhurst et al. 2004; Kolesch and Knoblauch 2019). In developing this research, I wanted to explore how different people in different contexts engaged with different forms of heritage, and this required qualitative interviews, rather than questionnaires that tend to ask visitors how much they agree or disagree with assumptions and statements made by the researcher. I wanted to get a sense of what visitors saw themselves as doing in their own words and terms. The aim was to get a sense of the inner musings or reflexivity of visitors as they interacted with heritage, to ask them what they were doing and what this doing meant to them.

To explore the constitutive and performative practices of museum and heritage site visiting across different genres of sites required a large sample of different types of museums and heritage sites. A substantial sample of visitor interviews was also required to see if different themes emerged in the data and if this corresponded to issues such as educational attainment, gender, ethnicity and so forth. Having a large qualitative dataset also required the application of statistical techniques to allow overall patterns and themes to not only be quantified but compared to visitor demographic data. In developing this research, I endeavoured to be reflexive about the questions I asked visitors and museological staff and to ask open-ended rather than leading questions. Before discussing the methodology and methods employed in detail, it is first important to briefly outline the history of this study. All research is an artefact of the methods used, not only in terms of how data is collected and measured and how samples are defined but also, as in this case, how the overall project developed.

History of the research

There were three distinct periods of data collection. The first of which, funded by a small British Academy grant, took place in 2004 when I and a group of research assistants interviewed visitors at country houses and labour history museums within England. This data was reported in *Uses of Heritage* (2006), which used simple descriptive statistics to make comparisons between the houses and the labour history sites. As the dataset was relatively small, no meaningful statistical conclusions could be drawn from the visitor demographics. However, what this data did reveal was that visitors to the house museums, or English country houses, were doing something very different to those visiting labour history museums.

In 2007, two opportunities presented themselves to extend this data further. The first was an invitation from various country houses or house museums in England to come and do further interviews. The invitation followed the development of exhibitions within each of the houses that were attempting to intervene in the comfortable and cosy narratives visitors tended to take away from such houses and that I had reported on in 2006. Exhibitions under the title 'Work and Play' were then being held in six country houses within Yorkshire, the aim of which was to highlight the history of domestic servants and estate workers and to engender an understanding of how much work went on to support the leisured bucolic lifestyle of the houses' past owners.[1] Interviews were carried out at three (Burton Constable Hall, Temple Newsam and Brodsworth Hall, Table 4.1) of the houses involved in this exhibition series. While this material tended to replicate the findings reported in 2006 for country houses, it also revealed a tendency for visitors to ignore or reject the interventions of the 'Work and Play' exhibitions to challenge the normative narrative of the country house. This finding was more decisively evident in my second opportunity in 2007.[2]

Under an Arts and Humanities Research Council (AHRC) Knowledge Transfer Grant in 2007, 1,498 interviews were conducted at eight exhibitions at museums and house museums across England, marking the 2007 bicentenary of the abolition of Britain's slave trade. The '1807 Commemorated' project (Smith et al. 2011) generated a variety of different datasets; the visitor data, however, was published in Smith (2010, 2011, 2015). The visitor data primarily revealed how those who

TABLE 4.1 Sites in England: genre, numbers interviewed and year of interviews

Nationalizing Narratives: Country Houses (House Museums) 2004 and 2007	N=	1807 Commemorated (legacies of enslavement) 2007	N=
Audley End, 2004	71	British Museum exhibition: Inhuman Traffic: The Business of the Slave Trade	206
Belsay Hall, 2004	103	National Maritime Museum Exhibition	205
Brodsworth Hall – 2004 Brodsworth Hall – 2007	37 70	Bristol Empire and Commonwealth Museum: Breaking the Chains	162
Harewood House, 2004	109	International Slavery Museum, Liverpool	339
Nostell Priory, 2004	86	Birmingham Museum and Art Gallery: Equiano Exhibition	165
Waddesdon Manor, 2004	48	Museum in Docklands: Sugar and Slavery	182
Burton Constable, 2007	23	Wilberforce House, Hull	148
Temple Newsam, 2007	97	Harewood House Exhibition[1]	91
Dissonant & Contested Histories: Labour History 2004	N=		
National Coal Mining Museum in Wakefield	85		
North of England Open Air Museum, Beamish	128		
Tolpuddle Martyrs Museum	60		

[1] In this instance the interviews were entirely about the 1807 exhibition and did not include discussion of the House as happened in the 2004 interviews at this same heritage site.

identified as White British tended to disengage or distance themselves from the dissonant and uncomfortable history detailed in the exhibitions. It also revealed how negative emotions, such as shame and guilt, underpinned cognitive dissonance and attempts by visitors to reinforce more triumphal narratives of English national identity. The data also revealed the different and often far more critical ways in which those who identified as African Caribbean or Black British responded to the exhibition, often using the exhibitions to assess the degree to which they as British citizens and the history of enslavement and abolition were being recognised or misrecognised during the bicentenary (Smith 2011). In addition, the patterns or themes in how people responded to and used the exhibitions did not vary significantly across the eight different sites.

Having already gathered a large database from English country houses, labour history museums and exhibitions detailing the history and legacies of enslavement, I was granted an Australian Research Council Future Fellowship in 2009 to amass similar data from Australia and the United States to compare with that already collected from England. This data was gathered between 2010 and 2013. Sites were chosen that were comparable to those sites from England so that labour history sites and house museums of the social elite were selected. In the United States, sites discussing the legacies of enslavement were also chosen, although permission to interview at such sites was difficult to obtain, and interviews were undertaken at the exhibition *Slavery at Jefferson's Monticello: Paradox of Liberty* at the Smithsonian National Museum of American History (NMAH) and the National Civil Rights Museum in Memphis, Tennessee. While the latter may appear not to be directly comparable to the English bicentenary exhibitions, the English exhibitions all had significant elements documenting the legacies of enslavement for England, including issues around the rise of civil rights (Cubitt 2010). As Australia did not have exhibitions or heritage sites marking chattel slavery, additional sites of contested history and heritage centring on Indigenous histories and immigration were chosen for comparison between Australia and the United States. Additional sites of nation-making were also chosen that lacked counterparts in the data collected from England; these included sites of the commemoration of war, celebratory frontier history and national parks. That certain types of sites are not included in the English data needed to be taken into consideration when undertaking the comparisons between the three countries in Chapter 5 and in the genre comparisons in Chapter 6.[3] While the number of questions initially asked of visitors in 2004 had been reduced by 2010, and noting that there were questions within the bicentenary study specific to the bicentenary, there was nonetheless a set of core questions (identified in the following section) that were asked across sites, and it is these core questions that are analysed and compared in this study.

Mixed methods research

The key aspect of MMR is the integration of qualitative and quantitative data (Creswell 2014, 2016). The integration of both sets of methods is undertaken to provide breadth and depth of insight into how visitors engage with heritage. Quantitative methods typically rely on numerical data analysed through statistical procedures that allow the examination of the relationships between variables and to quantify the salience or 'strength' of these relationships (Creswell 2014: 4; Brannen 2017: 5). This includes the quantising of concepts, in which an indicator, including nominal measurements, may stand in for a particular concept (Bryman 2012: 164; Collingridge 2013). With qualitative research, it is the nuanced meaning given to concepts and their interrelationships, rather than the frequency of variables, that is of interest; as McCracken notes, "qualitative work does not survey the terrain, it mines it" (1988, quoted in Brannen 2017: 5–6). Further, qualitative research in providing details of human experiences provides contextualisation for quantitative approaches in the social sciences that are often limited by their decontextualisation from the 'real world' of human experience (Castro et al. 2010: 343).

Originating in the late 1980s and early 1990s within the social sciences, MMR has been the subject of critique and debate (Creswell 2014: 218), not least of which concerns the 'incompatibility thesis' that questioned the effectiveness of using methods derived from contradictory ontological and epistemological assumptions (Mertens and Hesse-Biber 2012: 75; Hathcoat and Meixner 2015: 436). Two related issues are often stressed in response to this critique, the first of which has been the emphasis placed on the idea of the *integration* of methods to produce new insights rather than a simple addition of either qualitative and quantitative data to the other to produce multimethod research (Creswell 2016: 216, 218; see also Fetters and Molina-Azorin 2017; Fetters 2018). The second related issue has been to stress the importance of transparency in identifying the ontological and epistemological basis of the research; as Hathcoat and Meixner (2015: 438) note, no "inquiry is philosophically agnostic" (see also Shannon-Baker 2015; Fletcher 2017; Schrauf 2018). Indeed, a common dubious presumption in MMR has been to adopt a 'what-works' maxim in which researchers uncritically jump between different philosophical positions in adopting particular methods (Hathcoat and Meixner 2015).

Critical realism (see Chapter 1) is the philosophical position that frames this research. While not associated with specific methods (Fletcher 2017: 182), it does, however, provide a philosophical basis for integrating quantitative and qualitative methods. This is because, as Iosifides (2011: 47, 128) argues, it disassociates quantitative methodology from positivism and qualitative methodology from relativism that may be generated by versions of interpretivism and social constructionism. As Fletcher points out, critical realism does not simply rest with thick description of a given context but rather seeks also to engage in explanation and causal analysis, making critical realism "useful for analysing social problems and suggesting solutions for social change" (2017: 182). Indeed, qualitative methods are required in the frameworks of critical realism to "to address causality in the social world", a process facilitated by the integration of quantitative methods (Iosifides 2011: 90). The compatibility of critical realism and MMR also lies in the emphasis critical realism places on "uncovering diversity and relationships among people, events, and ideas . . . that allows for process-based causal inferences" (Shannon-Baker 2016: 330). The position that there is a material reality but that it may be understood in varying ways is, for Schoonenboom, the point where critical realism ensures integration in MMR takes place (2017: 3–4). She, however, rejects the utility of critical realism, arguing that it rests on the idea of a singular 'objective reality' (2017: 4). This is an over-simplification of critical realism, which recognises a social reality that has causal powers; indeed, the concept of ontological depth, foundational to critical realism, understands that the "object of study exists in a layered reality" (Bygstad and Munkvold 2011: 12).

The MMR approach used here is what Cresswell (2014: 219–223) terms a "convergent parallel mixed-methods design" in which both qualitative and quantitative data were collected under the same set of concepts and assumptions to look for convergence and divergence between the two sources of information. However, my use of MMR was not simply to verify, triangulate or give credibility to the findings (Kern 2018). The aim was also to seek, in keeping with MMR principles, a comprehensive account of visitor experiences, to look at the processes and structures of social life that influence visitor experiences, to provide both a generalised and contextual understanding of the performance of visiting and to open up the possibility of encountering unexpected results by integrating different methods (Bryman 2012: 633–634). Having laid out the methodological basis for the research, the following sections define the specifics of the methods employed in both data collection and analysis.

Genres of sites of heritage

Genres defined

As discussed in the history of the project section previously, the data was not collected in a single piece, but as funding opportunities allowed. Within the first set of collected data (2004–2007), I had perceived that visitors were engaging differently with different types of museums or heritage sites and had started to develop the idea of registers of engagement (Smith 2011). The sites fell into two broad categories: those celebrating and advancing nationalising narratives (country houses) and those representing marginalised and contested histories (labour history and histories and legacies of enslavement). Table 4.1 provides a full list of the sites where interviews were conducted in England.

On extending the study into the United States and Australia, the aim was to choose sites that also represented nationalising narratives and those that presented contested or overtly dissonant histories (Tunbridge and Ashworth 1996). As occurred in England, choice of sites within the two overarching categories in the United States and Australia was also determined by which sites granted permission for interviews to take place; some obvious choices of nationally significant sites and museums are thus absent in the database. Table 4.2 lists the sites chosen from the United States and Australia, grouped not only by the two categories but also by sub-categories. These subcategories define the genres into which the sites chosen for the study were classified. This classification was used as a variable in the statistical analysis (discussed later) of the interview data. The category of sites of consensus national narratives was broken down into eight genres. These constituted, in no particular order, 'house museums', which included English country homes,

TABLE 4.2 Sites in Australia and the United States: genre, numbers interviewed and year of interviews

Nationalizing Narratives: House Museums	N=	Dissonant & Contested Histories: Labour History	N=
Lanyon Homestead, ACT, 2011	60	Mt Kembla Heritage Centre, 2010	38
Rouse Hill Farm, NSW, 2011	42	Museum of Australian Democracy at Eureka, 2013	86
Vaucluse House, NSW, 2011	43	Museum of Work & Culture, RI, 2012	18
James Maddison's Montpelier, Virginia, 2011	112	The Youngstown Historical Center of Industry and Labor, Ohio, 2012	22
Hermitage, Tennessee, 2012	101	Rivers of Steel, Pittsburgh, 2012	20
War Commemoration		**legacies of enslavement**	
National War Memorial, ACT, 2011	63	Slavery at Jefferson's Monticello: Paradox of Liberty, NMAH, 2012	100
The Price of Freedom, NMAH[1], 2012	69	National Civil Rights Museum, Tennessee, 2012	101
Frontier History		**Indigenous History and Culture**	
Stockman's Hall of Fame, Qld, 2010	160	First Australian's Gallery, National Museum of Australia, 2010	106
National Cowboy & Western Heritage Museum, Oklahoma, 2011	110	Uluru Cultural Centre, NT, 2012	114
Other National		Mashantucket Pequot Museum, CT, 2011	94
Old Melbourne Goal, 2010	101	**Immigration History**	
Star-Spangled Banner, NMAH, 2012	100	Immigration Museum Melbourne, 2010	133
Yellowstone National Park, 2012	62	Ellis Island National Museum of Immigration, 2012	100
		The Lower East Side Tenement Museum, NYC, 2012	80
		Nordic Museum, Seattle, 2012	14
		Japanese American National History Museum, Los Angeles, 2012	38

[1] National Museum of American History, Washington D.C.

Australian stately houses and presidential plantations; sites of war commemoration (Australia and the United States only); Frontier history (Australia and the United States); 'Other National' which consisted of the Old Melbourne Gaol, *The Star-Spangled Banner* and Yellowstone National Park. Originally, Yellowstone National Park was paired with Uluṟu-Kata Tjuṯa National Park. However, following collection and coding of the interviews, it became apparent that Yellowstone's significance to visitors interviewed at the Old Faithful Visitor and Education Center was largely connected to national narratives centred on the fact that this was the world's first national park and that it upheld a national sense of American conservation and preservation values. The interview work at Uluṟu-Kata Tjuṯa National Park, undertaken at the Uluṟu Cultural Centre, which discusses both Aṉangu culture (the Traditional Owners of Uluṟu-Kata Tjuṯa) and what the centre's website defines as the Park's "natural environment" (Parks Australia 2013),[4] centred on issues of Indigenous history and culture and was classified with sites of Indigenous history and culture (Table 4.2). Sites of dissonant or contested history were divided into genres consisting of: 'labour history' (England, Australia and the United States), Immigration history (Australia and the United States), Indigenous history and culture (Australia and the United States) and sites addressing 'legacies of enslavement' (United States and England). Although both Uluṟu-Kata Tjuṯa National Park and Ellis Island are sites that sit firmly within national narrative templates, they also tell dissonant or contested histories of, respectively, Indigenous cultural survival in the face of colonisation and immigration to the United States. After preliminary statistical and qualitative analysis of the interviews at these sites, they were grouped, respectively, within the Indigenous and immigration genres. However, in some analyses (discussed later) that tried to highlight and quantify the differences between the broader grouping of 'national' and 'dissonant' sites, these two sites were grouped separately within their category that incorporated both national and dissonant narratives.

Interviews were scheduled to take place at each site across 4–5 days, and where possible or relevant, including both weekends and workdays. Selecting a weekend was not relevant when interviewing was undertaken during peak visitation periods over summer. Interview numbers varied considerably across sites; Tables 4.1 and 4.2 lists the sites with visitor interview numbers collected at them and dates of collection. Variations occurred for a number of reasons. In England funding allowed for research assistants, while the funding for the data collected in Australia and the United States specifically excluded the possibility of employing research assistants, and the interviews were almost all collected by myself.[5]

Further, the flow of visitors varied significantly across different sites and different genres; for example, visitor numbers to labour history sites in all three countries, but particularly the United States and Australia, were relatively low. My intention was to gather at least an arbitrary 100 interviews from each site; this was not always achieved either because visitor numbers were relatively low and this number could not be reached, or it was not reached when saturation was very obviously achieved prior to reaching this number (and this occurred specifically at both sites

94 Methods and quantitative findings

of War commemoration). At some sites where during fieldwork it was perceived that considerable variation in visitor responses was occurring, the number, if fieldwork times allowed, was increased (this was particularly the case at the Melbourne Immigration Museum and the Stockman's Hall of Fame), although it should be noted diversity during coding (see the following sections) was not always as extensive as perceived in the field. All sites at which interviews were undertaken were given a report about the findings particular to that site.

Details of the museums and heritage sites

As listed in Tables 4.1 and 4.2, interviews were undertaken at 45 different museums and heritage sites. Space does not allow detailed descriptions of each site, and the reader is directed to the websites of each institution. A general description of each site is given in the following, and notes are made about changes that have occurred since the time of the interviews.

House museums

House museums, either as country houses, stately homes, presidential and plantation houses, chateaux and so forth, all have a very similar and standard interpretive strategy – the house 'speaks for itself'. Visitors are often invited to stroll through the house to gaze at the furnishings and artworks, while the odd interpretive panel or guide will provide historic details about rooms, artefacts or previous owners. While guided tours were offered at some houses, the stress on the history of the houses is in general about their owners and/or the men who paid for their building. James Madison's Montpellier and the Hermitage differed from the Australian and English houses in that they also contained information about the enslaved who worked in the house and surrounding plantation as part of their standard interpretive information, while Lanyon provides some limited information about its convict history, and three of the English country houses (Brodsworth Hall, Burton Constable and Temple Newsam) had exhibitions about their servants and estate works at the time of the interviews. Harewood House, one of the 'Treasure Houses of England' was, like Brodsworth Hall, surveyed twice. Unlike Brodsworth Hall, the 2007 material is included in the enslavement legacies genre for statistical analysis because visitors were explicitly asked about the 1807 Exhibition at the house rather than about the house itself as was done in the previous survey work.

War commemoration

The Australian War Memorial, Canberra, is itself both a museum and a memorial to those who participated in Australia's armed conflicts (although it noticeably excludes commemorations of Australia's early land wars) and features both permanent and temporary exhibitions. The exhibition *The Price of Freedom: Americans at War* at the National Museum of American History (NMAH) provides a history of armed conflicts from the French and Indian wars to contemporary twenty-first-century conflicts.

Frontier history: Halls of fame

National Cowboy & Western Heritage Museum, Oklahoma City, previously the Cowboy Hall of Fame and Museum, recounts the history of the 'American West' detailing the history not only of 'cowboys' and other rural workers but also some history of American Indian culture and frontier violence. Included in the museum is an exhibition on the popular culture of cowboys as developed through novels, television and feature films. The museum also has an extensive collection of artworks depicting the American West. The Stockman's Hall of Fame is modelled on this museum and is located in the town of Longreach, Queensland, some 1,200 km northwest of Brisbane. The term 'stockman' is equivalent to the American cowboy. Opened in 1988 at the time of the Australian bicentennial, it aims to commemorate Australian pioneers and those 'who did so much in rural and outback Australia' (Anon 2010: 8). After criticism for neglecting Indigenous Australians and European women, refurbishments in 2003 attempted to redress this. Information on Aboriginal culture, frontier conflicts and the importance of Aboriginal 'stockmen' and the inclusion of histories of European and Indigenous women were peppered throughout the hall as it told the story of 'outback' or rural Australia. A feature of the hall is the biographical plaques of men and women who have been inducted into the hall of fame.

Other national sites

Old Melbourne Gaol, located in Melbourne's CBD, functioned as a prison between 1842 and 1929. The current building was constructed in 1852–1854, and its design was influenced by the Pentonville Model Prison, London. The site is managed and interpreted by the Victorian National Trust and consists of the Gaol, City Watch House and a magistrate's court. Interviews were conducted only about the Gaol, which at the time of the interviews had minimal interpretation, although small exhibitions were present in some of the cells on early Aboriginal occupation, women convicts and poverty and the use of the prison as a gaol during World War II for soldiers absent without leave. One of the main attractions was the death masks taken from executed prisoners and the replicas of Ned Kelly's armour and the actual gallows on which he was executed (Smith 2017a). This is classified as a national, rather than a dissonant site, as it is marketed, displayed and framed within Australian national narrative templates, specifically about Kelly and his symbolisation of the rebellious Australian identity (Tranter and Donoghue 2008; Barnwell 2019).

The Star-Spangled Banner: The Flag That Inspired the National Anthem at the NMAH features the original flag flown at Fort McHenry in 1814. It tells the story of the flag from 1814 to the present and is the first exhibition a visitor sees on entering the NMAH, as it is placed opposite the main entrance. Yellowstone National Park, Wyoming, was established in 1872 and is purported to be the world's oldest national park. The Old Faithful Visitor and Education Center, at which the interviews were collected at the request of the National Park Service, primarily discusses the geological and ecological history of the park, and at the time of the interviews, no information on Indigenous history was noted.

Labour history

Eight sites of labour history were included in this study, and sites in Australia and the United States had far lower visitor numbers than those in England. The National Coal Mining Museum in Wakefield, England, tells the story of that industry's history, including the 1984–1985 miners' strike. It is built over a decommissioned coal mine that visitors could tour accompanied by ex-miners. The North of England Open Air Museum, Beamish, County Durham, aims to preserve 'the everyday life' of North East England, though the interviews all took place at and asked visitors about the exhibit of the colliery village. Interpretation at the museum is carried out through what the museum referred to as 'demonstrators' and has been the subject of much discussion and debate (Smith 2006: 200). Tolpuddle Martyrs Museum, Dorchester, recounts the story of the martyrs' arrest, trial and transportation and the influence this had on the development of the trade union movement.

Australia has relatively few museums dedicated to labour history. The Stockman's Hall of Fame in part addresses the history of rural workers but does so within the narrative framework of frontier history and Australian national identity and is thus not grouped in this genre. Mt Kembla Heritage Centre is a small community-run centre founded in 2008 and tells the story of local coal mining. The interviews were undertaken during the annual heritage festival, which in 2010 was held in the local school, to mark the anniversary of the 1902 coal mine disaster that killed 96 men and boys. The Museum of Australian Democracy at Eureka, which opened in 2013, was located near the site of the Eureka Rebellion of 1854, Ballarat. The museum housed the original Eureka flag that was flown over the Eureka stockade as gold miners protested against unfair taxes and a lack of representation. As well as the story of the rebellion, the museum also contextualised this history in a wider narrative about Australian democracy, politics and political action. The museum closed in 2018.

The Museum of Work and Culture, Woonsocket, Rhode Island, recounts the history of the local textile manufacturing industry and the migrant workers who settled in the region. In addition, it features a reconstructed union hall and local schoolroom. The Youngstown Historical Center of Industry and Labor, Ohio, provides a history of the region's steel industry (Linkon and Russo 2002). The Rivers of Steel National Heritage Area, Pittsburgh, consists of a number of historic locations, trails, disused industrial sites and a museum. The interviews were all taken on site and immediately following a tour of the Carrie Blast Furnace.

Methods 97

Legacies of enslavement

The eight exhibitions of the '1807 Commemorated' sites in England have been documented elsewhere (see Cubitt 2009, 2010, 2015; Smith et al. 2011). As Cubitt (2009, 2010) has argued, the structure and narratives in these exhibitions were similar and focused on African culture prior to the slave trade, details of the slave trade (in particular the triangular movement of people and sugar), plantation life, resistance and abolition and the legacies of the contemporary trade including the rise of civil rights activism. The eight exhibitions were all opened in 2007 to mark the bicentenary of Britain's abolition of its slave trade; these were either temporary exhibitions, such as that at Bristol, Birmingham and Harewood House or permanent exhibitions such as those at the International Slavery Museum, Wilberforce House and the National Maritime Museum.

The temporary exhibition *Slavery at Jefferson's Monticello: Paradox of Liberty* was developed by the National Museum of African American History and Culture (then still under construction) and was thus housed within the NMAH during 2012. The exhibition looked at the history of enslavement at the Monticello plantation owned by Thomas Jefferson and presented details about the lives of six enslaved families, featuring evidence about Jefferson's genetic links to the Hemings family (see also Gordon-Reed 2008). While many of these exhibitions were held at national institutions, the interviews focused only on the dissonant exhibitions.

The National Civil Rights Museum, Memphis, Tennessee, is located at the Lorraine Motel, the site of Martin Luther King's assassination, and documents the history of the civil rights movement. While this is not a museum that features the history of slavery, it has been grouped, at least logistically for the statistical analysis, with exhibitions on enslavement history and legacies because it does address the ongoing legacies of the history of American enslavement. This museum does stand out, as the analysis in Chapter 6 reveals, for a range of reasons not only from the other sites in this genre but from other sites overall in this study.

Indigenous history and culture

The First Australians Gallery, the National Museum of Australia (NMA), looks at the history of Indigenous Australia before, during and after European contact and colonisation. It highlighted, among other issues, the history of frontier massacres and Australian systemic and institutional racism – in particular, the history of the Stolen Generations (see Wilkie 1997; Read 2014). At the exit to the gallery, a video of then Prime Minister Kevin Rudd delivering the 'Apology to Australia's Indigenous Peoples' (Rudd 2008) in the Australian Parliament was played on a continuous loop. The Museum opened in 2001 and was immediately heavily criticised in Australia's 'history wars' for this gallery, and the museum's portrayal in general of colonial history that 'failed' to 'celebrate' Australia's 'achievements' (see Casey 2001; Anderson 2002; Dean and Rider 2005; Morphy 2006). Although this museum is itself a national institution, it is this contested exhibition only that was the focus of the interviews.

The Cultural Centre at Uluru-Kata Tjuta national park is located at the foot of Uluru and outlines Anangu (the Traditional Owners of Uluru) culture, history and knowledge about the creation of Uluru. The material presented in the centre is provided by and managed by the Anangu. The content of the Mashantucket Pequot Museum, Connecticut, is also determined by its Indigenous owners. Owned and controlled by the Mashantucket Pequot Tribal Nation, the museum outlines the history, culture and knowledge of Indigenous north-eastern United States. A feature of the museum at the time of the survey was a large life-sized diorama of Mashantucket Pequot village life during the sixteenth century.

Immigration history

The Immigration Museum, Melbourne, opened in 1998 and challenged the conservative turn in Australian politics during the 1990s (Hutchinson and Witcomb 2014: 236). It emphasised the point that everyone in Australia whose ancestors had arrived after colonisation in 1788 were and are immigrants to Australia. Interviews at this museum addressed the entirety of the museum's displays and content; at the time of interviewing, a temporary exhibition about Australian Afghan cameleers was also on display (Jones and Kenny 2010).

Ellis Island, while a national landmark in the United States, is grouped nevertheless with other immigration museums. The Ellis Island Immigration Museum outlines the history of the island as a processing point for immigrants between 1892 and 1954 (Maddern 2004). A feature of the exhibition is the accounts of the stressful inspections migrants travelling steerage class to the United States had to undergo. In 2012, the pervasive message at the museum was that Ellis Island represented the opportunity for immigrants 'to attain the American dream'.[6] Maddern (2004) outlines curatorial intentions to acknowledge cultural diversity, though the museum has nonetheless been criticised for producing a master narrative of American patriotic sentiment (Kirshenblatt-Gimblet 1998, 177f). The Lower East Side Tenement Museum, New York City, is a preserved tenement building in which newly arrived migrants to the US lived and through which visitors are taken on guided tours displaying the working-class immigrant social and industrial history associated with the building and its surrounding district. The museum has attracted critical praise for its inclusive approach to social history and ideas of American citizenship (Abram 2007; Russell-Ciardi 2008). The Nordic Heritage Museum, Seattle, a small regional museum, provides a linear history of Scandinavian immigration to the Pacific north coast, extensively illustrated by dioramas and models. The Japanese American National History Museum in Los Angles documents both the history of Japanese immigration to the United States and the ongoing experiences of Japanese Americans. A feature of the permanent exhibitions was the Japanese experiences of internment during World War II (see Kikumura-Yano, Hirabayashi and Hirabayashi 2005).

Interviews[7]

Staff interviews

Interviews with staff were primarily used, alongside my notes and observations recorded during site visits, to determine the aims of exhibitions or interpretive content and the core messages curatorial or interpretive staff had intended. The purpose was to determine whether the curatorial or interpretive messages matched those that visitors were taking away while also providing myself with a deeper context of the exhibition or interpretive content and any specific exhibition techniques used to engage visitors. In addition, I also used websites, any available pamphlets or other material available at sites and exhibitions to provide further context. All interviews were undertaken with the assurance of anonymity. Semi-structured interviews were recorded and varied in length from 30 to 60 minutes. No extensive analysis of the staff interviews was conducted as part of this study, and they were used to provide background or contextual information. Staff who granted interviews were provided with a transcript of the interview.

Visitor interviews

The visitor interviews used a structured schedule with both qualitative (open-ended) and quantitative (closed-ended) questions. Technically, the structured schedule together with the number of the interviews undertaken would be classified as a qualitative survey undertaken to determine diversity (rather than distribution) of experience and meanings in the visitor population (Jansen 2010: 3). However, the number of open-ended questions and the often extensive responses and interest visitors had in talking about their visits often engendered the feel of an interview rather than the administration of a questionnaire, and for this reason, I use the term 'interview' rather than 'survey'. Issues of distribution were determined through coding and statistical analysis discussed in the following sections. The interview schedule, including the interviewer script of approach, consisted of:

> Preamble: *Hello, I am doing university research here today and I am talking to visitors about their reactions to name of place/exhibition. Would you be prepared to complete an anonymous questionnaire with me, it should take about 10 minutes? I have an information sheet here with details about the project, which you can have. I will record part of the survey if that is ok with you, if it is not I can take notes instead. Please know you can withdraw from the survey at any time and I will not use the information you have provided.*

1. Male/Female.
2. Age: A <17, B 18–24, C 25–34, D 35–44, E 45–54, F 55–64, G over 65 (a card was offered to the interviewee, who nominated the relevant letter of the alphabet)
2. Occupation:

3 Highest Educational Qualification (a card relevant to country in which the interview was being held was offered to the interviewee asking them to provide the number against their highest educational qualification, using a number was important as it reduced any potential embarrassment on the part of the interviewee):[8]
4 Have you travelled from home or from a holiday address?

- Home post[9]/zip code:
- If overseas, country:

5 How would you define your ethnic background or affiliation?:
6 Is this your first visit *to name of exhibition/site/institution* Yes/No. If no, how long ago did you last visit? (Prompt: < or > 12 months)?:
7 What are your overall reasons for visiting the exhibition/site? (A third card was offered and visitors were asked to choose only **one** reason).
   NOTE: *I now wish to ask you a number of open-ended questions, would it be ok if I turn on the recorder, this is a totally anonymous survey and the recording is just to help me take notes. If you would prefer, I can take written notes.*
8 What does the word 'heritage' mean to you?
9 Whose history are you visiting here?
10 Are you part of the history represented here?
11 How does it make you feel to visit this place?
12 What experiences do you value on visiting this place?
13 What does being here mean to you?
14 Are there any messages about the heritage or history of Australia/America/Britain that you take away from this place?
15 What meaning, if any, does an exhibition like this have for contemporary Australia/America/Britain?
16 Is there anything you've seen/read/heard today that has changed your views about the past or the present?
17 Is there anything left out of the displays you would have liked to have seen?
18 Is there any aspect of your personal identity to which this exhibition speaks to or links?
19 Is there anything you would like to add or tell me?
   Thank you very much for your time.

As noted, the interview schedule changed over time, although the schedule was the final version used. A longer set of questions was initially developed by myself and Gary Campbell and used in the 2004 interviews. This was reduced in 2007 to the core questions asked previously, and only these core questions were included in the statistical analysis. However, additional questions were also asked in the '1807 Commemorated' interviews specific to the bicentenary context (Smith 2010, 2011). Additional questions were also asked at many of the sites because the museum or heritage sites had requested specific questions be included to address issues of interest to them. For example, extra questions were asked about the 'Work and Play' exhibitions, and at some sites, such as James Madison's Montpellier and the Stockman's Hall of Fame, staff provided additional questions about new interpretive work. At a small number of sites, I also added extra questions specific to particular issues raised by a site – for example, at the Immigration Museum, Melbourne, a federal election campaign was occurring at the time of the interviews in which immigration issues featured, and I added a question specific to this. In each case, with the exception of the '1807 Commemorated' material, the additional questions were asked at the *end* of the schedule, although before question 19. Follow-up or questions of clarification could also be asked as required. While only the core questions were included in the statistical analysis, the additional, where relevant, were used for further nuance in the qualitative analyses discussed in Part III of the book.

The 19 questions asked previously represent the core set of questions asked at the sites; the exception to this was question 13, 'What does being here mean to you?' In 2007, this was removed in the cull of the longer set of questions asked in 2004 at the English houses and labour history sites and was thus not included in the interviews undertaken at the '1807 Commemorated' exhibitions. It was also thus not included in the initial schedule used in Australia and is missing from the interviews undertaken at the National Museum of Australia First Australians exhibition; the Immigration Museum, Melbourne; interviews and the Stockman's Hall of Fame. However, after interviewing at the Stockman's Hall of Fame, where being at the site was such an important issue for many visitors (Smith 2012a), it was reinstated in the interview schedule for all subsequent sites.[10] In reading the analysis in Chapters 5–7 in relation to this question, it needs to be noted that this was asked at fewer sites. How age was recorded changed from the 2007 data onwards. That is, in the 2004 data, age was recorded for decades ending in zero rather than five as defined; thus, the 2004 data in relation to age is excluded from the analysis in Chapters 5–7. The 1807 material recorded the youngest group as 16–24, whereas this was changed to 18–24 in later recordings; for the analysis in Chapters 5–7, the 1807 group 16–24 is equated to the 18–24 age bracket.

Background to the questions

The questions were designed to explore the sorts of memory and identity work that visitors were undertaking. The first set of questions of the aforementioned schedule, asked before turning on the recording device, were largely closed questions requiring simple one-word or short responses. The exception to this was question 5, which asked respondents to identify their ethnic background and affiliation. No list of standard ethnic identifiers was offered, and people gave their affiliation as they defined it. The demographic information collected was used in the statistical analysis and is also used when quoting from interviews. Thus, when visitor quotes are used, they are referenced first by an interview number that abbreviates the name of the site (see list of abbreviations) and the sequential number of the interview. This is followed by sex, age, occupation as self-described by the visitor and ethnicity as self-described by the visitor.

For questions 2, 3 and 7, visitors were offered cards from which the visitor offered either a lettered (in the case of age) or a numerical value in response to the question. Question 7 asked visitors to identify from a proffered list the reasons for coming to the site; the cards listed the reasons in order as recreation or leisure; education; taking the children; did not come specifically to see *site or exhibition name*, just in the area/museum; to find about *topic of exhibition/interpretation;* to explore what it means to be Australian/American/British; followed, where relevant, by one or two reasons specific to the exhibition or site; other. In coding this question (see section on coding) education and 'to find about' were eventually combined as an educational reason.[11]

Responses to the closed questions were written onto the interview schedule by the interviewer. After question 7, the interviewee was asked if it was permissible to turn on the recording device for the open-ended questions. Occasionally, the interviewee would decline, and the interviewer would instead take notes.

The wording of question 16, asking if visitor's views had changed, was workshopped with museum professionals in 2004. I wanted to measure what, if any, learning was being done without leading the visitor by asking a question that included the words 'learn' or 'education'. The museum professionals with whom I discussed this question argued that changing views were at the heart of the educational endeavours of museums. Education as a reason for visiting was offered in question 7; the aim was to see how many chose education as a reason for visiting and to compare this against the open-ended questions to see if issues about learning or education were offered unprompted or arose organically during the interview. Questions about objects and curatorial or interpretive strategies, techniques and content were also not asked, as the curatorial and interpretive practices and performances were not part of the aims of the study, although question 17 invites, while attempting not to lead the visitor, responses about these. The overwhelming response, however, to question 17, was no, and thus, this question has not been included in the analysis. The remaining questions were explicitly designed to explore the emotions engendered during the visit and the values, messages and meanings visitors associated with the site or that they were developing or mediating during their visit.

I have often been quizzed by colleagues about the complexity of the questions, who suggested that many people would have difficulty with them. The questions rarely had to be explained to visitors, although when a visitor did ask what was meant, the question would be rephrased. If that did not help, the question was then skipped. Overall, visitors did not have issues with the questions, the exception being 18, about which visitors asked for clarification more than any other question. Question 19, not formally part of the statistical analysis as the majority of respondents unsurprisingly said 'no, they had nothing else to add', was, however, an important question, as it occasionally allowed visitors to add issues that had not been covered and that were important to them. Further, it often proved to be the point at which visitors turned the interview around and asked the interviewer about the study, what they thought of the exhibition and so forth, which sometimes resulted in useful and enlightening discussions.

All questions were asked sequentially, although on occasion, questions were asked out of order; when visitors in response to a question early in the schedule raised issues relevant to a later question, that question would then be asked out of sequence to avoid the interviewee repeating themselves. Alternatively, if when answering an earlier question, the interviewee had answered a later question that question was then skipped, and a note was made to ensure that during coding, the earlier answer was referenced. Questions were occasionally skipped at the request of respondents.

During the open-ended section of the interview, the interviewer would also make notes on the interview sheet. Importantly, when more than one person was being interviewed, it was necessary to note who spoke first (to help the transcription process) and to link them to their discrete interview number and associated demographics. This was important, as each individual interviewed, regardless of whether they were interviewed alone, in a couple or a group was counted as a discrete interview. Couples and groups did not always agree with each other and could and did gave independent answers, indeed with some interesting debates ensuing; thus, being able to identify separate speakers was important. Discrete notes (often in coded form) were taken by the interviewer during or immediately at the end of the interview about body language or other notable observations, such as discomfort, annoyance or amusement at a question if the interviewee teared up or showed distress. On occasion, and in particular but not limited to sites and exhibitions of dissonant history, interviewees would become distressed. When this occurred, and on the few occasions that interviewees were annoyed by the questions, the interviewee would be asked if they wanted to stop. Neither I nor any of the field assistants reported that in these instances the interviewee wanted to stop. Indeed, on many occasions, distressed visitors nominated that they found the interview cathartic and actively wanted to continue. I have also had visitors, especially in the case of dissonant histories, say that they enjoyed the interview, as it allowed them to express their opinions and values about the heritage they were visiting. A handful of visitors also nominated that it had helped them organise their thoughts and responses to the exhibition, suggesting that an option to sit down and talk through a difficult exhibition with someone would be a useful service to offer at museums or dissonant heritage sites. One woman was so engaged with the interview that she left her young child behind with me when we finished the interview and I had to chase her through the museum to return her child, to her intense embarrassment!

Conducting the interviews

The interview preamble suggests that the interview would take about 10 minutes. This was correct if the interviewee gave one or two sentence responses to each of the open-ended questions. However, visitors often elaborated their responses, and interviews frequently took between 10 and 20 minutes, with a few interviews lasting longer. One museum had to ask a young man and myself to leave, as they were closing. The interview was already over 90 minutes long, and continued for another 15 minutes on the street at the insistence of the interviewee, as he was so engaged with the interview and the exhibition he had been visiting!

On the whole, I found visitors to be very interested in undertaking the interview, and respondents took their time to think about the questions asked. People often had the time, as they were by and large at leisure visiting heritage sites and museums, to do the interview, and many were clearly pleased to be asked. Spot checks on rejection rates suggest that rejection rates at the English sites were about 10%, while at both Australian and American sites, it was at most 30%.

Visitors were convenience sampled as they were leaving exhibitions or sites. Interviewers would stand near, but within, the exit to the exhibition, museum (when the whole museum was the subject of the interview) or the heritage site. Respondents were approached where there was seating so that they could sit if they wished. Interviews were generally collected between 11 am, usually an hour after the museum or site opened, to about 4 pm, usually at least an hour before closing time.

In England, as noted, I had research assistants or students who helped me collect interviews at the country houses (2004 and 2007) and labour history museums. During the '1807 Commemorated' project, Kalliopi Fouseki, Ross Wilson and I collected the majority of interviews, with further research assistants helping at larger sites. Gary Campbell also conducted interviews in 2004 and 2007. I undertook almost all the interviews in Australia and the United States.

All assistants were trained by me in the interview protocol. An important aspect of this protocol was to remain professional but *interested*. This was important even when, as happened, visitors were offering opinions and statements that the interviewer found abhorrent. I have had interviewees tell me that 'you won't want to hear what I have to say as you will disagree!' The response was always 'I'm interested in your opinion, I really do want to know what you think'. Those visitors were often quite correct – but maintaining a professional and interested persona was important as, after all, I had intruded on their visit and asked them for their opinion. The protocol also required that distressed visitors or visitors who appeared anxious, in a rush or otherwise worried during the interview, would be asked if they wanted to stop. An information sheet about the project was handed to interviewees in Australia and the United States.[12]

Transcriptions

All recorded interviews were transcribed verbatim. This included speech disfluencies, such as ums and ahs, pauses (short or long), laughter, trembles (indicating deep emotions), whispering or other changes in tone or volume during the interview. Where couples or groups were interviewed, each person speaking was distinguished in the transcript. Ellipses in the quotes indicate pauses by the speaker, while those enclosed in square brackets thus [. . .] indicated material excised from the transcript for brevity.

Coding and statistics

Coding

Each of the closed- and open-ended questions in the interview schedule was coded. As Saldaña (2016: 4) defines, codes in qualitative research are "most often a word or short phrase that symbolically assigns a summative, salient, essence-capturing, and/ or evocative attribute for a portion of language-based or visual data". The codes devised were nominal – that is, the codes had two or more categories, but there is no intrinsic ordering to these categories. For example, gender is a categorical variable having, for the purposes of this study, two nominal categories (male and female) but without any ordering of these categories. In the case of the open-ended questions, for example, responses to the question about how a visitor felt, the codes 'sad', 'angry', 'intrigued', 'disinterested' and so on were signified by nominal numbers representing different themes in visitor responses, but there is again no hierarchy or other value placed on their ordering. Coding for patterns was undertaken in the open-ended questions; that is, consistent or repetitive themes in each question were identified and assigned an arbitrary or nominal numerical code. Codes were used to quantitise the open-ended questions (Collingridge 2013) to enable summary statistics of the themes to be generated and to allow cross-tabulations between themes and demographic variables.

Codes were initially generated by myself and Gary Campbell as we read through the initial interview material in 2004. In the coding of that material, we read through a random sample of each of the open-ended questions, developed a code based on this and then, as we coded, new codes were added as themes emerged or codes were merged when what we had initially perceived to be independent themes were found to be variations of other themes. The resulting 'code sheets' were then used as the basis for the '1807 Commemorated' project, with the coding sheet being expanded and modified as new themes emerged from that data. It was also at this point that codes exploring the intensity, valence and conservative/ progressive registers of engagement (see Chapter 3) were introduced. Coding of '1807 Commemorated' data was in large part undertaken by myself, Gary Campbell, Kalliopi Fouseki and Ross Wilson. The expanded codes were then applied to the data from Australia and the United States by me and Gary Campbell; again, codes were added and merged based both on the nature of the new data and refined by the idea of registers of engagement. I want to stress that when codes were changed, previous data was again entirely recoded by me and Gary to accommodate this change, resulting in quite a lengthy coding process. Recoding is not an uncommon aspect of the coding process as codes are refined and reworked (Saldaña 2016: 11–12).

Coding and recoding were carried out by either Gary and me or by a small group in the case of the '1807 Commemorated' data. Coding will be influenced by the particular way a coder views the data (Seltzer-Kelly et al. 2012). Consistency was provided by the coding group engaging in detailed discussions both before and during coding about what each code meant and represented. This was also achieved through the development, via discussion and debate, of a shared analytical aim (Saldaña 2016: 9). While individual coders went through their own assigned interview data, coding was done collaboratively. That is, it was done in a group for the '1807 Commemorated' data, or was otherwise always undertaken by Gary and me together. This allowed us to discuss what codes to assign if we were unsure of a particular visitor response; it also facilitated consistency and critical acuity in the process, as we continually discussed what we were doing and why. Coding also requires scrupulous attention to language and nuance and reflection on what a speaker may mean, which is particularly important in cross-cultural and cross-national contexts (Schrauf 2018). English was spoken in interviews[13]; however, colloquialisms in and within each country are notoriously different, and as coders, we tried to be aware of this issue. Differences in terminology between the United States and England/Australia in terms of 'conservation' versus 'preservation' were also considered. Spot-checking of each other's coding was also undertaken to ensure consistency.

In addition, the interview sheet for recording demographic information was kept separate from the interview transcripts when coding the open-ended questions. Thus, coding of these questions was done blind from the gender, age, educational attainment, occupation, ethnicity and so forth of the respondent. The variables not kept blind were the country and the site of the interview. Each question was coded individually; however, the overall interview could be consulted to contextualise answers that drew on previous responses or to help the coders understanding the intent or meaning of the answer given.

Codes were also given for the demographic questions, for example, 1 for male and 2 for female and so forth. In relation to the codes for occupation, the British 'standard occupational classification' (SOC 2000)[14] was used. This was in place when we first started coding in 2004/2005, and as this was the code originally used in the English data, it was utilised for consistency across the Australian and American data. With respect to ethnicity, codes were ultimately defined to differentiate people who identified as being from a politically dominant ethnicity, non-dominant ethnicity or as a tourist to the country in which the interview was undertaken. Thus, those who identified as White British, Anglo Australian, Caucasian American, alongside those who identified simply as British, Australian, American, 'normal' or as having 'no ethnicity', were all coded as being from a 'dominant ethnicity'. Those who self-identified as Indigenous Australian or American, Native American, African American/Australian, Asian American/Australian, Latina American/Australian, Chinese Australian/American, or as Asian, Black, or African Caribbean British and other similar descriptors were coded as identifying as being from a 'non-dominant ethnicity'. 'Dominant/non-dominant' rather than 'minority' is used to specifically reference the political privilege held by certain ethnic identities against the political marginalisation of others. The use of the term 'minorities' is problematic; for example, in the United States, many 'minority' populations are not numerically minor while other ethnic populations can be low in numbers but wealthy and exert political authority. In some contexts, 'race' rather than 'ethnicity' would be used; the use of ethnic identity here does not preclude that issues of racism are not a factor in expressions of privilege or experiences of discrimination, while it also recognises that issues of xenophobia and other forms of prejudice can also contribute to the maintenance of privilege and discrimination.

Overall, we aimed to keep the number of codes to a minimum, although we often found this difficult for some questions. In developing the statistical analysis, codes often went through a further compression into categories; for instance, codes relating to issues of education or those relating to nationalism or to changed views (to give but three examples) were collapsed and merged to facilitate the analysis. The demographic variables were also often collapsed. For example, age became under or over 45 years of age; educational attainment became divided into have been to or have not been to university, ethnicity was collapsed to one of three codes constituting a member of the dominant ethnicity or non-dominant ethnicity where the interview was conducted or as a tourist to that country. This collapsing was done after statistical analysis revealed some patterning in relation to, for example, being younger or older than 45, coming from a dominant or non-dominant ethnicity or not having been to university rather than say what level of qualification was obtained and so forth. Collapsing the codes allowed for greater clarification of patterns in the data. While many patterns and tendencies in the data were intriguing, only those that were statistically significant are discussed in the following chapters.

Statistics

The coded demographic and open-ended questions were entered into the Statistical Package for the Social Sciences (SPSS) to derive descriptive statistics and cross-tabulations between variables. Nominal numbers or codes were used for each of the questions or variables in the interview schedule. The most appropriate statistical test for nominal variables is the Chi-square test. A Chi-square test is used when a relationship between two categorical variables needs to be examined (cross-tabulation). The p-value of a cross-tabulation is a measure of the probability of the relationship between the variables having occurred by chance. The p-value, as a probability has a value ranging from zero to one. For instance, if the p-value is 0.03, that means that only 3% of the results have occurred by chance. Hence, the term 'statistically significant' is used for results that are unlikely (at a certain level of probability) to have occurred by chance. Conventionally, it is deemed to indicate statistical significance when p is less than or equal to 0.05. It is essential to stress that a Chi-square does not inform about the strength or causality of a relationship: 'a statistically significant difference' means that there is statistical evidence that there is a difference. However, further examination then occurs to determine whether this difference is important or significant in the common meaning of the word. That is, it makes sense within the context of the research questions being asked. Where relevant, Fisher's Exact

108 Methods and quantitative findings

Test was also used in cross-tabulations, and in larger cross-tabulation arrays random samples of permutations were carried out through Monte Carlo re-samplings.

Cross-tabulations were undertaken between demographic variables and are discussed in Chapter 7. These were undertaken to see what overall patterns in visitors' memory and identity work could be discerned. Cross-tabulations were also undertaken for the different genres as defined, and the results are discussed in Chapter 6. Cross-tabulations were undertaken as well between the three countries and are discussed in Chapter 5. In addition, cross-tabulations were undertaken for the overall database for sites defined as either 'national', 'dissonant' or both (ie Uluṟu and Ellis Island), and the results are discussed in Chapter 6. The database was also separated into 'national' or 'dissonant' (excluding Uluṟu and Ellis Island), and cross-tabulations with demographic variables were again calculated to allow for a 'drilling down' into some patterns that were deemed to have been potentially obscured within the analyses of the entire database. Descriptive statistical analyses of specific genres or sites have also been performed (Smith 2017a, 2017b, 2020).

Limitations of the study

A sequence of research opportunities that brought together various and differing resources has created a unique database across three countries and many different genres of museums and heritage sites. The project has developed, again as opportunities arose, into an intensively comparative project between countries, genres and visitor demographics. In hindsight and an ideal world, a comparative study between the three countries and genres would have commenced as such. However, while this study has grown following the vagaries of funding and employment opportunities, it should be stressed that it also developed following the insights derived from each period of data collection.

The comparisons between the countries and the individual institutions at which interviews were conducted cannot be argued to be one to one; interviews from certain genres of sites, for instance, were not, for a range of reasons, able to be collected from some countries. Different institutions will have and did employ slightly different interpretive techniques, and each site within a given genre will have placed more or less emphasis on certain aspects of the overall histories they told. Any generalisations drawn from the data are limited by these factors, and I do not claim that these findings are necessarily relevant outside of the genres of sites I researched.

This study, it must be stressed, is not about how curatorial or interpretive techniques and strategies may or may not have influenced visitor engagement or reception. My aim was to find out what *visitors see themselves as doing* in different contexts. Thus, variables measuring curatorial and interpretive strategies are not explicitly considered. While curatorial and interpretive professional practices may themselves be understood as performative and affective practices of heritage and meaning-making, the aim was to focus on the individual visit as part of documenting the performativity of museum visiting. As argued in Chapters 1 and 2, 'visiting' is itself a constitutive practice and performance of heritage-making both for the individual and in terms of collective and repetitive practices. The concern was to consider and document the strategies, emotional and discursive, that visitors used to both engage with the histories, culture or heritage they saw themselves as visiting and discern the themes and patterns in this behaviour. Occasionally, visitors would organically raise particular aspects of the strategies or content of interpretation and exhibitions or identify particular objects that they thought were noteworthy or about which they had either a strong positive or negative reaction. Where relevant, I draw on these visitor observations, but I do not do so in a systematic fashion, as such issues did not often arise in what visitors had to say about sites and exhibitions. This may well be a factor of the questions I asked: there are no explicit questions about objects or exhibition/interpretive strategies, although question 17 attempted to nudge the visitor toward discussing these issues.

The nature of the data has limited the statistical techniques that can be used, and while this may be seen as a drawback in some contexts, the emphasis on qualitative surveys, which in many cases became detailed interviews, is beneficial in providing details about the diversity of visitor performances. The statistical techniques that were applied produced useful and practical insights into the data. Some readers may be concerned about the length of time across which the interviews were collected, and that the fact that the last interview included in this study was conducted in 2013. There is also the issue of regional diversity in the United States and England. The study may well be understood as a snapshot with long temporal and geographical exposure. Certainly, the study provides an overview and not a detailed dive into temporal, geographical or indeed institutional specifics. The length of time taken between the last interview and publication of this work rests both on the time needed for the analysis and the vagaries of not living in an ideal world.

Conclusion

All research is an artefact of the methodology and methods used. It is, moreover, an artefact of the philosophical position that underpins the methodology that is used to frame the selection of methods applied to address the research questions. This research, based on the philosophical position of critical realism, has adopted a mixed methods approach to document and understand the nature and material impact of the performance of museum and heritage site visiting. As part of the mixed methods research, a qualitative survey consisting of detailed structured interviews with visitors was used to document the potential diversity in the visitor population. Coding of the questions asked of visitors produced nominal measures that were used to help assess the distribution and frequency of themes within the qualitative data and to compare the relationships between various variables in the data. Descriptive and cross-tabulation statistics were generated by SPSS. The following three chapters outline the statistical analysis and comparisons between the three countries, genre and visitor demographics. The qualitative data is also utilised to illustrate and discuss the nuances and details of the themes.

Notes

1. Anon, 2007 Exhibitions in Yorkshire, Country Life, May 17, www.countrylife.co.uk/out-and-about/theatre-film-music/exhibitions-in-yorkshire-40141. Accessed 11 March 2019.
2. This material has not been previously published.
3. Material from this phase of the collection has not as a whole been previously published, although data from specific sites such as the Stockman's Hall of Fame and the Old Melbourne Gaol have been published (see Smith 2012a, 2012b, 2017a) as has material from the immigration museums (Smith 2017b), and some material from the labour history sites has been drawn on (Smith and Campbell 2017; Smith 2020), while other publications draw on aspects of the data to discuss issues of empathy and recognition (Smith 2016, 2017b, respectively), the responses of children (Smith 2013) and affect and emotion (Smith and Campbell 2016).
4. Parks Australia (2013–2019) Cultural Centre. https://parksaustralia.gov.au/Uluru /do/cultural-centre/. Accessed 13 March 2019.
5. In the 2009 round of Future Fellowships funded by the Australian Research Council, research assistants were excluded. The idea was that the grant would concentrate on the 'fellow'. This exclusion was revised in later rounds of the grant program.
6. A message also reinforced by the museum's website, see NPS http://www.nps.gov/elis/index.htm. Accessed 19 March 2019.
7. Ethics clearance was obtained for the English data through the University of York, my then employer, and through the Australian National University for the data collected during 2010–2017. The Smithsonian Institution also required additional ethics clearance before granting permission to interview, and permits were obtained to interview at both Yellowstone National Park and Uluru-Kata Tjuta National Park. It should be noted that it was not the intent to interview people under the age of 18; however, children were interviewed often as part of a family group, or when they approached the interviewer and permission was sought from a parent or grandparent accompanying the child (Smith 2013).
8. In all the interviews undertaken, I have only had one interviewee complain about the interview schedule to the museum or site at which I was interviewing. The complaint, to one of the 1807 exhibition sites, was about this question: the interviewee complaining that despite the use of numbers, they found this question insulting.
9. In England, the intention was to record only the first half of the postcode.
10. This schedule has also been used as is or was added to by Waterton (2011), Zhang (2016, 2020; see also Zhang and Smith 2019), Coghlan (2017, 2018) and Dudley (2017, 2019).
11. A much longer list was used in 2004 and the '1807 Commemorated' data but was recoded down to this list.
12. This was not a requirement for ethics clearance in England at the time but was required by the Australian National University. Although information sheets were offered to each interviewee, many visitors declined to take one, and those that did seemed not to read it.
13. One interviewee in fact chose to respond in Spanish and another in French. Both were translated and included in the analysis.
14. Office for National Statistics, see https://webarchive.nationalarchives.gov.uk/20160108030321/www.ons.gov.uk/ons/guide-method/method-quality/specific/labour-market/soc-2000-and-ns-sec-on-the-lfs/index.html. Accessed 21 December 2019.

5
OVERALL FINDINGS AND NATIONAL COMPARISONS

This chapter discusses some of the statistically significant[1] correlations observed in the data between countries. It also outlines the interview population, both in terms of the overall sample and the sample within the three nations. It examines the overall responses to each of the interview questions and compares those responses between the three nations. While some clear differences do occur in visitor responses that can be correlated to national contexts, particularly in relation to definitions of heritage, what emerges more strongly from these findings is the extent of the similarities between the three countries. In addition, responses that identify the performances discussed in Part III of the book are identified, and the apparent contradictory discourses about education and reinforcement are identified and discussed.

The interview population

This section describes the basic demographics of the 4,502 people interviewed; of these 1,143, 944 and 2,415 interviews were undertaken in the United States, Australia and England, respectively. The previous chapter summarised the numbers of people interviewed at each venue and discussed the reasons for variations in numbers of interviewees between sites.

Interview population from the United States

Of the 1,143 people interviewed, 45% were male and 55% female; 56% were 45 years old or older; 68% held a university degree at bachelors level or higher while 68% identified themselves as employed in professional, managerial, intermediate and own account occupations and 15% in lower supervisory-routine occupations (Table 5.1). Caucasian Americans accounted for 73% of the interview population and were the most numerous visitors at all interview sites except the National Civil Rights Museum and the Japanese American National History Museum. Overseas tourists accounted for 10% of visitors interviewed (Table 5.2). Most visitors had gone to their destination from a vacation address (66%), with 27% and 7% visiting from a home or business address, respectively. The majority (68%) of those interviewed were first-time visitors to the venue at which they were interviewed.

Interview population from Australia

Of the 944 people interviewed at Australian sites, 42% were male and 58% were female, 58% were 45 or older and 53% held a university degree. Sixty-two per cent identified themselves as employed in professional, managerial, intermediate and own account occupations and 20% in lower supervisory-routine occupations (Table 5.1). Anglo-Celtic Australians accounted for 72% of those interviewed and were the dominant visitor ethnic group at all the Australian sites, and 18% of those interviewed were overseas tourists (Table 5.2). As in the United States, most visitors (55%) had travelled to their destination from a holiday/vacation address, although the frequency in Australia was almost 10% lower, with 42% travelling from a home address and 3% from a business address (this may be a result of interviewing in the United States being conducted wholly in the summer months, whereas interviewing in Australia was spread out over different seasons). The majority of visitors (70%) were first-time visitors; however, the Australian War Memorial was the only site where repeat visitors dominated, with 67% of those interviewed being return visitors.

Interview population from England

Of the 2,415 people interviewed at the sites in England, 47.5% were male and 52.5% were female; 54% had been to university and 78% identified themselves as employed in professional, managerial, intermediate and own account occupations and 14% in lower supervisory-routine occupations (Table 5.1). As reported in Chapter 4, there was a change in recording of age between the 2004 and 2007 data, and the 2004 data is thus missing from the analysis; 72% of those in the 2004 data were over 40 while 52% of those interviewed in 2007 were 45 or older (while 63% of those at the house museums recorded in 2007 were 45 or over, only 51% of those at the British slavery exhibitions were 45 or over, representing a much higher proportion of younger people attending these exhibitions). White British accounted for 69% of those interviewed and were dominant at all museums and sites, with the exception of the Museum of London Docklands 2007 exhibition on the history of British enslavement. Overseas tourists or expatriates/non-permanent residents accounted for 22% of those interviewed (Table 5.2).

Where recorded[2], 69% had travelled to their destination from a home address, 31% from a holiday address and none had travelled from a business address; 58% were first-time visitors, a lower frequency than for the other countries (but note

TABLE 5.1 Visitor occupations per nation

		Occupation[1]							Total
		Higher management and professional	Lower professional	Intermediate occupations	Small employers and own account	Lower supervisory and technical	Semi-routine	Routine	Unemployed[2]	
USA	Count	246	360	94	62	46	21	97	200	1126
	% within nation	21.8%	32.0%	8.3%	5.5%	4.1%	1.9%	8.6%	17.8%	100.0%
Australia	Count	168	232	84	82	42	38	105	168	919
	% within nation	18.3%	25.2%	9.1%	8.9%	4.6%	4.1%	11.4%	18.3%	100.0%
England	Count	652	791	300	86	58	153	106	193	2339
	% within nation	27.9%	33.8%	12.8%	3.7%	2.5%	6.5%	4.5%	8.3%	100.0%
Total	Count	1066	1383	478	230	146	212	308	561	4384
	% within nation	24.3%	31.5%	10.9%	5.2%	3.3%	4.8%	7.0%	12.8%	100.0%

1 To facilitate the analysis, occupations were collapsed; the first four columns were grouped as 'higher' occupations, while lower supervisory/technical, semi-routine and routine were grouped together in 'technical/routine' occupations.
2 Unemployed also includes students and those retirees who did not give a prior occupation.

TABLE 5.2 Visitor ethnicity and overseas tourist frequencies per nation

			Dominant ethnicity	Non-dominant ethnicity	Tourist	Total
	USA	Count	835	195	113	1143
		% within nation	73.1%	17.1%	9.9%	100.0%
	Australia	Count	680	91	173	944
		% within nation	72.0%	9.6%	18.3%	100.0%
	England	Count	1656	232	517	2405
		% within nation	68.9%	9.6%	21.5%	100.0%
Total		Count	3171	518	803	4492
		% within nation	70.6%	11.5%	17.9%	100.0%

this question was not asked of the '1807 Commemorated' visitors), as many of the house museums and labour history sites had significant numbers of repeat visitors (repeat visitors accounted for 41% and 43% at house museums and labour history sites, respectively).

Overall visitor profiles of the interview sample

The established profile of visitors to national museum and heritage sites tends to be well educated, middle class, older and from dominant ethnic backgrounds (see Merriman 1991; Aston and Hamilton 2010: 83; Black 2012; Hooper-Greenhill 2006; Selwood 2006; Bennett et al. 2010; Bounia et al. 2012: 16, 52–75; Kinsley 2016). This profile is particularly evident at national museums and heritage sites; at smaller regional or community museums and sites, the percentage of visitors from working-class and/or non-dominant ethnic backgrounds may be expected to be higher, as found in this study. While data collected by the museums on visitor profiles from the museums included in this study could not be obtained, the overall profile of an older, white, well-educated and middle-class visitor is one that research summarised by Black (2012: 21–25) reports as dominant in the United States, Australia and the United Kingdom.

Women tended to represent the majority of visitors at most sites and were particularly dominant at house museums. Indeed, interestingly, younger men (that is under 45) are significantly under-represented at house museums. In the combined sample from the three countries, women represent 54% of those interviewed, but at house museums, women represented 59% of respondents. The only sites where women were not in the majority were at the English labour history sites, where men represented 51% of those surveyed and at the sites of war commemoration where men represented 54% of visitors. Overall, with one exception at the English enslavement exhibitions, gender was not a factor in influencing the way visitors responded to or used museums and heritage sites. The exception was from within the '1807 Commemorated' data, where women were more likely, especially if they identified as African Caribbean or Black British, to be emotionally engaged and using empathy than men (Smith 2010: 198). However, this pattern was not significant across the entire dataset. Those aged 45 and over-represented 58% of the overall sample, and older visitors tended to dominate at certain genres of site, most notably house museums, the halls of fame and labour history; while younger people were more numerous at the sites commemorating war histories. Overall, however, those over 45 represented 55% of visitors at 'dissonant sites' and 61% of visitors at 'national' sites. As discussed in Chapter 7, age appears to have some influence on visitor responses, particularly in relation to the types of connections people were making with the past, which is itself linked to different performances of intergenerational connection (Chapter 11).

Those from politically dominant ethnic backgrounds account for 71% of the overall sample, and it was only at some of the museums addressing the history of enslavement, the National Civil Rights Museum and at the Japanese American National History Museum, that visitors from dominant ethnic backgrounds were in the minority. As discussed in Chapter 7, the ethnic background or affiliation of visitors correlates to how people use and respond to exhibitions, and this correlation crosses national boundaries. Indeed, at those sites coded 'national', 85% of visitors identified as belonging to dominant ethnicities, while 7% identified as belonging to non-dominant ethnicities, and 8% as overseas tourists. At sites coded as 'dissonant', those from dominant ethnicities represented 61%, while those from non-dominant ethnicities represented 15% and overseas tourists 24%. That there were far more overseas tourists going to explicitly dissonant sites than the 'safer' and more obvious national sites is in itself interesting; however, this observation adds to an argument developed in Chapter 7, that overseas tourists were, on the whole, a little more critically engaged at heritage sites than, overall, those from dominant ethnicities.

Those who had some level of university education account for 57% of the people interviewed. Visitors with university degrees were most frequently found in the United States, where 68% of visitors had attended university compared to 53% from Australia and 54% from England. In the United States and Australia, visitors with university degrees tended to dominate at all sites, the exception to this was the Australian Mt Kembla labour festival where 47% had a university degree. However, in England, the educational attainment of visitors was far more variable. Those who had been to university represented 42% of those visiting house museums and labour history sites, and at neither genre of site did those with university degrees dominate. However, 61% of those visiting the English enslavement exhibitions had been to university. In the overall data, of those who identified as being from politically dominant ethnic backgrounds, 51% held some level of university degree, while 60% of those from non-dominant ethnic backgrounds held such a degree. Overseas tourists in each country were the most highly educated, with 76% of that group holding university degrees. At sites defined as 'national' and as 'dissonant', those who held a university degree accounted for 54% and 59% of visitors, respectively.

In Australia and the United States visiting the sites in this study tended to be done while on holiday or vacation, while in England most people travelled from home, a finding that is likely to reflect geography. Whether or not people had travelled from a home or holiday address, as outlined in Chapter 7, had some, but little, influence on how people engaged with what they were visiting (52% in the overall sample had visited while on holiday or vacation). Overseas visitors or those who identified themselves as non-permanent residents of the country in which the interview was conducted, hereafter referred to as 'tourists', made up 18% of the overall interview sample. As discussed in Chapter 7, tourists as a group responded more frequently to sites and museums in critical ways than did the population of visitors from dominant ethnic backgrounds belonging to the country in which the site or museum they were visiting was located. Visitors were also asked if their visit was their first visit or if they were a returning visitor; 66% of those interviewed were first-time visitors. While this variable was also cross-tabulated against the open-ended responses, it produced very little patterning.

Visitor responses and national comparisons

This section summarises the results of each of the interview questions outlined in Chapter 4 and then correlates visitor responses to national context to determine what, if any, differences there may be in visitor uses and registers of engagement between the three countries. Significant cross-tabulations of the nations within the datasets of sites classified as either dissonant or national are also provided. If this analysis is not identified in relation to each of the questions, it means that any patterns in frequencies of responses within nations did not significantly vary depending on the broad classification of the site as 'national' or 'dissonant'. Variations across the more specific genres of sites do occur and are discussed in the following chapter.

Reasons for visiting

Visitors were presented with a list of reasons (Chapter 4) for visiting and were asked to select that statement 'that most closely matched their reason' for their visit to the site on that day (Table 5.3). A quarter of visitors in the overall sample choose recreation; however, just under a third (31%) choose either 'education' in general or more specifically 'to find out about' the topic of the exhibition or heritage site being visited. Comparing the results across the three nations reveals no noticeable variation in the proportion choosing either education or 'to find out about'. However, 17% of visitors from the United States choose recreation compared to 24% and 28%, respectively, from Australia and England. Those in the United States were more likely to choose 'to think about' the topic of the exhibition or heritage site than visitors in the other two countries (12%, compared to 8% from both Australia and England) and to choose 'to explore' (6%, compared to 2% and 3% from Australia and England, respectively). While educational options were frequently selected by

TABLE 5.3 Reasons for visiting

		Frequency	Valid percent
Valid	Recreation	1093	24.6
	Education	825	18.6
	Taking the children	277	6.2
	Just in area, did not come specifically to see ...	41	.9
	To find out about ...	546	12.3
	To think about ...	395	8.9
	To explore or remember what it means to be ...	161	3.6
	Other specific to site	761	17.1
	Other specific to individual	345	7.8
	Total	4444	100.0
Missing		58	
Total		4502	

visitors, and education or learning was a response frequently given to the open-ended questions that explored the experiences visitors valued or the feelings that were generated during their visits, the extent to which learning occurred is called into question by the results of the question about the messages visitors took away and the extent to which the visit changed visitors' views.

The meaning of 'heritage'

The AHD is embedded in much of the heritage legislation, policies and practices of the three countries in this study and tends to reinforce material definitions of heritage. Although the AHD has been challenged by increasing recognition of intangible heritage, its international influence on policy and practice is still strong (Smith 2015; Smith and Campbell 2017b). A key assumption embedded in the AHD is that expert understandings of heritage as primarily material and representing such things as museum collections, archaeological sites, historic buildings and the like, is something ultimately shared by most members of the public, and may be assumed to be shared by visitors to the museums and heritage sites included in this study.

Table 5.4 records the coded open-ended responses of the 2,632 people in England, Australia and the United States who were asked 'What does the word "heritage" mean to you?' There are two points to note: first, the dominance of definitions that engage with what international heritage policy refers to as the 'intangible' and second, the differences between the three countries. The response 'material heritage' reflects the expert or AHD-driven definition that nominates such things as historic houses, archaeological sites and museum artefacts amongst others. Heritage as an 'act of preservation' is also a definition influenced by the AHD, in that 'heritage' was defined in these answers as something protected, or that should be protected, often by experts. 'Education' refers to definitions that linked heritage to educational values, values promoted by the AHD and the infrequent response that nominated

118 Methods and quantitative findings

TABLE 5.4 What does the word 'heritage' mean?

	Australia %	USA %	England %
Don't know	4	1	0
History/the past	29	16	21
Background/identity	33	35	12
Intangible references	5	4	20
Family	7	33	1
Material things (AHD)	9	1	12
Act of preservation (AHD)	7	1.2	29
Nationalism/patriotism (AHD)	4	3	0
Critical of idea/term	0.2	0.4	2
What Indigenous or other people have	1	0.1	0
Emotional response	0.3	0.7	0
Ethnic identity	0.3	5	0
My religion	0	0.2	0
Royalty/aristocracy	0	0	1
Education (AHD)	0.7	0.4	1
Total	911	1008	713

AHD: definitions framed by the dominant discourse.

an origin myth such as 'heritage refers to frontier settlement' is one also framed by the AHD. The response 'history or the past' is a vague 'I really can't define it' and was often offered as either simply 'history' or 'the past', and as such it is unclear if it is specifically defined by the AHD. Those definitions framed by the AHD represent only 19% of responses:

> I've got to admit that the first word that came to mind was a building, an old building.
>
> *(IMM64: female, 45–54, editor, Anglo-Australian)*

The idea that heritage is intangible, family, part of one's ethnic identity or most often part of a nebulous, but very strong sense of one's 'background', or more specifically cultural background are not part of the expert-driven AHD. Those responses coded 'nationalism/patriotism' also explicitly spoke of heritage as representing that feeling as opposed to the material heritage that represented that emotion. When people talked about heritage as their cultural background, ethnicity, family and so on, they were expressing strong values and ties to particular ideas of identity and meaning. Visitors often struggled with answering this question not because they did not understand it, but rather, found it difficult to express the sense of feeling or emotion they associated with the word. While some of the feelings and values that were expressed may fit all too easily with nationalising and authorised narratives of nation, the point here is that in those definitions listed in Table 5.4 as not identified with the AHD, people are referring to emotional rather than materialist-based understandings of the nature of heritage. Heritage is not perceived so much as a thing but as a *feeling of belonging*. Examples of responses coded cultural background, include:

> Heritage? Heritage to me is the history that has occurred from our forefathers and brought us to the point where we are today. Anything that's happened in the past, whether it's our culture, our particular family members in the past, that heritage is what, or history makes us who we are. How we feel and how we think.
>
> (NCRM29: *male, 55–64, retired military, Honkey Cat (American)*)

> I guess it means background. I think – it's actually quite a tricky word to describe, but I do think of it meaning where you come from, something more than history. More than facts, maybe more of a feel.
>
> (TM65: *female, 25–34, unemployed, German English American, hard times tour*)

> I guess the culture behind where we live and, um, the way we live today, I guess.
>
> (MK8: *female, 25–34, naturopath, Australian, 2010*)

The idea of 'background' is also very firmly incorporated into more specific definitions that reference family and ethnicity. Examples of definitions that emphasise family include:

> Heritage means *my* background, *my* ancestry, where I've come from.
>
> (NCRM16: *female, over 65, retired teacher, African American, 2012, visitor's emphasis*)

> My family line, what my heritage is, meaning if it tracks back from my grandmother to her mom and stuff. And I guess that would be the values of how I was raised.
>
> (NCRM53: *female, 45–54, postal worker, Black American*)

> Basically it's the history of your family the history of your area that you come from, the history of whatever you're interested in, um, if you haven't got that you don't understand why things happen, why things are done that way, why people think that way.
>
> (MK37: *male, over 65, retired miner, Irish French Scot Australian, 2010*)

Definitions that stress family directly contradict the stress on the nation within the AHD. This sense of 'background' and its influence is carried over into those definitions that emphasise ethnicity, for example:

> Probably my ethnic and geographic circumstance.
> *(NCRM27: male, 25–44, advertising, White American)*

> I always think about Africa, the black er – that's what it means to me. I'm African American – somehow I wish it was just American, but I come from Africa. My ancestry, we came – we most likely came over as slaves.
> *(NCRM31: male, 45–54, retired military, African American)*

The sense of belonging or 'background' identified in the responses is also strongly reflected in responses nominating the feeling of national belonging, as did definitions that drew specifically on the intangible. These nominated not simply a sense of tradition, but ways of life, values and social and cultural experiences:

> The common experiences of a group of people.
> *(NCM49: male, 40–59, local government, Welsh)*

> Heritage is, err, what I've travelled all over the world to see, all the different kinds, and I just enjoy knowing about other people and where they live and how they cope with what goes on in their everyday lives.
> *(NCWMH76: female, over 65, Caucasian American)*

What is evident in the responses to this question is that the expert-driven AHD is not representative of non-expert understandings of heritage. The idea that identity and links to belonging and wellbeing are *implied* in traditional AHD definitions of heritage and certainly the idea that heritage is linked to expressions of identity are well rehearsed in the literature and public policy. However, the lack of explicit definitional acknowledgement of the emotional aspects of heritage works to both obscure and ultimately deny the legitimacy of these feelings and thus fails to incorporate a specific understanding of the valence of heritage in curatorial and management practices. Materialist definitions of heritage privileged by the AHD not only delegitimises the validity of the breadth of diversity of understandings of 'heritage' in these three countries but it also misses the strength of *feeling* and utility people find in the concept.

The diversity of heritage definitions is found in all three countries; however, there are some notable differences. Definitions framed within the AHD are significantly under-represented in the United States, where heritage is closely tied to concepts of family and cultural background. This may also be linked to a tendency for the professional discourse to reference 'historic preservation', rather than 'heritage', as is the case in Australia and England. The idea of the family offered by a third of respondents in the United States clearly distinguishes respondents from that country from those in Australia and England and suggests an understanding of heritage that is quite personally orientated.

In England, responses framed within the AHD, particularly the idea of heritage as an act of preservation or conservation, were more frequently offered than in the other two countries. However, definitions that nominated heritage as intangible (often referencing ideas of tradition) were far more frequent in England than in the United States or Australia. In England, definitions that nominated the intangible were most often given at sites of labour heritage, a site type under-represented in the interview data in both Australia and the United States. A striking characteristic of the overall English definition of heritage is a tension between the AHD, where heritage is understood as being about protecting things, and the idea of intangible heritage. This division, as argued in Smith (2006), tended to reflect class differences in that people from self-identified working-class backgrounds more often nominated intangible heritage than definitions framed within the AHD. However, while non-AHD definitions in England were given more frequently at labour heritage sites, it needs to be noted that the trends identified across the three countries are nonetheless maintained irrespective of whether the definitions were given at 'national' or 'dissonant' sites.

In Australia, heritage, as in the United States, was frequently defined as expressive of cultural background, although respondents were more often unsure of their definition, offering the vague and throwaway response 'history' or 'the past' more frequently than in the other two countries. Australian definitions sit between England and the United States, in that Australia had a higher frequency of definitions sitting firmly within the AHD than the United States but had a much higher preference for nominating cultural background than England. The response that heritage is what 'Indigenous people have, but I don't', was a response recorded generally, but not entirely, at Indigenous sites particularly in Australia, which related to the idea that Indigenous heritage had both a deeper temporal and cultural depth than that of the, usually Anglo-Celtic or Caucasian American interviewee. This answer in Australia, although infrequent in the overall sample, tended to correlate to a misrecognition or appropriation of Australian Indigenous heritage that is discussed in Chapters 10 and 13.

Connection to heritage

Two questions in the interview schedule, 'Whose history or heritage are you visiting here?' and 'Are you part of the history represented here?' aimed to reveal not only how the visitor characterised the history and/or culture represented by the site or museum they were visiting but to also see if they had any form of connection to that history or culture (Tables 5.5 and 5.6). The results of both questions suggest that respondents in the United States have an overall stronger sense of 'ownership' of the heritage they were visiting than visitors in either Australia or England.

The most frequent response in all three countries to 'Whose history or heritage are you visiting here?' (Table 5.5) was to nominate 'everyone's' (United States 32%;

TABLE 5.5 Whose history or heritage are you visiting here?

		Frequency	Valid percent
Valid	Everyone's	1407	34.3
	Ethnic/class/group specific	779	19.0
	Person specific	467	11.4
	My own/my family's	394	9.6
	Local/regional/state	263	6.4
	Indigenous	239	5.8
	Issue-based history	174	4.2
	Period specific	93	2.3
	No one's	72	1.8
	Both Indigenous and non-Indigenous	64	1.6
	Critical of exhibition	32	.8
	Individual and a group	23	.6
	Architectural history	18	.4
	Natural history	7	.2
	Don't know	67	1.6
	Total	4099	100.0
Missing	99	403	
Total		4502	

TABLE 5.6 Are you part of the history represented here?

		Frequency	Valid percent
Valid	Yes – emphatic	1373	32.9
	Yes – unelaborated	737	17.7
	Probably/think so – hesitant yes	194	4.6
	Yes – but not personally	56	1.3
	No – unelaborated	1500	35.9
	No – different background	118	2.8
	No – do not have personal/family links	49	1.2
	No – I'm a tourist to country	44	1.1
	No – feel excluded	27	.6
	Dissonant, indicating discomfort	25	.6
	Don't know	50	1.2
	Total	4173	100.0
Missing	99	329	
Total		4502	

Australia 37%, England 34%). The second most frequent response was to nominate that it belonged to a specific ethnic or class group, a response more frequently given in England (United States 16%; Australia 11%, England 24%). The counterpoint to this response was to identify that a site was linked to a visitor's own or family history and was more frequently given in the United States (17%) and Australia (12%) than in England (5%). It should be noted that the responses in England are heavily influenced by the exhibitions on slavery where respondents most frequently defined those exhibitions as belonging to a particular 'ethnic' group or identified the exhibitions as representing a particular 'issue' rather than as a heritage relevant to the nation (countries/everyone's) or saw it as 'world history'. This response was part of a strong denial of what this history may mean to concepts of British national identity, which has been discussed elsewhere (Smith 2010), but is re-examined in Chapter 13 in light of similar responses to dissonant history in Australia and the United States. Visitors in the United States (13%) and England (14%) more often nominated that the history they were visiting belonged to a specific person relative to those in Australia (5%), although this tends to reflect responses to house museums, which saw the history of the house as representative of a particular American president or member of the English aristocracy or landed gentry.

In response to the question 'Are you part of the history represented here?' (Table 5.6) visitors in the United States were far more likely to offer affirmative answers than those in Australia and England. The majority of Americans, 74%, answered yes to this question, compared to 54% in Australia and 49% in England. Without the enslavement exhibitions, the frequency in England falls to 38%. This latter figure is influenced by a low affirmative response to this question from house museums in that country, a surprising result given that these sites are often defined as core elements of Britain's national heritage (Mandler 1997; Dresser and Hann 2013: xiii).

The penultimate question asked if any aspect of the museum or site being visited spoke to or was linked to the visitor's identity (Table 5.7). Once again, those in the United States were more likely to answer in the affirmative (58%), followed closely by Australia (54%). However, an affirmative answer was given by only 42% of respondents in England, in part influenced by the discomfort many White British people had with the enslavement legacy exhibitions (Smith 2010), though it also occurred at lower levels in other genres as well. Of the various positive answers offered to this question, the response coded 'this is part of my personal and/or family heritage' was most frequently nominated by Americans (19%) and Australians (21%) compared to England (6%). Interestingly, although the most frequent response to the question 'Whose history or heritage are you visiting here?' was to nominate the 'country's' or 'everyone's', only 6% in response to the question on personal identity nominated 'my national identity' (Americans, at 10%, offered this more frequently than Australians, 7%, or the English, 3%). The sense of ownership or closer personal connection to the heritage of the site or museum being visited by Americans is reflected in the definition of heritage offered in the United States, which privileged ideas of family. It may also reflect a characteristic of the way sites and museums were used in the United States to reflect on the present, an issue discussed ahead.

How does it make you feel?

The question 'How does it make you feel to visit this place?' (Table 5.8) produced marked differences between the three countries. The most frequent response in all three countries was the response coded 'interested/educated' (United States 18%, Australia 22%, England 15%). However, this does not necessarily mean that

TABLE 5.7 Is there any aspect of your personal identity to which this exhibition speaks to or links?

		Frequency	Valid percent
Valid	No, not linked to my personal identity	1811	46.4
	Not my history – active rejection	113	2.9
	Yes – trivial or platitudinous observation	106	2.7
	This is my personal/family heritage	509	13.0
	This is part of my national identity	221	5.7
	Though empathy with people in past and/or present	213	5.5
	This is my people's history (class/ethnicity/region/religion/gender etc)	194	5.0
	Critical reflection on past for commentary on the present	148	3.8
	Aspiration/cultural capital	101	2.6
	Social memory/commemoration/remembrance	100	2.6
	Hobby/interest connection	79	2.0
	I find it educational	67	1.7
	I appreciate the values the site represents	54	1.4
	Spiritual link	42	1.1
	Arcadia, rustic, bucolic (aesthetic link)	26	0.7
	Elicited tourist response	25	0.6
	Yes, but private	14	0.4
	Acculturation	8	0.2
	Conservation statements	3	0.1
	Don't know	67	1.7
	Total	3901	100.0
Missing	99	601	
Total		4502	

people *were* actually feeling educated. This is a response that, in general, although not always, was indicative of a level of passive engagement within the registers of engagement. Most of the responses in this code can be characterised as 'oh, I am just interested' or 'it's very educational' and were banal or flat responses that deflected the question and its request to examine one's feelings. There were two primary reasons; first, simply because the visitor was having a nice day out and did not want to explore the issues represented at the site too deeply and reflected a sense that education or interest *should be* the answer given. This is illustrated by a visitor to Vaucluse House in Sydney who observed:

> I don't know, I should say something that, you know, education, learning on a place like this, but to be honest, the experience that I'm valuing on this is just the beauty of the place and enjoying the gardens, and having a lovely lunch, things like that; having a nice day out.
>
> *(VH33: female, 25–34, graphic designer, Australian)*

TABLE 5.8 How does it make you feel to visit this place?

		Frequency	Valid percent
Valid	Nothing, nice day out, 'non-emotional' answers	342	8.2
	Interested/educated	724	17.4
	Making empathetic connections	391	9.4
	Dissonance, defensive, confronted	302	7.3
	Moved – vague emotional statement	266	6.4
	It makes me deeply reflective/emotional intelligence	235	5.6
	Comfortable/comforted	198	4.8
	Proud	197	4.7
	Humbled – positive sense	164	3.9
	Humbled – deferential sense	54	1.3
	Nationalistic/patriotic	121	2.9
	Shame/guilt	99	2.4
	I feel recognised, historical injustices are being recognized in my history	95	2.3
	Nostalgic – social memory	85	2.0
	Nostalgic – reactionary	51	1.2
	Creating/maintaining links/sense of belonging	82	2.0
	Glad I'm alive now/grateful things have changed	82	2.0
	privileged	83	2.0
	Awestruck/overwhelmed	70	1.7
	Depressed, distressed, anxious	61	1.5
	Deep emotional response, but unable to do anything with it	61	1.5
	Glad preserved or remembered	54	1.3
	Numinous/spiritual	51	1.2
	Let down/disappointed by exhibition/excluded	44	1.1
	Aesthetically engaged	43	1.0
	Confronted and conflicted but thoughtful, without elaboration or depth	39	0.9
	Inspired	29	0.7
	Cultural capital	22	0.5
	Embodied sense of being in place	20	0.5
	Reinforcing feelings/knowledge (explicitly stated by visitor)	16	0.4
	Relaxed/renewed	15	0.4
	Unresolved anger	6	0.1
	Jealous	5	0.1
	Lament/loss	2	0.0
	Pilgrimage	1	0.0
	Don't know	54	1.3
	Total	4164	100.0
Missing	99	338	
Total		4502	

The second was that the visitor was expressing socially acceptable cognitive dissonance with the interpretation featured at the exhibition or site. This issue is discussed more fully in Chapters 8 and 13. Nevertheless, some responses were offered by people who were feeling genuinely educated and informed. The frequency of these particular responses, however, is likely to be reflected in the low frequencies of visitors who responded positively to the question about changed views (discussed ahead).

A feature of the responses in England is dissonant responses, where visitors felt 'confronted and defensive'; 13% expressed this relative to 1% in the United States and only two people in Australia. This response was, in large part, a reflection of the exhibitions on the history of enslavement (Smith et al. 2011). These exhibitions were documenting a hidden history and, in the main, offering an interpretation that did not reflect the celebratory narratives of the majority of the British media and parliamentarians at the time (Cubitt 2009, 2010; Waterton and Wilson 2009). Removing these exhibitions from the analysis, however, does not entirely remove the dissonant response, as similar responses occurred at the 'Work and Play' exhibitions at house museums. These exhibitions attempted to unsettle the dominant bucolic readings of these houses that neglected the often oppressive history of domestic and estate workers (see Chapter 10). The negligible dissonant responses to this question from the United States and Australia is worth comparing to the responses coded 'confronted and conflicted but thoughtful' and 'deeply emotional, but unable to do anything with it'. Being confronted and conflicted differs from the dissonant response in that a visitor has recognised dissonance, but this has elicited a thoughtful rather than a dismissive response. Both codes register a deep emotional engagement, although with the former, the visitor has been able to become thoughtful and reflective; in the latter response, the visitor has not, at the time of the interview, been able to marshal their thoughts. In the United States, while only 3% and 4% of visitors, respectively, were coded as such, these responses are either absent or represent 1% or less from the English and Australian data.

While dissonance does not disappear from the English responses when the bicentenary data is removed, what does become almost completely absent is the response 'it makes me deeply reflective', which represents 4% of responses in both the United States and Australia and 7% in England. This response to the slavery exhibitions was not found at other English sites and was a response that, while not exclusive to non-dominant ethnic visitors, was over-represented by African Caribbean British respondents. Another difference highlighted by the removal of the bicentenary data is a drop in those responses that were empathetic; 12% of respondents to this question in England made empathetic connections relative to 5% and 6% in the United States and Australia, respectively. However, in England, this response was again over-represented by those respondents of non-dominant ethnic backgrounds at the enslavement legacy exhibitions, who are almost entirely absent at other site genres in England.

Actively dissonant responses to confronting historical topics appear to be a peculiar aspect of the English response. This response does occur in the other two countries, but it was to other questions in the interview schedule and/or was often more passively expressed, as discussed in the following. Other distinguishing responses in the English interviews is the degree to which people nominated feeling comforted or comfortable, which while present in responses from Australia and the United States, was not found anywhere near as frequently as in England (9% compared to 1% in the United States and 0.3% in Australia). This feeling was *exclusively* connected to house museums in all three countries (Chapter 10).

Interviews, in general, from the United States and Australia are marked by the coded responses that revealed passive or low emotional engagement: 'moved – vague emotional statement' (such as 'sad' or 'good' or 'happy') and 'nothing, having a nice day out'. These responses occur much less frequently in England (1% and 5%, respectively), and both responses in the United States (13% and 12%) and Australia (12% and 11%), while generally illustrative of passive engagement, could also signal passive dissonance with sites or exhibitions destabilising a visitor's accepted narratives. In contrast, the strong emotion of pride was marked in both the United States (9%) and Australia (8%), but relatively infrequently expressed in England (1%). Australian visitors were more likely than those in the United States and England to express a positive sense of humility in relation to achievements and events of the past (7% compared to 3% from both England and the United States).

In summary, and in response to this question, there is a sense that feelings of cognitive dissonance are responded to more explicitly and directly in England than in Australia and the United States; visitors in the latter two countries tended to be far more passive or guarded in their disagreement with the interpretive material. In the United States a strong positive emotion to being confronted is evidenced by a small percentage of visitors, which, although not always, tended to lead to reflection and thoughtfulness. Strong positive emotions occur in all three countries, pride in particular in the United States and Australia, while a sense of comfort is a feature of the English responses. These overall differences tend to be maintained within either dissonant or national sites within the three nations.

What experiences do you value on visiting this place?

This question, not asked at the England bicentenary exhibitions, produced some differences across the three countries, but as discussed in the following, some of these differences may have more to do with the genre of the site than the country in which the site was found (Chapter 6). Nonetheless, respondents from the United States far more frequently nominated seeing a particular aspect of the site or an artefact from the museum collection they were visiting as the valued experience than respondents in Australia and England (34% compared to 13% and 1%, respectively, Table 5.9). This may in part be the influence of *The Star-Spangled Banner* exhibition where respondents uniformly nominated seeing the flag, while in England at the house museums, the sense of being at a given house was more important than specific artefacts. In the English data, 25% of visitors nominated a holistic sense of physically 'being at' the site they were visiting (relative to 11% and 12% from Australia and the United States, respectively), while an overall sense of an aesthetic experience was recorded for 13% of visitors in England, but only for 2%

TABLE 5.9 What experiences do you value on visiting this place?

		Frequency	Valid percent
Valid	None	139	5.1
	Educational/informational	516	19.1
	Nominating a particular aspect of the site/seeing specific artefacts	468	17.3
	Physical sense of being at the museum/site	414	15.3
	Empathy	258	9.5
	Tourist/recreational	175	6.5
	Identity/memory work	168	6.2
	Platitude	139	5.1
	Aesthetic enjoyment	133	4.9
	Gaining cultural capital (explicit statements made)	78	2.9
	Ability to reflect on present/past	58	2.1
	Sharing past/an experience with my children	37	1.4
	Opportunity to show respect/recognition	34	1.3
	Reinforcing what already know/feel (explicitly stated by visitor)	29	1.1
	Reinforcing nationalism/patriotism	25	0.9
	Acculturation	1	0.0
	Don't know	30	1.1
	Total	2702	100.0
Missing	99	1800	
Total		4502	

in Australia and 1% in the United States. Explicit statements coded 'gaining cultural capital' were also far more frequent in England (9%) than in the United States or Australia (both less than 1%). The latter three responses in England tended to be more frequent at house museums than at labour sites where an active process of identity and memory work is far more prevalent (21% at labour sites relative to 2% at houses). The physical sense of 'being at a place', while recorded at labour history sites in England, was again most prevalent at house museums (Chapter 10).

In Australia, the most frequent experience nominated was being 'educated/informed' (26%), a response also frequently given in the other two countries (16% for both). As with the question on feeling, this response can measure a sense of educational achievement; however, it could also be expressed as a throwaway response when the respondent was either simply characterising their visit as a 'nice day out', registering low levels of engagement across the interview, or was confronted by the interpretive content of the site (this is explored further in Chapters 8 and 13).

An interesting response that occurred across all three countries were those who nominated 'empathy' as an experience they valued; this response represented 10% of the overall sample and 8%, 9% and 12% of responses in the United States, Australia and England, respectively. In both the United States and England, this response was found predominantly at dissonant sites, while in Australia it was more evenly distributed between national and dissonant sites. Respondents either talked about their empathetic responses to the site or talked about a desire to have an empathetic response. What this response says about the agency of some visitors and the way they are using sites is important and is explored in Chapters 11 and 12. Empathy was also an important element for those whose views of either the past or present was changed or significantly deepened at or by the site they were visiting, and this issue is discussed in Chapter 8.

What does being here mean to you?

As discussed in Chapter 4, this question was not asked at all sites. In response to this question visitors were, in order of frequency (Table 5.10), making some form of personal connection (either in active or passive forms) to the site or the history and culture it represented (21%). These responses were often linked to the performance of intergenerational communication and connection (Chapter 11) or they were having a nice day out (16%), commemorating the history or culture represented (15%), nominating that the site meant nothing to them (13%) or found it educational (13%).

Visitors in the United States were most frequently engaged in making some form of personal connection (24%) to the site or undertaking some form of commemoration (18%). It needs to be remembered this question was not asked at all of the English or Australian sites; however, Australians were less likely to make

TABLE 5.10 What does being here mean to you?

		Frequency	*Valid percent*
Valid	Nothing	255	12.9
	Personal connection (of which 11.3 passive / 9.7 active)	416	21.0
	Nice day out/touristic response	318	16.1
	Commemoration (of which 6.8 passive / 8.5 active)	303	15.3
	Education/information gathering	246	12.5
	Reinforcement (explicitly stated)	93	4.7
	Expressing nationalism/patriotism	83	4.2
	Embodiment (of which 2.4 passive / 1.0 active)	67	3.4
	Cultural capital/aspirational/acculturation	53	2.7
	A chance to reflect on past or present	50	2.5
	Spirituality	43	2.2
	Prevarication, ambivalence, discomfort toward complex topic	8	0.5
	Pilgrimage	8	0.4
	Don't know	31	1.6
	Total	1974	100.0
Missing	99	2528	
Total		4502	

connections than visitors in the other two countries (15% compared to 24% from the United States and 21% from England). Commemoration was far less frequently offered as a meaning in England (8%) than in Australia (21%) and the United States (18%). The frequency of making personal connections from the United States interviews may reflect and link back to the quite personal and familial definitions of 'heritage' nominated by visitors.

A response coded 'spirituality', while infrequent, was most often given in England (5% relative to 3% in Australia and 0.3% in the United States); this response included both direct discussions of spirituality and references to a god, but also a sense of the numinous as identified by Cameron and Gatewood (2012). It is this sense of the numinous that dominates here and is again a response that was given at house museums, as was the cultural capital/aspirational response (8%), which again was infrequent in Australia (1%) and the United States (1%). The 'nice day out' response was most frequently given in England (24%) and Australia (21%) while representing only 10% of responses from the United States.

An interesting response from the United States was 'a chance to reflect', which while accounting for only 4% of the responses from the United States, and most frequently at dissonant sites, is almost completely absent from Australia and England (1%, respectively). The idea that being at a site allows time and space for reflection is important in the United States, as responses to the question asking visitors to reflect on the 'meaning' of the site to contemporary Americans reveal that 8% of visitors in the United States used the site they were visiting to reflect on present-day issues.[3] However, as discussed in the following and in Chapter 7, this response is influenced by ethnic identity. Further, the response is linked to a performance of affirmative reinforcement (Chapter 9) rather than an educational response. However, for 14% of visitors in the United States and 13% in England, being at a site was about education or information gathering, although this represented only 6% of responses from Australia.

Are there any messages about the heritage or history of Australia/America/England that you take away from this place?

The idea that visitors will take away a particular message is a strong assumption embedded in the literature and museological and heritage interpretation practices. Overall, 30% of visitors stated or implied that they took away no message; a further 11% explicitly stated that their existing ideas or feelings on or about a topic had been reinforced, and a further 9% offered platitudes or thought-terminating clichés, indicating that the visitor was not engaging with or taking away an identifiable curatorial message (Table 5.11). On the registers of engagement, platitudes are indicative of low cognitive engagement.

The reasons underlying the 'no message' response are varied. Occasionally, it was an active oppositional response to, or rejection of, the content of the exhibition or interpretation. Sometimes it was a measure of a visitor's passive engagement. More

TABLE 5.11 Are there any messages about the heritage or history of Australia/America/England that you take away from this place?

		Frequency	Valid percent
Valid	No message	1220	30.2
	Reinforcing feelings and/or knowledge (explicitly stated)	436	10.7
	Platitude	363	9.0
	Critical engagement/reflecting on modern issues	405	10.1
	Gratitude, historical debt	256	6.4
	Social messages	225	5.5
	Recognition/gaining or showing respect	203	5.0
	Vague statements about how hard it was/is (no empathy/gratitude)	184	4.5
	Preservation message	175	4.3
	Nationalistic/patriotism/national identity	141	3.5
	Noting how society has changed	99	2.3
	Values of people in past to be taken up or reinforced in present	86	2.1
	Empathetic link made	67	1.7
	Vague connection to the past	62	1.5
	Educational for younger generations or other groups	42	1.0
	Just being here is important	25	0.6
	Yes, but unelaborated	23	0.6
	Critical of exhibition	14	0.3
	Sense of loss	13	0.3
	Spiritual message	5	0.1
	Cultural capital (explicit statements of attainment)	2	0.0
	Total	4046	100.0
Missing	99	456	
Total		4502	

often, however, the response appears to be simply reflecting that visitors do not see the need to, or have the desire to, take away a message. This may itself be a reflection of the extent to which the site was perceived to be reinforcing a visitor's entrance narrative (Pekarik and Schreiber 2012).

Collectively, the responses so far outlined to this question equate to 50% of visitors. These visitors were coded as having engaged relatively passively with the idea that the site or exhibition they were visiting may contain some form of message about the history or heritage of their country or the country in which they were a tourist. It needs to be noted that when visitors did nominate messages, this nomination in itself did not necessarily indicate that these were messages that they had 'learned' at the site, only what the site represented to them or, on occasion, what they thought the curatorial/interpretive message was, even if they were not engaging with that message.

The 'no message' response was most prevalent in English interviews (32%), followed by the United States (29%) and with Australia (27%) not too far behind. Previously, this response was reported as a feature in visitor interviews from the English bicentenary and enslavement legacy exhibitions (Smith 2010); however, the response is not confined to those exhibitions in that country. Those exhibitions had been explicitly designed to raise awareness of the neglected history of Britain's involvement in the transatlantic slave trade and aimed to engage audiences with messages about the legacies of this history (Cubitt 2009; Dresser 2009). The high 'no message' response was assumed to be a function of the degree to which visitors had been confronted by that contested and hidden history (Smith 2010). However, the results here suggest it is not necessarily a reflection of dissonance or discomfort with exhibition messages, especially as the 'no message' response is a little more frequent at national sites overall (33%) than at dissonant sites (28%). Rather, it suggests that 'messages' are not crucial to visitors' uses of sites and underlines the reinforcement performances discussed in Chapter 9.

Platitudes were also a feature of responses to this question in England (12%) and the United States (8%), but not quite as frequently in Australia (4%). If the bicentenary data is removed, the frequency of the platitudinous responses in England is significantly reduced to 1% of the responses in that country. The 'no message' response, however, only moves slightly down from 32% to 30% of responses in England. What the change in platitudinous responses indicate is that there is a far more positive and active engagement with English labour history and house museums than there was with the bicentenary and enslavement legacy exhibitions. The influences of the genre of the site on the results needs to be noted here and will be discussed in Chapter 6; however, in all three countries, platitudes are more prevalent at dissonant than at national sites (14% and 3%, respectively), reflecting discomfort with exhibition content.

A feature of the responses from the United States was that 7% of the messages were expressive of nationalism or national identity, compared to 4% of responses in Australia and 1% in England. However, this response in the United States is *only* found at national sites and not at dissonant sites, whereas it is present at both types of sites in the other two countries although in reduced frequencies at dissonant sites. Visitors in the United States (10%) and Australia (11%) were more often likely to nominate messages that suggested historical gratitude for achievements in the past than visitors in England (3%), although in Australia this was far more frequently done at national than dissonant sites (11% and 0.3%, respectively). Additionally, the offering of messages that went beyond historical gratitude and that represented a more reflexive form of recognition or respect was a feature of the Australian data with 11% of responses in that country compared to just 2% from the United States and 4% from England (in both England and Australia this variable occurred *only* at dissonant sites, but equally at both site types in the United States). Recognition or respect in Australia tended to be shown to Indigenous peoples at sites of Indigenous history and culture and towards migrants at the Immigration Museum. In England, it was again entirely a feature of the bicentenary exhibitions. This response on the register of engagement reflects a very deep and considered response and is discussed in detail in Chapter 12.

Reflecting on modern issues counted for 10% of responses. The issues reflected on were many and varied, ranging from topical events at the time of interview to longer-term issues such as racial or gender inequality, immigration, labour issues, among others. This response represented 12% and 11% of responses in the United States and England, respectively, and only 6% of responses in Australia. In England, this response only occurred at dissonant sites, whereas in the United States it occurred across all site types, although more frequently at dissonant sites. Critical reflection on the present is also a response that correlated with ethnic identity (see Chapter 7).

In summary, the most frequent response across all three countries was that messages were not taken away from the sites being visited. When messages were taken away, quite a range and variety were offered, and this perhaps reflects the range of genres of sites at which interviews were taken (see Chapter 6). However, variation across the three countries is not particularly notable with the exception that both visitors in the United States and Australia tended to reference historical gratitude more than was the case in England; messages about the nation were slightly more prevalent in the United States, and Australian visitors were more likely to offer positive forms of recognition. Outside of the bicentenary and enslavement legacy exhibitions, visitors in England were less likely to offer platitudes, suggesting a more active and positive register of engagement with house museums and labour history sites.

What meaning, if any, does an exhibition like this have for contemporary Australia/America/England?

While a wide range of responses were given to this question, 31% of visitors defined the meaning of the site they were visiting as an aide to memory, of which national memory dominated at 25%, while memories associated with either specific communities or personal and familial memories each represented 3% (Table 5.12). In the United States, 30% of visitors nominated the site as an aide to national memory, while 25% did so in Australia and 22% did in England. Platitudinous statements were also a frequent response across all three countries, representing 25% of the overall sample; this was slightly higher in the United States, representing 28% of responses, relative to 24% from Australia and 23% from England. This response may reflect the difficulty some people had with this question. However, the response from England is a reflection of the bicentenary exhibitions that many White British visitors found confronting. If the bicentenary data is removed from the English data, the variable 'platitude' drops to 10% of the English dataset, leaving labour history and house museums again characterised in often far more active and positive ways than the exhibitions on enslavement and their legacies. As is discussed in Chapter 6, platitudes were offered more frequently at certain genres of sites, particularly those addressing dissonant histories, than at others. However, in response to this question, platitudes do not always represent a dissonant response, as they may also be reflective of the question's request that the visitor considers the modern meaning of the site and the narrative schematic templates about nation are framing visitor responses; as discussed in Chapter 6, platitudes in response to this question are very prevalent at national sites.

Responses that identify sites as aides to memory for specific groups did not vary across the three countries, and those using sites as aides to personal memory were slightly more common in England, reflecting responses at labour history sites. The personal connections that Americans had made in response to other answers were frequently abandoned here in favour of national and nationalising narratives.

Using sites to reflect on modern issues was a related response to those coded aides to memory and represented 11% of the overall sample. In England, this represented 15% of the responses, but it was again *only* the exhibitions on enslavement legacies that were used to reflect on the contemporary issues of racism and multiculturalism. The critical response at these exhibitions was most frequently offered by African Caribbean British rather than by White British visitors (Smith 2010, 2011). In Australia, this response represented only 2% of visitors and occurred only at dissonant sites. Notably, in the United States, where 8% were using sites in this way, a range of genres of sites were used to reflect on modern issues, although this response was more frequently given at dissonant sites (16% relative to 3% at national sites). Reflection was often not in response to curatorial messages or prompts but was rather an organic response by the visitor. This reflexive response tends to signal but is not confined to, affirming reinforcement and performances of recognition (Chapters 8 and 12, respectively).

A notable response to this question was the 17% who identify the site being visited as having some form of educational value (Table 5.12). This was a response most frequently made in England (20%) and then most frequently at house museums (24%), compared to 18% in Australia and 10% in the United States. These responses, however, predominantly talked about the importance of these sites either for children or groups other than that to which the visitor belonged.

An associated response here, although relatively infrequent at 5%, is the lament 'it doesn't but it should', which is a concern that the social values that the site is seen to represent and/or its role as an aide to particular memories that it serves for the visitor, is perceived not to be shared by either the rest of society or by other groups such as the young or particular ethnic or migrant communities. This response was most frequently given by those from politically dominant ethnic backgrounds when engaged in performances of reinforcement and sit alongside the 'educational' response that inevitably references the need for people other than the speaker to be educated. Both reference a sense of discomfort and speak to a desire by the visitor that particular groups should assimilate the values the visitor considers the site represents. Further, they are also statements naturalising the meaning of the visit, which in turn helps legitimise the performances of reinforcement discussed in Chapters 9 and 10.

TABLE 5.12 What meaning, if any, does an exhibition like this have for contemporary Australia/America/England?

		Frequency	Valid percent
Valid	None	76	2.0
	Aid to memory – personal identity	123	3.2
	Aid to memory – regional, class or ethnic identity	106	2.7
	Aid to memory – national	942	24.7
	Platitudes or unelaborated yes	946	24.8
	Educational resource	646	17.0
	Reflecting on modern issues	407	10.7
	Conservation/preservation meaning	194	5.1
	It doesn't but it should	176	4.6
	Represents certain values that are relevant to the site	50	1.3
	Tourist resource	40	1.0
	Acculturation/cultural capital	3	0.1
	Embodiment in place	13	0.3
	Don't know	89	2.3
	Total	3811	100.0
Missing	99	691	
Total		4502	

In summary, visitors in the United States abandoned the tendency to make personal or familial links to heritage sites that they had done in response to previous questions to talk more frequently about the national meanings and values of the sites they were visiting. The meaning for memories of nationhood, patriotism and nationalism were more prevalent in the United States than in Australia or England but not strikingly so. While visitors in the United States also tended to offer platitudes slightly more often than visitors in the other countries in response to this question, they were also more likely to use sites to reflect on modern issues – something that was only done in England in response to the exhibitions on the history and legacies of enslavement and almost absent in the Australian data. The relative lack of platitudinous responses in England at labour sites and country houses references a far more positive and celebratory engagement with these sites than at the 1807 bicentenary exhibitions.

Is there anything you've seen/read/heard today that has changed your views about the past or the present?

There was no significant variation in response to this question across the three countries; overall, 80% said 'no their views had not changed in any way' (Table 5.13). At certain museums, such as house museums, this statistic was as high as 90%; the lowest frequency of 65% was recorded at the Immigration Museum, Melbourne. A simple no was the common response to this question; however, 20% of those who said no also went on to say, without prompting, that the site had reinforced

TABLE 5.13 Is there anything you have read/seen/heard today that has changed your views on the past or the present?

		Frequency	Valid percent
Valid	No	2386	60.5
	No – reinforced what already knew	779	19.7
	Yes – vague acknowledgement	132	3.3
	Yes – new (minor) information	244	6.2
	Yes – better informed, more aware seeing the physical reality	108	2.7
	Yes – new (major) information	101	2.6
	made me think about things in new ways	96	2.4
	Yes – empathetic link made	42	1.1
	Yes – epiphany	19	0.5
	Inspired to make a change in behaviour or life	4	0.1
	Don't know	34	0.9
	Total	3945	100.0
Missing	99	557	
Total		4502	

what they already knew or believed. 'Reinforcement', and its various synonyms, was not used in the interview schedule but was a very common way in which people talked about their visit, not only in response to this question but also to the questions asking visitors to identify any messages they may have taken away, how the site made them feel or the experiences they valued. Reinforced, affirmed or confirmed were all used in response to this question, for example:

> No, but it's reinforced it.
> *(TM59: female, over 65, system analyst, Jewish American)*

> I think it just reinforces the ideas I always had about it, it just confirms, you know...
> *(IMM029: female, 35–44, mother, Australian)*

> No, I don't think so. I don't know whether I'm that flexible. [laughs]
> *(AWM52: female, 25–34, legal policy, Australian)*

TM59's response is typical of the way people responded in this vein, and while 'reinforcement' as AWM52 suggests may be viewed in some instances as inflexibility on the part of the visitor or an unwillingness to engage, reinforcement is not necessarily negative or a 'failure' of the exhibition or interpretation to engage visitors. Reinforcement could be affirming with both progressive and conservative political implications (Chapter 9). However, the response to this question does tend to contradict the responses to the questions about feelings, valued experiences and 'being there' in which visitors frequently nominated education, information gathering or feeling interested and the frequency of the selection of 'education' or 'to find out about' in response to the question about reasons for visiting. As discussed in Chapter 3, 'learning' as commonly used in the museums and heritage educational literature measures some form of *change* or a marked deepening of understanding. While people may say that they feel or believe they are engaging in an 'educational' or learning activity, that is not necessarily what is happening. There is a strong commonsense perception in relation to both museums and heritage that they are 'educational' and that visitors, even if they are not visiting for educational reasons, consider that they *should* be doing so. What is also revealing, and is discussed in more detail in Chapter 8, and as outlined in response to both the questions about the contemporary meaning of a site and the messages taken away, is that when visitors do talk about visiting as an educational experience, they tend to talk about it in terms of the education of children or the education of groups of people *other than* the group to which they themselves belong.

The sense to which a discourse of learning was used to deflect dissonance or as a reflex response by those simply having a relaxing day out is also borne out by the results of this question. However, 19% did nominate some level of change in views. Relatively minor changes, such as a 'vague acknowledgement' that something had changed or the nomination of the attainment of new, but minor, information collectively accounts for 10% of responses. Of particular note are the 9% deeply engaged on the register of engagement who nominated that they had an epiphany, observed that the site 'made them think about things in new ways'; who talked about making empathetic links and the four people who intended to change their behaviour. As discussed in Chapter 8, the ability to sincerely and imaginatively make empathetic links, was integral in deepening or changing a visitor's understanding.

Discussion

A number of themes arise from the analysis outlined in this chapter. First, a strong discourse emerges that links visiting with an idea of 'education' or learning. Almost a third of all visitors selected 'education' or 'to find out about' from the list of reasons that best explained their visit and went on to raise, unprompted, the idea that information gathering or education were experiences they were seeking or what 'being at' a particular site meant for many visitors. Feeling informed or educated was also a common response to the question that asked people to explain how they felt at the site. However, this emphasis on the educational visit is contradicted by the frequencies with which people either took away 'no message' or offered platitudes or other flat responses that registered low cognitive engagement in response to the question about messages. In addition, very few people considered that their views had changed or deepened. Much of the museological and heritage educational debate stresses that the role of museums and heritage should be about influencing social views and debates, if not altering people's perceptions and basic historical and cultural understanding (see Chapter 3). What is notable here is that a discourse of 'reinforcement' emerged, not only in response to the question about changed views but also in relation to other questions. How do we make sense of the apparent conflict between the educational and reinforcement discourses that are evident in the interviews?

The idea that sites are educational is part of the polite and expected response, as VH33 quoted above illustrates. However, it is significant to note that when people did talk in-depth about the educational meaning or message of a site, they inevitably talked about the meaning in terms of its importance for people *other than* themselves. The learning discourse, as discussed in Chapters 8 and 13, can also be invoked when people feel negatively challenged by an exhibit or interpretation at a heritage site. This discourse can paradoxically be an indication of polite mild to deep dissent on the part of the visitor, particularly that visitor not wanting to be seen as being 'negative' about the exhibition or site they were visiting. It can, paradoxically, be used to legitimise and normalise performances of reinforcement (Chapters 8 and 9). The discourse can, most certainly, be what it seems, and may reflect that visitors see themselves as engaged in learning, even perhaps when that is not necessarily what is happening. The discourse of reinforcement is a more honest visitor response and reflects more closely what visitors are indeed doing than the educational discourse does. As argued in Chapter 9, this is not necessarily a negative or undesirable use of heritage. In certain contexts, the use of museums and heritage sites as cultural tools for reinforcing visitor views can be quite positive and politically powerful, while in other contexts it may indeed be cause for concern by curators and interpreters.

A second theme that is evident in the data is the degree to which the AHD does not frame the majority of visitor understandings about the nature of heritage. While the AHD does nod to the emotional elements of heritage, as argued in Chapter 2, this acknowledgement is oblique and entirely guarded. Visitors often struggled to define heritage, as evidenced by those who simply offered 'history' or 'the past' as their definition, but more frequently, the struggle centred on how to express complex feelings and emotions. Visitors talked about a sense of 'background' that often stood in for a sense of belonging, wellbeing and connection. Undoubtedly, the visitor responses to the question about heritage challenged the AHD as visitors drew on ideas of the intangible and family, but more generally, it was the sense that heritage is intimately linked to the way a person feels that challenged the AHD more specifically and illustrated its inability to define and engage with a non-professional or public understanding of the concept.

The third theme to draw out here focuses on national comparisons. An overall sense emerges that visitors in the United States tended on the one hand to make strong personal connections to the material they were visiting, while on the other hand, they might also make strong links to the nation. In response to the various questions exploring 'connection' and the question that asked what 'being at' sites meant, visitors in the United States evidenced a strong connection by more frequently claiming that heritage as their own or drawing personal links to it than visitors in the other two countries. A sense of connection or 'ownership' was also reflected in the degree to which Americans identified a sense of heritage with family. This link was reversed when visitors were asked what a site may mean to contemporary America/England or Australia. One of the more notable differences between the three countries is the tendency of visitors in the United States to make personal linkages to sites while also making strong statements about the sites' contemporary meaning for narratives and memory-making about the nation. While not a common response, a further feature of the response from the United States was a deep, emotional connection often tied to a positive and thoughtful response to having their entrance narrative challenged or associated with using the site they were visiting to reflect on the present social and political issues or experiences. American respondents were also less likely to see themselves as engaged in recreation when visiting heritage sites than visitors in Australia and England, once again suggesting an active and strong sense of connection to, and utilisation of, the sites being visited.

When visitors in the United States or Australia found exhibition or interpretive content confronting, they were more likely than those interviewed in England to express their dissent or dissonance passively through platitudes. Visitors in England were far more explicit in their dissonance with the exhibition or interpretive content than visitors in Australia and the United States. A sense of comfort and expressions of cultural capital were featured in the English data, and the strength of positive associations with heritage may point to why those in England were more strident in addressing dissonance. Visitors in England at sites where their entrance narratives were not being challenged were more likely to nominate that they had taken away some sort of message, suggesting a relatively active engagement with those sites they found comfortable or familiar.

The Australian data showed a greater emphasis or use of an 'education' or learning discourse and the socially progressive response 'recognition and respect'. Like visitors in the United States, Australian visitors tended to be more passive in their dissonance than those from England, while also, as in England, they made slightly fewer links to the nation than those in the United States. Like those in the United States, a feature of the Australian response was historical humility and gratitude.

Conclusion

While there were differences identifiable between the three nations, it is also important to stress the extent of their similarities. The differences between the nations is not, in general, stark, insofar as there are few variables or responses to sites that occur only or predominantly in the one national context. Although perhaps the most measurable difference is the degree to which visitors in America both referenced personal connections to heritage while also nominating that the contemporary meaning of the site they were visiting was linked national memory and narratives. It needs to be noted that there are difficulties in the comparison undertaken between the nations as certain genres of site type – in particular, Indigenous, immigration and enslavement legacy sites – do not occur across all three countries, while the numbers of visitors interviewed at labour history sites in Australia and the

United States are considerably lower than those from England. The extent to which some of the patterns observable here may be influenced by or reflect the genre of the site is explored in the next chapter.

What the overview of the data from the three countries does do, however, is draw attention to a number of features that need deeper analysis. In particular, the issue of both the use of museums and heritage sites as avenues for either reinforcement and/or learning are issues discussed in Chapters 8 and 9 and speak to an overall performance of reinforcement that visitors undertake. The issue of platitudes and their use, as well as more active forms of dissent and discomfort, are revealed as an issue of note and are discussed in Chapter 13. Platitudes and other forms of discomfort are defined as emotional and discursive strategies that signal an attempt to limit cognitive dissonance and that are deployed when the comfortable and comforting performance of reinforcement is challenged. The following two chapters provide further insight into where and why this performance is undertaken and provide background to the frequency and nature of the strategies of cognitive dissonance that are discussed in Chapter 13. How people are connecting to sites and exhibitions and how that connection is then used is also an emergent issue from the overall data and is discussed in depth in Chapter 11. Although a relatively infrequent self-conscious response in the overall dataset, the issues of 'recognition and respect' and the associated issue of misrecognition need further exploration and are discussed in Chapter 12.

Notes

1 See Chapter 4 on the definition of 'significance' used in this chapter.
2 The variables 'where travelled from?' and 'first visit?' were not recorded during the study of museums and house museums responding to the 2007 bicentenary of Britain's abolition of its slave trade. Thus, the data presented here is from the 2004 data and the 2007 'Work and Play' data recorded at house museums and labour history sites and represents 917 interviews.
3 The coding notes that the visitor was reflecting on contemporary issues not what those issues were.

6
GENRES OF MUSEUMS AND HERITAGE SITES

Comparisons

While there are some differences in visitor responses to museums and heritage sites between the three nations, the patterned variation in visitor responses and demographics between site genres is more striking. Chapter 4 outlines how and why the individual museums and heritage sites were first grouped into 'national' and 'dissonant' sites and then grouped into different genres. This chapter outlines, first, the variations in demographics between the genres, and second, key variations in visitor responses between the different genres. Two overall themes emerge from this analysis: first, patterns of variations in visitor responses do occur between the different genres. While the genres do share similarities in responses, the frequencies at which certain responses occur at different genres allows the identification of emotional and/or discursive 'signatures' or affective repertoires for different genres.

The second theme, which occurs across all genres, is the way particular emotional connections, or lack of connection, to sites influenced visitor reactions. The extent to which visitors feel personally connected or feel that a site engages with their sense of nationalism, or understanding of a national narrative, tends to reflect deep emotional engagements that then facilitate the performances of reinforcement discussed in Chapters 9 and 10. Genres, or specific experiences, which challenge a visitor's sense of self and/or national identity tend to elicit negative valence, which can, as discussed in Chapter 13, result in performances of misrecognition. Rather than looking at the details of the results for each interview question and the minutiae of variations, the following sections broadly outline the significant quantitative differences between the different genres.

Visitor demographics and genres of heritage sites and museums

Visitor profiles in relation to age, gender, educational attainment and ethnic identity were similar within the genres to the overall sample with some notable exceptions.

Visitors over 45 were over-represented at house museums (older: 67% vs. younger: 33%), at labour sites (68% vs. 32%) and the halls of fame (70% vs. 29%), while younger people were more numerous at the 'other' national sites (older: 41% vs. younger: 59%) and sites commemorating war (35% vs. 65%). Those over 45, as identified in Chapter 7, more often formed connections with sites reflective of the performance of intergenerational connections; as is illustrated ahead, these connections were particularly prevalent at labour sites, halls of fame and also immigration sites (Chapter 11).

Females (54% of the overall sample) and males (46%) occurred in roughly equal or similar proportions at the different genres and individual sites, except for females comprising 59% of visitors to house museums, 59% to immigration museums and 58% of visitors to Indigenous sites. Males dominated at English labour sites, though this trend was not replicated in either Australia or the United States, while 54% of visitors to sites commemorating war were men. Gender did not correlate significantly to patterns in visitor responses (Chapter 7).

Those who had been to university were in the majority at all genres of sites with the exception of the labour history genre and the halls of fame, where those without university degrees accounted for 55% and 60% of visitors, respectively. Both genres address working-class histories, as the halls of fame, while ostensibly addressing national narratives about the settlement of the American and Australian 'frontier', also speak to the histories and experiences of agricultural workers. The genre with the highest frequency of university-educated visitors (72%) was immigration sites, where the performances of familial intergenerational connections at this genre, as discussed ahead and in Chapter 11, show a sense of gratitude for the opportunities afforded by the descendants of immigrants.

Those who identified themselves as employed in the four 'higher' categories of employment (professional, managerial, intermediate and own account, Table 5.1) represented the majority of visitors in all genres (between 56% and 79%). The lowest frequency of higher professional/own account (56%) occurred at the war commemoration sites, which recorded the highest level of student (and younger) visitors. The highest frequency (79%) of these occupations occurred at the slavery legacy sites. Those from the 'technical/routine' occupations were the most prevalent at the halls of fame (29%), labour sites (23%) and Indigenous sites (20%); at all other genres, these occupations accounted for between 10% and 14% of visitors.

People from politically non-dominant ethnic backgrounds were recorded at all sites, except Yellowstone National Park, and made up the majority of visitors only at the National Civil Rights Museum, the Japanese American National History Museum and the London Museum in Docklands. Overall people from non-dominant ethnic backgrounds (who accounted for 12% of the overall sample) more frequently visited 'dissonant' sites and the sites categorised as both national and dissonant (Uluru and Ellis Island) than 'national' sites (see Table 6.1). That is, those from non-dominant ethnicities accounted for only 7% of visitors at all national sites, but 15% at dissonant sites. At specific genres, those from non-dominant ethnicities visited sites addressing the legacies and histories of enslavement (19% of visitors) and immigration (16%). At house museums and labour history sites, just 4% and 3%, respectively, of visitors identified as belonging to non-dominant ethnicities. As outlined in the following, more critical and emotionally complex responses occur at dissonant than at national sites, but as developed in Chapter 7, ethnic identity also appears to influence the registers of engagement (RoE) at sites.

Tourists were interviewed at all sites. As Table 6.1 reveals, tourists were far less frequent at 'national' sites where they accounted for 8% of those interviewed relative to dissonant sites where they made up 24% of visitors. The highest frequency of tourists was recorded at sites associated with the legacies of enslavement, immigration and Indigenous culture and history – 30%, 25% and 22% of visitors, respectively. Ellis Island, included in the immigration genre, is publicised as an overseas tourist destination; however, this site is not skewing the results in this genre, in that similar frequencies of tourists were recorded at most of the other immigration sites.[1] Counterintuitively, genres associated with national histories and nationalism, such as presidential or aristocratic houses, the halls of fame and their representation of frontier settlement, commemorations of war and so forth are not sites with high overseas tourist visitations relative to the other genres that speak to specific and dissonant accounts of history.[2] As identified in Chapter 7, tourists regardless of what

TABLE 6.1 Visitor ethnicity and overseas tourist frequencies per genre

			Dominant ethnicity	Non-dominant ethnicity	Tourist	Total
genre	Immigration history	Count	214	60	91	365
		% within genre	58.6%	16.4%	24.9%	100.0%
	Indigenous history and culture	Count	209	38	69	316
		% within genre	66.1%	12.0%	21.8%	100.0%
	Enslavement legacies	Count	816	305	478	1599
		% within genre	51.0%	19.1%	29.9%	100.0%
	Labour history	Count	414	15	28	457
		% within genre	90.6%	3.3%	6.1%	100.0%
	House museums	Count	971	48	73	1092
		% within genre	88.9%	4.4%	6.7%	100.0%
	War commemoration	Count	94	15	21	130
		% within genre	72.3%	11.5%	16.2%	100.0%
	Cowboy/stockmen halls of fame	Count	240	17	13	270
		% within genre	88.9%	6.3%	4.8%	100.0%
	Other national	Count	152	20	29	201
		% within genre	75.6%	10.0%	14.4%	100.0%
	Yellowstone	Count	61	0	1	62
		% within genre	98.4%	0.0%	1.6%	100.0%
Total		Count	3171	518	803	4492
		% within genre	70.6%	11.5%	17.9%	100.0%

genre they were visiting tended to display more elements of a critical RoE than did domestic visitors from dominant ethnic identities.

There was a marked difference in where people travelled from to get to particular genres of site. House museums and labour sites were visited most frequently by people who had travelled from a home address; this indicates a local connection to these sites and has implications for the RoE underpinning the heritage performances occurring at them. That people most frequently travelled from a holiday/vacation address to visit the remaining genres is not surprising. What is of note here is that while most people travelled to sites commemorating war from a holiday/vacation address, this genre of site had the highest recorded frequency of return visitors at 49%. While first-time visitors dominated at all genres, the other sites with relatively high-returning visitors were Yellowstone (47%) the halls of fame (37%) and house museums (36%).

National and dissonant sites

Comparisons between the two categories of 'national' and 'dissonant' sites revealed that sites framed by national narratives tend to have an overall RoE that is itself framed by celebratory commemoration. Those sites that present more dissonant histories feature responses that either engage empathy and tend to produce a more critical and engaged RoE of reflection and introspection or produce an oppositional and confronted response. Within these two groups, various genres also have their affective practices and performances (see the following).

The celebratory practice of visiting national sites was itself framed by definitions of heritage that referenced 'history' or a joyful and inclusive 'everyone's', which is belied by visitor demographics at such sites that tend to be dominated by well-educated domestic visitors from middle-class occupations and dominant ethnic backgrounds. Far more diverse definitions of heritage were offered at dissonant sites, reflecting not only the background of visitors (Chapter 7) but also the greater variation in performances of heritage-making occurring at these sites.

On the whole, visiting national sites is not about 'learning', with 'education' and 'to find out about' as reasons for visiting selected by just 18% of visitors at national sites relative to 38% at dissonant sites. This is also reflected in responses to the question on changed views, with 12% of visitors at national sites reporting they had changed their views relative to 23% at dissonant sites. Reasons 'specific to the site' were the most frequently selected for national sites (34% relative to 6% at dissonant sites). Additionally, educational options tended to be selected at dissonant genres when visitors also identified as not having personal or familial connections. Where visitors did have such connections, the RoE tended to underpin the performances of intergenerational communication outlined in Chapter 11. Genres that documented histories marginalised within the AHD, and whose place in nationalising narratives is contested, saw educational options selected a little less frequently in favour of options 'to think about' or 'to explore'.[3] This begs the question: Were certain sites seen as more 'educational' by visitors than others? If we consider the results of the question about changed views, and the degree to which people talk about 'reinforcement' (Chapter 9) within the interview data, it may be that the use of terms such as 'education', or more specifically 'learning', may be seen as both a rhetorical justification for visiting certain sites and not others and a polite expression of cognitive discomfort. This issue is explored further in Chapter 8.

Sites categorised as either dissonant or national sites have particular affective repertoires – for example, aesthetic engagement, feelings of jealousy, a sense of pilgrimage, feeling relaxed or renewed and creating overt cultural capital were variables that were *not* recorded at dissonant sites, while feelings of nationalism or patriotism represent only 0.6% at dissonant sites relative to 6% at national sites. Conversely, shame/guilt, unresolved anger and lament and loss were all absent from national sites but present at dissonant sites. Empathy and the variable 'deeply reflective' also featured at dissonant sites, representing, respectively, 13% and 10% relative to 2% and 1% at national sites. A feature of dissonant sites was also the variable 'dissonance, defensive and confronted', which accounted for 11% of responses at dissonant sites relative to 6% at national sites. At national sites, 10% of visitors offered vague statements about being 'moved' relative to 4% at dissonant sites. While some of the differences between the two groups are not large, there are nonetheless distinct emotional variables that characterise the two groups. Overall visitors to dissonant sites tend to express a more febrile valence on the RoE relative to national sites where either a calm or flat emotional tone or an intense but celebratory valence associated with patriotism tended to dominate. Looking further into the specific genres develops this distinction further (see the following).

A 'dissonant and confronted' response is recorded almost entirely at sites of dissonance and is, with only two exceptions, entirely absent for all the genres that link to national histories and narratives. The exception was one visitor at the exhibition *The Price of Freedom: Americans at War* who expressed dissonance with the celebratory nature of the exhibition, and 9% of visitors to house museums. In the latter case, this dissonance or discomfort entirely relates to the English 'Work and Play' exhibitions at some of the English stately homes and the exhibitions on enslavement that were included at the presidential houses and is not an organic feature of this genre. Rather, it marks the distress felt by visitors when the 'feeling rules' associated with this genre were disrupted (see Chapters 10 and 13).

In terms of messages, the 'no message' response tended to be lowest at genres where visitors had recorded the strongest personal connection to the site or where there was a strong connection to nation and a clear or unambiguous national narrative. The response was highest at sites where 'recreation' was the most frequent response for reason for visiting or at sites that represented particularly contested and dissonant histories. In short, messages were more frequently taken away at national sites and sites of dissonance, where the visitor was actively engaged through their own personal or familial connections. These messages could be those generated by the site but more often were those the visitor had brought with them and was reinforcing. However, where contestation occurs or where a visitor tends to see themselves as recreating, messages are either rejected or simply not relevant to the visitor.

Messages coded 'offering or gaining recognition and/or respect' were absent from all genres of nationalising narratives except the halls of fame. This variable was pronounced at Indigenous sites and occurred at the halls of fame in relation to Indigenous histories (Chapter 12). Counterintuitively, platitudes are relatively infrequent at sites presenting and/or commemorating national narratives when visitors discussed the messages they took away. It might be expected that hackneyed and overwrought messages about the nation, frontier advancement and patriotism may have been offered. While they were found, it was not as frequently as might have been expected. Rather, a range of more active messages were offered at such sites including active statements about national identity or patriotism that did not rest on platitudes. Thus, as with the 'no message' response, platitudes tended to occur at sites representing dissonant and contested histories and legacies and often in these instances took the following form:

> Well sure. We need to learn from our past, and from our past mistakes.
> *(SJM63: female, 35–44, homemaker, Caucasian American)*

As argued in Chapter 13, this response is about shutting down cognition by closing down difficult or uncomfortable emotional responses to history and heritage.

In general, visitors regarded the contemporary meaning of sites or exhibitions as aides to memory. Between a quarter and a third of visitors identified the individual site they were visiting as an aide to national memory.[4] The exception to this was the enslavement legacy and labour genres and Yellowstone. Unsurprisingly, at Yellowstone, 54% of visitors saw the site as having meaning for nature conservation. As noted in Chapter 5, in response to the question about the contemporary meaning of a site, there is a significant rise in the numbers of platitudes being offered across all sites. This may have been a response to the difficulty some visitors had with this question; however, as noted in Chapter 5, this was the point where visitors tended to abandon talking about personal connections in favour of discussing sites in the context of national narratives. The rise in platitudes in response to this question, rather than necessarily reflecting dissonance as it had with responses to the question about messages, does tend to reflect hackneyed responses. Platitudes were a feature at all the national sites, representing 28% of responses:

> Yeah, because, like, modern Australia, you've got to have a history before you can become a modern nation.
> *(AWM26: male, 18–24, comedian, Australian)*

Thus, the frequency of platitudes at national sites may correspond to the degree to which the national narrative templates define the meaning of these sites as, to paraphrase AWM26, representing the 'history' you have to have to be a 'modern nation'. The performative nature of visiting national heritage sites works to continually reconstitute and authorise ideas of the nation and its citizenship. It does so both relatively passively in terms of the forms of platitudes and also a little more actively in terms of characterising sites as aides to national memory. However, a relatively passive register in terms of characterising national sites as aides to memory dominates most national heritage sites. Overall, the performative RoE at national sites suggests an affective practice of visiting that is calmly and routinely reinforcing consensus ideas of national identity. The following sections discuss variations in the overall patterns identified in this section and identifies the more specific RoE within and between specific genres.

House museums

House museums stand out as locations for a relatively depersonalised and emotionally 'composed' or sedate and demure affective visiting practice, which tends to lead to active contemporary conservative meanings being attached to the houses. This practice commences with the definition of heritage most frequently used at such sites, which tend either to the vague 'the past' or 'history' to non-personal definitions that fell firmly within the AHD. Visitors tended to see themselves as recreating, with 31% selecting recreation as a reason for visiting, and 47% selecting 'for the experience of going to the house'[5], highlighting that house museums are not places where people seek or feel the need to talk in terms of learning. Relatively few visitors made or expressed some form of personal connection to the histories presented at the houses across the three questions that explored this issue. In identifying the history or heritage of houses, visitors nominated individuals (34%), often the person who paid to have the house built or was the most famous occupant of it, followed by an inclusive 'country's/everyone's' (24%), or a neutral identification of the aristocracy or other elite social class (20%).

House museums, across all three countries, had a particular emotional signature in that a sense of feeling comforted and comfortable (13%) was reported as being engendered by the site, a response either absent or all but absent at all other genres. Feelings of being privileged to visit and aspirational cultural capital, while reported in low frequencies, were additional specific markers of the house museum affective practice. The experience of being at a house museum was most frequently (24%) characterised by a physical and embodied sense of simply being at the house. However, in discussing what being at the house meant to visitors, 23% reflected on a nice day, and although 19% made some form of connection to the site, this was largely passive rather than demonstrating a more active sense of commemoration. Certainly, house museums, alongside the 'other national' sites, recorded the highest 'no message' response of 36%. This response, coupled with the 89% who stated that 'no change of view' had occurred, is perhaps expressive of the particularly comfortable reinforcing nature of the house museum performance that is discussed in Chapter 10 and that has been so heavily critiqued in heritage literature (Hewison 1987; Seaton 2001; Deckha 2004; Gable 2009). When active messages were taken from the houses, 18% of visitors explicitly acknowledged they were reinforcing existing feelings or knowledge (relative to 7% or less at other genres), while a further 9%, the next most frequent, took away messages about the importance of preservation. Like most national sites, house museums were most frequently seen as aides to national memory (33%), but this was most frequently expressed in politically conservative terms, far more than any other genre.

The holistic and physically comfortable humility of simply 'being at' houses is expressive of the RoE at this genre. Being at houses was itself acknowledged by some visitors as a form of reinforcement, often of socially conservative meanings. Interruptions or challenges to the house museum affective practice were largely met with resistance by visitors. In England, this resistance was expressed with overt distress and dissonance, while, as is discussed in Chapter 10, it tended to be met with less overt strategies, such as the deployment of platitudes, which emphasised indifference, in the United States and Australia (see also Chapter 13). This, as with the more overt dissonance from the sites in England, suggests that while the house museum visit is one that tends to be emotionally composed, depersonalised and primarily recreational, the meanings it has for people are nonetheless deeply and closely valued.

War commemoration

Sites commemorating war histories tended to be visited by those making strong emphatic connections to the idea of the nation but were otherwise expressing a relatively flat or subdued emotional register. Unsurprisingly, a strong theme throughout the interviews at these sites was one of the nation and a sense that visitors were commemorating their national identity while also expressing historical gratitude. A strong sense of connection was marked at these sites, with an emphatic yes response to the question 'Are you part of the history represented here?' offered by 52% of visitors relative to 12%–26% at other national genres, while 'being at' the genre was most frequently defined as about commemorating the histories of war (36%).

Like the composed emotional register at houses museums, which tended to produce low cognitive engagement in response to most interview questions (unless the affective practice of the house visit was challenged), the subdued register at the war commemoration genre also tended to produce quite passive messages and contemporary meanings. While only 11% took away 'no message', the lowest frequency recorded, this tends to suggest that commemorative consensus narratives easily generate a sense that a message has been received during the visit. The most frequent message taken away was the expression of gratitude and historical debt (24%), far more frequently than at other sites, and in keeping with dominant narrative templates in both Australia and the United States. Expressions of nationalism or patriotism were also a feature of war history sites (13%), as were social messages about the impact of war (13%) and the idea that the values of the past needed to be taken up in the present (12%). These values often reflected a sense of duty, selflessness and patriotism. While 33% of visitors saw the contemporary meaning of the genre as an aide to national memory, 35% defined the contemporary meaning with platitudes referencing nationalising narratives, again stressing the passivity of the RoE:

> If we ever forget what happened, it's bound to happen again, so.
> *(AWM40: male, 25–34, software developer, Australian)*

Unlike other genres in the national category, 46% of visitors, who in the main tended to be significantly younger at this genre, chose education as a reason for visiting. However, in concert with house museums, the war commemoration genre had one of the lowest 'change of views' response (12%), suggesting that such sites may be seen as 'educational'; the narrative templates of national gratitude they represent are reinforced by the visit.

The experiences valued while visiting were most often defined in terms of seeing specific artefacts or histories of specific battles (38%), while 14% nominated that they had experienced some form of empathetic connection, although on the RoE, these connections tended to be more passively discussed relative to those identified at dissonant sites, in that they were often discussed as fleeting and expected experiences generating flat valence. Emphasising the passive nature of many visits were the 16% who nominated that they valued no particular experience when visiting and the 20% who noted that 'being at' the site meant 'nothing', which are higher responses than at other national genres.

The emotional tone at war commemoration sites was markedly less intense than those recorded at most other sites. For example, at other sites of national narratives, overt nationalism/patriotism and a reactionary nostalgia were far more conspicuous, with 30% of visitors at war commemoration sites simply offering responses coded as 'vaguely moved'. This was followed both in frequency and in vagueness of feeling by an often unelaborated response of feeling 'proud' (14%). Indeed, a comparison of the emotional tenor between the National Museum of American History exhibitions *The Star-Spangled Banner* and *The Price of Freedom* in response to this question reveals a much stronger and explicit identification of clear and deep emotions by visitors at the flag exhibition than those visiting *The Price of Freedom* (see the following). This may, in part, be a response to being in the presence of the original Star-Spangled Banner, and the impact of seeing the flag was referenced by many visitors. However, the emotional tenor of Australian visitors to the Australian War Memorial is identical to visitors at *The Price of Freedom* exhibition, suggesting that a relatively flat or mundane emotional response may be the affective repertoire that was either generated by or seen as appropriate to express at this genre. This produced a strong but subdued valence in the ways in which the values and narratives around this genre were performed and reinforced through and by the practice of visiting.

Frontier history: halls of fame

The halls of fame, like the house museums, tend to be characterised by a discourse of recreation and having a 'nice day out', and a mixture of both low cognitive engagement, at least as evidenced by a high 'no message' response (33%) and low 'change of views' (10%), and a very active emotional engagement. The more passive response seems to be associated with the relatively high selection of recreation (36%) as a reason for visiting, the highest after Yellowstone National Park. The 'no message' response at this genre, in particular, may reflect the possibility that visitors are, unlike curatorial and interpretive staff, less concerned about messages, with 7% noting that simply being at the site was 'the message' for them. The mixed RoE at this site is most apparent in response to the question about the contemporary meaning of the genre. The variable aide to national memory was also coded passive/active, and the majority of the 28% who thus identified the halls of fame as an aide to memory did so actively; the halls were the only one of two genres where the active form was most frequent (the other being the Indigenous genre). Conversely, 25% of visitors also defined the contemporary national meaning of the site with platitudes, falling passively back to the received narrative template. There appears to have been, on the one hand, a passive reinforcement of and commemoration of narratives around frontier history and the social history of the cowboy/stockman, while on the other hand, this passive reinforcement was, at times, underlined by a more active emotional investment in the ideal of the stockman/cowboy frontier stories.

This emotional investment was in part evidenced by the degree to which, in Australia at least, visitors talked about their visit as a 'pilgrimage' (Smith 2012a), but was evidenced counterintuitively in both countries by a discourse of education/learning. Visitors to the halls frequently talked about their visit in educational terms, in that 31% selected education variables as a reason for visiting; 21% nominated feeling 'interested/educated' by their visit, and 28% said having an educational experience was what they valued. Additionally, 18% of people identified the meaning of the site for contemporary society as an educational resource, of which 13% identified it as educational for someone else. The educational/learning discourse that was a marked feature of these sites is largely about identifying these sites as resources through which children, urban dwellers and immigrants could learn about the importance of the frontier narrative to national identity, rather than marking any educational activity on the part of the visitor. This is linked to the 'it doesn't but it should' passionate lament in which 8% of visitors were concerned that the contemporary meanings of the halls were not understood by society. The idea that sites were educational for other groups was indicative of and expressed a considerable emotional investment in the meanings and social values the sites represented; this discourse not only naturalised the values that such sites represented to the visitor, they also indicated the strength of their commitment to them. A strong message that 13% of visitors nominated at this genre was the idea that the values the genre represented should be taken up in the present; these included the valuing of 'hard work' and 'determination' that were perceived as extending the Australian and American frontiers.

In common with labour sites, visitors to the halls also expressed feelings of historical gratitude (13%) and nostalgia (7%), although unlike at the labour sites, this nostalgia tended to be a conservative yearning for what is understood as 'better times with better social values'. Historical gratitude was also a message that 8% of visitors took away, while 13% passively noted how much society had changed. Of particular note are the 3% who took away or offered messages of recognition and/or respect. Although a small percentage, this was the only national genre where this was recorded, and it was offered in relation to recognising Indigenous peoples and the history of dispossession of land and other rights.

This genre has often come under strong criticism for presenting conservative and narrow visions of frontier history in both Australia and the United States. The degree to which they are perceived in these critiques as 'simply' touristic or recreational resources tends to facilitate their dismissal as 'real' museums and thus as being of less analytical concern. However, the results illustrate that, despite a visitor's sense that they are visiting for recreation, visitors nonetheless have strong emotional connections to these sites, which can, in turn, facilitate the reinforcement of treasured entrance narratives. In addition, emotions such as historical gratitude can also have considerable power in facilitating the maintenance of exclusionary national narratives as much as they can the more progressive historical messages (see the following) taken from labour history sites.

Other national sites and Yellowstone National Park

The genre defined as 'other' national reflects two sites that represent national narratives not otherwise defined by the halls, houses or the sites representing war histories. This miscellaneous genre, alongside Yellowstone National Park, shared aspects in common both with the halls and war history sites in that they were characterised as aides to national memory and expressed varying messages linked to commemoration and national celebration. This was evident at the exhibition about the history of the Star-Spangled Banner, which registered high emotional engagement with the flag and the narratives of the nation it represented, with the reason for visiting highly focused on 'seeing the flag'. Conversely, such national celebration was also evident at the Old Melbourne Gaol despite the very different register of engagement recorded at this site. At this site, visitors tended to express low or subdued emotional engagement and tended to talk about the visit as very much framed by a sense of recreation. Here, two different registers of engagement, one emotionally engaged and one far more emotionally flat or banal, produced similar results in terms of messages and the meanings constructed during the visit. Similarly, Yellowstone was defined as a recreational visit across a range of questions, while 15% of visitors took away a strong message of nationalism or patriotism from the park linked to its early conservation history. Interestingly, the visit to the park was also characterised as an opportunity to 'think about' conservation issues (18%), an infrequent to almost absent selection at other national sites. This selection perhaps influenced the 42% who took away a conservation message that was otherwise infrequent at other sites and the 54% who observed that the contemporary meaning of the site rested on its conservation values. The utility of including the 'other' national sites and Yellowstone National Park in the analysis is that they illustrate how either flat or more intense emotions linked to celebratory national narratives tend to produce a profile of visitor response that is markedly different from those genres where marginalised histories or explicitly dissonant histories are represented.

Labour history and immigration sites

Both genres have quite similar RoE, which are marked by close personal and familial connections and the critical, empathetic reflections that visitors make from them. As outlined in Chapter 11, performances of intergeneration connections are frequently made at these genres. This sense of connection is evidenced at immigration sites by a strong emphatic yes (50%) in response to the question asking if the visitor's history was represented at the site; while 36% identified the history or heritage they were visiting as that of a particular ethnic group (ie *not* that of the visitor's), a further 27% identified that history as their own or their familial heritage, and 29% offered an inclusive 'everyone's'. At labour sites there was a clear inclusive and assertive identification, often underscored by a sense of pride, that such sites were representative of working-class history and heritage (56%) or belonged to a visitors' own or familial heritage (20%), while 'being at' both genres was marked by the making of strong and predominantly personal or familial active connections (38% at labour and 24% at immigration). Visiting both genres was also framed by heritage definitions that reflected these connections. Heritage as 'family' was a feature of the immigration genre (34% of definitions), while at sites of labour, definitions that fell into the category of 'intangible heritage' featured (21%) and tended to include the identification of workplace knowledge and skills. Although this latter definition was particularly frequent at the sites in England, it was also a feature of sites in Australia and the United States.

Labour and immigration sites had a relatively low selection of educational options at 18% and 32%, respectively, in preference for the selections 'to think about' or 'to explore what it means to be' collectively representing 29% and 25%, respectively. These were options, with the exception of Yellowstone and the enslavement legacy sites, that were almost absent at all other genres. Nonetheless, education was a significant feature at immigration museums, with 25% of visitors nominating that they felt 'interested/educated' by their visit, and 24% nominating that having an educational experience was something they valued. Unlike at other genres, this concern with education did result in higher frequencies of changed views, with immigration museums (alongside Indigenous sites) reporting the highest frequency (28%) of people who considered their views had been changed by their visit. Expressions of empathy was also a feature at immigration museums, and as argued in Chapter 8, there is likely to be a causal relationship between this and the changing of views. The individual site across the study with the highest frequency of changed views was the Immigration Museum, Melbourne, where 35% of visitors considered their views had been changed in some way – a museum that has been positively reviewed for the ways in which it works to actively engage visitor emotions (Witcomb 2013; Schorch 2015).

Issues of education were also a feature of labour museums, but in a different way. The frequencies of those who changed their view at this genre did not vary from that recorded for the overall sample; however, 29% of visitors when considering the contemporary meaning of labour sites defined them as an educational resource. Specifically, they defined them as educational resources for children and other social groups, with a particular emphasis on the visitor's children. As at the halls of fame, this idea of education was often linked to the 'it doesn't but it should' lament that contemporary society does not value the history represented by the site. While relatively infrequent at labour sites (only 5%), this is a lament that underlines the sense in which particular experiences of heritage are regarded as under-recognised. This lack of acknowledgement may be reflected in the degree to which the labour genre was *not* identified as an aide to national memory, as only 19% nominated the genre had contemporary national meaning. At other genres, including immigration museums, between a quarter and a third of respondents identified sites as aides to national memory, the only other exception to this was the enslavement legacy genre (also only 19%). Labour sites were also characterised as aides to personal memory (17%) or as aides to 'group memory', specifically class memory (16%).

Critical, empathetic reflections were significant markers of both genres. The most frequent experience valued at labour sites was that of expressing or feeling empathy (25%), a feature also notable at immigration sites (15%) as well as the war commemoration genre. However, at the two former genres, this was more closely linked to a RoE that facilitated active and self-conscious familial remembering and identity-making than at the war genre. In reporting the feelings generated by sites, empathy was a feature at immigration sites (12%) as was the response 'it makes me deeply reflective' (9%); at labour sites, a progressive form of nostalgia linked with social memory (14%) and feelings of pride (9%) and historic gratitude for working-class achievements (21%) were a feature. This feeling of historic gratitude was also a feature at the halls of fame (see above) and tended to be connected to the labour history of agricultural workers represented by stockmen and cowboys and is all but absent at other genres. It should be noted that while gratitude was also a feature at war commemoration sites, this was largely in terms of the messages taken away, rather than being expressed as a feeling.

The emotional repertoires engendered and expressed through the connections made and imaginative empathy at these genres correspond to a relatively low 'no message' response at the labour genre (16%), alongside simple reflections on how hard life was or still is (21%) and deeper messages of historical gratitude and an enabling sense of humility (13%). Messages registering 'critical engagement/reflecting on modern issues' were a feature at both genres, representing 15% at immigration and 13% at the labour genre. This variable was found infrequently at all other genres with the exception of the enslavement legacy sites. While the 'no message' response was high (23%), but below the overall frequency, at the immigration genre, messages about historical gratitude (12%), offering or gaining recognition and/or respect

(10%) and making 'empathetic links' (6%), also featured at this genre. Immigration museums, in particular, were used by visitors to reflect on modern issues when asked to consider the contemporary meaning of the site (14%). While this variable occurred in higher frequencies at the enslavement legacy sites, it ranges from absent to less than 4% at all other genres, including labour sites (0.7%).

Both genres are marked by strong familial and personal connections that underwrite performances of intergenerational communication. At labour sites, this is itself underwritten by overt and self-conscious forms of remembering and identity-making, wherein sites were used as aides to class and familial memory. In opposition to immigration sites, these sites tend *not* to be used to reflect on the present but are more frequently used to measure and express various forms of historical gratitude and a sense of loss expressed by a desire that sites as educational resources would facilitate the social remembrance of past achievements. Labour sites are also marked by a form of nostalgia that is regularly more reflective and critical than the reactionary nostalgia that tends to be linked to house museums and the halls. It is a form of social memory that has been recorded in the context of other studies of working-class heritage in England (see, for example, Cashman 2006; Bonnett and Alexander 2012; Loveday 2014), but was found across sites in all three nations in this study. The immigration genre, where similar RoE focused on personal and familiar connections were made, was used more often to critically reflect on contemporary social and political issues, a complex critical engagement that informs how these sites were used as aides to national memory and in performances of intergenerational communication (Chapter 11).

Indigenous history and culture

The three Indigenous sites, the Mashantucket Pequot Museum, The First Australians Gallery at the National Museum of Australia and Uluṟu-Kata Tjuṯa National Park, are marked by a depersonalised discourse of 'education', which obscures the quite self-aware political use of these sites by some visitors. The Indigenous genre had the highest selection of the education options as the reason for visiting, at 58%. Additionally, 26% identified as feeling 'interested/educated' during the visit, 27% identified information gathering as the experience they valued, reinforced by 14% who noted that being at the site was about educational experiences. In assessing the contemporary meaning of the sites, 30% identified them as educational resources, although two-thirds of these visitors noted the sites were educational for someone other than themselves. While a significant proportion of visitors in defining the educational values of the sites did so in terms of its value to other visitors, nonetheless 27% of visitors at the Indigenous genre sites saw themselves as having changed their view – the second-highest occurrence after immigration sites.

While the educational uses of the genre are important, they also mark not only polite visitor cognitive dissonance but also the depersonalisation of the sorts of connections visitors made at this genre. Cognitive dissonance was a feature at this genre, as represented by the relatively high 'no message' response (35%) and by the offering of platitudes as messages taken away (10%). Cognitive dissonance was also measured by the lack of connection people made to these sites. For example, the majority (57%) of visitors did not see themselves as part of the history of the site, and 71% of visitors defined the heritage of the sites as belonging to a specific ethnic group other than their own. While this is in part about discomfort with the dissonant histories represented at the sites, it is also, however, more strongly reflective of a considered response that represented a hesitation on the part of the visitor, in the light of the history of colonial assimilation, to appropriate Indigenous culture and history to themselves.

This hesitancy was often connected to the performance of offering recognition and respect to Indigenous peoples discussed in Chapter 12. A quarter (25%) of visitors identified that 'being at' this genre was about 'making a connection' even though the majority did not see themselves as part of the genre's heritage. As argued in Chapters 2 and 12, the first step of offering respect or recognition requires non-Indigenous people to recognise themselves as possessors of colonial privilege. The desire to make a connection, and yet the hesitancy in doing so, is reflective not simply of dissonance, but more specifically of the degree to which visitors at this genre were self-consciously negotiating the politics of recognition. As discussed in Chapter 13 in relation to Uluru, this negotiation was not always successful and could be derailed to maintain misrecognition through a process of cultural appropriation, but what is significant nonetheless is the degree to which these sites were used as an arena to work through contested historical and contemporary issues. The performance of negotiating recognition is evidenced by 22% of visitors who offered positive messages about recognition and/or respect – a variable that only occurs, and then at much lower frequencies, at the halls of fame (again offered in relation to Indigenous peoples) and at immigration and enslavement legacy genre sites. It is also evident in the 25% of visitors who identified these sites as aides to national memory and then did so in relatively active and reflective ways. In coding this particular response as active/passive, the Indigenous genre was, alongside the halls, the only genre where active characterisations of sites as aides to national memory were dominant.

Legacies of enslavement

A wide range of performances and registers occurred at sites addressing enslavement legacies, however; within this genre, the ethnic background of visitors tends to correspond to particular registers of engagement, an observation explored further in Chapter 7. Overall, this is a genre with which people from a politically dominant ethnic background tended not to make close, personal or other forms of connections, while also engaging in a discourse of 'education' to frame what they claimed they are doing at these sites. A strong sense of dissonance and distancing from negative valence emerges from White British visitors in the English exhibitions, while in the United States, Caucasian Americans, in general, exhibit a less explicit or overt register of dissonance. Both these registers result in, and are reflective of, what may be termed a studied or explicit 'indifference' which facilitates, as argued in

Chapters 9, 10 and 13, the maintenance of privilege. The educational discourse that white visitors tended to use in discussing their visit is in marked contrast with the high frequency of 'no message' and platitudinous responses recorded for this genre. However, indifference is not the universal register of engagement at this genre for white visitors, where, despite being confronted, some visitors engaged in reflective and critical cognitive engagements. Empathy, deep reflection and critical reflections on modern issues and 'recognition and respect' were also features of this genre. While these were more often expressed by visitors from politically non-dominant backgrounds, they were nonetheless also voiced by visitors from politically dominant ethnicities. Visitors to this genre of site who identified as African American or African Caribbean British tended to make closer personal connections with these exhibitions than White/Caucasian visitors and tended to engage with the exhibitions with empathy and critical reflection.

After the Indigenous and war genres, education was most frequently (44%) selected as a reason for visiting; however, the selection 'to think about' (17%) was a particular feature of this genre. Additionally, 14% considered they felt 'interested/ educated' and a further 14% defined the contemporary meaning of the genre as an educational resource. While these are variables not particularly high relative to other genres, the significant issue here is that in both the United States and England, these responses were over-represented by Caucasian Americans and White British respondents at sites with a relatively high proportion of African Americans and African Caribbean British visitors. These responses were a mix of genuine educational aims but also, as argued in Chapter 13, polite dissonance.

Stronger dissonance emerged, however, across many of the questions. White British respondents dominated the 15% who were coded as feeling dissonant and defensive, while they also entirely represented the 6% who nominated feeling shame/guilt. While the latter does not necessarily reflect dissonance, as argued in Chapter 13, this negative valance tended to facilitate the development of strong opposition to exhibition narratives. Additionally, the absence of explicit discussions of these emotions in the American data also speaks to a more cautious and covert discussion of dissonance with the history of race relations in that country.

While the no message response was relatively high (32%), a marked feature of this genre was the high frequency (19%) of those who offered platitudes to the question about messages, a response again over-represented by Caucasian Americans and White British. Conspicuous by their complete absence, particularly in the United States, were messages about the national meaning of this genre. Such messages are present, albeit in small numbers at dissonant sites overall, but are only entirely absent at this and the Indigenous genre. Additionally, only 19% identified this genre as an aide to national memory, well below the frequency recorded for the overall sample and, except for labour sites, at other genres. This is in part influenced by the English data, where sites were far less frequently identified as aides to national memory than in the United States, but it nonetheless speaks to hesitation in seeing the history of slavery and its ongoing legacies as part of national narratives.

Platitudes were a significant response to the question about a site's contemporary meaning, and unlike at genres such as war commemoration, these were expressive of dissonance rather than of simple narration of national narrative templates. Platitudes represented almost a third (31%) of responses to this question. Breaking this down, however, platitudes accounted for only 8% of responses at the National Civil Rights Museum (where visitors from non-dominant ethnicities numerically dominated), but 46% at the *Slavery at Jefferson's Monticello: Paradox of Liberty* (where visitors from politically dominant ethnicities were numerically dominant) and 32% at the collective English Bicentenary exhibitions. Caucasian Americans and White British were significantly over-represented in this response, which was indicative of discomfort with, and emotional distancing from, the implications of this heritage.

This discomfort is also reflected in how people made connections to this heritage. While 'country's/everyone's' was also most frequently (32%) given when assessing whose history the site represented, the RoE was regularly mixed. On the one hand, this could express an inclusive sense of heritage, but more often, the response indicated a distancing of the visitor from the heritage of the site. That is, the response tended to more frequently signify 'it's everyone's; thus I need not regard the history at this site as part of my particular heritage', rather than the more inclusive registers found at national sites. Almost a quarter (24%) identified the heritage of this genre as belonging to a particular ethnic group, inevitably African Americans or African Caribbean British, and in the context of the exhibitions and how the statements were offered; they again tended to distance Caucasian American or White British respondents from considering the legacies of this history. A feature of this genre is the 12% who identified the heritage at the sites as a dismissive 'issues-based history', a variable not recorded at any other genre. These were statements that once again facilitated visitor detachment, which in turn insulated the visitor from deeply engaging emotionally or cognitively with this history, and were again dominated by visitors from dominant ethnicities. While there was a high positive response to the question 'Are you part of the history represented here?' with 60% saying yes, this needs some unpacking. At these sites, African American and African Caribbean British visitors were over-represented in the empathic yes response, while the no and a hesitant yes response were dominated by Caucasian American and White British visitors. However, a yes response, when given by those from politically dominant ethnic groups, was more frequently given in the United States by Caucasian Americans than was given in England by White British visitors.

Although dissonant visitor responses are a feature of this genre, a far more positive response is also a significant finding. A feature of responses to the question on feelings was 'it makes me deeply reflective' (11%), a response that utilised emotional intelligence to reflect on both the historical and contemporary issues associated with racism and was a response in which African Americans and African Caribbean British were over-represented. Expressions of empathy were the most frequent response (18%) to the question on feelings, again over-represented by African Americans and African Caribbean British visitors, who also entirely accounted for the response 'I feel recognised' (6%), a response only otherwise found at 1% or less at the Indigenous, labour or houses genres (in this case about exhibitions on English servants). In terms of critical messages, 14% were critically engaged in reflecting on modern issues, 10% offered social messages, often politically progressive (2% vs. 8% conservative/progressive). Both these variables were again dominated by those from non-dominant ethnicities and in particular by people who, in their interviews, saw themselves as closely socially or politically linked to the history of the civil rights movement. A further 7% of visitors saw themselves as engaged in acts of recognition and respect. The latter sentiment, unlike at other genres where this featured, was expressed in two ways. First, by those from dominant ethnic backgrounds offering recognition of the legacies of racism and disenfranchisement of people of African ancestry, and second, by African American or African Caribbean British visitors using the exhibition to judge the extent to which they were being recognised or misrecognised by the museum and wider American or British society (Chapter 12). At the National Civil Rights Museum, the first response dominated and was offered either by Caucasian Americans or tourists.

Additionally, in characterising the modern meaning of the genre, 24% of visitors did so while reflecting on modern issues. This response is relatively infrequent at other genres, representing 14% at the immigration genre, but less than 5% at all other genres. This response was particularly evident at the National Civil Rights Museum where it accounted for 24% of responses but is under-represented at the *Slavery at Jefferson's Monticello: Paradox of Liberty* where it accounted for only 5% of responses. As noted in Chapter 5, this variable most frequently occurred at sites in the United States, but in both countries and especially in England, it is again over-represented by those from politically non-dominant ethnic backgrounds.

Despite the number of people reporting education as a reason for visiting, those who had changed their view did not vary significantly from the overall frequencies defined in Chapter 5. The sites in England were slightly more likely to see changes of view than the sites from the United States, in that 84% and 83% of visitors at the National Civil Rights Museum and the *Slavery at Jefferson's Monticello: Paradox of Liberty*, respectively, stated that their views had not been altered, relative to 74% from England.

Making connections

One of the issues that does cut across genres, and is the second theme to emerge from the comparisons, is the way the degree of feeling or making of personal or familial connection with a heritage site or museum facilitates how visitors engage with sites. While the banality of having a nice day out correlates to platitudes and low message take-up is not surprising, what is also important to note is that platitudes and low message take-up also occurs at genres or instances where visitors do not perceive themselves as being personally connected or linked to the site, even if they see themselves as linked through national identity or citizenship. When visitors express low emotional connection or affinity, there is a corresponding increase in responses that tend to work to maintain indifference or the status quo. On the other hand, where visitors express connection and affinity to the history on display, there is a corresponding expression of empathy, critical reflections, active message-making and a greater frequency of changed views. While this means that certain genres reflect a wider variety of affective practices occurring at them than others, it also suggests that genre is not the only influence on visitor responses. How this process works is examined in more detail in Chapters 8–13, while the following chapter unpacks these observations further by correlating visitor demographics against visitor responses.

Conclusion

Particular RoE can be witnessed at different genres or groups of genre depending on whether they represent celebratory or commemorative nationalising narratives or express dissonant or politically marginalised histories. National context does not account for the differences between genre, and while national context had some influence on variations within genres, in particular, the genre of enslavement legacies, the similarities that occurred within genres and across national contexts were more marked. The RoE at different genres also reflects different affective practices and performances ranging from the banal and the composed to the empathetic and meditative. These registers and the heritage performances they underwrite will be explored in more detail in the following chapters; however, it must be noted that while patterns emerged between genres, some similarities and patterns appear to occur across genres.

The extent to which visitor responses tended to vary according to ethnic identity at the enslavement legacy genre sites raises the question of to what extent ethnicity and other demographic variables influence visitor responses either within or across the genre and/or national context. Visitor profiles in relation to gender, age, ethnicity, occupation and educational attainment do vary between the genres, appearing to influence the choice of genre visited. It is clear that sites telling national stories, but except for those telling the histories of war, tend to attract lower frequencies of visitors from politically non-dominant ethnic backgrounds. Immigration and enslavement legacy sites attract visitors with broader ethnic diversity than other genres, and labour sites recorded higher numbers of visitors without university degrees. This may reflect the degree to which such museums or sites attract visitors who perceive that these sites represent their own history and heritage; conversely, the lower diversity with regard to ethnicity and educational attainment at genres that link to various forms of national narratives indicates the degree to which such places do not reflect a shared national identity. As Stuart Hall (1999: 4) argued in relation to national storytelling in museums, the imagined community of nation depends on a shared understanding of cultural meanings that binds individuals into the larger national story and its heritage, and that 'those who cannot see themselves reflected in its mirror cannot properly "belong"'. Visitor demographics and their influences on the results of the interviews are the subject of the following chapter.

Notes

1 Tourists accounted for 19% of those interviewed at Ellis Island; 29% at the Lower East Side Tenement Museum; 23% the Immigration Museum, Melbourne; 13% at the Japanese American National History Museum and 0 (of 14 visitors) at the Nordic Heritage Museum.
2 All frequencies were bellow or well below the 18% of the overall sample so that overseas tourists/expats accounted for 16% at sites of war commemoration, 14% at other national sites, 7% at house museums, 6% at labour sites, 5% at the halls of fame and 2% at Yellowstone.
3 At Immigration sites 'to think about' or 'to explore' collectively constituted 25% of responses, 22% at enslavement legacy sites, 29% at labour sites, 19% at Yellowstone, 10% at halls of fame and between 0% and 6% at all other genres.
4 The breakdown of 'aide to national memory': Immigration 32%, Indigenous 25%, houses 29%, war commemoration 33%, halls of fame 28%, 'other' national 24% and legacies of enslavement 19%.
5 In Table 5.3, this selection was quoted within 'other specific to the site' and only separated out here for the analysis of this genre. The experience of simply 'being at' the house was a theme replicated in response to other questions for this genre.

7
DEMOGRAPHIC VARIABLES AND VISITOR RESPONSES

This chapter compares visitor responses against demographic variables. Each of these variables was cross-tabulated using SPSS against visitor responses recorded for each of the open-ended questions. The aim was to determine if the variations between genres identified in Chapter 6 are also influenced by visitor demographics and to determine if particular visitor characteristics correlate to particular responses or frequencies of responses. As discussed in Chapter 5, there are some significant variations nationally in the demographics of visitors interviewed in the three countries, although as Chapter 6 also demonstrated, particular demographic profiles did correlate to the genre of site. As genre was identified as a significant influence on visitor responses, more so than national contexts, the data was also again broadly divided between 'national' and 'dissonant' sites and cross-tabulations were run against each question in all of these categories against the demographic variables. This was important, as some demographic variables became eclipsed within the overall database, as they had different influences depending on the category or genre of the site.

In discussing the results of these comparisons, only those variables that produced statistically significant and meaningful results are identified. The broad patterns revealed are identified rather than a complete question-by-question outline. Gender and whether or not the visitor was a returning visitor had few meaningful correlations; the only significant correlation with gender was visitor numbers at some of the genres discussed in Chapter 6. Age, educational attainment, distances travelled and occupation, all had some influence on responses. However, the most consistent demographic variable to influence visitor responses was the variable 'ethnicity'; that is, whether or not a visitor identified as a member of either a dominant or non-dominant ethnic identity or was an overseas tourist to where the interview occurred. The results outlined in this chapter suggest that social privilege – most specifically based on ethnic identity, and possibly to a more limited extent for class identity – has the greatest influence on visitor heritage performances.

Comparisons between demographic variables

A comparison of age against the other independent variables showed that those aged 45 and above were much more likely not to have been to university; 48% of that age group did not have a higher degree, compared to 36% from the younger age group. Those 45 and over were more likely to be a return visitor (28% under 44, 38% over 45), but less likely to be overseas tourists (24% under 44, 13% over 45). Those who had been to university tended to be younger and were far more likely also to be domestic travellers as well as more likely than those without a university education to travel from a vacation or holiday address. As noted in Chapter 5, overseas tourists and those visitors from politically non-dominant ethnic backgrounds more frequently held higher degrees than those from dominant ethnic backgrounds. Those who had travelled from a home address were far more likely to be return visitors than those travelling while on holiday or vacation.

As outlined in Chapter 5, the demographic variables do not differ significantly across the three countries, except in relation to educational attainment and occupation, with visitors in the United States having been to university more frequently than in the other two countries. Conversely, however, (Table 5.1) those who were employed in higher management and higher professional occupations were a little more frequent in the English sample than in the United States or Australia. These tendencies are in part influenced by the genre, in that those from higher managerial positions were more frequently found at enslavement legacy exhibitions, a feature of the English data, whereas routine occupations were a feature of the halls of fame (Chapter 6).

Age

Visitors aged 45 and over were, overall, less likely to change their views than younger visitors, suggesting perhaps a greater investment in particular readings of the past than some younger visitors. Of those 44 and under 77% had not changed their views, while 84% of those over 45 had not. However, breaking this down further, those aged 18–24 were the age group most likely to change their views, with 28% nominating that their views had been changed to some extent. Those aged from 35 to over 60 were far more likely to report that their views had not been changed than those 34 and under. This was mirrored in the degree to which those 44 and under were slightly more liable to feel 'educated' by their visit. Respondents 44 and under were more likely to choose an educational option than older visitors (35% vs. 25%, respectively), who were more likely to choose options specific to the site or the individual visitor.

More significantly, however, those 45 and over were, particularly at the labour genre sites, more likely to engage in active and self-conscious memory work and to make active connections to what they perceived as their history; much of this done as part of a performance of intergenerational communication. In response to the question asking visitors to identify the experiences they valued, those 45 or over tended to nominate answers coded identity/memory work a little more often than younger visitors (i.e. 7% compared to 2% of those 44 and under). However, this was particularly marked at labour history sites where 20% of older visitors were actively engaged in active identity/memory work relative to 6% of those 44 and under, who more often saw labour sites as 'educational' (25% relative to 13% of older visitors). This may indicate a sense of personal connection held by older visitors to sites that often represented the histories of deindustrialisation experienced by older generations and tends to reinforce the degree to which personal connection fosters active RoE. In terms of defining what 'being at' sites meant, those 45 and over talked about 'making connections' a little more frequently (23%) than younger visitors (18%). Although, not a large difference, it was again particularly the case at labour history sites. These responses by visitors tended to be associated with the performances of intergenerational connection discussed in Chapter 11, as older visitors tend to engage more often in active familial memory and identity work, which is perhaps not surprising, given the nature of that performance.

Travelled from a home or holiday/vacation address

Those who had travelled to the site they were visiting from a home address were more likely to select recreation and less likely to select either of the educational options than those who had travelled from a holiday/vacation address. That is, 28% who had travelled from home selected recreation, and 20% selected education compared to 22% and 28% who had travelled from a holiday/vacation address. In addition, 46% of overseas tourists selected one of the educational options, while 24% selected recreation. This suggests that those who had engaged in some form of travel, either domestically or internationally, are either invested in or are legitimising that travel by invoking education as the reason for visiting. As I have stressed, domestic or international tourists are often dismissed within much of the heritage and museum literature as engaging in banal or mindless visits (Graburn and Barthel-Bouchier 2001: 149; Ashworth 2009). It may be that those perceiving themselves as 'tourists', having travelled away from their homes, draw in the rhetorical power of the benefits of education to differentiate themselves from the cliché of the ignorant tourist or understood themselves in engaging in an educational pursuit. However, those who had travelled from a home address or who were returning[1] older visitors (see the section on age) were less likely to regard their visit as educational, possibly because of either familiarity or some sense of personal connection to the place. While home or holiday/vacation address did not meaningfully correlate with other questions, it is interesting to note that questions that had 'educational' responses were consistently approximately 6% more likely to be nominated by those who had travelled from a holiday/vacation address. Although this is not a large difference, it was sustained in each of the relevant questions, as was the tendency for about 6% more of those who came from home than from a holiday/ vacation address to nominate 'reinforcement' when this occurred as a response to a question. This point about connection, whether, as in this case, it is geographical or otherwise, is worth stressing. The idea of 'visitors' discussed in Chapter 3 tends to be underwritten by an often unacknowledged assumption that visitors, unlike the discourse around community groups or the community of experts, lack connection or knowledge or understanding of the heritage being 'visited' – as they are 'visitors' who pass through the site.

Ethnicity

The most consistent pattern in responses correlated to ethnicity and while the differences were not on the whole large, they were nonetheless statistically significant and were persistent through many of the questions. The results indicate that those from non-dominant ethnic identities tended to be more critically active in the RoE than those from dominant ethnic identities, who tended to be over-represented against variables measuring passive or less critical engagement or variables measuring discomfort at dissonant sites. This pattern occurs regardless of whether or not the site being visited belongs to any of the different genres considered by this study or to the overall categories of 'national' or 'dissonant'. Ethnicity, of course, does not correspond exactly with different RoE, but there is a consistent pattern across the genres and the three countries of the study. Overseas tourists as a group, and regardless of their ethnic identity, also tended, overall, to be a little more active in their engagement than domestic visitors from dominant ethnicities. Although, as a group, they shared some of the passivity and discomfort of those domestic visitors from dominant ethnicities, they also proportionally more often were represented by active and critical variables. The following thematically works through relevant interview questions that produced statistically significant results to explain the details of the correlations between ethnicity and RoE.

Those from non-dominant backgrounds tended to both make more personal connections and to do so empathically to the sites they visited, often drawing on more personal definitions of heritage to do so (definitions that nominated family, ethnicity and inheritance). Thus, visitors from non-dominant ethnic backgrounds tended to offer definitions of heritage that referenced family identity more than those from dominant ethnic identities (24% vs. 15%, respectively).[2] In addition, those definitions identified in Table 5.4 as sitting comfortably within the AHD were offered more frequently (21%) by those from dominant ethnic backgrounds than those who were not (11%), while the vague it is 'history' or 'the past' response was a little more frequently given by those from dominant backgrounds (23% vs. 16%). These definitions were similar between the categories 'national' and 'dissonant' sites, with those from dominant ethnic backgrounds and tourists tending to offer definitions that on the whole were quite generalised ('history/the past'), material and preservation orientated but also stressing the intangible, while those from non-dominant backgrounds referenced families, ethnicity and inheritance/

legacy. While these groupings of definitions are not necessarily more active than the other, the definitions favoured by those from non-dominant ethnicities tended to be more personal.

This personal definition is also reflected in how connections to the histories and heritage were made at museums and heritage sites. Of visitors from politically dominant ethnic groups, 58% said yes when asked if they were 'part of the history' represented by the site they were visiting, compared to 71% of visitors from non-dominant ethnic backgrounds who said yes. Those from non-dominant backgrounds were far more likely to be empathic in their positive response (55%) than those from dominant backgrounds (30%). While visitors from non-dominant ethnicities were more likely to say yes to this question at both national and dissonant sites, there are some differences worth highlighting. At national sites those from non-dominant backgrounds represented only 7% of visitors, compared to 15% at dissonant sites; however, of those who chose to visit national sites, 61% said yes, relative to the 57% of those from dominant ethnicities. At dissonant sites this margin increases to 77% relative to 58%, while at dissonant sites those from non-dominant ethnicities where far more emphatic in this yes (66% relative to 40%). At national sites, relatively few visitors were emphatic on this point, with 29% and 20% of non-dominant and dominant ethnicities, respectively, being unequivocal on this issue. That those from dominant ethnic backgrounds were, on the whole, a little less likely to actively see themselves as part of the history or heritage they were visiting is an important issue. What emerges here is a more active register of engagement by those from non-dominant ethnic backgrounds relative to those from dominant backgrounds, *regardless* of the type or genre of the site being visited.

This is reinforced when visitors were asked if any aspect of the site spoke or linked to a visitor's personal identity. Those from non-dominant ethnic backgrounds again tended to define some link to the site they were seeing with only a third (33%) of that group saying no to this question, compared to 49% of those from dominant ethnic groups. Those from non-dominant identities were more likely to identify that link as either familial or as part of their ethnic or other group identity than dominant visitors (34% vs. 31% and 15% vs. 4%, respectively). Again, these responses and relative differences are maintained at both national and dissonant sites. The majority (61%) of tourists, however, said no, it did not link to their identity, with slightly more saying no at national sites.

In terms of reasons for visiting, visitors from non-dominant backgrounds were more likely to have selected 'to think about' than those from dominant backgrounds (18% relative to 7%), while those from politically dominant groups were more likely to choose recreation (27% relative to 11%). Overseas tourists were also more likely, but to a lesser extent, to select 'to think about' (12%). These choices were also maintained regardless of whether the genre or categories of sites were 'national' and 'dissonant'. The 'to think about' choice suggests a more thoughtful and potentially more engaged response, which is confirmed through the open-ended questions.

For the educational options, 26% of visitors from politically dominant ethnic backgrounds chose these options in comparison to 36% from non-dominant ethnic backgrounds and 46% of overseas tourists. In reflecting on whether or not a visitor considered their views to have changed, 25% of overseas tourists nominated that they had changed their views to some degree, compared to only 17% of domestic visitors who had nominated this. The differences between dominant and non-dominant ethnic backgrounds were not notable for the question on changed views.

In response to the questions about how the site made visitors 'feel', one of the key differences was that visitors from non-dominant backgrounds were over-represented in the response that addressed recognition in terms of either feeling recognised or feeling glad that recognition was being done by the museum or site visited, with only 1% of those from politically dominant backgrounds offering this, relative to 9% from non-dominant backgrounds. This difference is not particularly surprising, as 'feeling recognised' often requires the speaker to be aware of being in a politically marginalised position, but it is notable that this issue was far less frequently commented on from those in positions of relative privilege. Those from non-dominant ethnic backgrounds were slightly more prone to be making empathetic connections (12%) relative to those from dominant backgrounds (8%), while tourists (15%) were again more likely to make such connections. Those from non-dominant backgrounds were 3%–6% more frequently let down or disappointed with an exhibition, making deep emotional responses and being deeply reflective than those from dominant backgrounds. Those from dominant ethnic backgrounds and tourists were both 4% more likely to express dissonance and be defensive about being confronted by exhibition content. While these differences are individually not major in relation to each of the variables listed in Table 5.8, they are suggestive and tend, at least in terms of ethnicity, to be reproduced in responses to other questions. In grouping the variables in response to this question according to, in a relative sense, how active or passive they are, then emotionally active responses were provided by just over a third (35%) of the visitors from dominant ethnic backgrounds and just over half (51%) of those from non-dominant backgrounds. The active response for tourists at 44%, while less active than that for visitors from non-dominant backgrounds, is more active than those expressed by visitors from dominant backgrounds.

In defining what 'being' at a site meant, domestic visitors from non-dominant backgrounds were more active in response to this question than those from dominant ethnic backgrounds, identifying the visit as a form of commemoration, by 26% and 14%, respectively. Those from non-dominant backgrounds were also more likely to identify that being at a site was a chance to reflect on either past or present (8% vs. 2%). They were also less likely to passively nominate that it was about a 'nice day out' (6% vs. 17%) or less likely to state that they were reinforcing what they already knew or believed (1% vs. 5%) than those from dominant backgrounds. Overseas tourists frequently nominated that being at a site meant nothing in particular (26%) or was a nice day out (20%).

The 'no message' response to the question about messages was evenly distributed between those from dominant or non-dominant ethnicities, although 40% of overseas tourists stated that they took away 'no message'. This result may not be surprising if we assume both that tourists and this response are passive, but in response to other questions, tourists were relatively active and critically engaged, perhaps highlighting the idea that a more complex issue may be underlying the 'no message' response than a simple lack of engagement. Those genres with sites where visitors made close links with the history on display tended to have a lower 'no message' response, suggesting a more active engagement. Thus, the equal frequencies of the 'no message' response from visitors from both dominant and non-dominant ethnic identities are surprising, given that those from non-dominant backgrounds more frequently made active connections to sites. This suggests that genre rather than ethnic background is a stronger influence on the 'no message' response. Indeed, the 'no message' response and use of platitudes did not vary significantly between ethnicities at dissonant sites, while those from non-dominant ethnic backgrounds offered the 'no message' response slightly more at national sites (38% relative to 32% of dominant ethnicities). While this latter result may reflect some discord with national sites by those from non-dominant ethnicities, these results may also again suggest that taking a message away from a visit may not be a point of concern for some visitors or visitors at particular types of site. In terms of active messages being taken away, the visitors who identified as coming from politically non-dominant ethnic backgrounds were slightly less likely to reinforce their feelings or knowledge than those from dominant backgrounds (9% vs. 12%, respectively) but were much more likely to be critically engaged and reflecting on modern issues (17% vs. 9%). They were also, although only slightly, more frequently engaged in making empathic links (4% compared to just 1%). Those from dominant ethnicities were slightly more often expressing gratitude and historical debt (7% relative to 5%).

In response to the question about what meaning a site may have for contemporary society, those from non-dominant ethnic backgrounds were again, alongside tourists, tending to show recognition and respect (8% in both cases) more frequently than those from dominant ethnic backgrounds (4%), who were more often actively reinforcing what they felt or knew (10% relative to 4% each for non-dominant ethnicities and tourists). Those from non-dominant backgrounds and tourists were also more likely to be critically engaged and reflecting on modern issues (14% and 19%, respectively) than those from dominant backgrounds (8%). Again, there is a tendency for those from non-dominant backgrounds to be more active on the RoE. However, this is contradicted by the variable 'aide to national memory', where 31% of visitors from non-dominant backgrounds identified the site they were visiting as an aide to national memory relative to 24% of those from dominant backgrounds. In general, this response tends to reproduce consensus narratives or the respective nation's narrative template about nationhood and national identity and appears to contradict the personal links being made by those from non-dominant backgrounds described previously. The active register that those from non-dominant backgrounds had tended to utilise for other questions seems reversed here, especially as in offering this response, those from non-dominant backgrounds were more likely to do so passively than those from dominant ethnic backgrounds (22% vs.7%, respectively). The passivity of this response may be a rote or expected response being given to a white interviewer asking about the meaning of the site to the nation, particularly at authorised sites of nation-making. Alternatively, it may also be influenced by a desire for those from non-politically dominant groups for the issues they see represented at certain sites to be taken up within national memories. Certainly, if the response is broken down further and coded as politically neutral, conservative or progressive/liberal, those from non-dominant backgrounds are far more likely to offer statements assessed as progressive/liberal renditions of nationalising narratives. While responses coded politically neutral were the majority response for both groups, 55% and 56% for dominant and non-dominant ethnicities, respectively, 21% of visitors from dominant ethnic backgrounds offered politically progressive/liberal responses relative to 40% of those from non-dominant backgrounds. Tourists also tended to offer progressive/liberal responses (42% of their responses) more often than domestic visitors from dominant ethnic backgrounds.

In summary, those from non-dominant backgrounds in making more personal connections to the sites they visited were also more often engaged in empathy, reflection on both the past and present-day issues and politically progressive commentary. They were also most often seeking and/or offering recognition and respect to other social groups. Conversely, those from dominant backgrounds were often more passive in their engagement, more often using platitudes and generalising, more likely to be explicitly observing that they were reinforcing, more often expressing historical gratitude and more often found themselves feeling defensive or confronted at sites and exhibitions dealing with dissonant history. Those who identified as overseas tourists (either from dominant or non-dominant ethnicities in their own countries) as a group sat between the two groups of domestic visitors, and were themselves a group that was over-represented at dissonant sites relative to national sites (Chapter 6). This group frequently expressed some of the more critical and active variables expressed by those from non-dominant backgrounds, while also sharing some of the more passive attitudes of the dominant ethnic groups within the country they were visiting. Overall, however, they were a little more active on the RoE than those domestic visitors from dominant ethnic backgrounds.

So, the question arises: What is at stake, what might explain the result between RoE and ethnicity? What is both at stake and in operation is a sense of social privilege. While overseas tourists can be quite platitudinous and simply engaging in a 'nice day out', they can also show quite deep engagement. They are doing so, however, in contexts where they are a visitor to the country in which the site is located – that is, their sense of national, cultural or social identity is not at risk, or is at least not at the same level of risk, as those domestic visitors from dominant ethnic backgrounds.

Those whose historical and contemporary social and cultural experiences are not, as Stuart Hall (1999) notes, 'mirrored' in dominant national narratives, tend to regard their visit less often as simply recreational or as having a 'nice day out' and tend to make relatively strong personal links to heritage sites and museums. They are also more likely to engage in deep reflection, to use the site to reflect on the present, to engage critically and to utilise empathy in the connections and reflections they make and to frame the meaning of the site in politically progressive ways. Those from politically non-dominant ethnic backgrounds are often presented, within the context of the AHD, with fewer choices in the way they may express and remember their own cultural and social identities than those from politically dominant ethnic backgrounds. Both this lack of choice and the tendency for their own contemporary and historical experiences to be excluded from nationalising heritage may account for the correlation reported here with those visitor responses that are more self-consciously critical and empathically reflective.

Those from politically dominant ethnic backgrounds are less likely to be actively critical and reflective relative to both those from non-dominant ethnic backgrounds and overseas tourists. Overall, a sense emerges here of a relatively less self-conscious and more habitual engagement with sites, particularly sites linked to nationalising narratives, which speaks to a routine reinforcement and affirmation of privileged historical and contemporary experiences – in other words, a performative rehearsing of white social privilege. This does *not* mean that *all* visitors from politically dominant ethnic groups are undertaking performances of privilege, just that many do. There are many examples in the following chapters of those from dominant ethnic backgrounds engaging in critical and reflexive identity work and indeed examples where visitors from such backgrounds are engaged in *both* performances of privilege and deeper critical reflection in the one visit. However, the quantitative data identifies that there are some differences based on ethnic identity that bears further examination and elaboration, both in terms of qualitative analysis of the data (following chapters) and also in terms of further research and study. The numbers of visitors from non-dominant ethnic backgrounds do mean that any influence that they have on the data is swamped by the larger sample of those from dominant ethnicities, and new studies that aim to address that limitation are needed to assess the results reported in this book. What the following chapters do, however, is to flesh out both the banal and active engagements of those from both dominant and non-dominant identities, and the indications here is that empathy and other-oriented emotions are important issues. However, it is also useful to define the more frequent and passive or habitual performance that tends to be undertaken more frequently by dominant ethnic groups. An important issue here is the discourse of reinforcement that emerged in Chapter 5: What exactly is being reinforced, and how and what are the consequences of this performance? These are issues that are addressed in Chapters 9 and 10.

Educational attainment and occupation

A complicating issue in understanding the response of domestic visitors from dominant ethnic backgrounds is the issue of educational attainment and occupation. Educational attainment and occupation also correlated with certain differences in the data, with the greatest differences recorded in response to the questions what 'being' at a site meant and what 'experiences' people valued; although differences in responses to other questions were persistent, they were not as pronounced. Those with university degrees, and those in professional and managerial occupations, tended to generalise and to discuss sites in terms of their national values and meanings or within nationalising narrative templates (Wertsch 2008a) slightly more than those who did not hold a degree. Visitors who have not been to university and/or occupy less prestigious occupations tended to engage in more active connections to sites, active and self-conscious memory and identity work and utilised empathy and social memory more often. These differences, it must be stressed, are not large in the overall database where they tend to be overshadowed by other influences; however, they are consistent. In such a large database, certain variables can become dwarfed, and it is not unusual in such cases to then drill down into the data to determine if or where these differences become more pronounced. The differences between occupation and educational attainment became far more pronounced at dissonant sites and then more specifically at the labour genre. Labour sites have relatively high visitation from white visitors with low educational attainment. Visitors to these sites tend to identify close and strong links to their personal histories and performed quite reflective and critical engagements. While there are clear patterns across ethnic identities, a similar but weaker pattern of critical engagement and strong personal links also emerged at sites of dissonant or marginalised heritage, and more specifically, at the genre of labour history, associated with educational attainment and occupation. The point to emphasise here is that while a sense of ethnic privilege and exclusion influences visitor responses, so too may experience of class privilege and exclusion. The results that point to this conclusion about class privilege are outlined ahead.

Those from the top four occupations listed in Table 5.1 are more likely to nominate, in response to the question 'Whose history or heritage are you visiting here?', 'everyone's' (36%) than those from the lower three occupations (27%), the latter group being slightly more likely to identify the history or heritage as their own or their families (13% vs. 9%). Similarly, those who had been to university were slightly more likely to nominate 'everyone's' (31% vs. 25% who did not hold a university degree). What this indicates is those from higher occupations and those with higher educational attainment were, on the one hand, more inclusive but also a little more likely to generalise and be less specific about whose history or heritage they were visiting.

In identifying the experiences valued at sites, those who had been to university were twice as likely (22% relative to 11%) to nominate a particular aspect of the site as the experience they most valued. This response was relatively banal on the RoE. Conversely, those who had not been to university were more likely to value empathetic engagement, particularly at dissonant sites where the relative frequencies were 19% and 15%. Those without a university degree were also more engaged in active identity/memory work at dissonant sites (15% relative to 5% of those who had been to university). These differences were also pronounced at labour history sites, where those without a university degree tended to be more engaged than those with university degrees in active identity/memory work (21% vs. 9%) and empathy (29% vs. 20%), something also shared by older visitors at this genre (see section on 'age'). The differences identified between educational attainments were also mirrored for occupation: those from higher-level occupations reflected the response of those who had been to university, while those from lower supervisory-routine occupations were also more likely to be engaged in active identity/memory work at dissonant sites (18% relative to 9%) and labour sites (28% relative to 14%).

In identifying what 'being' at a site meant, educational attainment correlations did not show large differences (between 4% and 6%) but tended to reinforce responses to the question on experiences, in that those who had been to university were more likely to say 'nothing' or make passive connections or connections to nation, while those who had not been to university were more likely to make active connections while also reinforcing. While these differences are small within the overall database, they are more pronounced at dissonant sites, and in particular, at labour history sites, where those without a university degree tended to be more engaged than those with university degrees in making active connections (39% vs. 28%) and were less likely to nominate that being there meant 'nothing' (6% vs. 11%). As with the preceding question, occupation again mirrored the differences between educational attainments with those from lower supervisory-routine occupations engaging in making active connections (28% relative to 14% of professional/own account).

In defining the meaning of a site for contemporary society, education had a limited correlation to results in that those who had been to university were a little more likely to identify the meaning of the site they were visiting as an aide to national memory (27%) than those who had not been to university (22%). This result is also reflected at labour sites, where 17% of those who had been to university identified the site as an aide to national memory relative to 9% who had not been to university. These results indicate that educational attainment may facilitate viewing the past as having national significance, as the AHD tends to emphasise. Conversely, however, the possession of a university education appears also to encourage critical reflection on the present, in that 13% of those with university degrees did this as opposed to 7% without those degrees. However, this latter difference may be reflective of ethnic identity, as those from non-dominant ethnic backgrounds more frequently held university educations (Chapter 5) and reflected on modern issues (a variable that is all but absent at the labour genre, see Chapter 6). At the labour genre, 18% of those with university degrees identified the site they were visiting as educational relative to 37% without university degrees, many of these linking the educational value with a sense of loss, nominating that such sites were educational for people other than themselves. This sense of loss may energise the degree to which those without higher degrees tended to be undertaking active identity/memory work during their visits, particularly to sites within the labour genre; ethnographic work in deindustrialised communities has tended to emphasise the link between loss and active heritage work (Dicks 2000; Cashman 2006; High and Lewis 2007; Mah 2012; Loveday 2014; Taksa 2019; Berger 2020).

The results are indicative and point to the need for further work. It is difficult to untangle correlations that may be defined as class related (as represented by educational attainment and occupation), particularly as issues of genre, ethnicity and age may also have influenced the results. Further work on issues of class and the use of both heritage sites and museums is certainly required; nonetheless, the idea that class may also influence the overall performances of privilege and those performances undertaken in the context of social and political marginalisation and misrecognition is suggestive.

Conclusion

Social experiences of privilege and exclusion appear to influence visitor responses and use of heritage sites and museums in so far as ethnicity tends to correlate with differing RoE across all sites and national contexts. This is mirrored, but to a less clear extent, by educational attainment/occupation. Those without university degrees and from lower supervisory-routine occupations, as with those from non-dominant ethnic identities, all represent minorities within the database, representing, respectively, 42%, 15% and 11% of those interviewed, the latter two being particularly under-represented in the data. Given their under-representation, further research is needed to explore the differences and patterns being identified here around ethnicity and class. Nonetheless, from the overall patterns identified in the data, it is postulated that there are overall performances of privilege and social exclusion that influence and underlie the more specific performances of heritage-making that visitors undertake.

This idea is explored further in the qualitative analyses outlined in the following chapters, and how performances of exclusion and privilege may underpin and inform heritage-making is most explicitly explored and exemplified in Chapter 9. Performances of privilege are also identified as being based on affective practices that reinforce particular social experiences as being so common as to be banal, or as a form of Gramscian 'common sense', hardly worthy of active reflection unless that sense of commonality or banality is disrupted. The following chapters identify these affective practices, in particular, one of 'indifference', in Chapters 10 and 13 that, it is argued, helps maintain performances of privilege and the heritage-making they inform. Performances that may be defined as navigating social and political exclusion and inequity linked to both ethnic and class experiences are also explored and are most clearly exemplified in performances of affirming reinforcement and certain forms of intergenerational communication that focus on familial identity and imagined conversations. Age also appears to link to particular performances of familial and intergeneration communication and connection, and this is also explored in Chapter 11. Additionally, throughout this and the preceding two chapters, observations have been made about discourses of 'education' or 'learning', the arguments about the uses of these and their role in particular heritage performances, and the RoE they signify are also developed in the following chapters, and in particular, Chapter 8.

Notes

1 The variable 'new/returning' visitor had little to no correlation to visitor responses; the only question where it was significant was that returning visitors who also tended to be older were less likely to choose education as a reason for visiting. While it may be assumed that returning visitors may have deeper connections or investments with sites they have returned to, this was not evident in the data.
2 The most marked difference concerning the question about the meaning of the word 'heritage' correlated to country as discussed in Chapter 5; however, responses to this question also correlated to ethnic identity, which also was maintained across the three countries. Thus, there was both an influence from national identity as well as ethnic identity in how people defined 'heritage'. For example, the definition 'family', while influenced by ethnic identity, does not entirely account for the degree to which it was more broadly offered in the United States (see Chapter 5).

PART III
Emotional heritage
Themes and performances

8
REASSESSING LEARNING
Changing views and deepening understanding

The educational role of museums and heritage sites is important. The idea of learning, particularly the notion of lifelong learning, continues to energise debate about the role and pedagogical significance of heritage within museological and the wider heritage studies literature (Falk and Dierking 2000; Kelly 2002; Falk 2005; Morse et al. 2016). However, education and learning are not necessarily synonymous. Drawing on the work of Gert Biesta (2009, 2013), this chapter aims to reassess the utility of the idea of learning and heritage. The aim is not to dismiss learning, but to suggest that as a pervasive discourse, it may not be constructed or deployed in useful ways.

Specifically, the chapter develops two intertwined arguments. The first is to support the utility of Andrea Witcomb's (2013, 2015) concept of a 'pedagogy of feeling', while concurrently emphasising Zembylas's (2018) point that museum and heritage sites have the *potential* to be useful places to work through difficult emotions. As argued in the following chapters, the normative emotional embodiment engendered by visiting, particularly for national sites, tends to be celebratory. This often results, as Chapter 13 illustrates, in the handling of 'difficult' emotions in ways that maintain misrecognition and inequity. Zembylas's point, which echoes Witcomb's underlying contention, is that emotion cannot be ignored in exhibition and interpretive design and development. Emotions are central not only to the performances of meaning-making discussed in this volume but also to the practices of learning. This argument is developed through an analysis of those visitors who, as identified in Chapter 5, considered that their views had changed or their understanding had deepened. It is also based on a consideration of why certain individual sites and genres of sites, as identified in Chapter 6, had higher frequencies of visitors who considered their visit had altered their views or understandings. The chapter, thus, identifies what it was that facilitated the learning process.

The second intertwined argument draws on the apparent absence of learning within the dataset. In particular, it examines the seeming discrepancy, identified in Chapter 5, between the extent to which visitors identified education or learning as important motivations for visiting yet did not engage in learning. It also considers the extent to which, as identified in Chapters 5–7, visitors talk about the educational values of sites for groups other than the one to which they belonged. To understand these issues it is important to look at the learning discourse, and the practices and performative nature of learning, to understand not only what this discourse does but also how it limits not only the educational role of museums and heritage sites but the role of such institutions and sites in wider social debate. I commence with this argument as it ultimately frames not only why I consider that there is an absence of learning in the data, but it also underlines the importance of learning when indeed it was something in which visitors engaged.

What is meant by learning?

As was established in Chapter 3, learning is an important concept within and the aspiration of both museums and heritage site interpretation. As with wider definitions of learning, the definition employed within the museology literature references a desire for 'change' (see Chapter 3; M. Smith 2018). Although what, exactly, is being changed and to what is an interesting question. Additionally, the idea of 'lifelong learning' is one that appears particularly apposite for museums and heritage sites, not only in promoting a desire and behaviour in children to learn for life but also to engage adult visitors as 'learners'. The language of learning has become ubiquitous in the education field and within public policy, so much so that it has attained the status of common sense (Biesta 2013; Bayne 2015; M. Smith 2018). Indeed, as Biesta (2013: 8) argues, learning has become so naturalised as intrinsically good and desirable that it is "on a par with breathing and digestion". As Ambrose and Pain have stated, learning in museums is "something we *do*" (2018: 67, emphasis in original), but as Biesta (2013) argues, both the doing and its apparent inevitability needs interrogation. As Yosef-Hassidim (2016: 222) notes, Biesta's oeuvre aims to ask what is educationally desirable; however, in his asking, Biesta found the dominant discourse of learning to be unequal to either framing or answering this question.

For Biesta (2015: 234), learning is not inevitable, and as a language, it refers to "processes that are 'empty' with regard to content and purpose", while the idea that we should be lifelong learners "actually says very little – if anything at all". Noting also that to say that the point of education, or in our case of visiting museums and heritage sites, is to 'learn' is not only unhelpful, it removes agency from both the 'learners' and 'teachers', or in our case, curatorial and interpretive professionals (Biesta 2013, 2015). In response to this situation, he has identified, using what he notes is a purposefully ugly term, the issue of 'learnification' (2009: 38).

Learnification, or the proliferation of a language of learning that has, throughout the twenty-first century, framed educational practices, has developed due to a combination of issues. These include the importance of constructivist theories of learning that place students/learners at the centre of educational practices, the critique of the idea that teachers ought to control these practices, the rise of practices of informal learning and the rise of neoliberal policies that stress that the responsibility for learning falls on the learner so that lifelong learning is constituted as being less of a right and more of a *duty* (Biesta 2009: 38). On the positive side, this has seen education become less didactic and, seemingly, more dialogical. However, the emphasis that learning is something we inevitably do and that it is individualistic – it can only be done for oneself – has seen a shift away from relationships in educational processes and practices, making it "far more difficult to explore what the particular responsibilities and tasks of educational professionals, such as teachers and adult educators, actually are" (Biesta 2013: 6). It has also, counterintuitively, made it less dialogical, as it obfuscates the politics of education. The political work that Biesta sees learnification doing is particularly explicit in relation to lifelong learning and the duty of citizens to continue learning for life. Lifelong learning is predominantly about the development of human capital to facilitate "changes in the global economy and the world of work" (2013: 7). Additionally, it is also about advancing social cohesion in such a way that any tensions between economic development and the world of work and between democratic practices are occluded (2013: 7). Learning, Biesta argues, has been hijacked for the service of a particular segment of society (2015: 236). In the context of heritage sites and museums, the discourse of learning, and lifelong learning in particular, reinforce both Bennett's (1995) arguments about the regulatory role of museums in constructing the 'good citizen' and Janes's observation that museums are the keepers of the status quo (2016: 230).

In addition to learning becoming a 'duty' that cannot be avoided, constructivism places self-comprehension, and thus the learner, at the centre of the process and, in doing so, "turns the world into an object for the self" (Biesta 2015: 237). This constructivist position facilitates uncritical relativism – any change in comprehension is rendered 'good', as learning has been achieved. It also, however, means that it becomes difficult for both the natural and social world "to speak on its own terms"; the positing of the learner as the centre and origin of the relationship with the world means that any opportunities for decentring and disrupting the learner's sense of place are limited (Biesta 2015: 237). The 'emptiness' of the language of learning, in which learning is defined as natural, individualistic, intrinsically good and a continual process – where outcomes are measured by reference to vaguely defined changes in comprehension, without ever enumerating if change is good or not – does two things. First, it defines learning as purposeless; learning is good in and of itself. Second, it makes it difficult to evaluate critically educational (or learning) aims and outcomes. It is a language, like that of 'community', that gives us a warm feeling of 'good works' (Biesta 2013: 13; see also Bauman 2001). The overall result then, is, as Biesta (2009: 37) argues, the maintenance of the status quo, as counterintuitively, the language of learning constrains discussion and dialogue.

Bojesen (2018: 929), in her critique of Biesta's arguments, makes the plea for the unsought moment of inspiration, "the getting-carried-away by something outside of ourselves, *without* recourse to purpose". Having an unsought inspiration does not, however, mean that what was learned did not have a purpose or a utility; would something be learned, and by inference retained, if it did not achieve something or have meaning for us? The discourse of learning not only obscures debate over *what* is learned – what has been changed – but also what it was learned *for* (Biesta 2009: 39). The emphasis in the learning discourse, particularly that exemplified by lifelong learning and the idea of an ongoing individualistic process, not only deflects questions about the direction and purpose of learning, it also renders the relationship between the learner and 'teacher' difficult to define and enumerate (Biesta 2012). Teachers, or in this case, curatorial and interpretive professionals, become facilitators for the needs of the learner (Biesta 2004, 2012). The learner, in effect, drives the learning process through the requirement of the facilitator to meet their needs (Bayne 2015: 16–17). Again, this detracts from the agency of debates about the purpose of learning, and indeed, education. In the case of museums and heritage sites, this sets up a dynamic where the institution should morally meet the needs of customers or consumers as 'learners', if they are to 'learn'. Once again, any debate about educational directions is impeded, especially when professional judgement runs counter to the 'needs' of the learner (Biesta 2004: 249). This has implications for museums and heritage sites, as the predominance of the discourse of learning allows for a sense of 'good works' being achieved while facilitating the maintenance of what Janes (2016: 230) has identified as a culture of denial about the role of museums in maintaining the social status quo.

As 'learners', visitors are rendered both passive and active: passive receivers of the museum's message and active as dutiful learners who have changed their behaviour. Any idea that visitors are doing something other than learning is lost in the moral imperative of the learning discourse. Moreover, any sense of the relationship between the interpretive content of the museum or heritage site and what the visitor is doing is also occluded – the material, and its provision by staff, are simply there to facilitate the learners' needs, and a linear relationship between institution and visitor is reaffirmed. Critically and conceptually, the ability to frame and understand what visitors might be doing during their visit, and how they *use* museums and heritage sites, is lost as visiting has become equated with learning.

Going back to the point that learning is not inevitable, Biesta argues that there is any number of contexts and reasons why someone may choose not to learn. As he states, a refusal to learn:

> can help make visible that calling someone a learner is actually a very specific intervention, where the claim is made that the one is being called a learner lacks something, is not yet complete or competent, and therefore needs to engage in further 'learning activity'.
>
> *(2013: 9)*

Biesta admits there may be specific cases where it is legitimate to make these assumptions – for example, if a person has an aspiration to learn a particular skill or understanding. It is, however, nonetheless important that the learning identity is confined to such instances – that it is understood as a "pragmatic, time-bound and situation-bound *choice*, and not a natural state of affairs" (2013: 9, original emphasis).

While the following chapters discuss the choices visitors have made about the meaning their visits have for them, this chapter aims to engage both with the choices visitors made to learn and to unpack the learning discourses visitors themselves used. A final point from Biesta's (2009: 44) work is his plea that discussions around the aims of education are framed by far more critical use of the language of learning, which allows for considerations of "learning 'of what' and 'for what'", but to which we might add 'for whom'. In short, the consequences of learning need to be an integral part of any conceptualisation or consideration of learning in a museum or heritage context.

In using the aforementioned consideration of learning, the apparent absence of learning in the dataset may be understood as precisely that: an absence. It speaks to the choices visitors made. The answers given to the question that asked if the 'visit changed your views about the past or present' should be regarded on face value as meaningful – people in exercising both agency and choice responded candidly about what if anything may have changed and thus may have been learned. The fact that the majority said no, or that their views had been reinforced, reflects what visitors understood of their relationship with the site they had visited.

The aforementioned framing of learning also tells us about the apparent contradictions outlined in Chapter 5 between those that choose from the proffered list of reasons for coming the variables 'education' or to 'find out about' and those who offered education or learning as the reasons for being at a site or the experiences they valued, and yet said no, nothing had changed. Rather than being a contradiction, it reveals the pervasiveness of this discourse first, as something that 'should' be done, and second, as the political work visitors themselves were doing with the discourse of learning. This discourse was used in several ways, to authorise their reinforcement of their valued narratives and social positions (Chapters 9 and 10), to identify their desire to see other social groups become socialised within dominant narrative templates and associated social values and to mask the choices they made not to learn (Chapter 13).

As noted in Chapter 7, the language of education/learning tended to be used more often by visitors who had travelled from holiday addresses, the suggestion being that this may have helped justify the visit in those cases where visitors did not choose to engage in learning. More importantly, however, invoking 'learning' works to help strengthen the legitimacy of what is being reinforced. Those who nominated that the site had reinforced their views often talked about the importance of the site as an educational resource. A typical example from the Stockman's Hall of Fame is provided by visitor LR118 who responded to the question on changed views with "Uh, not for me, it just reinforces a lot of the stuff I think" had, in response to the previous question on the meaning of the site to contemporary Australia talked about how the site "teaches the Australian, or anyone who visits, what Australia's all about and [. . .] what they endured in the past and hopefully [visitors will] continue to learn" (female, 45–54, registered nurse, Australian). The extent to which visitors talked of the need for people other than themselves, or groups other than that to which the visitor identified, to 'learn' justified their performances of reinforcement. The learning discourse authorised their choice not to 'learn', to in effect reinforce what they knew and valued, as to talk of the need for others to 'learn' underlined and naturalised the importance of what the site represented to the respondent. In this process, certain social experiences, and the values they embodied, were normalised both in history and in contemporary society as legitimate and of importance. For 'others' to 'learn' about the significance of this experience was a demonstration of their socialisation and their 'good citizenship'. Certain visitors, particularly those engaged in the conservative performances of reinforcement, discussed in Chapters 9 and 10, are thus using their visits to emotionally invest in and embody the legitimacy of maintaining the status quo – and they do so precisely through the discourse of learning.

Finally, the discussion of learnification provides an important framing for the following section of the chapter, as while the agencies of individual visitors in making choices about what was learned is acknowledged, it does not render museums or heritage sites as simple facilitators. Any identification of those aspects of the exhibition or interpretive content that facilitated learning needs to be considered in terms of its consequences. It underlines the importance of clear pedagogical agendas, not only to assist clear reflection and dialogue but also to enable understanding of how certain pedagogical techniques interact with specific registers of engagement to either facilitate or constrain those agendas. It also repositions visitors as *part* of, and not simply subjects of, the performative process of heritage-making that museums, heritage sites and their staff undertake.

Emotion and learning

If learning is a purposeful choice, what facilitated those who considered their views had changed to make that choice? What was the moment of inspiration that Bojesen (2018) identifies as important, and what made those moments meaningful and useful enough so that visitors considered that a changing or deepening of views, or learning, had occurred? Witcomb (2013) has argued that the simple walking and reading of texts, or the passive listening to interpretive content, is insufficient to the task of producing a critical pedagogy for museums and heritage sites. She calls for a 'pedagogy of feeling' that acknowledges the importance of affect/emotion in how people learn and engage with heritage (Witcomb 2015). Emotion, as Trofanenko (2014: 35) also argues, is part of the multifaceted range of influences that frame how and why people choose to engage in learning. However, the emotional authenticity, or what Morton (2002) refers to as 'emotional truth', of visitor interactions with heritage may also be significant in this choice. Of the 19% who nominated that their views had been changed or deepened in some way, 10% nominated that they gained new, relatively minor, pieces of information (Chapter 5). However, this section draws specifically on the remaining 9% of visitors who nominated a significant deepening or alteration of understanding to identify what triggered these responses and to outline the ways visitors then navigated their affective responses to sites and exhibitions.

Four visitors (Table 5.13) identified that they felt sufficiently motivated to change their behaviour. It is important to stress that they were not simply reminded that they should behave in ways that confirmed pre-existing views, but rather act in new ways based, in all four cases, on a deeper and new appreciation achieved through their visits. All four talked in a holistic sense about the impact of their visit of the embodied physicality of being in place, of not simply visually or textually witnessing history and culture, but emotionally engaging with it.

A teacher, who stated she had driven with her children over 4,000 km to visit Uluṟu – "it was the centre of our trip" – noted that when she was younger, the place had been called Ayres Rock. She remembered when the site was handed back to the Traditional Owners feeling "annoyance and, you know, what was this?" when the name changed. Throughout the interview, she continually referred to the beauty of the place, the connection to the place she had seen Indigenous people make, and how overwhelmed she felt by simply being there. When asked if anything had changed, she noted, "Yeah, everything really". She noted that watching a historical film clip at the cultural centre had brought back memories for her, that she "remember[ed] those images on TV" and "the racism that was so apparent then". She notes "watching them now, with the experience of hindsight, and going 'wow, Australia's changed so much'. You know, the cultural views have changed". She goes on to reflect:

> I personally – I teach English at a high school in Sydney, and I actually am responsible for our 11 Indigenous students, and actually, for me it's – I'm going to look at them differently I think going back because there's an understanding that wasn't there perhaps before. Just – yeah, it's funny.
>
> *(U87: female, 35–44, teacher, Anglo-Australian)*

The film triggered a reflection about how Australian society and her views had changed. However, the sense of being 'overwhelmed' and in awe of the site, its history and Indigenous culture was important in underlining that moment of reflection. Similarly, a visitor interviewed after the Rivers of Steel tour of the Carrie Furnace and another visitor at the National Civil Rights Museum were both overtaken by deep empathetic responses to the hard work that, respectively, labour and the civil rights movement had engaged in to bring about social and political change. The visitor at the Rivers of Steel site felt inspired to "not necessarily work more – but like work *on* things, like improve our society" (RS4: male, 45–54, engineer, Canadian). While a Caucasian teacher at the Civil Rights Museum noted: "Seeing how hard students had to work to get to go to school makes me feel like I need to work harder teaching", a sentiment reinforced by the links she drew between her personal experience and the site:

> I think it probably speaks to a very southern heritage in a home that I grew up in that knew prejudice was part of the conversation, to the place where

I am now, where I am *the* white teacher with my group of students, helping them learn and helping them be able to make a difference, so, anyway. . .

(*NCRM38: female, 45–54, teacher, Caucasian American, her emphasis*)

The fourth visitor, who was visiting Yellowstone National Park drew on the idea that the park was representational of national achievements in conservation to observe that his visit "changes my perspective on how I go about things in my daily life, with the environment and situations like that" (Y13: male, 45–54, military, Caucasian American). While the visitor at Uluru nominated that film images prompted a specific reflective moment, like the other three visitors, it was the cumulative emotional authenticity of being at the sites that was important. However, all four evidenced important imaginative responses to the sites that underpinned their learning. Y13 draws imaginatively on the idea that Yellowstone is representational of national achievement, while the Uluru visitor invokes changes in Australian society and imagines changes for her future interactions with her Indigenous students. At the Rivers of Steel site, the visitor is in awe of the size of the site reflecting in response to the question on feelings "I look at these huge pipes or I look at the tiny valves or stuff, I just always think of the people who built this place and who were working there for so many years"; this is an imaginative, empathetic response. The visitor at the Civil Rights Museum draws imaginatively on her own experiences of southern privilege by juxtaposing that with what she has seen in the museum and her own experiences of teaching African American students. An imaginative empathy was important, as Johnson (2005: 42) notes, to imagine alternative futures and presents, new ways of being and acting.

The holistic sense of embodying being on a site that is already important to a visitor – they have after all chosen to visit – was often referenced by those who expressed a sense of being 'better informed' or of deepening their understanding. As this example illustrates, physically being on site can facilitate the imaginative links people needed to deepen their understanding:

Yeah, it's interesting, you know, you read about it in a book, but it's interesting to actually be able to see it and make it a little bit more tangible, to be able to really understand what it was like. You know, it wasn't new, but it was nice to be able to see it.

(*TM67: female, 25–34, engineer, German English American*)

Those coded in Table 5.13 as 'better informed' tended to note that rather than having a significant change in understanding, being at the site brought clarity; "I didn't have as clear a picture of what [immigrant] life was like until I took this tour" (TM50: male, 45–54, lawyer, Jewish American). Being in place allowed some visitors to make the imaginative leaps that they needed to deepen their engagement with particular issues or topics. While specific artefacts, as will be identified, can facilitate or spark learning, as Dubinsky and Muise (2016) point out, artefacts are not always central to a visitor's experience of a site. Rather, in feeling better informed, visitors often noted that being at a site met their expectations in providing an emotionally authentic and thus imaginative rounding out of their understanding. This deepening of understanding, however, could coincide with curatorial aims, as was the case for TM50 and 67 at the Tenement Museum, who developed a more empathetic understanding of immigrant experiences. Alternatively, it may not coincide with curatorial aims. This is exemplified by a visitor at the Hermitage, discussed in Chapter 3, who noted that his understanding of slavery was deepened: "[I learned] how well the slaves were taken care of" (H14: male, 25–32, student, Argentinian American). The emotional and imaginative authenticity of place provided H14 with a learning experience that, for him, was as meaningful and useful as were the experiences for TM50 and 67. It may be argued that H14 was reinforcing his prejudice, but, equally, it has to be asked to what extent TM50 and 67 themselves leaned toward empathetic compassion. A pedagogy of feeling that acknowledges the work that emotions/affect plays on understanding is important; however, as Trofanenko (2014: 36) points out, emotion interacts with other factors such as ideology, prior knowledge and social experiences to develop individual understanding. The encouragement of certain affective states or responses cannot be conceived as leading to universal responses in understanding. Affect is socially mediated; to draw on theories of affect that are based on ideas of pre-discursive states of being will misapprehend the social mediation and consequences of affect within pedagogical practices (Chapter 2).

As Chapter 6 illustrates, dissonant sites, particularly Immigration and Indigenous sites, had the highest frequencies of people who considered their views had changed. Dissonant sites also engendered higher levels of imaginative or deep empathy than national sites. These sites, far more than national sites, utilised what Rowe et al. (2002) refer to as 'little narratives'. In their study of history museums, they argue that personal narratives carry not only the authority of the 'eye witness', but more importantly can "convey what social reality feels like rather than what it should be like" (Bodnar 1992, quoted in Rowe et al. 2002: 103). These little narratives, through both the personal and emotional links they can make, facilitate critical reflection about larger narratives of nationhood. Little narratives may, depending on how they are used and how visitors engage with them, maintain or disrupt larger narratives of imagined communities (Rowe et al. 2002: 103–104).

As this visitor from the Tenement Museum reveals, little narratives facilitated the imaginative connections that deepened understanding and then facilitated reflection on larger narratives:

> Just seeing the living conditions, I think was very eye-opening. Actually, learning about the families on an individual basis, I thought that was a very effective way of making it more personal.
> *Why is the personal important, do you think? Why was it good to make it personal?*
> I think when you hear a lot of, when you read a lot about the immigrant experience, and it's sort of more as a whole. And to actually hear an individual person's story and how they researched it, you know, for the museum, what

happened to, you know, the children, or the family, how they struggled for certain jobs. It was, it made it, you were more connected to it, I think. That was something that you could really envision yourself.

(TM21: female, 45–54, journalist, Pakistani German)

Through the personal narratives told about individuals and families at this site, the visitor engaged with the larger narrative of the immigrant experience, making it personal in such a way that she could imagine how it may have felt for herself to be in that situation. She revealed, she had herself been an immigrant to Germany in the 1970s; however, her experiences as an immigrant had been very different to those discussed at the site. The personal stories had allowed her to imagine a different historical experience. This is imaginative empathy that led to this visitor deepening not only her critical understanding of the significance of the history of immigration, but as she goes on to reflect:

> Immigrant issues are becoming more difficult in Germany, especially after September 2001. I'm from a Muslim context, and it never meant much to me, but now people ask me if I am Muslim all the time. I used to not identify as such, but now I do. People worry about immigration too much; now, it has become a real problem. And I wonder as a journalist how much I may contribute to this unfortunate worry about it. These are issues I was thinking about during the tour [of the tenement museum].

The higher levels of empathy recorded at dissonant sites, together with the higher rates of changed views, was relational. As Wildt (2018: 77) argues, based on her experiences as a curator at the Amsterdam Museum, exhibiting individual stories about the communities with which she had worked "means building a relationship". Additionally, it also means building relationships with visitors. Objects, as Wildt (2018: 79) notes, may have powerful resonance; however, "stories are mediated through texts, audio or video", and it is the personal stories that facilitate deep and imaginative empathy. When visitors did point to elements of an exhibition that affected them, that facilitated deep empathetic engagement, it was to stories with which they could make a personal and emotional link. Most frequently noted by visitors were the voice recordings at *Breaking the Chains*, British Empire and Commonwealth Museum, of an actress, reading the diary entry of a young enslaved girl, sold away from her mother; reading the letters written by Dr King at the National Civil Rights Museum, or film clips of old news items at the Uluru Cultural Centre. At the Historical Centre of Industry and Labor, Youngstown, Ohio, it was the individual stories of workers that were important in one person's self-identified choice to learn:

> I was always on the management side [...] especially when I graduated from college, one of the questions asked of me when I went to work for Rover Express because they were having some strike issues, what did you think of it? And my answer was, 'lock the doors, keep them out.' But when you go

through a museum like this and you see how impoverished the people were, that they were literally owned by the company's store, and the value of the person was irrelevant, and the importance was how much production can we get out of this body, and how little do we have to pay them? And so it changes, even at my age now.

(IL2: male, over 65, retailer, American)

This visitor, who had, when younger, been on the side of 'management', noted that the museum had helped him learn about the issues faced by workers. He noted that his turning away from his previous views was not new, "I felt this way for quite a while, that, yes, there's a need for unions", but the museum had helped him along his path to changing his view. Here, deep empathy again underlay the shift in views, but the self-identified learning undertaken at the museum had purpose: it had been useful for helping him think through his larger reflections on his society; he concludes his lengthy musing about the history of organised labour and the need for unions with, "I'm afraid our humankind, our nature, is still such that – we certainly see it in our country today – greed is destroying our nation". As other chapters illustrate, many visitors engaged in reflection similar to this visitor and those previously mentioned but did not identify what they were doing as learning. Reflection, on the whole, was undertaken as people mulled over and engaged in 'self-talk' (Archer 2007) about the legitimacy of their existing views and experiences. In the aforementioned case, however, this visitor is engaging in a longitudinal change of views; he is reflecting, but it is part, for him, of a learning process that has resulted in quite a radical change of position. Indeed, this is perhaps where museums and heritage sites are most realistically effective, not in the epiphanies (although these did occur) but in the provision of space and time for individuals to work through complicated emotional and ideological changes in position – a point returned to later.

Epiphanies, moments of sudden realisation, did occur at the museums, representing 0.5% (Table 5.13) of responses to the question about changed views. When this occurred, and they only occurred at dissonant sites, visitors spoke of being overawed by both the informational content of the site, but also by the empathetic impact of stories told. Deep empathy engaged imagination, and visitors worked through their feelings to inform the changes in views they were making and the judgements that both informed and had resulted from those changes. Empathy, as both emotion and skill, was often felt as distress and compassion for the other, as was the case with this visitor to the International Slavery Museum, Liverpool:

Yeah everything for me, everything for me, absolutely everything has changed a lot for me. Erm, it's opened my eyes up, to be honest, and to take an interest in it, I knew we had slaves and that, but I didn't know they actually. . .

(ISM305: female, 35–44, receptionist, White British)

This visitor admitted to knowing and understanding very little about the British slave trade; emotionally, she is overcome, trailing off, as she admits to being deeply shocked and unsure of how to think through what she has learnt. She notes she wants to come back, speaking approvingly of the videoed reconstructions in the museum as it was these that "touched me", noting, "it's interesting when someone is talking, it makes you feel as if you're there". She is overawed with her distress, but not so much she does not engender sufficient compassion and self-reflection to know that "everything has changed" for her understanding of this history. Empathic feelings, however, did not always rest on feelings of distress but could also be felt as anger and rage for the injustice experienced by others, as the following visitor to the exhibition *Slavery at Jefferson's Monticello: Paradox of Liberty* illustrates:

> what they say is not true. Because I mean in school they basically really taught you that, you know, Thomas Jefferson was the one that, you know, basically began it all for, you know, African Americans to be free, but as you actually come here and learn that he actually owned lots of slaves himself, that really did change my views about the past and who he was.
>
> *(SJM24: male, 18–24, barista, southern American)*

Drawing once again on the stories of individual experiences of enslavement, note SJM24's palpable anger – "[the exhibition] was a little damn emotional for me" – is directed at both what he was taught at school relative to what he has just seen in the exhibition and the ongoing injustice of treating people as "second class citizens". As discussed in Chapter 13, desires to resist difficult or uncomfortable emotions alongside aspirations to uphold valued entrance narratives, were instances where people chose, consciously or otherwise, not to learn and to maintain misrecognition and injustice.

Introducing what Simon (2011) calls 'difficult knowledge' to museums, particularly sites of national narrative–making, requires breaking through habitual and established repertoires of celebratory emotional expression. It requires visitors to engage with uncertainty and ambiguity, emotions that are often difficult to navigate within conservative ideological frameworks (Jost et al. 2003; Jost 2019). Simon (2011: 434), in his analysis of exhibitions based on the photography of American lynching, notes that knowledge will become difficult when "one's conceptual frameworks, emotional attachments, and conscious and unconscious desires delimit one's ability to settle the meaning of past events". In such contexts, he argues, sense of self can become undone, in much the same way as was experienced by the visitor to the Liverpool exhibition. This may not only turn a visitor away but can result in confusion, disorientation and anxiety about knowing how to respond. Thus, for Simon (2011: 447), pedagogies of provocation require an assessment of what might be risked by them. However, it is not simply the traumatic that can arouse risky destabilisation; 'difficult knowledge' can be far more prosaic. What may be perceived as not difficult for some may be seen as risky by someone else. Risk may occur, for instance, when self-understanding of the universality and legitimacy of a person's sense of social privilege is called into question. As argued in Chapter 13, this particular risk underlines many of the performances of misrecognition discussed in that chapter. However, it is worth noting here the ability to navigate difficult emotions/knowledge is predicated on the long-term success of conciliatory politics (Hutchison and Bleiker 2008: 387).

Zembylas (2018: 207) argues for the need to understand the intended and unintended consequences of the possible emotional regimes that may be invoked in museum education based on pedagogies of feeling. He observes that "empathy and emotion sharing are not uncontested 'goods', whatever the context" (2018: 208). This is because emotional regimes give meaning, as he notes, to the educational work of museums and heritage sites, but the boundaries of these regimes are fluid and changeable. Agreeing with Simon (2011), Zembylas (2018: 208) calls for new vocabularies and practices when dealing with the affective regimes of difficult heritage. However, such a call should not stick at difficult or dissonant heritage/knowledge, as what constitutes 'difficult' or dissonant heritage is itself changeable and fluid. Rather, the point to stress is that any pedagogy of feeling needs to be self-consciously aware of the broad and flexible field of affective regimes it hopes to invoke, and, more specifically, the registers of engagement that mobilise and give meaning to how museums and sites, and their educational practices, are used. Additionally, any rethinking of educational practice within heritage needs a more self-aware and critical engagement with who the audiences are; that is, how experiences of social privilege, inclusion or exclusion define what is or is not 'difficult knowledge', dissonant heritage or uncomfortable emotions. As findings in Chapter 7 indicate, the social context of visitors helps frame affective practices and heritage performances of meaning-making.

The interlinked fluidity of emotional responses and concepts of difficult knowledge or heritage is underlined by comparisons of the examples listed previously of reflexive learning coupled with the performances of affirmation and those of positive recognition outlined in Chapters 9 and 12, respectively, against the emotional recoiling from difficult and contested histories that underlies performances of misrecognition detailed in Chapter 13. These juxtapositions illustrate the different registers of engagement that visitors mobilise to produce different meanings from the same experiences – from visiting the same site or exhibition. While some performances may be more prevalent at particular site genres, nonetheless an array of registers of engagement and meaning were found at each site. As Zembylas (2018: 208) notes, the issue here is not the restraining of certain emotions, such as "downplaying the suffering of the victim in the name of reconciliation or fostering empathy" or ignoring the possibility of negative emotions, such as shame or guilt, by those from historically privileged positions. Rather, it is understanding the potential repertoires of affect, and of "creating spaces where grievances can be freely expressed, and corresponding emotions can be productively worked through" (Zembylas 2018: 208). In this sense, the educational aims of museums and heritage sites may be more usefully crafted towards the provision of arenas for engaging with and coming to terms with the positive and negative emotional valences of history.

The most effective example of how visitors engaged with a museum's educational aims, exhibiting significant changes in view while working through what

190 Emotional heritage

were for them difficult emotional responses, was a family of four adults at the Immigration Museum, Melbourne. This museum had the highest frequency of those who considered their views had, in some way, changed (Chapter 6). A pedagogy of feeling was evident in how aspects of the museum's exhibitions had been developed (Witcomb 2013). Analyses in particular of the permanent exhibition 'Identity: yours, mine ours' have discussed its self-aware engagement with affect and its positive consequences for visitors (Witcomb 2013; Schorch 2015; Mulcahy and Witcomb 2018). At the time of the interviews for this study, however, this exhibition had not been opened. The family of four's sense of self had been undone by the provision of a role-play room that, like the later exhibition studied by Witcomb and Schorch, was designed to engage visitor emotions (Figure 8.1). On entering the room, visitors were invited to take on the persona of an immigration officer interviewing potential migrants to Australia. Visitors could choose scenarios from a range of different periods in history representing different periods of Australian immigration policy. These scenarios consisted of videos, recorded by actors and showed potential immigrants being interviewed by an immigration officer. At the end of the video, the visitor could then vote on whether or not to allow the applicant entry. The visitor is then told whether the immigration officer in the video, using the relevant policies for the period chosen, would have let the person into Australia or not, and the reasons for that decision.

FIGURE 8.1 Visitors engaging with the interview interactive in the *Getting In* exhibition, Immigration Museum, Melbourne.

Source: Museums Victoria. Photographer: Benjamin Healley.

I had come upon the family in the museum's café, animatedly discussing this room, and they were more than willing to be interviewed. The family had emigrated from England to Australia in the late 1950s when the now-grown children had been young. Their own experience of being immigrants was not, however, identified as a reason for the visit, but rather an opportunity to socialise for the mother's 80th birthday.

This family had chosen a contemporary scenario featuring an Iraqi refugee. At the end of the interview, the family had collectively decided that the story told by the Iraqi had been suspiciously inconsistent. Thus, they rejected his application. The voice-over then explained that the Iraqi would have been granted entry into Australia. The inconsistencies in the story, it was explained, were explicable by the trauma the man had experienced:

How does it make you feel to visit this exhibition?

>   FATHER: A bit nostalgic, going back to the earlier times when we first arrived.
>   MOTHER: Yeah.
>   DAUGHTER: I really enjoyed it, the educational aspect of understanding other views.
>   SON: And just that interview thing there where we kicked that poor bloke out of Australia! [laughs]
>   DAUGHTER: The interview, yeah, I feel really bad.
>   SON: And I think I'm soft and it turns out to be the opposite! Whoops! [laughs]
>   (IMM54: male, 45–54, engineer, English Australian; IMM55: female, over 65, mother, English Australian; IMM56: female, 45–54, public health, English Australian; IMM57: male, over 65, retired, English Australian).

At this point in the interview, while the daughter admits to feeling 'sad', the son's sense of himself has been challenged, something he appears to take lightly. However, by the time we get to the question about messages, the son reveals, while uncomfortable, that he is reflexive:

>   SON: I reckon like, I think just how hard it is to decide when a person is a refugee or not; for me, I reckon it just must be such a tough job.
>   MOTHER: Yeah, it's impossible, isn't it?
>   SON: Yeah, I mean, you have an obligation to...
>   MOTHER: Do the right thing.
>   SON: And help those people, but you don't know if, you know, you don't know if you've been had! [laughs]
>   DAUGHTER: Yeah, yeah, and if you have been had and something bad happens, does it fall back on that poor person who accepted him? That one person, yeah, so yeah.
>   FATHER: But it doesn't matter what precautions you tend to take, you still get it wrong.

SON: Oh yeah, yeah.
MOTHER: Oh you can, yeah, well we got it wrong, didn't we?
DAUGHTER: And that's not something we do! [laughs]
FATHER: I'm thinking more of the bigger things, such as the blowing up of the Trade Centre. I mean, that was done by a doctor that had been living in the country for goodness knows how long and somebody got it wrong letting him in.
DAUGHTER: Yeah, but then did they get it wrong when they let him in or was that an after-effect that he decided to turn? Who knows?
FATHER: Well, we don't know.
DAUGHTER: Yeah.

They are all working through difficult emotional responses to the exhibit. The role-play has unseated their sense of self, it's hard to do the right thing, and as the mother notes they "got it wrong", but as the daughter exclaims "that's not something we do!" This is a destabilisation of self that Simon (2011) notes can be elicited by difficult knowledge, but they work through this. At this point, the family is empathising with the immigration officer and discussing how difficult that job must be. There is an attempt by the men to justify their decision to exclude the applicant, the spectre of the World Trade Centre is recalled, and the son worries they may have been "had" by the inconsistencies in the Iraqi's story. They engage with uncertainty; they "don't know", but they do know their decision in this instance was 'wrong'.

From this point of uncertainty – they were not as "soft" as the son had thought, they were wrong even though they thought they were doing "the right thing" – they entered into a lengthy and thoughtful discussion about what the history of immigration had meant for Australia:

SON: I mean this is like the history of Australia and how it's built up. I mean the Snowy Mountains thing must have been one of the major engineering feats at that time and basically pulled people from all over the world ... so to me, it's really important.
DAUGHTER: This is what Australia is.

They moved to a discussion of the impact of colonisation on Aboriginal people, with the mother observing, "I feel a bit more sorry for the Aborigines now than I did before" – to the way Australian immigration policy had changed over time, the inconsistencies within those policies and their ongoing effect on the population. They then moved on to reflect on a current national election debate about refugees, especially those asylum seekers arriving in Australia by sea, who the media was negatively referring to as 'boat people'. When probed about this last point, a very lengthy debate ensured among the family about media portrayals of refugees:

DAUGHTER: Yeah, so instead of the media concentrating on the boat people coming over, and blowing that all out of proportion, maybe if they looked at the refugee camps where they're coming from and start to really see where the problem is [...] all they do is stimulate the racial prejudice.

Their debate continued about the hardships faced by refugees in refugee camps and their poor treatment in Australian detention centres. They talked about the historical mistreatment of Chinese immigrants and how each new ethnic group in Australia faced prejudice. They noted the sometimes desperate measures, including the use of smugglers, which people took to obtain entry to Australia. They discussed the idea of 'queue jumping', which onshore asylum seekers had been accused in the media of doing, and wondered what this so-called practice meant in terms of the desperation refugees must feel. They lastly spoke of their desire to see the Australian government review refugee claims more effectively, to shorten the unjustly long processing times for claims:

> FATHER: In other words, you have to get back to the root cause and speed that process up, do something in that area.
> SON: And make it fair.
> DAUGHTER: And make it better, that's right, so they [refugees] don't need to do that [i.e., use people smugglers and travel by unsafe boats], yeah.

The son's reference to "making it fair" is important here, the rhetoric of giving people a 'fair go' is pervasive in Australia. As the daughter states, being unfair is "not something we do", the 'we' referencing both her family and Australian society, in general. Self and the values of having a 'fair go' were destabilised, the family rising to the challenge this offered to reflect on and question what they knew and assumed. While initially, they attempted to justify their decision to exclude the Iraqi refugee, they managed to move past that to enter into a wide-ranging debate among themselves that lead to insight about historical and contemporary Australian immigration policies, Australian racism, media portrayals of refugees and Aboriginal issues. Empathy began with the immigration officer, and while never quite alighting on the imagined Iraqi refugee, it nonetheless was extended to the idea of refugees in general, actual on- and offshore asylum seekers and Indigenous Australians. As the mother noted about the museum experience, "I think it's grounded me better in Australia".

This section has focused on the 8.5% who nominated deepening of understanding or changes in view. Museums and heritage sites, it needs to be acknowledged, were also used as sources of information by visitors. Included in the percentage were the 2%, who while not necessarily changing their views, took away major new information. While much of the minor information visitors nominated tended to be about dates or sequencing of events and so forth, sites as authoritative and accessible repositories of information could be used in revealing ways by visitors. Although not a firsthand account, this frequent visitor to the Japanese American National History Museum, in discussing the museum's meaning for contemporary America, recounts his own observations at the museum:

> Every new immigrant group that comes into the United States, especially from countries where there's a lot of conflict, and should we be attacked by another country, the impact is going to be pretty grave. It's like the Iranian

situation, Iraqi situation. I remember when that first came up, a lot of the local Iraqi and Iranians came to the museum to kind of see what they could experience.

(JANM: male, over 65, retired FBI, Japanese American)

The gathering of information can be part of the learning process, although as this example suggests, learning information is done for a purpose. The family at the Immigration Museum, Melbourne, may have experienced Bojesen's (2018) unsought moment of inspiration, but the family took advantage of the opportunity the role-play room afforded them because it had meaning for them. It helped them navigate complex contemporary debates in Australia; it grounded them more, as the mother stated, in Australian society – it had a purpose – it was applicable to them. Engaging in eliciting emotional responses requires purpose and direction. Understanding the purpose of visitor uses of museums and heritage sites is integral to the development of pedagogies of feeling and the utilisation of museums and sites as arenas for working through difficult emotions.

Conclusion

Embodiment, imaginative empathy and the intensity of either the positive or negative emotions that were felt by visitors were important registers in learning. Importantly, the scale at which these registers occurred were frequently at the personal but were negotiated in such a way as to broaden the scope of visitor engagement to encompass broader issues that included the prospect of behavioural change, a critique of national narratives, and national policies and racism. What was changed was not always what the institutions involved intended, nor was change always 'good' and what was changed was framed and mediated by ideology, which in turn framed the purpose and meaning of what was learned. Conversely, embodiment, intense valance and empathy do not inevitably lead to visitors making a choice to learn.

As Zembylas (2018) argues, the emotional repertoires that may be invoked by pedagogies of feeling and provocation will shift and change depending on the multifaceted contexts of visitor experience and their skills in recognising and mediating their emotions. Practices within pedagogies of feeling inevitably expose a complex emotional landscape, but this does not mean that Witcomb (2013, 2015) is not correct in drawing attention to affect. Rather, what is required is a reworking not simply of the vocabularies and practices of addressing affect/emotion, as Zembylas suggests, but also a reworking of how learning in museums and heritage sites is defined. As Biesta (2013) argues, learning is a choice. Ideological resistance to negative valance is evident in the performances of misrecognition discussed in Chapter 13. Additionally, education, and indeed learning, is enabled by critically self-aware relationships, which are undermined by the notion that the role of museums and heritage professionals is largely to 'facilitate the needs' of 'lifelong learners'.

To come back to the point with which this chapter commenced. The educational role of museums and heritage sites is important, and it is not a failure of professional-pedagogical aims that not all visitors use sites to learn or as educational resources for themselves. The educational role of museums and sites remains an important professional, aspirational aim, but it is an aim subject to ongoing reflexive dialogue as to its purpose, content and practice. The language of learning, learnification, masks the variety of ways in which visitors use sites. It is a discourse that needs opening up to facilitate not only engagement with emotions but also the enablement of professional practices that explicitly address and build relationships with other forms of visitor engagements and uses of heritage that are not based on 'learning'.

9
PERFORMING REINFORCEMENT AND AFFIRMATION

'It just reinforces a lot of the stuff I think'[1]

Visiting museums and heritage sites framed within the AHD is a decidedly white middle-class activity. Studies of the history of museums and early critiques of the development of the so-called heritage industry have stressed how museums and sites, particularly those framed by consensus national narratives, speak to a visitor profile dominated by the well-educated and those from ethnic political majorities (e.g. Hewison 1987; Merriman 1991; Bennett 1995; Kohlsted 2005 among others). Despite decades of attempting to develop more inclusive exhibition policies, the profile of visitors to national museums and heritage sites tends to remain resolutely white and middle class (Bennett et al. 2010; Black 2012; Bounia et al. 2012; Conrad et al. 2013; Chapter 5). This is not to say that regional and specialised museums and heritage sites, such as those addressing labour history or histories of immigration, do not attract a more diverse visitor profile as identified in Chapters 5 and 6, but that on the whole, those sites and museums that fit comfortably within the AHD and associated nationalising narrative templates speak to a particular class and ethnic experience.

The dominant profile of museum visitors is important to keep in mind to understand the performance of reinforcement that emerged from the interview data. In response to the question about changed views, 20% of visitors nominated unprompted that the museum or heritage site they were visiting had 'reinforced' their knowledge, views or feelings. Additionally, 11% of visitors in response to the question on messages similarly noted that their views had been reinforced. The word 'reinforce' (or its various synonyms such as confirms, strengthens or validates) was also used in connection to questions about experiences, feelings, what being there meant to visitors and how the site may have linked or spoken to a visitor's sense of identity (Chapter 4). A rough search[2] of the interview transcripts found approximately 390 additional instances of people talking about reinforcement, confirmation or other synonyms; that is, roughly 9% of the interviews explicitly used such terms. Reinforcement also occurs, however, without the explicit use of such terms. Indeed, reinforcement is the most frequent heritage performance that visitors undertake, often informing other performances of heritage-making.

In explicating the expression of the 'performance of reinforcement', this chapter argues that there are two versions of this performance that have two different registers of engagement and ideological outcomes. The first is a performance typically, as suggested in Chapter 7, performed by well-educated visitors from dominant ethnic identities and is reinforcing interlinked experiences of privilege and national identity. The intensity of the register of engagement may be either deep or shallow, while the valence will be emotionally banal in that the emotions will be commonplace or well trodden by the person expressing them, and no matter the intensity of their expression, they will work to reassure, calm or comfort the visitor. The ideological outcome is to confirm the legitimacy of the social experiences of the visitor within a reinforced national narrative; this legitimacy is not overtly pronounced but simply rehearsed and affirmed by the very act of visiting. This act sustains the sense to which certain understandings and experiences of both the past and present become so much taken for granted or 'common sense' in Gramscian terms.

The second version of this performance is one of affirmation, which, unlike the previous version, is more self-consciously undertaken and based on personal acts of remembering and is specifically an active seeking of affirmation of one's political and social values. As argued in Chapter 12, one of the variants of performances of recognition is a seeking of a sense that a visitor's identity and social and historical experiences 'matter'. While this reinforcing or affirming performance may, at times, overlap or underlie performances of recognition, the performance of affirmation is explicitly tied to a reinforcement of the political values held by a visitor. It is also more often undertaken by visitors who do not fit the usual visitor profile, who identified as belonging to non-dominant ethnic identities or who had not been to university or occupied lower supervisory/routine occupations. Its register of engagement is not only more self-conscious, but it is also generated by discomfort, if not individual or communal experiences of injustice, and unlike the other performance of reinforcement, it does not seek to bring comfort to the visitor-only affirmation. While its ideological consequence can be either politically progressive or conservative, it tends to the politically progressive.

Theorising visiting

Various arguments, particularly about museums, have been put forward to theorise the nature and consequences of visiting. Three interrelated arguments, in particular, have influenced academic and policy debate in both museum and heritage practices and are briefly reviewed in the context of the performances of reinforcement. The first argument draws on Bourdieu's idea of 'cultural capital' and identifies museum visiting as a performative statement of the social and cultural capital required to appreciate and 'understand' the value and significance of the cultural material on display (Merriman 1991; Pearce 1992; Fyfe 2004; Hanquinet 2016). This argument is supported by the survey work carried out in Britain by Nick Merriman in the late 1980s that identified the extent to which those from what he called 'high status' groups felt comfortable and at ease in museum contexts and were more concerned with impersonal national values narratives, while 'lower status' groups were more concerned with engaging with personal aspects of the past (1989, 1991). As outlined in Chapter 7, the extent to which politically non-dominant groups tend to draw on personal connections with the past supports this observation. Survey work by Bennett and colleagues that analysed the extent to which Bourdieu's ideas about the links between cultural tastes and class could be identified in Britain also revealed the extent to which those from the professional-executive class are far more likely than working-class and intermediate occupations to visit museums and other cultural institutions (2010: 180–1). Indeed, Bennett et al. argued that participation in public cultural activities was the most distinctive feature of both the professional-executive class and those members of the middle class in possession of university degrees (2010: 193). As they note, educational experience is a principal source of cultural capital, and the increasing need to obtain university degrees to acquire middle-class jobs has resulted in increasing cultural engagement in middle-class behaviour, which in turn becomes a tool in social positioning; as they state "culture matters to the middle classes" (2010: 194). Additionally, while class can be significant in the negotiation and mobilisation of cultural capital, particulars of its expression will also be influenced by ethnic identity (Banks 2017).

Engagement with museums and heritage sites is a performative statement of taste and class positioning and social privilege and is reflected in the well-educated profile of visitors to national sites and museums. It is also, as the second interlinked argument about the nature of museum visiting attests, not only about legitimising the social identity of the museum visitor but also about socialising and regulating the conduct of visitors (Bennett 1995). Drawing on Foucauldian ideas of governmentality, Bennett (1995) has argued that national museums engage in the management and regulation of social behaviour and concepts of citizenship. More recently, drawing on 'assemblage theory', he has stressed the role that museums play, not as self-contained 'knowledge/power apparatuses' but as part of regulatory assemblages that help intervene in and govern particular social problems (Bennett 2015: 16). Calls for museums to engage in social debates (e.g. Sandell and Nightingale 2012; Kidd et al. 2016; Janes and Sandell 2019, among others) speak directly to the regulatory role of museums.

The idea that museums play a part in the regulation of identity, social problems and, as Autry (2017: 190) argues, the construction of a "consensual version of the past as a shared past" also underpins the educational function of the museum. This stress on learning in museum and heritage debates (Chapters 3 and 8) links directly to the regulatory role of museums in the management of ideas, expressions of citizenship and collective identity and is linked to the idea of the performance and acquisition of cultural taste. That is, the emphasis on education and more specifically, a discourse of learning speak to university-educated museum and heritage professionals and visitors as a continuation of both expressing and acquiring cultural capital. In this sense, learning may be less something that is done, and more of an expression or justification for displaying and acquiring cultural capital. Nonetheless, the point here, however, is that the performance of reinforcement may be understood as an expression of both the regulatory role of museums and their role in the negotiation of cultural capital and social identity. These roles of both museums and heritage sites are often unacknowledged within professional practice. This is in part because they are so much understood as what is done and in part because this is uncomfortable to admit within the progressive turn of museological practice, as represented by new museology. The learning discourse is one that obfuscates these roles but is nonetheless part of the continuation of both the practices of museum professionals and visitors. It is also worth noting, and as becomes clear in the following, reinforcement is not learning, not only is it not learning in terms of the definition of learning used in museum and heritage studies (Chapter 3), but it is specifically about reinforcing a position of belief and emotional commitment to particular understandings that legitimate collective and individual identity. It is this emotional work and re/commitment that makes this performance powerful. The affective practices of this performance also work to make the first version of this performance commonplace and banal (Billig 1995), while making the second version more individual in expression and personally affirming.

The dominant profile of both museum visitors as white, well-educated and employed in professional, managerial, intermediate and own account occupations (Chapter 5) supports the idea that the performance of reinforcement has consequences for the regulatory role of heritage and negotiations over cultural capital. What is important here, however, is the extent to which various studies have reported that the dominant audience profile of visitors to national museums finds museums to be highly trustworthy institutions (Rosenzweig and Thelan 1998; Aston and Hamilton 2010; Cameron 2006, 2007; Conrad et al. 2013). This trust, it is argued, centres on the idea that museums provide reliable and authoritative information about history and culture. It may also relate to the idea that museums are characterised as 'safe places' (Gurian 1995, quoted in Cameron 2005: 214). The phrase that museums are 'safe places for unsafe ideas' is a well-worn one in museological practice (Coles 2016: 39), though Gurian herself, who the comment is attributed to, sees the sentiment, given the current political situation in the United States, as far more complex than she first thought (Anderson and Gurian 2018). This sense of trustworthiness and safety aligned to the dominant visitor profile is noteworthy and suggests that this confluence may not be as benign as may be assumed. Indeed, ideas of safety may speak less to the notion that museums are safe places to explore unsafe or radical ideas and more to the fact that they are safe and comfortable places for certain types of visitors, as this visitor to Harewood House attests:

> I feel safe here with the kids, as the same sort of people visit here – there is no danger – it's relaxing.
>
> *(CH58, female, 30–39, lunchtime supervisor, British)*

As argued about the English country houses (Smith 2006: 153), seeing people like yourself, from the same class and ethnic background, at the sites you were visiting was often discussed in terms of feeling 'safe' and comfortable. The idea that museums are 'safe' is highly problematic and works to facilitate the reinforcing performances, as this sense of safety and comfort will be defended by visitors. When a visitor's sense of safety is challenged – that is, when the reinforcing performance is confronted – visitors can and do engage in an array of emotional and discursive strategies to maintain a sense of emotional safety and the reinforcement of their entrance narratives. Additionally, the idea of museums as safe places also misunderstands that museums and other forms of authorised heritage sites are not 'safe' places for certain types of visitors, particularly for those who do not fit the dominant visitor profile – a point Gurian elaborates on in her interview with Anderson (2018).

Having argued, however, that the performance of reinforcement may be understood in terms of the arguments about museum governmentality and cultural capital, that it is overall a performance of social and political privilege, it is also important to note that there are nuances and variations in this performance as well and that it is not always politically or socially negative in its consequences. This point can be emphasised by drawing out the affirmative version of this performance.

Performing reinforcement

At *The Star-Spangled Banner*, NMAH, I interviewed a mother and her adult daughter who were deeply engaged in the exhibition. So engaged were they that when I asked how the exhibition made them feel, the daughter burst into audible sobs, while her mother, intervening for her daughter, stated: "Well I will answer for her. Very emotional, and actually for myself too, it's emotional". When I got to the question about what meaning the exhibition had for contemporary America, the daughter responded, tearing up as she did so, "I think so. I think it creates a link to the reason we became a country" (F30 18–24, student, Caucasian American). By the time she had finished this sentence, she had become so affected, she had excused herself sobbing, and disappeared to collect herself. Her mother was more collected in her responses to my questions and noted that the exhibition meant "history to me, and American pride", when asked if her views had been changed she stated it:

> Just supports my strength for our country even more. The patriotism.
> *(F31: 5–54, teacher, Caucasian American)*

A short time later, I happened to interview the father of the highly affected young woman, who had separated from his family to go through the exhibition at his own pace. In response to the question on the contemporary meaning of the exhibition, the question that had so overcome his daughter, he stated:

> Um, my 21-year old daughter is bawling like a baby right now because she went through that exhibition, yes. So yes, it does have meaning. You've got to force people to remember.
> *(F32: male, 45–54, self-employed, Euro-Caucasian American)*

This was a very affective exhibition for Americans – a point picked up by an Australian visitor who had come to the exhibition to "To try and find out what makes Americans tick", concluding, as she noted the extent of the affect the flag had on the Americans around her, "It's still a puzzling race of people" (F40: female, over 65, auditor, Australian). For the American family, visiting the Star-Spangled Banner was a performance of reinforcement; what was reinforced was their emotional commitment to their identities as Americans and their sense of patriotism – as the mother noted, this was what was being strengthened by their visit.

In talking about the mother and daughter at a conference presentation, I was approached by an American member of the audience, concerned that I had not understood how affecting seeing the original Star-Spangled Banner was and that I was somehow dismissive of their emotions. My point is not that this emotional response is 'wrong'[3], but rather that both the intensity of the patriotic emotion of the daughter and the more mildly expressed patriotism of the parents were both doing the same work of reinforcing national identity and patriotism. The second point is that the 'hot' or intensely embodied affective experience of the daughter does not, of necessity, lead to critical reflection. Indeed, every American I interviewed at that exhibition expressed patriotic feelings in varying intensities, and it seems that the feeling rules (Hochschild 1979), or affective repertoires (Wetherell 2012) within both American society and the exhibition itself compel and legitimise such affective responses. The affective repertoires or feeling rules for this exhibition were established not only by the interpretive content and display of this very large flag strikingly displayed in dimmed lights (for conservation reasons – but this nonetheless contributes to a sombre atmosphere) behind a large sloping glass case that visitors file past – but also by how the visitors are responding to the exhibition and, importantly, to each other. Visitors commonly commented during interviews about the behaviour of other visitors noting with approval or otherwise people's behaviour in exhibitions.

They also regularly commented about the importance of an exhibition to other groups in society, commonly lamenting that people who do not come to certain exhibitions or sites was evidence that other groups do not see the importance of the values and narratives the site represents. This concern was encapsulated in the 'it doesn't but it should' lament coded in response to the question about the contemporary meaning of sites and is evident in the father's "You've got to force people to remember". Many visitors at this exhibition were concerned that what they saw as American values or heritage was being lost and that more people should visit this exhibition to remember, as F86 asserted, "what America stands for" (female, 55–64, housewife, American). The father's concerns that others too should remember what he found important were shared by other visitors when discussing the contemporary meaning of the exhibition, for example:

> People have lost the sense of our own heritage and history, and I wish more people would take the time to come and see and explore.
>
> *(F9: male, 35–44, attorney, American)*

> I think it does. A lot of people don't get to see stuff like this, or they don't *know* about this, and they're not educated about it. But when you see this, it makes you, like, more interested in your culture and be proud to be American, and a lot of people, if you don't see this, you just don't care. But if you see this, it's really nice.
>
> *(F23: female, under 17, student, American)*

> Yes. I think that it's very important for modern-day Americans to understand. I wish everybody took civics, and I wish they took it again as adults. [. . .] I wish that people could walk through this and see why it's so important that we have what we have.
>
> *(F56: female, 25–34, writer, White American)*

The expression of the desire for others to come and visit the exhibitions a visitor finds important is a tacit acknowledgement that the affective practice of visiting is an embodiment of the values and narratives the site visited is held to have. It is a performance of reinforcing what is considered important, "it's really nice" as F23 states – it is comforting – to see people like yourself performing and emotionally investing in the values you cherish. The performances of reinforcement may be individually performed, but they are also a collective performance. Visiting particular sites reinforces your commitment to particular values and narratives, not simply because you individually have gone to a museum or heritage site that represents those values to you but because you have also perceived other people doing the same thing. Of course, not everyone may be taking away the same meaning as yourself, but the power of seeing others 'like yourself' at the sites you also value reinforces the legitimacy of one's commitment to those values. As work by Coghlan (2017) demonstrates, visitors can be engaged in what she calls 'imagined conversations' with other visitors, a sense that they are not only sharing a mutual experience but that they are in 'communication' with each other as they tour an exhibit about what it means and the values it represents. This facilitates the maintenance of an 'imagined community' of national and social affiliations (Anderson 1991), as expressed by these visitors to James Madison's Montpellier; the International Slavery Museum, Liverpool; and the Tenement Museum, respectively:

> Being here means again, it strengthens, I think, who we are, who I am as an individual, and being an American citizen.
>
> *(JMM106: male, 45–54, case management supervisor, American)*

> Well, it just reinforces our view of the world, being aware that more people are knowing about what we already knew.
>
> *(ISM262: male, 16–24, student, Spanish)*

> I think it's an important reminder to modern-day America or modern-day folks to be aware of the past, and the difficulties, realities, trials, and I think

it's an important place, an educational institution to support people's understanding of being a good citizen, I think.

(TM38: male, 55–64, college professor, Irish Canadian)

What 'America stood for' at *The Star-Spangled Banner* exhibition, what was hoped would be remembered, was for many an ill-defined sense of 'freedom', as illustrated by these responses:

Probably just freedom.

(F36: female, 35–44, nurse, Caucasian American)

The price of freedom isn't free.

(F45: male, 35–44, professional, Caucasian American)

You know, it's, like, we're Americans, we're proud of being Americans, we have freedom, and the flag represents our freedom.

(F58: female, 55–64, teacher, White American)

These responses are platitudes, thought-terminating clichés. The performance of reinforcement is, on the whole, not a critical one; it is one that elicits emotional wellbeing, a comforting confirmation that your views are 'right' and legitimate, and this is perhaps most prevalent when national identity is reinforced. It needs to be stressed, however, that although I have drawn on a particular exhibition, reinforcement of nationalism or patriotism was neither the preserve of *The Star-Spangled Banner* exhibition or American visitors. Reinforcing performances of nationalism occurred at all other national sites; for example, ideas of 'freedom' were also expressed at presidential houses and *The Price of Freedom* exhibition. At Ellis Island the enduring myth that the United States "was a real melting pot, it still is" (EI17: male, 55–64, marketing director, American) was being reinforced for many visitors. At the halls of fame, Australian and American national narratives of frontier values of hard work and tenacity were reinforced, while at English house museums a national affection for the aristocracy was rehearsed. As the following examples from, respectively, the Stockman's Hall of Fame and Nostel Priory in England, illustrate, in this reinforcement, there is an underlying sense of quiet, if not banal, reassurance and comfort being invoked:

Each time we come to a place like this, it just reinforces what I've seen and just makes me feel good to be an Australian. [. . .] I don't think I'll take anything new um [away] . . . at all, but it's [my knowledge and views have] been reinforced. Reinforcement is really what I take away.

(LR9: male, 55–64, manager, Australian 2010)

How unique and special history is – of great houses and gardens – reinforces the unique English history.

(CH191: female, over 60, retired bank manager, English, 2004)

This sense of comfort visitors felt at sites was very pronounced at English country houses, as I have previously argued (Smith 2006: 140–142); however, visitors outside of this context talked, again unprompted, about how certain sites made them feel comforted. For example, this visitor to the Stockman's Hall of Fame, in response to the question about how the site made her feel, responded, "Comfortable I would say" (LR89: female, over 65, retired farmer, Australian). When asked if she could explain, she stumbled a bit, noted this was not her first visit to the site and she and her husband referenced the large and iconic statue of a stockman that stands outside of the museum (Figure 9.1), as LR89 went on to state "I guess we could say a sense of pride or a sense of belonging perhaps, maybe." Both she and her husband were retired farmers, and the history of stockmen may have been close to their sense of personal history, but their sense of comfort spoke to the reassuring narratives of the nation. Other visitors reinforced this point at other sites:

> Proud, comfortable, included within society.
> *(F75: male, 55–64, architect, American)*

> Oh, it's comforting. It's a nice area. I could probably envision living here [The Hermitage] in those days.
> *(H3: male, 45–54, retired military, American)*

FIGURE 9.1 Bronze statue of a stockman, titled 'The Ringer', with saddle over shoulder and bridle in hand outside of the Stockman's Hall of Fame, Longreach, Queensland.

> Only my identity as an Australian. So generally, it's pretty iconic as a place for Australia because an Australian – and the colours are very Australian; they feel very comfortable and . . . yeah.
>
> *(U6: female, 35–44, manager communication centre, Australian)*

The repetition of visiting places, as LR89 noted, adds to the sense of comfort, but repeatable acts of visiting also add to the maintenance and power of Wertsch's (2007) concept of national narrative templates – templates that, as he argues, tend to be ideologically conservative. The repetitive practice of visiting also rehearses various affective states: in the cases above, the comfortable and comforting sense of national belonging and the social and political values perceived to underlie this. The comforting rehearsing of national narratives is both an expression of and a reinforcement of conservative nationalising ideology. As Jost (2006) argues, ideology influences what a person cares about and how they are affected. Moreover, the comforting affective practices underlying the reinforcement of national identity is linked not only to the tendencies for those with conservative ideologies to simplify, be selective in the information they process and to rely on intuition (Jost and Krochick 2014) but also to their affective repertoires based on fear of change and ambiguity (Jost et al. 2003: 351). This is a performance wherein particular forms of social privilege and experiences are not only legitimised through the repetition of museum visiting but also through the repetition of experiencing specific affective states of being – in this case, comfort and safety. The repetition of these affective states renders these emotions 'banal' in Billig's (1995) meaning of the term – that is, as to be so commonly reproduced and experienced as to become unremarkable – and thus work to in a stealthy way reinforce an emotional validation of the narratives and beliefs and meanings given to both past and present social experiences to which they may be linked. While Billig's analysis was specifically undertaken in terms of nationalism, and while the national in the cases previously mentioned is what is being referenced, the banality of particular emotions and practices of remembering can also work to reinforce and legitimise other narratives and forms of identity-making.

The repetitive acts of visiting, particularly at sites of national heritage-making, have a further consequence for understanding the relative passive performance of reinforcement. The social privilege that is comfortably rehearsed is facilitated by the repetition of visitors seeing people like themselves both visiting and within museological and other heritage displays. As Reni Eddo-Lodge (2018: xvii) points out, "In culture particularly, the positive affirmations of whiteness are so widespread that the average white person doesn't even notice them. Instead, these affirmations are placidly consumed". Underpinning the repetitive and passive acts of reinforcement at national museums is the presumption "that to be white is universal" (Eddo-Lodge 2018: xvii).

The performances of reinforcement discussed earlier were often deeply affecting to the visitors expressing them. Additionally, the examples chosen so far have had a 'knowing' sense about what they were doing. The sense of wellbeing and national celebration that underpinned and were a result of the performances discussed so far cannot be understated. However, the reinforcement of views, knowledge and feelings occurred in response to less intensive affective engagements with exhibitions and sites. Visitors often talked about how sites 'reinforced' what they had already known, for example:

> No, I think it's really reinforced views that I've held for a long time.
> *(NMM13: male, 45–54, nurse, White British)*

> No, not really [changed], my knowledge and experiences were relatively similar to this before that so I think it's just reinforced my ideas on it already.
> *(NMA33: male, 25–34, teacher, Anglo-Saxon Australian)*

> I would say no [change]. We're pretty educated already about American history, I would say. So it was more of a reinforcement, I think, for us, is what I would call it.
> *(F89: female, 18–24, student, Caucasian American)*

> How does it make [me feel?] [pause] I mean we have visited several houses before, so this is why we – it is just as a comparison. It's finding what we knew before, confirmation.
> *(BC14: male, 35–44, journalist, German)*

The confirmation of knowledge, identity or belief was often a casual statement made by visitors, taken for granted that that was what they were doing. BC14, visiting a stately home in England, noted the simple repetition of visiting house museums was about confirming what was previously known. This quiet or matter-of-fact sense of reinforcement is particularly prevalent at house museums and its nature and consequence are discussed in more detail in the following chapter, but it is also something that was often done quietly in passing at most sites. For example, at the Australian War Memorial and *The Price of Freedom* exhibition in the United States, 'pride' was a dominant theme in visitor's interviews. However, this was often expressed in terms of 'of course', this is what is felt; the feeling rules in this context required this and was presented in the relatively flat and mundane emotional repertoire, identified in Chapter 6, that was associated with this genre. Examples of matter-of-fact pride expressed either in response to the question about changed views or how the exhibition made people feel include:

> No [views not changed], I'm still a very proud Aussie.
> *(AWM007: female, 35–44, home duties, Australian)*

> Just proud to be an Australian.
> *(AWM050: female, over 65, retired teacher, Australian)*

> It makes you very proud to be an American.
> *(W8: male, 35–44, director of operations, nuclear power plant, Caucasian American)*

The affective state of visiting both of these sites reinforced how conflicts are understood as part of both country's narrative template of nation-building and identity. While the emotional repertoire of this genre was relatively flat and limited, there are two points to be stressed here. The first is that most performances of reinforcement are quite routine, matter-of-fact and unremarked. Second, in most cases, the performance of reinforcement was undertaken within the feeling rules and emotional repertoires associated with a particular site. Whether it was the more febrile emotions engendered by *The Star-Spangled Banner* exhibition or, the more sombre emotions of the war commemoration exhibitions, the associated emotions become repetitive in the specific contexts of the exhibitions or sites at which they were experienced, underpinning the taken-for-granted and banal nature of this performance.

Reinforcement could also be quietly maintained even in the face of curatorial attempts to destabilise that performance. Chapter 13 discusses in more detail visitor tactics and strategies for neutralising curatorial interventions and feelings of discomfort as they work to re-assert a celebratory reinforcing performance. However, it is important to note here, as it helps illustrate what this performance does for visitors and how strong it is. For the first example, let us return to LR89, the retired farmer at the Stockman's Hall of Fame that found the site so comforting, as it engendered both pride and a sense of national belonging. At this site, staff had added some questions at the end of the interview schedule, asking people to comment on the material on Aboriginal history that had been added in the redevelopment of the exhibition, and to get their views about whether or not the hall should increase that content. LR89 stated "Oh, it was very interesting what we did see but . . . some things are very hard to see", implying that those sections of the exhibition were in poorly lit areas. It should be noted that this material was interspaced within the exhibition and no more physically hard to see than other aspects of the history on display. While she claimed to be 'interested', she was not interested in 'seeing' this material, as to really 'see' this contested history of exploitation and dispossession would require a challenge to her sense of pride and belonging. The mythology of the heroic 'stockman' tends to work to suppress acknowledgment of frontier conflict (Menzies 2019: 213–214), facilitating the visitor selectively 'seeing' and processing.

A second example comes from an exhibition on the British slave trade held in 2007 at the National Maritime Museum, Greenwich. In this instance, the visitor had earlier in the interview expressed unease with the exhibition, with what he defines as "its too one-sided point of view", noting he had wandered into the exhibition because "I just thought it was an art gallery". While he noted he liked seeing "the objects" and getting a sense of "the suffering that obviously happened", he went on to state that the exhibition needed both "more emphasis on the suffering and how much it meant to the African people to be ripped from their native country" and "the significance of the slave act being abolished" by the British. Thus, while confronted by the exhibition he wanted more emphasis on suffering to accentuate the heroics of the British in ending their trade; when asked how the exhibition made him feel, he first avoids the question, then, when the question is repeated he goes on to state:

> It just confirms a part of what I knew already really; I don't feel any empathy or anything like that, I still feel the same.
>
> (NMM89: male, 35–44, banker, Caucasian British)

The visitor, denied his expected comfortable reinforcement of British achievement and national celebration, negates any empathetic feelings towards the enslaved and insists what he knew previously has been reinforced. When asked about the meaning of the exhibition for modern Britain, he states "it's good to show people, young children as well, how this country was built, the importance of the sea, very important, as a sea-faring nation" and, thus, any potential discomfort is forgotten and the nationalising narrative of the Maritime Museum has been reinforced and left unchallenged by the exhibition on enslavement.

Similarly, a visitor to the Hermitage, President Jackson's plantation, when confronted by a temporary exhibition on the site's history and Jackson's involvement in enslavement, noted that they felt:

> Gratified, I guess. I noticed a lot of insinuations about him [Jackson] about the slavery weren't too good, but I think for that period of time I think he was probably an okay guy. I didn't think he was a bad guy. I think he had a hard life, you know, [...] early in life. I think he did well for himself.
>
> (H75: female, 55–65, civil service, White American)

While not acknowledging that she is reinforcing her views, it is what she is doing. She notes that the experience she most values is the enjoyment she got from looking at the house's architecture and the gardens. This enjoyment reinforced her entrance narrative of Jackson as a heroic founding father. She goes on to defend that narrative when pressed to discuss the exhibition on enslaved African Americans by the idea that Jackson "lived through a hard time in his life and that [slavery] was just part of their life".

While the performance of reinforcement is banal, and undertaken unremarked and almost unconsciously as a matter of course, it does not mean that visitors are not making choices. Choices were made in what to visit and not visit both in terms of the choice of which institution to visit and, once at a museum or site, what aspects of an exhibition may be 'seen' or ignored. Choices were also made in how visitors engage; sometimes cognitively the choices were not clear or fully realised, but an element of choice is important as reinforcement was not a mindless default setting, but something people chose to do. As one visitor to the Stockman's Hall of Fame truthfully noted in response to the question on changed views:

> I guess one looks for things that reinforce them [views].
>
> (LR148: female, 45–54, drafter, European Australian)

Performing affirmation

Another form of the reinforcement performance is 'affirmation'. Affirmation, of course, is what overall the performance of reinforcement is doing, whether it is an affirming of national identity, knowledge a visitor had of a topic or their social identity. However, a particular version of the performance of reinforcement is worth differentiating, as it is explicitly more self-conscious; personal and, importantly, linked to a critical reflection on both past and present. Those who identified as belonging to non-dominant ethnic identities or as having relatively low educational attainment were over-represented in this performance.

Further, the visitors engaged in this performance regularly went on to make critical assessments of contemporary politics and social justice issues. In these more explicit performances, what is affirmed is the political values held by the visitor. This can be closely linked to performances of recognition discussed in Chapter 12, performances that centre on the sense to which a visitor's identity and social and historical experiences 'matter'. Indeed these affirming performances of reinforcement are also often a prequel to performing certain types of recognition. Examples of affirmation from the National Civil Rights Museum include:

> It brings out some bad memories, but it also validates what kind of people we are to go through that and yet be who we are. So I find strength even from the struggle.
>
> *(NCRM58: male, 45–54, pastor, African American)*

> It reinforced, basically, what we went through during that time. I graduated from high school in '68, that was the year he [Dr King] got killed, so I went through shootings, we were having meetings, and so it just bring back, bring back a lot. You know, I was telling my husband a few minutes ago, you know, it *saddens* me to have seen, to have gone through it. It's just like you're reliving it again, you know?
>
> *(NCRM66: female, 55–64, social worker, African American)*

For the last speaker, as for other visitors at this exhibition, this affirmation was sometimes saddening, if not distressing, as they reflected on experiences they or their parents had lived through or as they acknowledged continuing discrimination and injustice; however, it was also, as NCRM58 asserts, validating. As NCRM58 went on to state being at the museum was "for me it's empowering" to affirm his memories and experiences in the civil rights movement and to remember what Dr King had accomplished. As many older African American visitors noted, the museum did not change their views, but rather provided an opportunity to remember and validate their memories of their experiences. Such affirmations were quite self-consciously personal and left space for critical reflections on the meaning of the past for the present. For example, NCRM15, noting that her views had not changed because she "pretty much lived through this", went on to reflect on the poverty she had seen while driving through Memphis and that poverty had been a concern of significance to Dr King; she goes on to reflect:

> I think Barack Obama is looking at that issue. The reason people call him a socialist is because – the distribution of wealth is so off-balance. There are just too many poor people in such a rich country. [...] the issue of poverty is still not addressed in this country, and it needs to be. There's just no way that people should be living the way that they're living, and have such small groups of people who have all the wealth, you know? I just think that, to answer your question [about the meaning of the museum] that we need to re-think the distribution of wealth in this country.
>
> (NCRM15: female, 55–64, teacher, African American)

Yet, another visitor who stated that their visit had been an "affirmation" noted that "it has been a very long struggle with a lot of work still to be done. Discrimination has taken new terms, and it's like evil is looking for a new place to turn" (NCRM32: female, 55–64, manager, Black American). While another visitor whose personal memories were affirmed observed:

> I still feel like I'm going through what they [were] going through. The fight still goes on, and there's still voting disparity. Disenfranchisement. There's still job discrimination. The pay divide is still, it is just as great as it used to be. We need to – the change still needs to come. It's going to come.
>
> (NCRM31: male, 45–54, retired military, African American)

Younger visitors to this museum could not draw directly on personal memories of the civil rights era as represented by the museum. Nevertheless, they drew on a range of other personal links – for example, confirmation of their own experiences of discrimination, communal or familial memories or "because I'm the future of that history that we made" (NCRM24). These personal connections led to deeper and personal reflections on the past and present:

> Yes. It means that I need to work harder and to teach my children more so they can do more to achieve the equality that was fought for.
>
> (NCRM24: female, 35–44, secretary, Black American)

> That there is an importance in community. No matter where you go if you have a strong community you can – you're able to have power to, you know, have your voice heard.
>
> (NCRM72: male, 18–24, student, Nigerian American)

> Be proud of what you are. Remember the past so you can get on with the future.
>
> (NCRM94: male, 18–24, college student, African American)

Not to give up as far as the struggle for equality, and really taking it to heart, and now the meaning of what really took place and that they had a lot of people who lost their lives. And it's almost in vain if nothing continues to change.

(NCRM43: male, 35–44, pastor, African American)

Another couple who found the museum highly affecting explicitly because they were visiting to remind themselves about racism in America noted their views on this topic had been affirmed, stating, "it's re-affirming but, you know, it's certainly invigorating too" (NCRM27: male, 25–34, advertising, White American). This affirmation was part of the reason he and his partner, who was too overcome to respond to many of the questions, had come to the museum as it represented an opportunity:

as a white American, it's important thinking about this stuff. I mean from the standpoint of how we contribute but also how we created the situation that led to – or how we created the situation, yeah. […] [it would be good to have a discussion, about] racial issues in America [but] you have a lot of people who are embarrassed to – in some sense – realise that they have had a role in creating the discrimination. So I – it's always – I think it would be great to sort of start that discussion.

(NCRM27: male, 25–34, advertising, White American)

While this latter couple were not, as many of the African American visitors to this site were doing, drawing on personal memories or shared experiences of discrimination, their visit was a self-conscious reinforcement of their personal politics. As the tears of NCRM28 in response to many of the questions revealed, and her simple response of "frustrated" to the question about how she felt indicated, this was neither a celebratory, banal or comforting experience (female, 25–34, education, White American). This is not to say that it was a bad experience; it was affirming, but the affirmative version of the performance of reinforcement was less about comfort than it was about resolve. As another Caucasian American visitor stated, the museum visit:

reminds me of the importance of standing up for what's right, even if it's not necessarily safe or comfortable.

(NCRM45: male, 45–54, park administrator, American)

While I have drawn on the National Civil Rights Museum, this affirming performance of reinforcement was not confined to this museum, although it occurred predominantly at sites of dissonant history. At sites of labour history, Indigenous culture and history, immigration history and the English exhibitions on the British slave trade, personal and familial memories alongside current experiences of discrimination were also actively affirmed or reinforced, which again led to both personal connections and critical reflections in the ways exemplified previously. To give one example of a couple from the museum of Industry and Labor, Youngstown, who were visiting to remember their fathers – hers had worked in the Youngstown steel mills, and his had been a coal miner in Pennsylvania – he notes that his views had not changed:

> No, [...] – being from a labour orientated family I know a lot of those histories of some of this stuff. Having been a union representative, and what have you [...]. It's a lot of history, and it's part of the growing up of the cultures of the area.
>
> *(IL5: male, over 65, retired auto industry, American)*

When asked if the museum spoke to any aspects of his identity, he embarked on a lengthy analysis of what organised labour had achieved for American society, which was made in the context of his visit having affirmed both "It's our livelihoods from our parents and our past generations" and "the diligence of people working to make a living, and the struggles they had to endure in order to survive".

Affirmation, however, was not always facilitated through personal or familial memories, or necessarily through personal experiences of injustice or discrimination; rather, personal links could also be actively made through a visitor's social and political values. At the Mashantucket Pequot Museum, for example, reinforcement of non-celebratory emotions and understanding again facilitated critical reflections:

> It just reinforces my inner feelings that for people to come to another land, escaping religious persecution there, and then to do what they did here is pretty arrogant because they don't understand another culture. It makes me ashamed.
>
> *(PM72: female, 55–64, real estate agent, Italian American)*

Here the visitor drew not on personal experiences of discrimination, but an empathetic connection made to the colonial histories of Indigenous disenfranchisement and her sense of morality.

How visitors used personal ideological positions and values to make personal and reflective links is illustrated by examples from the Museum of Australian Democracy at Eureka, a museum included in the labour history genre. The values used here to make connections, and which were thus affirmed, were associated with organised labour. The 1854 flag that flew over the Eureka Stockade and displayed, in much the same way as the Star-Spangled Banner (although smaller than the American flag, it too was displayed in a darkened room behind sloping glass), was a symbol of defiance by gold miners at the restrictive nineteenth-century government licencing system and has since become a contested symbol of both the union movement and the far-right in

Australia (Beggs-Sunter 2015). It too, like the Star-Spangled Banner, elicited strong affective responses, for example:

> when I first came in the presence of the flag, I was quite taken aback emotionally. [. . .] I didn't realise that the flag still existed, and having read the story and then turning round the corner and seeing the flag, I actually just felt I needed to sit here quietly for five minutes contemplating all that it represented.
> *(MADE26: male, 45–54, barrister, WASP Australian)*

In contemplating what the flag meant, he noted that his views had not changed but rather reinforced his political views:

> No, not really. I've always been a democrat. I've always been a democrat and someone who believes that oppression needs to be fought, in whatever way. And that comes through in my work. I don't necessarily always act for the downtrodden [as a barrister], but having everyone having the right to have their day in court, so to speak, is an important factor in what I do.

Another visitor who visited the museum because it was part of his history as a union member, dressed for the occasion as he had brought his hat, emblazoned with his union affiliation (CFMEU), *specifically* to wear to the exhibition. The performative nature of the visit reminding him of, and thus affirming, his commitment to:

> Remember the fight for workers' rights [. . .] and be strong in negotiation in the Enterprise Bargaining Agreements.[4]
> *(MADE28: male, 35–44, crane operator, Australian)*

This affirmation was contextualised by feelings of "pride [for the] conditions I am working in that have been fought for since the days of the Eureka Stockade, rostered days off, eight hour days and so on" and a critical assessment of what was still left to be achieved by organised labour.

It is important to note that while there is a strong tendency for affirming reinforcement to occur at sites of dissonant history, it is not inevitable that this will occur at such sites, as it is not necessarily only the site that is defining this response, but rather, how visitors are also using the sites. Further, it is not inevitable that progressive critical reflections will be an outcome of affirming performance. Two examples, drawn from the Tenement Museum, New York, illustrate quite conservative critical reflections on contemporary society made by visitors:

> Well, they weren't quitters, and they weren't looking for handouts, they were trying to make their own living and doing the best they could. They weren't waiting for somebody to bail them out.
> *(TM14: female, 55–64, elementary educator, American)*

> The importance of assimilation and there are still many groups [in America] that are not assimilated. We have still a long way to go to achieve assimilation. Museums like this are important facilities of assimilation [then talks negatively and at length about the Deferred Action for Childhood Arrivals [DACA] program that the Obama administration had announced a month earlier]. But integration is important, and museums like this show the importance of integration.
>
> *(TM63: male, over 65, IT, Irish American)*

While TM14 is making a negative reflection on people reliant on welfare, they note that while their views have not changed, they have no personal connections to the museum "because none of our families came from the big cities. [. . .] I can't relate to the [. . .] stories [told at the museum]". This example shows not only that dissonant sites do not lead inevitably to progressive reflections but also that personal connections may be important for progressive affirming, as opposed to the less personal and more conservative reinforcing performance of national identity. However, the second example is based on the museum's affirming of that visitor's father's history as an Irish American. TM63, having taken the museum's tour of the history of Irish workers in New York, states that "I sympathise with them [the Irish] and their plight". While his familial history of hardship has been affirmed, his critical reflection on contemporary social and political issues has politically conservative implications, not simply in terms of his critique of DACA, but the assimilationist position tends to deny the legitimacy of cultural and social diversity within a nation.

Conversely, national museums and sites do not inevitably result in the kind of depersonalised nationalising reinforcements discussed earlier in the chapter and are again influenced by how visitors choose to use them. One visitor to *The Price of Freedom* at the NMAH noted that his views had been reinforced and drew a personal and critical connection to the exhibition "as an American, and as a responsible and contentious American that we have used our culture and wars to impose our desires on to the rest of the world". He noted that his presence at the exhibition was an "ethnographical look at how war is portrayed in history, and [the way] it's written for a very specific audience", which he defined as "middle class suburban white folks". His analysis of the exhibition worked to affirm both his political values and his concerns that the "exhibition is very conservative, it portrays certain American values to a particular white middle-class audience", noting that he "understood why they [museum staff] do it, but it has cultural implications for all Americans", the visitor offered a critical and reflective scrutiny of American conflicts stating:

> That we need to be mindful that war is not just a construct that just sort of happens, that we're all responsible for the things that our governmental leaders put together. And that we need to be mindful of these political messages that we get through media, through government official channels.
>
> *(W20: male, 45–54, retired telecom worker, Asian American)*

Conclusion

There is an interrelationship between the genre of museums and other heritage sites and how an individual visitor uses those sites. National sites tended to be locations for a comforting performance of reinforcement, and dissonant sites promoted a more critical affirming performance. However, that interrelationship was not inevitable or entirely driven by curatorial and interpretive content but was also by the choices visitors made in the way they engaged with and used particular sites. These choices were, in turn, influenced by visitors' ideological positions and by the emotional repertoires associated with particular ideological positions and social experiences of privilege or disenfranchisement.

Further, the emotional repertoires of particular exhibitions and interpretations will in part reflect socially mandated feeling rules and in part will facilitate how curatorial and interpretive staff display or present objects and content, such as how the Star-Spangled Banner and the Eureka flag were presented. However, the emotional repertoires of exhibitions or heritage interpretations also require audience participation. Visitors individually and collectively worked to define and embody what were or were not, acceptable or useful affective experiences at particular sites. Indeed, visitors, as argued in Chapter 13, could work hard to maintain certain affective states that may have challenged or reversed curatorial or interpretive intent. Understanding the registers of engagement that underlie particular performances are thus integral for understanding the social consequences and the cultural and political 'work' that visiting museums and heritage sites does.

The two performances unpacked in this chapter, while not inevitably determined by visitor demographics, were nonetheless often informed by ethnic and class experiences. The visit is ultimately working to reinforce and affirm those experiences and their implications for the meaning of the past in and for the present. The first and more frequent performance of reinforcement was over-represented by the prevailing visitor demographic, those from well-educated and politically dominant ethnicities, and was often undertaken as a matter of course. Its primary consequence was to comfort and reassure the visitor and to reinforce their social and ethnic identities often in the context of a reinforced sense of national identity and the political and social values that underpin ideas of nationhood and citizenship. The performance reinforced prior knowledge and belief and was based on the embodiment of either febrile or calmer affective states; however, the emotions engendered were well rehearsed and so routine as to be banal to the individual expressing them. The banality of the emotions experienced in turn facilitates the emotional legitimacy of this performance and the memories, identities, narratives, values and knowledge that were reinforced. Indeed, there was an emotional *investment* in the narratives and values enacted by this performance. This, in turn, saw both a buttressing of and investment in the sense of comfort and security found in having narratives and values reinforced.

The implications and consequences of the reinforcing performance are not simply the maintenance of certain narratives, particularly nationalising or patriotic ones, but also the extent to which visitors who engaged in this performance felt included within society and the nation. This performance had a particular emotional strength and power that derived from the routine of its individual and collective practice and from the simple sense of comfort it gave. As is demonstrated in Chapter 13, this was a performance that was often strongly defended. This is because it is a performance of social, ethnic and political privilege and as such was often, although not exclusively, based within a conservative ideological emotional repertoire that worked to maintain or effect a state of indifference to the experiences of others who may be less socially privileged. It was also a precursor to and underlined the performance of misrecognition discussed in Chapter 13, as it is its role in the maintenance or encouragement of indifference that worked to ensure the continuation of misrecognition and lack of respect and regard given to people and groups to which the visitor did not belong. The relationship of this performance to indifference is developed further in the following chapter.

Affirmation, the second version of the performance of reinforcement, builds on historical and contemporary experiences of exclusion and disenfranchisement. Consequently, it was often more self-conscious in its practice and unafraid of confronting discomfort and dissonance; it primarily sought to have a visitor's social and political values affirmed in the context of community history rather than in the contexts of reinforcing national identities and narratives. The ability to make personal connections could be important in this performance; these connections were based on personal or collective communal memories, contemporary social experience, sincere, empathetic links and/or a sense of personal morality. It was a performance which, while not confined to those from non-dominant ethnic backgrounds or those without university degrees, was over-represented by visitors from these backgrounds – in particular, the former. Once again, visitors were emotionally investing in particular narratives and social and political values, and the individual and collective practices of visiting worked to legitimise these. Unlike the first performance of reinforcement, it tended to facilitate and underpin critical reflections on the past and the present, drawing out individual or collective implications of the past for the present and future. It was a performance that could have either progressive or conservative political implications, although the former was more frequently expressed at the dissonant heritage genres investigated in this study.

The performance of affirmation was one that also facilitated and underlay various performances of recognition that are unpacked in Chapter 12. It was also a performance that suggests that 'reinforcement' should not of necessity be seen as a negative outcome of visiting museums and heritage sites. If adult education or lifelong learning is a role or aim of curatorial and interpretive professional practices, and if it is accepted that reinforcement, as explicated in this chapter, is not 'learning' as defined within the frameworks of heritage and museological practices, then it might be perceived that reinforcement is antithetical to professional aims. The performance of affirmation fits within the progressive agendas of new museology, although it is a performance that once again cannot be entirely determined by professional practice, as visitor choice and personal connection is crucial to it.

Nonetheless, the performance is predicated on the existence of museums, exhibitions and heritage sites that provide the resources and spaces for such acts to occur. These performances in themselves reinforce the importance of those museums, exhibitions and heritage sites that seek to challenge and recognise heritage that sits outside the AHD and to acknowledge the historical and contemporary experiences of those from non-dominant positions in contemporary societies. The comforting version of reinforcement should not, however, be ignored. It is how museums, particularly national museums, are most frequently used by visitors. Understanding the emotions underlying and generated by this performance may provide insight into the ways it may be challenged or subverted, and thus, understanding how this performance is defended against curatorial challenges is the subject of Chapter 13.

Notes

1 LR118: female, 45–54, registered nurse, Australian.
2 This search was very approximate and conducted through a word search through Word documents. I had originally intended to use qualitative data management programs to do this form of search; however, the database of interviews was too large for these programs.
3 Canadians may, however, have a different position on this; the Star-Spangled Banner is associated with the war of 1812, the history of which is quite differently remembered in the two countries.
4 Enterprise bargaining is a negotiation between employers and employee bargaining representatives (usually a union) to agree on workplace conditions and relationships.

10
EMOTIONAL BANALITY AND HERITAGE-MAKING

The banality of grandiloquence revisited

In his 1938 novel, *The Code of the Woosters*, P. G. Wodehouse, described the *bien-être* of the country house: "The cup of tea on arrival at a country house is a thing which, as a rule, I particularly enjoy. I like the crackling logs, the shaded lights, the scent of buttered toast, the general atmosphere of leisured cosiness". The physical sense of being at a country house, stately home or presidential plantation is a forensic marker, as identified in Chapter 6, of the historic house visit. Visitors commonly discussed the importance of the physicality of simply being in place, more than they did for any other genre of site. The leisured cosiness of the visit, the languid procession through house and grounds, with or without a tour guide, engenders the comfort and security of the performance of reinforcement as outlined in the preceding chapter. This chapter unpacks what 'being at' a historic house means to many visitors and the specific memory and identity work that visitors do as they tour the sites. As a form of heritage 'The Big House' is iconic in many countries. In terms of the registers of engagement, the valence of the house museum visit is almost always positive. Indeed, the affective repertoires of this site are quite narrow, and the emotional tenor expressed at house museums tends to the banal, in the sense that it is well worn and familiar to those who are expressing it. The intensity is relatively passive to neutral, but it is heavily embodied in that being at the site means a lot – exactly what, however, was often difficult for the visitor to articulate. The meanings and narratives performed at house museums will tend to be highly conservative, although while some visitors did produce progressive/liberal readings of the house, overall the implications of the visit are the continual reconstruction and vindication of conservative historical and contemporary narratives.

Although these houses are used largely by visitors engaging in the performance of reinforcing both middle-class and national identity, house museum visits are worth analysing in detail because of how national insecurities and uncertainties are rendered 'safe' in this performance. This chapter argues that the specific sense of comfort and pride of the house museum performance of reinforcement defuses and offers redress to historical and contemporary social insecurities and facilitates the maintenance of emotional indifference to issues associated with social diversity. In house museums in England, it is insecurities linked to class; in Australia, it links to issues of the relative depth of time of Indigenous and non-Indigenous histories and the implications this has for sovereignty. In the United States, it is linked most specifically to the history and legacies of enslavement and its contemporary implications for the ethos of the American Dream and its notion of 'freedom'.

Unpacking the house museum version of the performance of reinforcement adds insight into what can be at stake for visitors when curatorial interventions jeopardise their sense of comfort and safety. While this chapter focuses on house museums, the broad arguments developed here about reinforcement are also relevant to other sites of national heritage-making. Additionally, understanding what can politically and emotionally be at stake is important for understanding and contextualising the performances of misrecognition and indifference, discussed in Chapter 13. This chapter draws in particular on interviews from Australia and the United States, drawing comparisons with previously published (Smith 2006: 115–161) analyses of the English country house performance and subsequent English interview material.

The house museum as a theatre of memory

As Raphael Samuel (1994) argues, museums and heritage sites are 'theatres of memory' in which the embodiment of being in place becomes focal to both public and private performances of remembering and forgetting. The physical and embodied sense of simply 'being' at a house is, as argued in Chapter 6, a marker of this genre and is linked routinely to a sense of 'having a nice day out'. On the registers of engagement, the house museum visit is largely passive, with little overt discussion by visitors about the memory or commemorative work that is being done by or during the visit. Nonetheless, the visit has a lot of meaning and significance to many visitors, even if that was often hard for many to articulate. It is also a visit that is highly repetitive; while house museums had, alongside sites from other national genres, relatively high frequencies of repeat visitors (36% of visitors), interviewees also regularly acknowledged that visiting this type of site was a routine leisure practice. For example:

> No [my views have not changed], I don't think so, we've visited quite a lot of houses, and you do get to know what to expect.
> *(BH53: female, over 65, secretary, English)*

> So they [houses] start, though all individual, you know, you start to gather a feeling . . . yeah, there's a similarity to them all.
> *(VH20: female, 55–64, unemployed, Australian)*

> H42: Well, and we also try to come to all the presidents' houses.
> H41: Yeah, we've been trying to hit the presidents' houses, and this was one of them.
> *Why the presidents' houses in particular?*
> H42: Because they're the president.
> (H41: female, over 65, retired teacher, White American; H42: male, over 65, volunteer, White American)

As BH53 acknowledges in stating "you do get to know what to expect", house museums are quite predictable in how they are presented, often with minimal written interpretation, visitors often touring through the gardens, house and outbuildings at their leisure or as part of a guided tour. Habitually, the servants' quarters or those of the enslaved and their workspaces will have been turned into offices and cafes or are otherwise not available for viewing, although the tendency to overlook such histories has started to change within this genre. At the two presidential plantations and the English country houses discussed in this chapter, the histories, respectively, of the enslaved and servants and estate workers were explicitly discussed and exhibited. Nonetheless, as VH20 notes, touring through houses engenders a sense of familiarity; you know what to expect. While visitors often noted that going to house museums was simply something that they enjoyed, many found it hard to explain the attraction. VH20, while knowing what to expect when visiting a house museum when asked what being there meant noted, "Well, that's an interesting question, yes, it must do because we chose to come here, and I think that I do enjoy that sense of connection to the past". As the following speaker also illustrates, although she does not quite know how she feels about visiting, visiting houses is nevertheless something that she does:

> I don't know [how I feel]. Because we've seen – we've been to Monticello, we've been to Mount Vernon, and we went [to] White Forest, Washington's birthplace, and this – I don't know, it's kind of neat to see part of history, how people lived. How things got done politically back in the time frame.
> *(H89: female, 45–54, legal secretary, American)*

The repetition of visiting such places, as argued in the preceding chapter, facilitates the performance of reinforcement, which further works to strengthen the sense of comfort obtained from that performance. As one visitor to an Australian house museum noted, this repetition of visiting means "I am now [part of the history of the house]. Because part of present history is the people who visit Lanyon, and I'm one of them. It becomes who you are" (LH2: female, 55–64, retired teacher, Australian). However, the comforting feature of the performance of reinforcement is enhanced further at house museums because of how the bucolic aesthetics of place works to engender a sense of comfort. For example:

> It's very peaceful here.
> *(JMM51: female, 55–64, speech pathologist, Caucasian American)*

> Um . . . it gives me a great sense of peace actually and a sense of history and a sense of almost timelessness in a way because it came from the past and yet it's still here, and it's still going.
> *(RH30: female, 58–64, academic, Australian)*

> I love the gardens and where they were buried. I thought that was, you know, a beautiful place and very quiet, and of course the house. I love the house.
> *(H63: female, 45–54, mammographic technician, American)*

> They had beautiful surroundings to live in. I mean, imagine waking up every morning and looking at that view even if you were a scullery maid.
> *(TN49: female, over 65, retired teacher, Anglo-English)*

House museums, like other genres of sites, were often used as places 'to take stock' and think about certain issues, as this visitor notes:

> Um, I think grateful, and I think um, kind of peaceful, I guess that's a weird word to use but just kind of getting away from the hustle and bustle of life and, kind of, just thinking about things that are important.
> *(JMM108: female, 25–34, executive assistant, Caucasian American)*

However, what the peaceful and bucolic space of the house museum provides in this context was, for the majority of visitors, a security rendering sense of belonging to the nation, as these examples attest:

> Being here means again, it strengthens, I think, who we are, who I am as an individual, and being an American citizen.
> *(JMM106: male, 45–54, case management supervisor, American)*

> We like England, [the house] it's true England through and through.
> *(TN32: male, over 65, retired engineer, English and Scottish)*

> Yes, yes, for contemporary Australia, it means we have to remember where it all began and what kind of people shaped us to what we are today.
> *(VH19: female, over 65, retired office worker, Australian)*

While house museums were often defined as representing national identity, the sentiments tended to be passively expressed, particularly in Australia and England, with little intensity or marked emotion, and were often given either as passing comments that took for granted that this is, of course, what the houses meant or as platitudes such as, "I think that you can't know where you're going unless you know where you've been, isn't that a cliché?" (VH8: male, 18–24, student, Anglo-Australian). Exceptions to this lack of intensity occurred at both American sites, where some visitors would momentarily tear up and express intensely felt patriotic sentiments towards Madison's role in developing the constitution and Bill of Rights or Jackson's contribution to the presidency and his status as a war hero. However, these moments of intensity were often fleeting and appeared entirely familiar to those experiencing them. The following sections unpack what is specifically remembered and forgotten in the house museum performance of reinforcement within England, Australia and the United States and how the comforting repetition of the house museum visit works to allay national insecurities and fears.

What's mine is not yours: class and the house-museum

In previous visitor research at English country house (Smith 2006: 115f), I argued that Mandler's (1997: 1) assessment that such houses represented "the quintessence of Englishness" was all too accurately reflected in the meaning of these houses to the majority of their visitors. The aristocratic country houses in England at which I previously examined visitor identity work were Harewood House, Nostell Priory, Waddesdon Manor, Audley End, Brodsworth Hall and Belsay Hall; subsequent work associated with exhibitions on servants' and estate workers' lives carried out at Brodsworth Hall, Temple Newsam, Burton Constable Hall and, in association with an exhibition on enslavement, at Harewood House (see Chapter 4). Based on the original research, I argued that the English country house performance engendered a sense of comfort and security not only about a visitor's sense of national identity but quite specifically in terms of knowing one's place in English society.

The visit was a well-established performance of social deference, with the visitor demonstrating that they knew they were 'visiting' the great house, and paying a form of envious homage to those who had the wealth and sensibilities to own such comforts and create the aesthetics of the house and the landscape in which it sat. This humbling sense of deference acknowledged and offered respect for the nation-building achievements that the aristocracy claim for themselves. Pride in what the English country house represented for national identity was often emphasised by peculiar visitor claims that other nations in Europe and North American did not have such magnificent houses and the traditions they represented (Smith 2006: 160). However, the reinforcement of national narratives and identity was not the only consequence of the visit. The visitor, in possessing the cultural capital to read and appreciate the bucolic aesthetics of place, was simultaneously asserting their English identity and their place within the nation and as a member of the English middle classes. Visiting country houses, as visitors commented "is a middle-class thing to do", and people felt a sense of comfort in seeing people like themselves at such properties (Smith 2006: 142). This was also a performance that visitors frequently nominated that they had enjoyed as children and continued the family tradition of visiting with their children, furthering the sense of middle-class identity and cultural capital they derived from the visit. Indeed the collective performance of visiting engendered a sense of 'community' among visitors, which together with the emotional authenticity of the sense of comfort and security provided during the visit rendered the class distinctions in England 'comfortable' and legitimate

(Smith 2006: 158). As one visitor so succinctly put it, the country house visit "gives us something to tip our hats to" (Smith 2006: 150). The emotional accuracy of the visit lent credence or authenticity to the collective remembering occurring at the houses and the politically conservative narratives about nation and class it both produced and reinforced.

In this section, I do not want to rehearse further how visits to English country houses constructed national and middle-class identities but instead look at the subsequent interview work undertaken in the context of exhibitions that attempted a more inclusive and dissonant acknowledgement of English history. While the overall English country house performance was one of comforting national identity, this does not mean that some visitors did not critique the absence of interpretive material on servants and the common inability to tour the servants quarters and other less aesthetically pleasing areas of the house museum (Smith 2006: 155). In drawing on the subsequent material, the aim is to reveal the depth of emotional commitment to the performance of heritage-making that at its heart is about the reinforcement of national and class identities. The depth of commitment is belied by the relatively passive register of engagement that underlies the house museum visit, as identified in Chapter 6. In examining the emotional investments made, what is at stake for visitors when attempts are made to challenge or subvert this performance is revealed.

The 'Work and Play' exhibitions at Brodsworth Hall and Temple Newsam were found on exhibition panels throughout the houses, while at Burton Constable Hall, a room was given over to the exhibition, which aimed to highlight the degree to which servants and estate workers underpinned the leisure or 'play' of the historical owners of these houses. At Harewood House the exhibition that detailed the history of the Lascelles/Harewood family's engagement in the slave trade, and the source of much of the funding for building and maintaining the estate, occurred in the first two rooms through which visitors had to traverse as they commenced their tour of the house. The degree to which many visitors failed to 'see' either the 'Work and Play' or the Slave Trade exhibitions is important, as the following visitors noted when asked if they had seen the exhibitions:

> I didn't notice it – I like the portraits [of the owners].
> *(TN75: male, 35–44, window cleaner, White British)*

> To be honest with you, I haven't even noticed it; I just look at the paintings.
> *(TN77: female, 35–44, civil servant, White British)*

> *Did you happen to see the 1807 displays in the house?*
> HH85: If it's all in the entrance hall, there's a bit in the library that brings your attention to the display, but we were more interested in the house rather than the 1807 exhibition, with it being our first visit we're paying more attention to that. I mean was it the Liverpool Museum that had an awful lot about the slave trade . . . but that was a big part of the actual museum, so you

pay more attention to it, where the 1807 exhibition is just a sidepiece to us visiting the house today.

What for you is Harewood House about?

HH86: Well, we've been going round some stately homes and we just like the gardens and we like the decorations.

(HH85: male, 45–54, manager, White British; HH86: female, 35–44, bank manager, White British)

As the last visitor indicates, an exhibition on enslavement is appropriate at the International Slavery Museum, Liverpool, but extraneous to the house performance. Another visitor offered a more blunt and angry assessment: "Irrelevant to this, completely irrelevant, completely irrelevant [to our visit], we haven't come to see this" (HH45: Female, 55–64, retired manager, White English). This failure to engage with material that attempted to subvert the comforting reinforcement of the visit was a relatively passive way of protecting the visitor's sense of certainty in the narratives of the nation they had come to reinforce. However, HH45's anger is a far more active rejection of interventions into the house visit. As she notes, she had come "for the house" which she found to be impressive and to be a "very beautiful house […] you can imagine someone living here". When pressed by the interviewer to consider the slavery exhibition, she tersely acknowledged that she had heard a recording in the exhibition "that the wealth was based on slavery, yes, slave trade"; when asked what she thought about that, she very angrily and loudly claimed, "we don't have a view really". Although she was pressed twice about the exhibition, the visitor's anger was largely about what she saw as the irrelevancy of this history, even knowing that the house was built on the proceeds of the slave trade, she could proclaim the irrelevancy of the information simply because it did not conform to her sense of not only what visiting a house is meant to mean but how emotionally it is meant to feel. The affective state that she wanted to be engendered was the feeling that it is a "nice, small house to go around", while Harewood House is anything but 'small' – the meaning implied here is that it is cosy and home-like.

The 'homey' qualities of house museums, even as homes for wealthy elites, were often commented on by visitors seeking to make a link to the history of the site, "I get a very good feeling here. It feels like a family home" (HH74: female, 55–64, manager, Australian), with the aristocratic owners of the houses often being referred to as 'the family' in place of terms that acknowledged their class and power – a practice that facilitated the cosy and comfortable feeling engendered by the visit (Smith 2006: 137; Palmer 2008). The idea that this is a 'family home', that makes visitors 'feel good', works to create a point of connection between visitors and the history of the great house. The family home is a mundane characterisation of the grandiose; however, it concurrently creates a point of connection between the history of the house and its owners to the visitor – everyone has a home – while gently and nonthreateningly emphasising the differentials of social positioning and power. Bringing servants and the enslaved into the family home, however, threatens that connection and thus the assurance given to a visitor's sense of place. This destabilisation is evident in the degree to which visitors sought to offer the idea that workers were 'well treated' at the house they were visiting. For example:

> I think the lives of these estate workers compares very fairly with everything we've seen before; they seemed to be better treated and better housed.
> *(BH12: female, 55–64, accountant, Anglo-Saxon British)*

> The people who lived here appear to have been quite good to their servants. The servant's quarters appear to be quite comfortable.
> *(BH68: female, over 65, bookkeeper, British)*

> Well, it's a great contrast [between owners and servants], and on the other hand, it gave them a living on the estate, they had security there, those who worked for a big house. But of course, there's a tremendous contrast between the house and the estate workers and their conditions. But they were fed and clothed and educated, and it was like a big community, wasn't it?
> *(BC3: female, 45–54, self-employed, British)*

> Well I thought it very interesting you know, below stairs, it must have been a fairly hot place to work, apart from that it seemed to me it was probably a fairly good working conditions, it seemed to be pretty or fairly well looked after.
> *(HH67: male, 25–34, teacher, White Irish Finish)*

The trope of the well-treated servant is pervasive in the house museum interviews and increases in frequency in response to the challenges to the performance of reinforcement. It works to negate any negativity brought about by recognising the privilege and power that the presence of servants in the 'family home' demands. Indeed, the class-based paternalism of the cosy community that BC3 constructs for herself works to negate the social and economic implications of her acknowledgement that there was a "great contrast". The last extract was given at Harewood House in response to a question simply asking the visitor if they had seen the exhibition on the slave trade; the speaker while not identifying if he has seen the exhibition or not immediately responds with how well looked after the servants were. Although the Lascelles/Harewood family were extensively involved in the British slave trade (Walvin 2005), enslaved Africans were not held at Harewood House. This leap to the well-looked-after servant disputes the negativity of acknowledging the history of involvement in the trade associated with the house; the implication is that because the servants were 'well looked after', the house's 'family' may be assumed to be benign in other areas of their business interests. This trope of the 'well-treated servant' occurs not only in the English interviews but also in the context of Australian house museums, while it is rendered as the 'well-treated slave' at the American house museums in this study. What this trope, however, specifically does is to render class distinctions, the great contrast that BC3 noted, less malignant and reassures visitors about the benevolence of their social positions as members of the middle class. As another visitor to Harewood House and its exhibition on the slave trade observed, [the message I take away is] "Only the fact that our beautiful houses were built off the back of slavery, which is a shame, but nevertheless we are here to enjoy them" (HH50: male, 55–64, train officer, White British). The enjoyment of visiting the bucolic and grandiose setting, and what it means to a visitor's sense of place, is unhampered by the discomfort of its history as the well-rehearsed pleasure engendered by the house visit is reasserted.

The house museum visit is, at its core, a performance about middle-class identity. While visitors frequently define such places as aides to national memory and identity, underpinning this reinforcing performance is the comforting security of the performativity of middle-class belonging and sense of social place. Although middle-class identity was often explicitly linked by English visitors to the activity of visiting house museums (see Smith 2006: 152), class was not explicitly raised in the interviews undertaken at house museums in Australia or the United States. Class is more readily discussed in England than either of the other two countries, who tend to adhere to myths of 'classless' societies or, as is particularly the case in the United States, the mythos that hard work will allow individuals to achieve social and economic progress (Thompson 1994; Zweig 2000; Samuel 2012). Visiting particular types of museums is about the negotiation of cultural capital and affirming the social and cultural confidence associated with the middle classes (Bennett et al. 2010). While the anxieties of class inequality were explicitly mediated at the English house museums even in the face of attempts to destabilise the historical narratives of the houses, reinforcing class identities also underlies the practice of house museum visiting in the United States and Australia. However, in the following two sections, I turn to an examination of how the house museum visit mediates other national anxieties, specifically around Indigenous challenges to sovereignty in Australia and American anxieties about the so-called paradox that lies at the heart of that nation's notions of 'freedom' and the history of enslavement.

Securing a sense of place and depth of time: alleviating colonial anxiety

Three Australian house museums were included in this study. Lanyon Homestead lies just outside of the southernmost end of the Canberra urban development; the 1850s homestead sits within a carefully managed formal garden, itself set within rolling acres of pastoral land that shields the house from views of the encroaching suburbs. The formal statement of significance defines the site as having a range of values to both Aboriginal and colonial histories. The house, however, at the time of the interviews was entirely interpreted in terms of its pastoral history, and visitors may tour the gardens, house and outbuildings at their leisure. However, like many such houses, much of the servants' quarters and workspaces have been turned into offices and cafes and are not available for viewing. Vaucluse House, a nineteenth-century mansion, once owned and developed by the explorer and politician William Wentworth, sits within extensive gardens in the Sydney suburb of Vaucluse and, as its website proclaims, it became "Australia's first official house museum" in 1915[1]; kitchens, where servants worked, are also open to visitors. Rouse Hill House and Farm, dating to 1819, was one of the early colonial farms granted to Sydney's early elites. Owned by six generations of the Rouse family, the house and land now sit within the western reaches of greater Sydney, and visitors can tour the house and farm outbuildings, including a restored schoolhouse.

As with the English house visitors, the overall register of engagement at these sites was relatively passive, with the majority of visitors seeing themselves as recreating or having a nice day out. A sense of banality was predominant, in which recreating visitors made well-worn passive and languid connections to the house and its history. These connections were predicated on defining the history of place as largely that of white settlers. For example:

> Early white Australian settlers, yeah, farmers.
> *(LH20: female, 35–44, lay minister, Anglo-Saxon Australian)*

> The settlers, pioneers, [...] People who established the farms in Australia.
> *(LH59: male, 55–64, engineer, Celtic Australian)*

> The Australians, the convicts, and the people that first discovered this country.
> *(VH35: male, 25–34, doctor, European Australian)*

Early Australian history is a history of Indigenous dislocation and disenfranchisement; the early land wars, particularly those around Sydney, have tended to be ignored within historical and contemporary consensus historical narratives (Clark 2018). The process of forgetting and historical denial, as Attwood (2017) argues, is a foundational part of national myth-making, and historical denial in Australia relates to insecurities over Australian sovereignty. Indigenous land was claimed by the British Crown, a departure from previous practices of purchasing land through treaty – an occurrence that left settlers "without a truly satisfactory way of legitimising their claim of possession" (Attwood 2017: 25). Acknowledging horrors around dispossession lends insecurity, doubt and ambiguity to Australian patriotic expressions of national identity – an issue that underpins the very public 'History Wars' in Australia over the interpretation of colonial history (Macintyre and Clark 2013). House museums and their cosy nomination as the history of white 'settlement' and, as VH35 nominates, "the people that first discovered" Australia are tacit renderings of a consensus reading of Australian history that excludes the horrors of colonial invasion of Indigenous Australia.

This cosy reading of Australian history, as represented by the house museum could, occasionally, be more critical:

> Well, this is a settled property, I mean there's very little about the Aboriginal, you know, antecedents in this area, so for me, it's more the white settlement

of this area, um, yeah um because it is a pastoral property obviously, so I think there's much obviously much more of a focus on that in this particular site.

(LH25: male, 35–44, defence analysis, Northern Indian Australian)

The houses in presenting or indeed being read by visitors as presenting an unambiguous account of early Australian history allowed celebratory connection to Australian identity:

Definitely, definitely, we're Australian born so [...]. Well yeah, that's right with an English background, you can relate to it.

(LH43: female, 45–54, law librarian, Maltese/English Australian)

LH44: Oh it's just wonderful, really it just, just shows what our pioneers...
LH45: It reaffirms where we are as Australian as what we've been and what we should be.
LH44: What we can achieve basically, from scratch.
(LH44: male, 55–64, painter and paper hanger, Australian & LH45: female, 45–54, retail, Australian)

The connections being made here were facilitated and expressed in terms of both pride and comfort. Concerning the latter, as with both English and American houses, this emotion facilitated a humbling connection to sense of place and was engendered by the aesthetics of place and setting, providing a sense of calm, comfort and renewal:

Just the beauty of it, nature, the trees, grass, and the wind, the lovely house and the stables, everything.

(LH2: female, 55–64, retired teacher, Australian)

Being here? Oh yes to me it's like a time out, it's a restorative thing, particularly after I've been shopping and all this sort of stuff, I come here, and it's like 'shhhhh' gives me a beautiful relaxed feeling for the rest of the day, so it goes beyond just the beautiful old house and the lovely tall trees and the fantastic coffee and all that sort of stuff [laughs].

(LH40: female, 55–64, technical writer, Australian)

The house is providing not only a historic sense of place, a connection to the past, but the restorative affective moments of pleasurable recreating engenders a sense of comfort that facilitates the legitimacy of the house as an Australian theatre of memory. The embodied experience of being in such comforting surroundings reinforces particular understandings and remembering of history and place as not only white/European but as also classless or at least allows a certain misrecognition of issues of class:

> The servants weren't that hard off; they had got freeboard. Especially single women. It was good for them to work here or places like this.
> *(LH56: male, over 65, retired public servant, Anglo-Celtic Australian)*

This is not to say that some visitors were not critical of this bucolic reading of the house and the humbling sense of place it generated; indeed some, but only a small proportion of visitors, used the house to reflect critically as this person is doing:

> It [heritage] [. . .] it's worthwhile recording, and again it's worthwhile recording with an *awareness* of what it cost everyone around to support these few people in a privileged lifestyle. You could go on to say that this is what *we* as Westerns have to face now, as affectively we've got half of Asia working like the servants in this house to *support* our luxurious lifestyles, and we should be aware of that it's quite a luxurious position we're in, and the only reason we're here is because a lot of people are working *very very* hard under difficult circumstances so we can live this life [laughs].
> *(LH40: female, 55–64, technical writer, Australian, visitor's emphasis)*

The overall languid emotional sense of relaxation of the house visit works to, as one visitor put it, 'restore' a particular sense of place and belonging. Underlying this performance, however, is tension or insecurity revealed through how some visitors were making connections to the houses. These were made in two ways but focused on issues of acculturation. The first was made by expatriate British or recent immigrants from the UK. These visitors nominated that visiting Australian houses were part of a tradition of visiting country houses that they had enjoyed back in their home country and were thus maintaining or remembering through their visit:

> Um, look for me, personally, I, um, visiting historic houses in the UK was something I did a lot, so it means an affiliation of um replicating what was sort of, what I would be doing at home.
> *(LH9: female, 25–34, online marketing manager, White British)*

> I'm quite interested in Australian history because we've only been living here a year, so, you know, we're just trying to find out a little bit more about the heritage and the people's journeys and how they came to settle, and obviously we are trying to settle here ourselves, yeah, it's quite interesting.
> *(VH1: female, 35–34, scientist, White British)*

As argued, the English country house visit is a performance of both British nationalism and a statement of belonging to the English middle-class. This performance of visiting, as these next two speakers illustrate, is being carried on to help the speakers acculturate themselves to where they now live:

> LH29: How would you put that I don't know I think it's just. . .
> LH30: I just feel as if I'm part of it because we live here now, this is part of us now, like is our heritage now because we live here, even though we come from England.
> LH29: And I love going to, and I love visiting things like this, because we brought up in England with it, been in Tassie [Tasmania] and seen all that, come here and seen this and I been to Adelaide and seen all those buildings too, and I just like churches as well if there's any.
> LH30: Yeah they've got to keep places like this open.
> LH29: Yeah they've got to otherwise if it all goes then there's nothing for people to visit and sit down and relax.
> (LH29: female, over 65, house cleaner and nanna, English, and LH30: female, 55–64, housewife, English)

The performance of visiting genteel historic houses was translated to the Australian context; however, for one expatriate British visitor, the meaning invoked was slightly different to that in England:

> Oh, I think everything is so much older, there is a real disconnect between the houses that you see there and the houses that you see here. So, um, here they are still very new and at home, they are so incredibly old, so they have a bit more of a 'wow' factor in the UK because they are really old and they still exist and whereas over here it is sort of about, you get a feeling about, a bright young future, you know, you feel like 'ah this is cool' and you know I think for Australia it's really about looking forward.
> *(LH9: female, 25–34, online marketing manager, White British)*

It is at this point that the insecurity underlying the Australian historic house performance is revealed. Australia is not as old as other countries, and more particularly Britain. As various visitors noted:

> Well, I think it's important for us to keep our heritage homes, and so there's history for ongoing generations because we don't have a very long history compared to Europe so. . .
> *(LH33: female, 55–64, unemployed, fifth generation Australian)*

> Australia doesn't have the really ancient history, well it does sort of in that way, but not the European sort of old history as the buildings don't go back that far, so I think it's really important to keep the ones that were built then.
> *(LH32: female, 55–64, retired business administrator, Caucasian Australian)*

This is as close to history as we get in this country, because, we don't have any um, you know cities or towns that are three and four hundred years you know, as in Europe or, or even places in Asia so. . .

(LH20: female, 35–44, lay minister, Anglo-Saxon Australian)

I think if you look at it now, I mean you can imagine that there's still a chance it will be here in 50 years' time or 100 years' time and I think that's important to say that there is some history in Australia and that, you know you've got to start preserving it now.

(RH14: male, 45–54, engineer, Australian)

The importance of preserving these houses becomes tied up with a sense of anxiety about the length of non-Indigenous history in Australia. Thus, the importance of the site as an aide to national memory is about reminding visitor's that there *is* an Australian European heritage. These houses as 'old' places lend legitimacy to a Europeanised sense of place. What this remembering does in terms of its forgetting of ethnic, class and cultural diversity in Australia is notable, but it is also specifically a forgetting or a historical denial of the land wars and other acts of forcible dispossession that are inextricably part of Australian colonial history. Australian house museums, as arenas for a comforting performance of reinforcement, passively and covertly reassure visitors that the Australian past and national identity is legitimate and unambiguous. Further, it is also unchanging, as one visitor to Rouse Hill notes, "Things are changing all the time, but I mean that [won't] always be if they leave it there" (RH13: male, 45–54, software engineer, Australian). The existence of these houses provides a RoE that addresses and is based on a conservative ideological emotional register that seeks security and eschews change and ambiguity.

The power of the house museum in Australia to engender security about national identity is illustrated further by the degree to which these sites were used by immigrants to the country to make connections to Australian national identity. British immigrants were singled out; however, immigrants from other backgrounds also used these sites, although they did so not with a sense of familiarity with visiting house museums as the British did, but because of the unambiguous vision of Australian identity they offer. As a visitor to Rouse Hill stated, visiting was "partly a civic duty of knowing what Australian roots are all about" (RH18: female, 45–54, business trainer, Filipina Australian). Notably, it was only at house museums and Ellis Island that I noted immigrants using sites to perform and affirm their adopted national identity – a testament to the nationalising narratives they represent. As one visitor to Vaucluse House, who identified as Anglo-Australian, excitedly observed:

I think it's a crucial part of our [history] . . . I was just walking in the door, and I saw two Asian tourists walking back, and I thought this is gold – a good absolute tourism experience to come here. That's exactly what I was thinking when I was walking in the door and saw them walking out. If I was [from] a foreign country and was coming to see this, I would be thinking that I'd nailed it.

(VH34: male, 35–44, real estate, Anglo-Australian)

232 Emotional heritage

There is pride in this statement that overseas tourists will have 'nailed' their understanding of Australia and its history, a history that for him "inspired [...] such ingenuity and creativity" to build the edifice that is Vaucluse House. This is a process of assimilation in which Australian experiences of ethnic and class diversity is neutralised alongside histories of dissonance and Indigenous presence. The performance of reinforcement ultimately nullifies the insecurities of sovereignty and nationhood that lie at the heart of Australian identity.

Freedom, liberty and indifference

The seventh US president, Andrew Jackson (1829–1937), purchased what became known as the Hermitage in 1804, living there until his death in 1845.[2] Jackson was committed to the institution of slavery (Cheathem 2011: 330) and, at the time of the interviews, an exhibition about those Jackson enslaved at the Hermitage and its cotton plantation was prominent in the interpretive centre through which visitors had to pass on the way to the house. Jackson was also responsible for the 'Trail of Tears', the forced dispossession and relocation of Indigenous Americans from the south-eastern United States to designated 'Indian Territory' west of the Mississippi River (Minges 2001; Sturgis 2007). The Hermitage is now within the metropolitan area of Nashville, Tennessee. James Madison's Montpellier, Virginia, the second American house museum included in the study, was the plantation house of the fourth president. Madison is considered to be the 'Father of the Constitution' and author of the Bill of Rights and was himself a slave owner.[3] At the time the interviews were collected, reconstructions of slave quarters located close to the house and ongoing archaeological excavations of their foundations, although not then part of the official tour, were on display.

As has been well documented, plantations as house museums have tended to disregard the historical presence of slavery (e.g. Butler 2001; Seaton 2001; Gable 2009; Bright et al. 2018), and the development of material on the enslaved at both sites appeared to be relatively new at the time of the survey. Visitors to house museums, like most national American museums, tend to be dominated by white, well-educated middle-class Americans (Black 2012; Levitt 2015) and, as Bright and Carter (2018: 25) argue, about plantation sites; this profile tends to be happy with the exclusion of the history of enslavement. Indeed, at the two American sites, overseas tourists accounted for only 2% of visitors, and those from non-dominant backgrounds 4% (of which one identified as African American and had visited while his wife was being interviewed for a job at the site). As was the case at the English and Australian house museums, most visitors interviewed at these sites were undertaking, through a relatively passive register of engagement, a performance of reinforcing a homogenised collective understanding of class, ethnic and national identity. For example:

> No, I think, it just reinforced my belief in the forefathers.
> *(JMM112: male, over 65, own business, American)*

That our country enjoys the freedom that it has today because of men like Andrew Jackson, and others who gave their lives so that we could.

(H45: female, over 65, own business, American)

I enjoy the freedoms that were created by the person who lived here, yes.

(JMM7: male, 45–54, teacher, Caucasian American)

The messages taken away or the meanings that these sites had as aides to national memory are summarised by one visitor at James Madison's Montpelier who stated that the message taken away was "Freedom, freedom, unity" while going on to observe that the meaning of the site lay in its ability to provide a "grounding, centring" sense of national identity (JMM10: female, 55–64, postal service, Caucasian American). In addition to the narratives of nationhood represented by references to 'freedom', the grandiose and bucolic nature of these house museums also invokes, as Bright and Carter (2018: 27) argue, the narrative underlying the novel and film *Gone with the Wind*, that the antebellum South "is a noble and honourable institution". Many visitors to the two sites, but at the Hermitage in particular, drew links to the sites through their 'southern heritage'.

While the register of engagement for these two sites was overall quite passive, many visitors demonstrated fleeting moments of deep emotion. Unlike the house museums in Australia and England, these sites did engender tears – with many visitors becoming momentarily teary-eyed when they talked about what they saw as the positive achievements of both presidents. While these moments could be intense, they were often momentary and reflected well-rehearsed and comfortable feelings of patriotism. Intertwined with the nationalising narratives of 'freedom' taken from both sites was a further intertwined narrative that links explicitly to the dominant underlying mythology of American identity, that of the American Dream. The underlying ethos of the dream is central to American national narratives and the idea that an individual's "station in life is earned rather than inherited" and is a foundational principle of the United States (Samuel 2012: 3). Interlinked with concepts of 'freedom' and the idea that citizens have the right to pursue happiness is the belief that through hard work, social mobility and opportunities for prosperity and achievement are all possible (Graham 2017). At these sites, a theme in visitor discussions about the meaning of the site was a celebration of the achievements of the presidents, and in particular, Jackson's 'humble origins':

Yeah. I think we have a lot to learn about work ethic from these people [Jackson], and I guess that would be it. It would be just the work ethic, that they really needed to work to survive. That there wasn't anybody enabling them to live. They had to do it themselves.

(H9: female, 55–64, university administrator, Caucasian American)

Oh absolutely. I certainly think that being aware and conscious of your history certainly gives you a context for appreciating where you are, and their responsibility for creating a future too because – obviously, President Jackson was an orphan and went on to do some pretty amazing things. Unfortunately, there were some other controversial things he did too, related to the Native Americans and slavery that we can't advocate at all. But, no, I think it's pretty neat. He started from nothing, as part of the Irish immigrants, so it's a pretty amazing story.

(H37: male, 35–44, sales, Caucasian American)

The celebration of the 'hard work' of the elites at these houses reinforced visitor's belief in both the dream and its underpinning position in American national identity and patriotism. Simultaneously, however, and counterintuitively to the ethos of the dream, this celebration also constructed a sense of humility and deference for the social elites represented by the houses. The ethic of hard work was something that was identified by visitors at all national museums in the United States and was often part of politically conservative readings of the museums of labour and immigration histories.[4] However, at these plantations, it takes on an explicit power to facilitate the exclusion of the hard work of the enslaved. H9, for instance, in discussing the ethic of hard work is referring to those in the Big House, her conclusion that there was no one there to enable the work of Jackson – that he had to do it himself – illustrates the power of the dream to frame the way the past is remembered and forgotten, and to exclude and include. On the other hand, H37 notes the controversies of Jackson's involvement in slavery and his dispossession of Indigenous Americans, but once acknowledged, this is forgotten as he transitions back to feeling comfortable about the 'amazing story' of the American Dream that he defines Jackson as representing.

The comforting idea of the dream and the motif of 'hard work' by the elites allowed some visitors to glide over challenges to their entrance narratives and their celebratory embodiment of being in place. However, other visitors, in addressing the hypocrisy, or what some refer to as the 'paradox', underlying the national narrative of 'freedom' and the history of slavery and its legacies were a little more active in maintaining their sense of comfort and security and, in this context, the nobility and patriotism of the performance of reinforcement. In maintaining their consensual understanding of a shared southern or national heritage, some visitors emotionally disconnected themselves from the enslaved, a response that also tended to reinforce ethnic paternalism and racist stereotypes:

> Well, I don't know that I really look at it [exhibition on slavery at the Hermitage]. I just read it just for information, but having grown up in the deep south, whose grandparents had – they didn't have slaves, they had sharecroppers on their property, I think to some degree slaves were treated better than history wants to say that they do. History tends to dwell on the bad part of slavery – not that there was anything good about it, but it gave many of these people a place to live, and a place to work and many of them were freed after the Civil War. So. . .

(H45: female, over 65, own business, American)

This response was given at the end of the interview. I had asked if they had noticed "the interpretive material on Enslaved African Americans" and having received an affirmative response, had asked her what she had thought of it. The response is telling; this resident of Mississippi had earlier told me that the history she was visiting was that of her grandparents and that the visit "makes me feel very proud of our country and our leaders". However, she stated that she did not know that she really looked at the exhibition on slavery, having read it for "information" only, referring to it in a 'non-emotional' cerebral register – it had not altered her affective practice of visiting. The response is also an example of what has been identified as covert racism (Coats 2008; Chin 2015); the racism is, however, clear and invokes the idea that enslaved Africans somehow 'benefited' from their captivity.

Others also referenced ethnic paternalism in ways similar to visitors in Australia and England who referenced class paternalism to cosily and unthreateningly assimilate the histories of class inequality into national narratives. The paternalism at these sites was expressed through the motif of 'the kind slave owner' and the cosy idea of 'community'. For example:

> It [slavery] was a part of their day to day existence, a big part, and I think that, you know, some of that stuff that you read, you know, a small community like this where people become family . . . you saw that even after the emancipation that a lot of them stayed, and this was their home, so yeah, I think it's an important part of the information here.
> *(H30: female, 35–44, construction manager, White American)*

> I thought it was well done and informative, personally. It kind of – it said right on they weren't exactly on the same level as far as living conditions and what have you, but at the same time they were still treasured members of the little community, I think.
> *(H31: male, 35–44, railroad manager, White American)*

> I thought it represented some fairly decent homes for the slaves and how they lived and how they treated them [. . .] I think it helps the folks that had to endure slavery come back and see what their forefathers had to endure and see how they were treated, and some people didn't treat them as bad as they thought.
> *(JMM112: male, over 65, own business, American)*

The cosy community motif works here, as it did at the Australian and English sites, to render the complexities of the past unthreatening to a visitor's sense of wellbeing derived from consensus and unambiguous national narratives and identity. Tensions over diversity and the histories of inequality and injustice and the legacies these have in and for the present are neutralised in the motif of the 'good' master of slave or servant, who is himself identified as 'hard-working', and in the motif of a benevolent 'community' that this underpins. Indeed one visitor at the Hermitage went so far as to project her sense of cosy safety onto the enslaved, noting how she liked the Jacksons' "sense of family and how hospitable they were to other people", observing about the enslaved, "I felt like they, you know, they felt like this was a safe place to be" (H36: female, 35–44, dental hygienist, Caucasian American).

The historical ambiguity of the so-called paradox of slavery and founding concepts of American freedom and the insecurities to a national sentiment that this represents was, for many visitors, not challenged or rendered 'understandable' to those visitors seeking reinforcement of national narratives. Jackson was known for having a violent temper (Belohlavke 2016), and examples of that temper in his treatment of the enslaved were identified in the exhibition, as one visitor noted, but went on to dismiss as "it was a bad time in our history, but there are a lot of reasons why it did occur. And Africans were enslaving their own people. It wasn't that white people just went over and grabbed a bunch. That's not the case at all" (H47: male, 55–64, oil field equipment sales, American). This visitor, although hesitantly acknowledging that slavery and Jackson's treatment of the enslaved was "not particularly. . . [good]", dismisses the information apparently learnt in the exhibition about Jackson's treatment of the enslaved and its destabilisation of his performance of reinforcement by, ultimately, blaming the victim, one of the tropes or self-sufficient arguments identified as part of the oeuvre of the language of racism (Wetherell and Potter 1992; Hill 2008; Augoustinos and Every 2010; Krishnamurthy 2013; Chapter 13).

In another example a visitor, while conceding the continuation of injustice in the United States through the information he has gained from the exhibition at the Hermitage, works to dismiss both the significance of this information and its ability to challenge his entrance narrative. He notes, "In some ways, Jackson appeared on the surface to be a fairly decent slave owner. Reading some of the information, he allowed them to grow their own crops [. . .] he was very protective of them as part of his family. Obviously he, if one of them acted up, he treated them harshly, as anyone would of any kind of property" (H82: male, 35–44, structural engineer, European American). This visitor then goes onto a lengthy discussion of the exhibition text on enslavement moving back and forth between noting that enslavement was not good, but there were benefits, observing as he does so, "I've worked for companies who thought they owned me [laughs]" engaging here in what is defined in Chapter 3, as shallow, insincere empathy. Shallow empathy works to dismiss the significance of the historical experiences of the enslaved and to validate their status as "property". He eventually acknowledges that the history of inequality is "part of American culture", but goes on to immediately claim "so the whole issue of slavery is still there [worldwide]. I mean in Africa they're still selling slaves, they're selling young ladies into slavery, prostitutional slavery, so it should be addressed, there's no doubt about it". Any concern about the legacies for American culture is deflected into a concern that contemporary forms of slavery are occurring in other regions of the world (he named both Europe and Africa); this then became his focus and prioritised as an issue for 'addressing'.

The reading here for H47 and H82 of the exhibition text, and others engaged in reinforcement, is not about the 'persuasive power' of historical evidence; it is about sustaining their emotional commitment to their sense of wellbeing about their place in contemporary society. The house museum performance of reinforcement legitimises and maintains privileged indifference to past injustices and their contemporary legacies. Certainly, as H47 and H82 illustrate, what is reinforced are racist stereotypes and paternalism, which appear to be more than 'indifferent', given the power they have to maintain contemporary inequalities. However, indifference is the counterpoint to the emotional register of the comfortable humility and national identity that is sustained by the performativity of 'being at' these house museums. Indifference facilitates a reading of the exhibition text that reinforces the idea of the 'kind slave owner' and alleviates historical complexity and uncertainty and any implications it may have for unsettling a visitor's entrance narrative. Being indifferent has considerable power; it facilitates the ability to ignore or dismiss that which threatens the social and political comfort of the performance of reinforcement.

The overall register of engagement at the presidential houses was passive, contributing to the majority of visitors performing reinforcement; however, as was the case in Australia and England, not all visitors were either engaged passively or were reinforcing. Other performances of heritage-making also occurred at these sites, including quite complicated acts of recognition (see in particular JMM85, quoted in Chapter 12). Visitors also used the house museums in the United States to remember the horrors of slavery, "and I don't want to hear that someone was kind to them. It doesn't work for me" (H69: female, 55–64, teacher, American). As H34, quoted in Chapter 3, reveals when he noted that you cannot "sugar coat" the past, some visitors engaged in quite significant and critical historicising of contemporary issues of racism and national identity. Others worked through "the hypocrisy of the Founding Fathers" while critically reflecting on "that huge gap of wealth that the institution of slavery created" (JMM86: female, 45–54, teacher, Hispanic American). Others used the sites to reflect on modern politics, particularly at James Madison's Montpellier where a few visitors reflected on contemporary issues associated with the constitution that was then in public debate. While for others, the visit "reinforce[d] [. . .] the teaching I received about American history was very slanted. It doesn't always present the whole picture as far as our influence on African Americans and how we treated the Indians" (H65: female, 55–65, teacher, American).

Conclusion

The practice of visiting particular types of heritage sites or museums is a performance of meaning-making in which the past is brought to bear not only in constructing contemporary personal and national identity but also in mediating and legitimising both a sense of place in society and aspirations for the future. Heritage performances, either individually or collectively, are explicitly about utilising the past to make sense of and address contemporary social and political issues or problems. The performativity of the house museum visit is based on modes of engagement whose affective consequences are feelings of comfort, safety and deferential humility that are generally quite neutral in intensity but which work together to reinforce conservative narrative templates of nationhood and national identity. This performance works to facilitate a sense of wellbeing both individually and collectively in visitors about their social position and place. In achieving this, issues of inequality on which the histories of The Big House ultimately must rest, and the specific inequalities between the elites and those whose land was stolen and those who worked to maintain these houses as either servant or slave – the 'great contrast' that one visitor identified – are occluded. To achieve wellbeing, empathy for historical experiences of inequality is either withheld or offered in shallow and insincere forms. In turn, this facilitates the restriction or withholding of sincere empathy and compassion to those in contemporary society who are the inheritors of the legacies of discrimination, prejudice and economic inequality.

Thus, the historical context for understanding contemporary class and racial inequalities and the ongoing implications of Indigenous loss of land in both Australia and the United States is rendered emotionally 'safe' through the construction of imagined 'cosy communities' of paternalism. The discursive tropes of 'the family home', 'the family', 'the good master' of the servant or enslaved underpin the sense of comfort and comforting history of the imagined community of The Big House across all three countries. In Australia, these tropes are also joined by a comforting sense of time-depth that helps locate and authorise non-Indigenous or 'settler' history. The similarities in the performance across the three nations demonstrate the power generated by the banality of the well-rehearsed and repetitive nature of the house museum visit and ultimately the power of this genre of heritage.

Part of the power of this performance also lies in the way it speaks to the emotional repertoires associated with conservative ideologies: in particular, fear of change and ambiguity. The performance, in generating an unambiguous national narrative, also provides the affective and narrative tropes of the 'community' of The Big House to keep at bay any challenges to or interventions into the narrative and to alleviate national insecurities. Autry (2017) argues that while museums construct collective and consensus narratives and memories, it is also their role to facilitate the way these narratives and memories may be shifted or reworked to form narratives that, while they may be again based on consensus, are nonetheless more inclusive and reflexive. The performance of reinforcement, and particularly that at house museums, reveals the curatorial challenges at facilitating any shifts within the national narrative template.

These challenges stem not only from the power of the performance derived by the banality of its repetition but also by both the well-worn or banal emotions it generates and the degree to which those emotions link to and reinforce conservative ideologies. The emotions generated by the visit are authentic both within the context of the visit and the ideological positions that frame that visit. This authenticity or the accuracy of these emotions lend further legitimacy to the acts of remembering that are undertaken by the embodiment of 'being at' the house museum. The sense of comfort and social wellbeing that is thus expressed works to belay national insecurities and requires the maintenance and reinforcement of indifference. Oppositional to sincere and deep expressions of empathy, indifference ensures that the social wellbeing of the visitor, reinforced and authorised by their engagement with certain forms of heritage, is maintained. What then is at stake for visitors in this performance of reinforcement is the need to maintain certainty and the social safety and comfort that certainty brings. Historical certainty provides, in these contexts, a comforting bedrock from which to understand and address contemporary social and political needs and issues. Ultimately, what is at stake is the maintenance of indifference.

Notes

1 Sydney Living Museums, Vaucluse House, https://sydneylivingmuseums.com.au/vaucluse-house. Accessed 17 July 2019.
2 Andrew Jackson's Hermitage, https://thehermitage.com/. Accessed 4 December 2019.
3 James Madison's Montpelier, The Life of James Madison, www.montpelier.org/learn/the-life-of-james-madison. Accessed 9 December 2019.
4 At labour sites, the narrative of 'hard work' would be used to negate the need for organised labour, as it was hard work that would ensure achievements and better pay. At immigration sites, the narrative of hard work was used to justify the status of the visitor or the visitor's ancestors as legitimate migrants while negating the legitimacy of contemporary migrants. For example, this visitor talked about the hard work of his grandmother and what she had achieved, noting, "My grandmother came when she was 16, alone, not with anybody else, and she was a cleaning lady in Tacoma, [there were] thousands of people that were willing to do something like that to make a better life for themselves. Where today nobody would even think of doing something like that" (NHM7: male, 55–64, pastor, Scandinavian American).

11
INTERGENERATIONAL COMMUNICATION AND CONNECTION

"My son married a Japanese woman, and they have just had twins!" was the reason a woman who identified as Jewish American gave for visiting *Common Ground: the Heart of Community*, a central permanent exhibition at the Japanese American National History Museum in Los Angeles. Visiting from out of state, she went on to explain that her son's maternal grandparents, her parents, had been interned in European concentration camps during World War II, while the grandparents of her daughter-in-law had themselves been interned in American concentration camps, the history of which was an important part of the exhibition she had come to see. She had chosen to visit to take time out to "think about what it would mean for the twins to have family on both sides who had experienced concentration camps" (JANM17: female, retired, over 65, Jewish American).

The assumption that museums and specifically ecomuseums, cultural keeping places or other forms of community museums, alongside community-focused heritage sites, are places that facilitate the transferal of intergenerational knowledge and memories is well established in the literature and professional practice. Indeed, such places are often defined as important for "raising youth awareness of and regard for [local] cultural heritage, with the aim to instil pride and knowledge in their past" (Song and Hayashi 2016: 161). In much of this literature, it is implicitly assumed that such transference will come from the stories the curatorial or interpretive staff will have constructed through the objects and stories told by the exhibitions and other forms of interpretive practices. As one docent at the Museum of Work and Culture, Woonsocket, Rhode Island, stated when discussing the messages he hoped visitors would take away, the museum "teaches what values those people [in the Woonsocket community] had, you know. What values they have and try to pass on to their children and to their grandchildren" (interview, 2012).

This chapter in mapping how visitors engage in intergenerational communication and connection reveals both the complexity and the multitude of ways visitors undertake this form of memory work. The idea of heritage as a communicative act has been developed by Bella Dicks (2000), and the concept of 'intergenerational communication' used here draws on the synergies between this idea and my wider thesis that heritage is a performative action of making meaning in and for the present. Communication is not, as Dicks (2000: 219) has argued, a simple linear equation with visitors being "on the receiving end of messages emanating from within the exhibition"; neither, however, is it necessarily a process reducible to visitor "interaction with the texts" or objects. As Dicks (2000) has argued, visitor constructions of self/other, their biographical, social or cultural relations and their memories and experiences influence how different individuals undertake communicative and performative practices. As this chapter illustrates, museums and other sites of heritage become localities that while facilitating practices of remembering and commemoration do not necessarily determine the scope or meaning of those practices. The new grandmother was entirely knowledgeable about and understood the history of Japanese American internment in the United States before her visit; her mission to the museum was not to further her learning about this. Rather, the act of visiting allowed her to take the time and space to engage in an embodied performance of remembering, which helped her mediate familial identity in response to the arrival of a new generation.

Mapping the terrain

How visitors engaged in inter- or cross-generational interactions and communication and the connections that were then made were very diverse. Museums and heritage sites themselves actively engage in this process through various school education programs, and while there were parents or grandparents in this study who identified that they had taken children with them so that those children may learn about 'history' from the museum itself, my focus is on the more complex and active ways in which intergenerational communication occurred. This does not negate the fact that children were brought to museums so that they could learn about the past from that museum, but on the register of engagement, this was a relatively highly passive form of intergenerational interaction in which the parent or grandparent assumed that an interaction with the objects and exhibits would ensure the transference of knowledge and understanding. While such interactions may have resulted in the desired learning on the part of the child, this was not always the case, as illustrated by one family at Rouse Hill house museum in Sydney. I interviewed them just as they finished a tour of the house and grounds, a tour the parents had hoped would impart a particular message to their child:

FATHER: [child's name], did you enjoy the tour? What was the best bit?
CHILD: Feeding the chickens!
FATHER: Was it nice to see the old house? Inside the house?
CHILD: Yes.

MOTHER: And do you think that you're lucky now? Living like you do? Or do you think they were lucky back then?
CHILD: I don't know. Lucky back then.
FATHER: No, we are lucky to live today.
MOTHER: This is how the rich people lived not how the poor people lived.

(RH14, male, 45–54, engineer, Australian; RH15: female, 35–44, mum, Korean Australian)

While it could indeed be argued that the child entirely got the message that an opulent Big House tends to offer – that in occupying such a place you are indeed lucky – the point here is that on the registers of engagement, this was the most passive form in which such intergenerational communication occurred. A slightly more active form occurred in which children 'learned to visit' – that is, they learned that visiting certain types of museum or heritage sites was something that they 'did' as part of familial, class or ethnic identity. Moreover, as part of this process, children also learned that the embodiment of particular emotions, that particular registers of engagement, was associated with such visits.

Far more active forms of intergenerational communication occurred in which family values, memories and familial identity were transferred and mediated by those visiting with family members. This process could revolve around an implicit transferal of social and political privilege or a more explicit and conscious transferal of progressive political values and occurred at both national and dissonant sites. Further, active registers of engagement occurred around quiet moments of reflection by individuals or couples visiting sites to mark or negotiate the meaning of changing family circumstances, such as the grandmother previously mentioned. Other acts of very active remembering occurred around familial politics of recognition; these acts undertaken by older visitors were about asserting their self-worth in the history of their own families.

Perhaps one of the most frequent acts of intergenerational communication and connection occurred in the 'imagined conversations' (Coghlan 2017) that occurred between adult children and absent or deceased parents or grandparents. These performances were most often done by individuals aged 45 or over, marking a particular life stage when the familial past and sense of connection becomes more pressing in the face of the aging or death of older family members, or as a process of mediating a visitor's mortality as illustrated by the woman at Ellis Island with whom I started this book. As identified in Chapters 6 and 7, these forms of intergenerational connections were not only most frequently made by those 45 or over but also most commonly occurred at sites of Labour and Immigration histories.

In the following sections, each of these various forms of intergenerational communication and connection are illustrated and expanded upon and the registers of engagement that underpin them identified. In doing so, I aim to first illustrate the breadth and complexity of how museums and heritage sites become familial 'theatres of memory' (Samuel 1994). The second aim is also to demonstrate the agency of visitors, as they make choices to use museums and heritage sites in these ways.

Third, to reveal how individuals utilise familial memories and identity to negotiate their sense of place within society, and finally, to consider the consequence of this process for ongoing individual and familial experiences of privilege or exclusion.

Intergenerational connection as 'imagined conversations'

Coghlan (2017), in work with visitors at the Museum of Australian Democracy Canberra, demonstrates that visitors can engage in what she calls 'imagined conversations'. These imagined acts of communication occur with other visitors, curatorial staff and contemporary politicians who were the subject of, or otherwise linked to, the exhibitions of that particular museum. It is a form of imaginative connection a visitor makes with those who are not present and where there is no real chance of actual physical communication (Coghlan 2017). This idea recalls Archer's (2007) idea of reflexivity, those internal deliberations or 'self-talk' that are engaged in as people interact with the world, but in which an imagined interlocutor has joined internal conversations. In the cases reported ahead, this process is about mediating a form of emotional connection with absent family members, in which time is telescoped and connections with lost or absent family members are not simply remembered but re-embodied and emotionally re-experienced. As the following visitor observed, the act of visiting allowed a time and place to remember absent family often not recalled in a person's day-to-day life:

> I don't spend much time thinking about what was it like for my grandparents or their parents when they came here [to America]. How much time does one devote to that? Here you do. You think, you remember, you understand better. It's a good thing.
> *(NHM1: female, 55–64, writer and social worker, Dutch/Irish American)*

The museum or heritage site as a space allocated for remembering not only provides a time and place that facilitates engagement with personal and collective memories of community and nation but, as is occurring here, those of family. Moreover, such sites also provide the space for people to 'feel', to embody the emotions that underpin and affirm those memories. The emotional accuracy, or emotional authenticity discussed in Chapter 2, gives validity to the memories recalled while recursively buttressing the valence, intensity and authenticity of the emotions being embodied. The emotions thus embodied most frequently lead to the strengthening of familial bonds with both present and absent family members. Emotions of positive valence were strengthened rather than created by the visit, and the positivity of these emotions would be taken away by the visitor into their day-to-day lives. However, museums and heritage sites could also, as places where people came to 'feel', be used as arenas where certain emotions could be 'left behind'. For example, one former coal miner I interviewed in 2004 at the National Coal Mining Museum, Wakefield, England, still traumatised by the 1984/1985 Miners' Strike, could only talk to his daughter about his own and wider familial history as miners at the museum. As he explained, his daughter who was eager for family history would, as he phrased it, 'drag' him to the museum so he could pass on his memories; doing so at the museum allowed him to leave the negative emotions that these recollections provoked behind at the museum. Not all intergenerational communication was celebratory, and such interactions could as frequently be used to mediate not only distressing family histories (e.g. Kidron 2013) but also to work through familial humility, obligation and dissonance. However, whether the emotional valence was positive or negative, acts of intergenerational communication were always intensely embodied and imaginative. For example, a tourist to the Tenement Museum, New York, defined her visit as an opportunity to re-embody past experiences of visiting a now-deceased family member, noting that the visit made him feel:

> Extremely interested. [. . .] I see the apartments here, the housing, I saw the same thing with my grandmother who died in 1992. She lived in [rooms that looked the same as these] in Belgium in 1992, so for me, it's like just visiting her, my grandparents' house again.
> *(TM17: male, 45–54, consultant, Belgium)*

Many visitors drew links between the site they were visiting or the artefacts on display and the memories that they triggered, and what that then meant for individual or familial identity; for example:

> Personal identity. My father worked in a machine shop all of his life, so when I see some of these tools and different implements, it reminds me of my father.
> *(IL1: female, over 65, school librarian, Italian American)*

However, more than simply triggering memories, the connections that were then made with absent parents or grandparents were often actively sought and embodied as visitors engendered a sense of deep familial connections, which worked to assert identity and sense of place. This is illustrated again by examples from the Tenement Museum:

> My mother grew up in New York, so she used to talk – she's no longer living, but she used to talk all about, and my grandmother, talked all about living in New York and all the various areas. It just gets me in touch with feelings of where I came from and who I am today. [. . .] [Being here] means feeling connected.
> *(TM30: female, over 65, teacher, Jewish American)*

> I was very moved. We went into the Italian American apartment, and I saw a lot of things in there that reminded me of my great-grandfather's home, with the saints on the wall, the cans of tomato sauce, even the photo of Franklin Roosevelt on the wall. My great-grandmother was very much wanting

to become Americanised, and she had a photo of Abraham Lincoln on her kitchen wall. So it's very emotional for me, and I certainly appreciate the sacrifice that they made coming here, and to give me the life that I'm able to have today.

(TM68: male, 35–44, social worker, Italian American)

Oh, I was there. That was me. I grew up – I slept on a couch in a bedroom, okay? My mother and grandmother sat in front of the stoves that I saw there. I remember all these things that they described in these rooms, I mean, it's one of ours.

(TM18: male, 55–64, sales, Jewish Lithuanian American)

TM30 is rekindling feelings of connection with her mother and grandmother through the stories they told of living in New York tenements, similar to that on display, and in doing so, is asserting to herself her familial and individual identity. TM68 invokes his sense of familial gratitude for what prior generations had done and achieved and the legacies thus left to him. While "it's one of ours" that is asserted by TM18 speaks to the power of both his own and his maternal family's history – that this history matters and has familial moral worth in underpinning his identity. This sense of connection not only speaks to an individual's sense of identity, continuity and place in the world, it also has considerable moral power. This is illustrated by TM41 who identified the history that he was visiting as "clearly my family's on both sides who emigrated to the United States from Russia and Eastern Europe". He had noted that being at the museum reminded him of the stories told by his grandmother, who had migrated alone from the Czech Republic around 1919 when she was just 16 years old: "she was very brave and determined". He goes on to discuss his feelings about visiting the Tenement Museum:

> A little bit excited, but also sad and in some ways, stronger.
>
> *Would you mind elaborating on that a little?*
>
> When I said stronger I mean in the sense that being able to relate one's present experiences with the past experiences of individuals or groups of individuals, be those families or larger communities, allows me anyway to draw more of a direct line between who I am and how I'm living my life today, and how that may relate back to people in communities that inform again who I am and what I'm doing.
>
> *What does being here mean to you?*
>
> It's sort of as a continuation of what we were discussing, yes, in the sense that, you know, grabbing the banister going up the first two flights of stairs – allows me to feel more connected, that's a meaning for me, to my roots.
>
> *(TM41: male, 45–54, insurance broker, Jewish American)*

The moral self-worth, the strength drawn from this visit, derives in part from mediating both positive and negative emotions; TM41 is both sad and excited, sad for the hardships ancestors had endured, but excited about the physicality of being in place, of "grabbing the banister", of making the embodied affective links to his 'roots'. It is also, however, in part reinforced by the depth of connections made through the telescoping of the past and present. The connections being made are not simply through physically being at the museum but also through the recollections of family stories and history, the imagined communication this individual visitor had with the grandmother whom he sees as brave and determined.

Storytelling to one's self or other present family members was an important way in which familial connections would strengthen. Visitors engaged in telling family stories in a variety of ways, often to younger generations, but also to a partner or to someone from a similar age group who was accompanying them on the visit. It was not unusual when interviewing a couple or a larger family group for the partner or a child to chime in during an interview she/he was 'just telling me about' some aspect of family history or a family story. Storytelling is a way of connecting with the listener, of organising knowledge and of working through and examining issues that confront but that also help define a sense of self and belonging (Ochs and Capps 2009). Family stories facilitate the negotiation and assertion of individual and family identity not only among family groups as they tour a heritage site relevant to that family's history but also for the individual visitor, as such stories were silently rehearsed and remembered as they toured a site. That this was occurring was demonstrated by the degree to which individuals readily and eagerly recounted such stories to the interviewer who interrupted such internal musing, for example:

> Oh, yes [there are links to my identity]. My grandmother worked in the garment industry, and an aunt – we now know when she died, she died of brown lung disease in her 90s – but as a child, she was also in the garment industry and in violation of the child labour laws, and she would speak about the fact that when the inspectors would come they would hide her underneath the clothing, the materials, so that the inspectors wouldn't see any underage children, and then she would be brought back out to work. So yeah, it's very real to me.
>
> *(TM59: female, over 65, computer programmer, Jewish American)*

> Absolutely [I am part of the history here]. My father grew up in one of these buildings here, and he was born in 1911, sixth of seven children from Russia. Grandfather pushed a cart with apples, grandmother scrubbed floors, five daughters slept in one bed, father and uncle slept on chairs, just like they said, yeah. So. . . [. . .] Very emotional, yeah. I mean I got kind of choked up. [. . .] [tearing up] it did feel like, you know, revisiting my parents' history.
>
> *(TM77: female, 55–64, librarian, Jewish American)*

These are just two short extracts, but I would be told quite detailed and lengthy narratives about family histories, or amusing anecdotes, as individuals affirmed their sense of self and familial belonging. These stories, however, were not simply rehearsed to reinforce familial connections, as the emotions engendered by these stories were used to make sincere, empathetic links to wider communities, in the instances mentioned to American immigrants and their children. In the case of TM59 the meaning of her family's history and the emotions it engendered lead her to muse "that the ugly things about the past aren't that far away, and can become today's reality again". TM77, who was deeply affected by "revisiting [her] parents' history", used her familial memories to reflect on the hardships of both past and contemporary immigrants to America, noting also "how people just sacrificed so much and lived in such horrible conditions for their children and grandchildren, who are us!"

The act of visiting sites authorised as 'heritage' lends not only space and time for such acts of remembering and reflection, but it also helps to affirm the legitimacy and worth of the processes of imagined and actual intergenerational communication. The power of the institutional authority of museums and other sites of heritage-making was particularly important in supporting the moral self-worth embodied by the imagined conversations with absent ancestors. This authority was also important for the next instance of intergenerational communication.

Self-worth and familial recognition

The moral self-worth that was defined as a consequence of the imagined intergeneration communication with absent family members can, in turn, be utilised to assert the historical and moral worth of individuals – that they 'matter' in terms of family history and identity. The next chapter discusses the performances of recognition that are informed by the 'politics of recognition' discussed in Chapter 2. These are performances that have both emotional and material consequences in the wider arena of negotiations over issues of social justice and exclusion/inclusion. While those performances tend to play to or reference a larger social audience, there are also more private and personal appeals to recognition that occur entirely within familial contexts; while these can also have wider social significance as discussed in Chapter 12, they will also have personal and familial implications. The moral self-worth that was defined as a consequence of the imagined intergenerational communication with absent family members will also be utilised to make demands for familial recognition.

An example of familial recognition occurred at the Immigration Museum, Melbourne: an older woman accompanied by her grown daughter talks about how she feels sentimental nostalgia about her voyage to Australia by ship. Her daughter, deflecting the question I had asked about how she feels, notes that the museum "reinforces the ideas I always had" (IMM39: female, 35–44, homemaker, Australian). The mother interjects, concerned her daughter does not understand the importance of her personal experiences. They negotiate the legitimacy of the mother's nostalgia; the daughter worried that her mother would find reminders of her experiences as a migrant "depressing". However, the mother notes that it is "pleasing to see that the immigrants are recognised and the contribution they've made" (IMM30: female, over 65, retired own business, English Australian), the mother pointing out the validity of familial history and its place in Australian economic development that has been provided by the museum and their visit to it. The daughter then acknowledges the contribution of immigrants to Australian society is "greater ... than you [that is, she] would have anticipated"; the mother, in response to her daughter's recognition, expresses pride, and exclaims, "We are ... we are everything".

Such interplays, while a consequence of performances of intergenerational communication, are also heavily reliant on the institutional authority of museums. This authority is illustrated, again at the Immigration Museum, Melbourne, where a visitor was mediating her own recognition of her father and potentially that of other family members. On entering the museum, the visitor described encountering a naturalisation certificate, which "triggered" deep but unspecified emotions; she goes on, "my father's generation spoke very little about their emotional experiences um ... and it's understandable when they were displaced from Europe" (IMM8: female, 45–54, university lecturer, Australian). She prosthetically embodies occluded familial emotions. The significance of her father's voyage is brought home to her, as she states, by the documents in the museum, and by the authority and physicality that such material has for her. This authority is reinforced by the idea that migrant history matters, one of the curatorial messages of the museum that she acknowledges she has read, but also as she notes because it is all housed in a building of "classical English architecture", the imposing façade of which asserts its authority.[1] She wants to share her insights into the importance of her father's experiences with her family, noting she was going to tell her brother to bring his children to the museum so that they too might experience the same sense of familial recognition.

In these examples, the museum and visitor have worked in partnership, the museum providing the arena and authority for the negotiations of recognition in which the visitors have chosen to engage. This is a very active and considered use of the museum in which there is an interplay between the physicality of the museum and the visit and the authenticity and authority of the emotions embodied. However, familial acts of recognition were relatively rare and need to be differentiated from performances of reinforcement. There is a multitude of examples from sites of immigration and labour as well as sites of national narratives that use the sense of self-worth generated by the visit to invoke laments that younger generations do not 'understand' and need to recognise what previous generations achieved and 'went through'. For example, one couple at Ellis Island who were engaged in recollecting and celebrating absent grandparents who had been processed as immigrants at the site noted that being on the Island was highly emotional: "I can't explain it [the emotion]. It's just emotion" (EI99: female, 45–54, dental hygienist, Jewish American). They then lamented that the emotional significance of Ellis Island and what it represented for them was not understood by "the kids I see day-to-day – I would drag them in there [museum] and force them to stand there just to see what it was like [...] they have no clue what their ancestors went through" (EI100: male, 45–54, building services, Jewish American). As discussed in Chapter 12, this may on one level be a plea for emotional and historical recognition; it is, however, fundamentally a lament that the visitor's social values are not being understood and is indicative of the performance of reinforcement discussed in Chapter 9. Rather than a sincere plea for recognition, it is a demand others should share their views and values, and the statement references the power of seeing others reinforce the values you hold. The sense of familial identity that underwrites such demands can, however, also underwrite the transferal of family values and identity discussed in the following sections.

Quite reflections: marking and remaking familial identity

As the new grandmother at the Japanese American National History Museum illustrates, sites were used by individuals and families to reconcile or mark significant changes in both personal and family identity: a process that was frequent at sites that tended to have personal connections to visitors, in particular sites of labour or immigration history; however, sites of national heritage-making could also become embroiled within familial identity. National sites without direct personal or familial connections to a visitor can, nonetheless, become important through the frequency with which such sites are visited – they become part of 'what we do as a family'. A complex example of the power of quiet reflections occurred at Lanyon house museum where the visitor's connection was less about the house's representation of an aspect of Australian history and more about family history developed through the practices of visiting and bringing his children to the site while they were growing up in nearby Canberra. Although he makes links between New Zealand history, where he was born, and Australian history, he comes to conclude that Lanyon is part of his personal history:

> Well, I guess, well because I'm born and bred in Kiwi land, Christchurch, so there is a link. There's obviously a link [between Australia and New Zealand] in terms of the forces, the armed forces, there's always been a link, and I think a lot of the things that happened in both of the nations are quite alike because of the culture. I don't think I'm part of the history, but I think I'm part of the new offering [laughs], having had kids here now, and the family's here, we've actually lived down in this part of the woods for over 19 years, so I think we're a part of this history of this sort of place and a part of Lanyon. And, you know, history, if you want to say in terms of we've always, when our kids were small it's been a part of our experience this place here in terms of Christmas carols [held at the site] and just bringing the kids down here so, yeah.
>
> *(LH52: male, 45–54, business coach, Indian Australian)*

The importance of Lanyon to his familial history is revealed when he is asked 'what does being here mean to you':

> Well, funny actually that you should say that [laughs] but I was actually having a bit of an emotional moment because my two boys are doing their first big overseas trip in about a week's time, and it's actually funny you should

say that in that there's a lot of history of our family here and I'm realising my, the 16-year old who's the youngest of the two is becoming a man, and I'm thinking 'oh my god, my time's up', not my time's up, but he's talking about leaving Canberra in about two years and doing uni in Boston, and funny actually I was walking around here it kind of made me think. Oh, I was going back to those moments when I was holding his hand and walking around here [laughs], so yes, yeah.

Connections to the nation, Canberra and family become intertwined in the repeated performance of visiting Lanyon over the years. There has been an accumulated impact of the act of visiting for himself and his sense of family; it is a place where he has mediated a range of meanings and ideas of belonging that ultimately allow him to use the site to reflect on and reconcile changing relationships with his sons.

Transferring familial values and identity

Intergenerational communication as actual communications between family groups, and most specifically between a parent/grandparent and a child/grandchild (whether as an adult child or as a minor), was a common use of all genres of sites. In these instances, families were engaged in the development or cementing of familial collective memories, or what Landsberg (2004) refers to as prosthetic memory. This transference relied not simply on the storytelling of older family members but also required the generation of emotional responses. The storyteller often assessed and arbitrated on the emotional authenticity and empathetic and imaginative responses of their familial audience – it is the ability to imaginatively and emotionally engage with another's stories and memories that facilitates the transference of collective memories (Landsburg 2004; Keightley and Pickering 2012). Thus, older family members as storytellers often worked to facilitate what they judged as the appropriate register of engagement in their audiences in much the same way that the mother negotiated the emotional registers of her adult daughter at the Immigration Museum, Melbourne. Museums were, as also noted, used as arenas that provided the authority and space to engage in such acts of communication. However, the transference and bolstering of familial memories also, both implicitly and explicitly, included the strengthening of familial values and identities.

As with many heritage performances, ideological as well as emotional registers played a role in what sort of museum and heritage sites families chose to visit for such activities. And this transference was not without wider social implications, as the cementing of particular familial values has political consequences. For instance, the parents of the young woman discussed in Chapter 9 who, as her father indulgently described, "bawl[ed] like a baby" in response to seeing the Star-Spangled Banner, nonetheless validated that response. While that family was engaged in a performance of reinforcement, intergenerational communication was also working to facilitate that broader performance. Similarly, the postal worker at the National Civil Rights Museum, discussed in the book's introduction, was also actively engaged in passing on familial values to her son. However, in this instance, the act was far more knowingly undertaken than the parental validation achieved by the parents of the young woman at *The Star-Spangled Banner* exhibit. In both cases, the intergenerational communication worked to facilitate acts of reinforcement and affirmation, which, as argued in Chapter 9, have wider implications for either challenging or maintaining social inclusion and exclusion.

In the active forms of intergenerational communication, parents of either adult or younger children used museums and heritage sites self-consciously to address issues either within the family or wider society. One very active example of this was a Caucasian same-sex couple at the National Civil Rights Museum, whose decision to come to the museum was triggered by a discussion they had had with their African American tenant when they were "having a couple of cocktails by the fire" with him when he recounted his experience of that day. He told them that he had been out walking when he noticed a white woman coming the other way; he recounted how he had turned away from her as they passed so that he "wasn't threatening". As one of the women stated this was "not anything I would have, you know [realised], just – it really bothered me, so I thought it was important to bring the kids here" (NCRM49: female, 35–44, nurse, Caucasian American). As she had noted, "my ancestors were racists, and I strived very hard not to be, and I want to instil that in my children, so that's why I felt it was important to bring them here". Her partner agreed with the importance of bringing their children, noting, "being a gay person [civil rights] it's something that we're fighting right now, just to see what [African Americans] had to do to have their rights versus us [. . .] we're not on the outside like African Americans [were], so it's inspiring that, you know, they came a long way and so will we" (NCRM50: female, 25–34, grad student, Caucasian and Native American). They went on to talk about marriage rights (at the time not universally legal in the United States) and doubted that they would see gay marriage accepted in their lifetimes, with NCRM49 stating:

> we have children, and that someday, you know, they'll talk about their great grandparents, they were one of the first married gay couples that were legally married in the state of Wisconsin, you know, so, that's our goal.

There is a complicated mix of memory and desired familial inheritance occurring here. While both parents were affirming their commitment to fighting against the inherited racism within their family, having been concerned about their privileged ignorance, they were also actively using the visit to engage their children in affirming new and more progressive family values. Additionally, they were imagining and affirming their sense of the values and achievements they hoped to bequeath their descendants.

This imaginative sense of active inheritance was also evident in how an African American clergyman recounted a childhood incident as he considered what meaning the National Civil Rights Museum might have for contemporary

America. He recounted an event that occurred when he was nine years old in Louisiana, how he had:

> got on the bus, sat next to a white man, and I seriously attempted to engage in conversation with him, at nine years old. And I heard my mother say 'Where's Johnny?', and somebody said 'He's sitting in the van next to that white man'. I don't know what happened then. My mother came forward, grabbed me by the right collar, and my feet were literally in the air as she dragged me to the back of the bus, and my mother and the rest of the people that were with us – there was about seven, maybe ten of us sat frozen, and I couldn't understand what was going on until we got off the bus, and they said, 'Wow', and I had no idea of the potential that could have [had].
>
> *(NCRM22: male, 55–64, clergy, African American)*

In considering this story he went onto note that "unlike Jewish parents, who teach their children about anti-Semitism, our parents don't teach us because they want to guard us against the hurt". His ignorance at nine having put his family at risk had underpinned his resolve, "I'm making a point to teach my kids, but teaching them hatred is not the way. And at the same time, lethargy will get you nowhere". Here family values are actively renegotiated across the generations; this visitor was himself deeply moved, asking me at times to turn the recording off so he could gather himself, drawing some solace from re-imagining the development of intergenerational experience and inheritance. As he had noted in defining heritage, it was "culture, values, passed on from our forebears".

Sites of dissonant history, such as the National Civil Rights Museum, were particularly used by parents "to share history and teach the children history" (NCRM60: female, 35–44, library assistant, Caucasian American). However, in this form of 'teaching' parents were not passively assuming that their children would 'pick things up' from the exhibits; rather, as one parent explained, being at the museum reminded her that when the children "have questions about things like [racism] that they know that they can talk with me or their dad about that" (NCRM63: female, 35–44, education, Caucasian American). Parents or grandparents unaccompanied by their children would sometimes use their visits to affirm familial values, and, as with NCRM63 and the clergyman, resolve to pass these on to their descendants, a further example from a labour history site:

> I think having been involved with unions in Australia; I think that knowing that really this event [Eureka Stockade] was the foundation of the union movement, and that's something special, that's something I'll take away from [here] and explain it to my children as well.
>
> *(MADE59: male, 45–54, principal, Anglo-Australian)*

Dissonant sites were often simultaneously utilised by older family members to reflect on the values and familial memories they had experienced and to either affirm or rework these as they both engaged in imagined intergenerational communication with their ancestors and actual intergenerational communication with their descendants. On the register of engagement, these were very active uses and interactions with sites; however, the examples so far have come from sites of dissonant histories, and it must be noted that equally active uses of both national and dissonant sites occurred in which largely politically conservative family values were transmitted. For example, the following visitor, implicitly questioning the value of organised labour, stated that they wanted the children accompanying them to take away a "work ethic", going on to explain a set of family values embedded in a version of the American Dream:

> Well, we have three pretty simple rules in our house: we don't quit, we don't whine, and we never get embarrassed. And these were folks that worked tirelessly with nothing, for nothing more but the promise of a better tomorrow. I think that exemplifies what helped build this country. I hope that we all remember to keep that close to our heart. I'm not so sure that everybody does any more.
> *(WC5: male, 55–64, chaplain, French Canadian Irish American)*

A less active or explicit version of intergenerational communication, however, tended to occur at national sites. Where, as with the parents of the tearful young woman at *The Star-Spangled Banner* exhibit, parents affirmed familial values not only of patriotism but values and familial identities based on self-assurance in the embodiment of specific affective states. This was particularly expressed by parents or grandparents nominating that they were taking children to particular sites so that they could experience the emotions that they had felt and considered important. Here the issue was not so much the information that might be gained by the child, but rather the affective response the parent or grandparent wanted to mediate, for example:

> I love bringing the grandchildren because they're having the same experience I had as a child.
> *(AWM25: female, 55–64, office manager, Australian)*

> I've brought my children here when they were very young, and [. . .] my grandchildren, when they get a bit older, I'll bring them here too, so they appreciate [what the site stands for]
> *(AWM27: male, over 65, accountant, Australian)*

These visitors were at the Australian War Memorial and the experience or appreciation that both visitors hoped the children would have was the promotion of pride, humility and gratitude not only to servicemen and servicewomen generally but also to past family members who had fought in Australia's wars. While the feeling rules at sites of war commemoration centred on feelings of patriotism and gratitude, the less complicated celebratory nature of other forms of national sites were issues parents also sought to reproduce. For example, one visitor at the First Australians Gallery at the National Museum of Australia noted:

> there's not as much engagement [of children] in here as I've seen in other galleries [. . .] It's not a very exciting gallery for children, it's very dry, and we're meant to, I think we're meant to be very serious in here but have some laughter, have some fun um . . . this might be missing out of this, of course, there's the solemn aspect to contact relations, but there's also the celebration I mean of all kinds of things and just having fun.
>
> *(NMA58: female, 35–44, lecturer, Australian)*

The gallery tells the story of Indigenous history in Australia, including the periods before, during and after colonisation. The "contact relations" being referenced here include the histories of the early land wars, Indigenous segregation and the histories and legacies of the Stolen Generations[2], the latter being a particular focus of the gallery. This gallery of dissonant history, contained within Australia's national history museum sited in the nation's capital, has been a target of Australia's history wars and criticised for failing to provide the appropriate celebratory tone (Casey 2001; Bonnell and Crotty 2008). At sites of national storytelling, celebration was something, as NMA58 indicates, parents wanted their children to feel, the "just having fun" of going to a museum working in itself to transmit not only certain family values but also reinforcing that visiting museums is simply enjoyable fun. I am not discounting that museums and heritage sites should not be 'fun' or entertaining, but in this context, the issue is that NMA58 identifies celebration as the appropriate feeling rules for a national museum and that children need not only to be able to feel this but must have the self-assurance to do so.

This performance of intergenerational passing on of self-assurance was facilitated by parents and grandparents seeking and reproducing similar affective responses to sites with their children/grandchildren. While parents sought particular affective responses from children in terms of the more active performances of intergenerational communication discussed in the preceding sections, the 'celebratory self-assurance' that some parents sought at national sites for their children was the end in itself. Marianne Hirsch (2012: 108) defines what she calls 'inherited trauma'. Trauma, she argues, is transmitted as 'postmemory' and exercised in families so deeply and in such a way that it can become deeply constituted as a descendant's own memories and sense of self (2008: 107). Similarly, 'inherited privilege' can become equally constitutive of individual memory and identity and can be seamlessly transmitted through the acts of visiting certain types of museums and heritage sites. This is because the act of visiting certain types of heritage sites can itself become constitutive of a visitor's individual and familial identity. In the case of national sites, dominated by white middle-class visitor profiles, and where celebratory self-assurance is embodied, it is privilege that is being transmitted and inherited. The inherited privilege is also quietly reinforced by how visitors, explored in the following, learn or are trained to visit.

Visiting to learn or learning to visit: taking the children

In 2005, when my children were quite young, I was asked by a staff member if I would please leave the museum I had been visiting with my family – my children were creating too much noise. It was a French regional archaeological museum, and we were in a gallery dedicated to describing how prehistoric stone tools had been made, and my kids were entranced. Excitedly calling out "mum, come and see *this*", their delighted squeals as they saw tools they recognised from a site we had visited earlier on our trip would not be moderated – thus, I was firmly told to *sortir du musée*. Almost eight years later, while surveying at another museum, this time in the United States, a noisy bunch of schoolchildren were talking excitedly to each other about the diorama in front of them. A member of the floor staff came up to me to lament the children's behaviour and to talk about how much she appreciated parents who teach their children 'how to visit'. Startled by this assessment, as obviously I had lacked such skills, I asked her what she meant. Well, she explained, parents who teach their children to be quiet and not rush about, to not only think about other visitors but importantly in this museum professional's considered view, that they showed respect for the objects and the exhibition. In short, they moderate the intensity and emotional expression of their register of engagement.

The repetition of visiting certain sites by families, or parents who take children to visit sites they experienced in their childhood, become part of familial identity. As one couple at the Old Melbourne Gaol noted positively in response to my question 'Are you part of the history represented here?' that yes they were, not because they had ancestors who were convicts, but simply because they had both been visiting the site for 40 years, first as children themselves, then as parents, and now as grandparents. When asked about the messages they hoped the grandchildren with them would take away, they were vague and uncertain, offering the platitude that "it is important to learn about your heritage and your history because obviously our children are Australian, our grandchild's Australian" (OMG20: female, 55–64, housewife, British Australian). The platitude masked the fact that taking away 'a message' was not a relevant issue for them; the issue was rather simply being at the site and what that meant for familial continuity of a tradition. They went on to note that they hoped their grandchildren would "be able to come one day themselves [with their children]". As a visitor at Rouse Hill house museum noted, visiting was a tradition that she was reclaiming, "we've lost so much of our rituals and our connection with the children and I think it's very important to try and get some of that back" (RH011: female, 25–34, allied health, Australian). Others echoed this sentiment:

> my mum used to often take me to historical houses, like she's been down to Elizabeth Farm and things like that, Rippon Lea in Melbourne, we used to do a lot of that with my parents but I haven't really done that with the children, so I want to start taking them to things like this 'cos I think it's great for them to realise how people used to live.
>
> *(RH08: female, 45–54, nurse, Australian)*

My father when I was a child used to take me to a cultural site every Sunday, and that interest has always stayed with me [I have] been to over 100 houses, [I] visit one a week.

(CH328: female, over 60, housewife, British)

The tradition of visiting thus becomes entangled with familial and individual identity as a visitor to an English house museum illustrates when he defined 'heritage' as "Coming here with my mum and Dad when I was a kid" (CH118: male, 30–39, police officer, British). Visitors here have learned that visiting particular types of heritage site is something that they 'do'. Visiting, particularly national museums and heritage sites, is a resolutely middle-class activity that is intergenerationally transmitted, the success of which is evidenced by the longitudinal maintenance of the middle-class visitor profiles at national museums and heritage sites (Black 2012).

Additionally, learning 'how to' visit national sites is more than establishing a familial and individual habit. It is also about establishing the appropriate register of engagement for a particular national site, whether that be the humble gratitude at the Australian War Memorial, the intensity of patriotism demonstrated by the tearful young woman at *The Star-Spangled Banner* exhibit, or the more ubiquitous and quieter forms of national celebration at sites of national storytelling more generally. These registers work to facilitate the inheritance of ethnic and middle-class privilege, which buttresses the indifference that underpins certain types of performances of reinforcement discussed in Chapters 9 and 10.

A visitor interviewed at the Uluru cultural centre illustrates this process of embodying privilege and indifference; Uluru is both a site of significance to its Traditional Owners, the Anangu, and Australian national narratives of frontier exploration. At the time of the interviews, visitors could climb Uluru[3], although highly visible signs at the start of the climb asked visitors to respect Anangu cultural values and knowledge by not climbing; the cultural centre also elaborated on this request. The visitor in question, an older Anglo-Australian visiting with his children, stated that they had come to Uluru not simply because it was an icon, but to broaden his and his children's awareness of Indigenous people and culture, as he goes on to note, "it's important for them [his children] just to understand more about where the country came from and how to look after it too" (U27: male, 55–64, accountant, Australian). Asking if he had undertaken the climb, he affirms that he had done so on his previous visit 24 years earlier, but on this occasion only went "up about 100 metres [. . .] But my children went up there, all three of them did". In asking him if he knew that the Anangu prefer people not climb, he dismissively affirmed, "yeah, yeah", going on to explain that he wanted his children to climb because "I think it's a great way to understand how big the rock is". While his avowed reason for visiting was in part to broaden his children's awareness of Indigenous people and culture, the act of climbing undermines that intent. In starting the climb and facilitating his children's climb, the visitor has transferred his unstated assumptions of privilege as a non-Indigenous Australian to his children. Indifference to Indigenous values is maintained and transmitted while a celebration of the national iconic status of

Uluru is preserved and embodied in the act of climbing. While this is an overt example of how people visiting certain sites can undercut interpretive or curatorial messages, in this case, the messages offered by the Anangu about cultural respect, it nonetheless illustrates that *what* sites people visit as much as *how* people embody the visit – the registers with which they engage – is learned and transmitted across generations.

Conclusion

Intergenerational communication is an important and complex use to which visitors put both museums and heritage sites. This performance can occur for its own sake – for example, those acts of quiet reflection or imagined communications with absent family members. Or it can, for instance, in the case of transmitting family values, underpin other performances such as reinforcement, affirmation (Chapters 9 and 10) and recognition/misrecognition (Chapters 12 and 13). While these performances are facilitated by museums and heritage sites and the authority they represent, this is not a passive process. Visitors make explicit choices about the particular 'theatres of memory' they attend and explicit or implicit choices about how they then use and engage with the sites. While visitors may gain intergenerational awareness, familial pride and knowledge about the past, this occurs through active individual visitor mediation of the meaning of the site to themselves and their family. Artefacts, displays or the site itself are used as familial *aide-mémoire* to construct familial narratives and acts of intergenerational communication – imagined or actual.

The performative aspect of intergenerational communication constructs and transmits familial stories, memories and identity and the social and ideological values that inform and underpin these. The embodiment of affective and imaginative experiences that facilitate this transference can itself be arbitrated for younger visitors by older family members drawing on the institutional and cultural authority of museums and heritage sites. Younger family members are also actively trained in the feeling rules of visiting certain types of sites. Consequently, the registers of engagement 'appropriate' to that site are learned alongside the social values and ideological meaning of the site to a familial sense of place and belonging.

This process can be both overt and covertly achieved. At sites of dissonant history, self-conscious and overt intergenerational transmissions tend to be more evident, while at sites of national narratives, the process tends to be more taken for granted and, thus, covert as particular forms of familial experiences of privilege are embodied and reinforced. In turn, this works itself to facilitate those performances of reinforcement, identified in Chapters 8 and 9, which tend to lead to the maintenance of indifference to a cosmopolitan sense of diversity and social justice. While the more taken-for-granted transferences of inherited privilege can underpin performances of reinforcement, they can also facilitate the more active performances of misrecognition of other groups in society. The more active and self-aware forms of intergenerational interaction occurring either at sites of dissonance or national narratives can also inform and facilitate performances of recognition. The following chapters turn to an examination of how visitors build upon not only the performances of reinforcement and affirmation discussed in Chapter 9 but also individual and familial identity-making to engage in performances of recognition and misrecognition. As the following chapter argues, performances of recognition or misrecognition are grounded on the transmission and affirmation of familial experiences of either privilege or disenfranchisement.

Notes

1 The building is an example of renaissance revival architecture, having been completed in 1876 for use as the state of Victoria's Customs House, see: https://museumsvictoria.com.au/longform/customs-house/.
2 Stolen Generations refers to those Indigenous children forcibly removed from their families under various State parliamentary 'protection' acts (Wilkie 1997; Read 2014).
3 After decades of debate, the Uluru climb was permanently closed in October 2019; for further details see 'Please don't climb Uluru', Parks Australia website, https://parksaustralia.gov.au/uluru/discover/culture/uluru-climb/; and McGrath (2016).

12
HERITAGE AND THE POLITICS OF RECOGNITION

Heritage and identity – the two concepts – are inextricably linked. However heritage is defined as 'cultural background', 'family', 'material things' and so forth (Chapter 5); the idea that it is representative or even constitutive of identity remains strong. To understand what this relationship *does*, I draw on debates over the politics of recognition and diversity. In Chapter 2, I argued that in understanding how the power and consequence of the interrelationship between heritage and identity intersects with struggles over recognition and redistribution reveals why heritage can *matter*, to the extent that it becomes embroiled in conflicts ranging in scale from the local to the international. Heritage can be understood as a resource of power and justification in conflicts over social justice and access to social and economic resources.

Museums and heritage sites are arenas of justification in which identities are asserted, negotiated and continually re/justified. As argued in Chapter 2, this then has a consequence for negotiations over recognition and misrecognition. The authority of material heritage as providing tangible and evidential legitimacy is important here as is the institutional authority of museums in in/validating particular expressions or representations of identity and historical narratives. Collectively and individually museums and heritage sites may become themselves, as institutions, implicated in the politics of recognition and misrecognition. They are also important arenas of justification for individuals to engage with issues of recognition and misrecognition. As such, they are used in a range of ways by individuals to understand and assess the political contexts in which they express their sense of identity and renegotiate their sense of place in society.

This chapter applies the arguments developed in Chapter 2 about recognition and redistribution and teases out the different and nuanced ways in which this is collectively and individually played out by visitors at museums and heritage sites.

It is argued that there are particular heritage performances undertaken that can be understood either as having a consequence for the politics of recognition, or may themselves be understood as individual or collective performances of recognition – or indeed of misrecognition. As argued in Chapter 2, the first steps of recognition must be self-recognition – that is, recognition of and by an individual or collective that they are the inheritor of privilege or marginalisation. For those seeking recognition the assertion of moral worth and self-esteem, celebrating and commemorating one's own identity is not just an empty gesture of identity politics, but a foundational position from which to move to seek parity and equity and to get governments and policymakers to listen to claims for redress. For those from dominant or hegemonic positions in society, the ability to question received narratives and social values that underpin privileged identities is necessary before there can be a move to acknowledge and recognise difference and any associated inequity and injustice. While these may be foundational, or first steps, that help build or provide opportunities for a politics of recognition to occur in wider social contexts, visitors may also actively and self-consciously use museums and heritage sites as they work through and engage in self-conscious critical acts of recognition. Additionally, performances of recognition tend to be built on affirmative performances of reinforcement discussed in Chapter 9 and on the more active and aware registers of intergenerational transmission of familial identity and history discussed in Chapter 11.

Recognition and heritage-making

The politics of recognition addresses the increasing importance of identity claims within political struggles in democratic societies. Within this formulation, historical legacies of injustice associated with different social or cultural identity claims are advanced as requiring recognition. Rather than simply being calls for acknowledgement, Nancy Fraser (1995, 2000) argues that recognition claims are part of material struggles for groups to have greater access to policymakers. This, in turn, may increase parity of participation in government policies regulating the redistribution of resources such as welfare, education, land and other forms of reparations. While Fraser's work is central to the idea of the politics of recognition that I draw on, Axel Honneth's (2005: 122) arguments about the importance of seeking respect and self-esteem add an important dimension to recognition as I am defining it. Esteem here is tied to the extent to which plurality and diversity of social and cultural values are not only accommodated by society but the degree to which the values of those seeking recognition may become accommodated and respected. For Honneth, as for Charles Taylor, respect and esteem speak to the emotional wellbeing of individuals and groups; however, recognition does not rest here. As Fraser (2010) argues, lack of respect and esteem are part of the consequence of misrecognition and should be understood as important in mobilising action in struggles over redistribution. Sayer (2005), for instance, argues that various emotions are important in propelling groups or individuals to seek recognition – particularly, the formulation of self-esteem and moral self-worth. Additionally, he also draws attention to the emotions that may underlie the moral judgements needed to offer recognition.

Heritage is linked, on the one hand, to feelings of belonging and senses of geographical and social place and, on the other hand, to processes of authorising historical narratives and the identities they inform. As such, it can become imbricated in the politics of recognition and struggles over not only claims for recognition but the moral judgements made to offer or withhold recognition. Moreover, heritage as a powerful affirmation of belonging demonstrates the foundational and emotional power of asserting individual and group self-esteem upon which groups may launch claims for recognition. Additionally, a strong personal sense of 'self-recognition' as either the inheritor of injustice or privilege is needed for individuals and groups to engage in negotiations over recognition and redistribution. Struggles over recognition are also ongoing complex negotiations, in which recognition claims can be denied, ignored or met with counterclaims for recognition, while any successful claim may be met with counterclaims or may itself initiate unforeseen acts of injustice that trigger further struggles (Tully 2000).

The concept of the politics of recognition, as developed in Chapter 2, has utility for not only understanding the consequences of how professionals engage in exhibiting and interpreting the past for public consumption but also the consequences of the collective affective practices of visiting museums and heritage sites. In teasing out individual performances of visiting as framed within the politics of recognition, my intent is not to claim that these performances are fully rounded engagements within the politics of recognition, only that they intersect with and have a consequence for such struggles. My aim is twofold. First, to identify the potential consequences that individual and collective acts of visiting certain sites of heritage-making can have and thus pinpoint what can be at stake for certain visitors in how museological and other professional heritage practices interpret the past for the present. The second aim is to illustrate the agency revealed by how people deploy the registers with which they engage with heritage.

Affective performances and practices of recognition or misrecognition were deployed in several ways and occurred, in various ways and extents, in all museums and exhibitions included in this study. However, responses to various interview questions coded as 'gaining or showing recognition' or 'feeling recognised' among others were particularly prevalent at museums dealing with histories of immigration, enslavement and its legacies and Indigenous culture and history (Chapter 6). There are five different and nuanced expressions of this performance to be elaborated. The first variant looks at the idea of self-recognition and the variety of ways it was expressed in this context. A particular issue here is the assertion or seeking of self-esteem and moral worth, as second, some visitors declared an active desire for recognition that energetically drew on assertions of self-worth. A third expression was the offering of recognition or respect from visitors from dominant ethnic, class or gendered positions to others. A fourth very active occurrence was the way museums, in particular, were used as a 'barometer' by some groups to measure the extent to which the museum, and its role in representing wider societal values and understandings, was or was not offering recognition. Associated with this assessment were those visitors who identified that they felt either recognised or misrecognised by either the site or the behaviour of other visitors. Finally, the collective and social performances of recognition that visitors overtly or covertly engage in are outlined and the implications this has for understanding the function and consequence of both heritage and museums are identified.

Self-recognition

Various forms of 'self-recognition' are, to a great extent, what visitors do at museums and heritage sites. Chapter 9 looked at the various ways in which identity, amongst other issues, was not only continually reinforced but also affirmed in one of the most common ways in which museums and heritage sites are used. Not all performances of reinforcement or affirmation lead to or can be understood through the politics of recognition. It is also worth stressing, and this is discussed in more detail in Chapter 13, that performances that reinforce positions of privilege in society will tend to impede the granting of recognition. Nonetheless, there are aspects of affirmation and self-recognition that can be usefully understood within this framework, and these particularly relate to the affirmation of self-esteem and self-worth from which claims for recognition may be built upon. In the following, for instance, visitors are not simply expressing their own identities, they are explicitly doing so in identified contexts where they perceive a lack of recognition:

> As an immigrant myself, this is the people who really built New York, and by connotation America. Those stories are never told.
> *(TM5: male, 55–64, bank regulation, African American)*

> I have been to Mount Vernon[1] [. . .] with a white tour guide. I was angry, all the African Americans were angry. The white guide made jokes about the chains [. . .] But here I feel there is respect and objectivity, even the whites walking round [the exhibition] have respect.
> *(SJM45: female, 55–64, federal government, African American)*

> [I feel] Wonderful, you know, this is something [history of enslavement] that should be replicated in every main town, city and in every museum.
> *(ISM179: male, 25–34, military officer, Black British)*

The positive emotion expressed in the last example relates directly to the sense that he is feeling recognised by the histories of the slave trade exhibited at the International Slavery Museum, Liverpool. As identified in Chapter 6, visitors, particularly at labour history, immigration and enslavement legacy sites, used their visits to remember and assert pride and self-esteem in their heritage or that of familial or group identities as discussed in Chapters 9 and 11. As one visitor at the National Civil Rights Museum observed, the museum made him feel "proud, and ready for the future" and that it was important to "be proud of what you are. Remember the past so you can get on with the future" (NCRM94: male, 18–24, college student, African American). The energisation of garnering self-esteem evident in this response facilitates the underpinning of contemporary and future aspirations.

The visit in these instances is an affective embodiment of pride and self-esteem in which the physicality of the site reinforced and legitimised a sense of the moral worth of the visitor. The authority of the physical existence and power of representation of heritage and the museum here is important and is illustrated by this response at the Mashantucket Pequot Museum from an Indigenous American visitor to the question about messages, in that, for him, the museum represented:

> We're still here.
> *Who's we can I ask?*
> The Native, Indigenous people are still here. They're still a lot of us even though maybe a lot of them are uprooted, but...
> (PM57: male, 45–54, unemployed, Native American)

In another example, this time at the Japanese American National History Museum, one frequent visitor to the museum identifies his commitment to the museum as an institution that tells a story 'that needs to be told' and that he sees as working to uphold and validate his Japanese heritage:

> [what does] Being here [mean]? Well, it's just that I support and I not only physically support it, but I financially support it. I think it has a story that needs to be told, for future generations, and even some of our present people that know Japanese ancestry, they know very little about the history and the background, and I think with this museum here you will retain [that history] [...] my children are into it and they know pretty much all of what the history has produced for them. But there are a lot of people that need to know, I think this museum will play a very valuable part in that respect.
> *(JANM13: male, over 65, engineer, Japanese American)*

In this example, he is effectively calling for solidarity both across generations and from others with Japanese ancestry so that they may also recognise and know their identity and history. The authority of the museum can of course also work in negative ways to dismiss recognition and/or to maintain disregard and misrecognition as this example from the British Museum's exhibition on enslavement and the slave trade reveals:

> Firstly, it is important to admit what we did long [ago]. [...] It's the British Museum. It's important that the exhibition was so small [...] nobody sees it you know, I mean you should have [the exhibition in] a big room [...] it's part of Great Britannia you know, I feel [they] [...] put [it in] this room just to say that we have the room on slavery, but [they] make it as small as possible so that less people can see it, maybe I am wrong but...
> *(BM184: male, 16–24, French)*

264 Emotional heritage

The temporary exhibition that marked the British Museum's nod to the 1807 Bicentenary of Britain's abolition of its transatlantic slave trade was mounted in the vestibule in front of that institution's numismatics department. It was, as this visitor identifies, a small room in which to mount an exhibition about a nationally commemorated event. As this visitor picks up, the message this sent was disregard and lack of recognition of this history and its ongoing legacies of racism and injustice.

As illustrated, the authority of the museum can both uphold and undermine claims of identity and pride and wellbeing, but so to can particular definitions of heritage. In asserting self-recognition as a member of a group seeking affirmation of self and ultimately wider recognition, ideas of heritage could also pose a barrier that individuals have to overcome, for example:

> Heritage I think in this country to me [said dismissively] it's just a couple of old buildings here and there, shacks that haven't been demolished, but heritage [. . .] is everything, it's my mother, my father, my family, yeah that's my heritage and I will leave something behind in my grandchildren.
>
> *(IMM99: male, over 65, pensioner, Italian Australian)*

> When you hear a lot about heritage, it's not usually the heritage of the whole country; it's exclusive, it excludes people. Such as stately homes, they represent the upper echelons of society and not the majority; here [Tolpuddle] it is more inclusive of people's heritage.
>
> *(TP35, female, 40–59, teaching assistant, English)*

These statements may be seen as challenges to the received professional and museological definitions of heritage as material objects; however, they need to be understood as more than that. In claiming that heritage is more than buildings – 'old shacks' – a claim is being made that the speaker's experiences of heritage matters, as those experiences are part of wider individual experiences and knowledge that have been discounted or not recognised. On a very personal level, the first speaker mentioned, an Italian Australian at the Immigration Museum, Melbourne, used his visit to reclaim his self-worth to himself as an immigrant of a group, often referred to with the offensive term 'wogs' in Australian society (Hage 2012):

> Well I want to prove to my grandchildren and my children and this is the beginning, they can see those photos and I was one of them, I'm not in there [actually in the photos] but I was 21 years old, blah blah blah and that's where we started our future.
>
> *(IMM099: male, over 65, pensioner, Italian Australian)*

This assertion of self-worth, embodied by his visit to the museum, formed the basis from which to claim recognition from his own family (Chapter 11). He identified the women in his family, who had chosen to go shopping while he was at the museum, as failing to respect his contribution to the family, as granddad going on and on, 'blah blah blah', as he states:

> I'm going to find those women, and before we go home tonight, I'll say 'I've been there' now remember, my girls [...]. That's it!

While he states he is seeking recognition simply from his family, this example raises an important issue for how we understand the politics of recognition. It reinforces the importance of having assurance in the legitimacy that individuals hold in their identity and in the experiences that form and underlie that identity – assurances that these things do matter and count. Especially as those claiming recognition place themselves at risk, and thus confidence and assurance are necessary (Sayer 2005: 955; Butler and Athanasiou 2013: 87). It also illustrates the importance and fragility of group solidarity, and that as Tully (2000: 474–475) argues, there will be continual interplay and negotiation within groups of who in the group matters, their position and of the meaning and nature of group identity. Additionally, the ability to place oneself in a 'community' and to seek communal or familial recognition of identity and deprivations and marginalisation associated with that group is important.

Self-recognition was not only pursued by those from marginalised communities and identities but was also sought by those from positions of privilege. Although this form of self-recognition was far less frequent than those described so far, these are nonetheless emotionally complicated and active re-assessments of received narratives that work to express recognition of themselves as the inheritors of privileged positions:

> Well, you know, you would say sadly like you guys [Australians], you know, we as the white people, we're the people that were the invaders. You know, brought the disease, brought the killings and all that stuff.
> *(PM39: female, 45–54, teacher, Caucasian American)*

> It makes me feel good that they [the Pequot] were able to do something and not lose it [their culture]. Sometimes it makes me feel ashamed as a white man for what Europeans did.
> *(PM43: male, 55–64, retired human services, Caucasian American)*

> That we're [whites] really biased and judgemental.
> *(NCRM74: female, under 17, student, White American)*

Such recognition is not easy, as it requires an ideological commitment to progressive political positions and a sense of justice. These sorts of identity reassessments or acknowledgements of privilege were relatively rare in the overall interview sample. Most people who engaged in acknowledgement of their privilege, it is important to note, did so based on a commitment to ideological positions held before entering the museum or heritage site. Occasionally alteration of views or deepening of understanding was obtained through the visit (Chapter 8), but most used the museum or heritage sites as space and time to reflect on issues about which they already felt strongly. As one woman at the National Cowboy and Western Heritage Museum stated when asked what messages she took away:

> I don't know if this what you mean: it's always on my mind as to how the Indians were so mistreated in this area, and how that affected them. I think of that more than... [trails off, indicating the exhibits]
> *(NCWHM104: female, over 65, retired telephonist, Caucasian American)*

In her response, she is not thinking about museological messages in a museum that, while it touches on some aspects of American Indian cultures, is largely dedicated to cowboy and frontier memorabilia, but is rather choosing to remember colonial injustice. Other examples of visitors using museums and heritage sites specifically as places to reflect on and reinforce their progressive political positions are discussed in Chapter 9 as performances of affirmation. However, another point to be made here is that the ability to acknowledge identities based on, or that incorporate historical and contemporary privilege, also requires the emotional intelligence to navigate not only issues of shame and guilt but also deal with the emotional ambiguity of both negative and positive aspects of your own identity. As discussed in Chapter 13, visitors from dominant ethnic backgrounds often raised issues of guilt and shame directly or obliquely during interviews at exhibitions and sites of dissonant history as emotions they did not want or most definitely made sure they were *not* going to feel. Some visitors passively or actively avoided negative emotions when confronted with dissonant histories and contemporary experiences, and, as discussed in Chapter 13, this avoidance, alongside a distrust of ambiguity, is a characteristic of people who identify as conservative (Jost et al. 2003). In terms of the politics of recognition, however, the nuances of the facility certain individuals and groups have to maintain and the need to maintain unambiguous emotional identities are important to consider (Chapter 13), as is the emotional dexterity of those who can address the ambiguities of recognising their privilege.

A visitor to the Immigration Museum, Melbourne, illustrates the emotional intensity of this process of self-recognition and of offering recognition. The visitor moves from self-recognition of herself as an immigrant, albeit from England (she is thus a member of a privileged immigrant group in Australia), to recognition of other less privileged and respected groups:

> I'm very fond of this museum because, I think it's, I'm going to cry, people think of museums as being sort of stuffy, artificial places and this one deals with real people and, I am going to cry ... It's because it's really powerful because it's the history of real people and the white settlers of Australia, both

you know the immigration side which is an enormously powerful story anyway having immigrated from England myself and knowing what it's like to leave your entire family behind and come over. That's the connection I have with that. But the Cameleers[2], for example, there's a little bit of history and as the film says upstairs, they, you know, they left no trace but their importance to the exploration and development of this country is phenomenal and these are just the little bits of history that get lost and I think this museum's really important in preserving these little bits of social history that often, in the great global scheme of political history, often get lost so I think it's very important.

(IMM106: female, 55–64, radio producer, White Australian)

Both positive and negative emotions are used in the examples to reflect on self-identity. In some cases, shame, as Sayer (2005) anticipated, was used to mediate and recognise self and a visitor's place in a hierarchy of political and social experience. In the last example, empathy was the emotion that was first used to recognise self and then to extend that recognition to the Afghan Cameleers, an often unacknowledged and ignored migrant population in Australia.[3] Moving to offer recognition and respect to others was often facilitated by the ability of a visitor to not only feel deep empathy as part of their register of engagement but also to have the skill to utilise that empathy in imaginative ways.

Some recent migrants undertook another form of renegotiating identities within processes of self-recognition to Australia and the United States. They used their visits to perform, demonstrate and work through their identities as citizens of a new country. Two sites, in particular, were used in this way, Ellis Island in the United States and Rouse Hill Farm in Australia. The latter is a house museum from Sydney's outer western suburbs, which attracted repeat visitors from local migrant communities. A visitor to Rouse Hill, who defined visiting as a 'civic duty', noted in response to the question about messages:

It's probably about, you know, being a migrant and knowing how to survive. I mean, for them [people in the past] especially knowing that there were no amenities or anything or technological advances during the time, but they were able to actually try . . . it's more than just a message, I can relate [to this history].

(RH18: female, 45–54, business trainer, Filipina Australian)

Other migrant visitors to this site noted with pride that they always brought family members visiting from overseas to this site of early European settlement so that they too could understand and experience Australian history and identity. This is a form of assimilation, an explicit and self-conscious renegotiation of identity in which the visitor is taking on Australian normative understandings of national identity while acknowledging that diversity appears to be downplayed. Her statement 'knowing how to survive' has two meanings here: on one hand, she is talking about the difficult struggles of early settlers to survive in a difficult and very alien physical landscape; on the other hand, she is navigating a difficult and alien social landscape of inclusion and exclusion. She is assessing the normative representations of Australian identity as represented by her local heritage site at Rouse Hill and adapting her identity accordingly – she is learning how to survive.

While this does not fit with the positive characterisation of the politics of recognition discussed in Chapter 2 as a struggle for the acceptance of diversity, what it illustrates is the power of normative identities. In one sense, this may be understood as misrecognition by normative Australian cultural narratives. It can also be understood as a pragmatic choice of compromise by someone seeking recognition as a member of Australian society who has moral worth as a new citizen and thus legitimate access to the rights of that citizenship. It is a performance of belonging and a simultaneous claim of a particular right of parity of participation in Australian society. In this claim for recognition, diversity may be downplayed or compromised, but parity of participation is nonetheless the goal. The performative aspect of this is important for embodying and demonstrating a new identity to others but, more importantly, as a reminder and demonstration to self. Ellis Island, a site of national significance in the United States as an immigrant gateway, acknowledges the histories of immigrants, but as Kirshenblatt-Gimblett (1998: 177) argues, tends to subvert the acknowledgement of diversity by blending their history into an assimilating national narrative. In the following example, a recent immigrant to the United States engages in an embodied assertion of her new identity, much like the visitor at Rouse Hill:

> Um, definitely. The whole American journey I feel I'm connected to, you know. As I told you before, I'm Jamaican – coming here, it was struggles, difficulty, and just like the journeys others have made before, that if you really put a lot, or put 100 per cent into what you're doing and be consistent, be diligent with it, that you can succeed. So a part of my history, you know, is really embedded in the message that was here today.
>
> *(EI7: female, 45–54, nurse, African American/Jamaican)*

The visitor is explicitly assimilating and embodying the American Dream in which hard work will lead to success. This performative demonstration takes on extra meaning and poignancy juxtaposed to those responses at Ellis Island from the descendants of immigrants who noted that the importance of the site to new immigrants was: "So that they can see how much easier it is for them than it was for [. . .] our ancestors" (EI11 female, 45–54, teacher, American). A message that some from immigrant families took away was "it makes you realise how easy we have it" (EI57: male, 55–64, CPA, Irish American) or "we have such an easy time. It makes you very – to know how blessed you are – and I think we tend to forget that" (EI30: female, 55–65, teacher, American). While these sentiments may be entirely true for these individual experiences, the broader message that immigration and life are easier now is a misrecognition of the intensities of continuing discrimination that contemporary migrants face, much as they did in the past, and of ongoing experiences of racism and xenophobia. While assimilative strategies may be a form of misrecognition and are oppositional to the multicultural and cosmopolitan aims of redistribution and diversity, it reveals conforming can be an individual strategy in the politics of recognition.

Claims for recognition

What the assimilatory strategies discussed also reveal is the importance of building a positive and self-affirming self-recognition as the basis from which to make broader claims and demands for recognition. I do not want to make grand claims that people were using their visits to museums and heritage sites to launch political movements. Rather, I aim to illustrate how some visitors mediated the meaning of their visits in the context of not only their misrecognition but continuing experiences of injustice and inequity. Sometimes this was expressed by what they hoped other visitors to the museums would take from their visit:

> To me, America still needs to work on treating everyone [with] equal rights. There is still a lot of racism and biases today and America still needs to learn that we are all one people [...] Americans need to learn to understand each other's heritage and to understand each other and learn to live together.
>
> (NCRM40: female, over 65, electronics, African American)

> I think it gives the message to remind people to treat people to be aware of where we buy our things or how we live our lives and I think it's also a message that this country did get there on the back of others [...] I think too many people are very nationalistic at times, they forget that this country was built on the sweat of others [...], it didn't just happen in sort of like glamorous Jane Austen type way.
>
> (BECM144: female, 35–44, sales assistant, Caribbean British)

> I think it's absolutely vital that below stairs people [domestic servants] are recognised and that their history is recognised [...] I don't particularly need my conscience raised to it [grandmother was 'in service'], but I think it's really important that the general public do.
>
> (BC16: female, 35–44, scientific research, Anglo-Saxon Protestant British)

The museum visit in these cases was a reminder to the visitors of inequities and their desire that others would make the attitudinal and material changes needed for their recognition. There was often a sense that seeing other people, especially people different to themselves, engaging with the exhibitions meant that those other visitors were being educated about ongoing inequalities which, in turn, would lead to changes in attitudes and recognition. This, of course, often misunderstood the degree to which other visitors engaged in both reinforcement and continuing misrecognition.

Claims for recognition do not always come from subaltern groups, and as Fraser (2008) and Tully (2000) note, claims and counterclaims may be made from dominant groups to reassert or maintain privilege. A good example of this in action comes from interviews at the Stockman's Hall of Fame and Outback Heritage Centre, in Longreach, Queensland. Dedicated to telling the story of Australian frontier expansion, the Hall celebrates the history of both pastoralists and agricultural workers. While it endeavours to incorporate Indigenous lives and histories into its exhibitions, the reputation of the site is that it tells a masculine story of colonial 'outback' perseverance and survival. It is also a site of pilgrimage. Many visitors identified their visit as a secular pilgrimage, and the difficulty of getting to Longreach, some 1,200 kilometres from Brisbane, defined it as an embodiment of their commitment to the meaning the Hall had for them (Smith 2012a, 2012b). It was also a site at which many visitors, themselves inevitably from rural areas west of the Dividing Range (i.e. 'outback' Australia), made claims for recognition, for example:

> Ah definitely. I think um … I think modern-day Australia needs to, probably come out of the cities if you like, and come and make a pilgrimage here and really appreciate what made modern Australia.
> *(LR116: male, 55–64, pastor, Australian)*

> You've got to have a bit of a feel for the outback don't you really and a lot of people in big cities they … I don't think they'd really know or would really care. I'm not sure.
> *(LR43: male, 35–44, head stockman, Australian)*

> Modern-day? If you're off the land, yes. I think if you're from the city, I think um … minor, but I think the city people still need to know what the heritage of Australia or the bush feeds our nation as well you know and I think, yes, they need to be told and we need to be seen … um, we need to promote ourselves really, yeah.
> *(LR22: male, 45–54, farmer, Australian)*

These visitors, all identified as living within the Australian 'outback' represented by the Hall, are forcefully demanding that urban dwellers, those from the cities, recognise their rural identities. There is a strong sense that urban Australia has forgotten the outback, failed to recognise their importance and provides insufficient respect. The context of these demands is, of course, continual conflicts over rural subsidies, drought relief and infrastructural support. Alongside the demand for respect of the historical worth of the outback for opening up the so-called frontier and recognition of the historic economic obligation of the nation to the agricultural sector, is a demand for the legitimacy of maintaining or increasing the distribution of rural subsidies. These demands are further emphasised and legitimised through a strategy of not only expressing pride in outback identity but also specifically claiming the authority and legitimacy of that identity as 'Australian'. In the following examples, citizens of the outback not only take pride in their own identities but work to naturalise outback identity as the national identity of Australia while actively undermining the legitimacy of other identities as they explain the meaning of the Hall:

> Even city folk once they've seen somebody in a Driza Bone, in a big floppy hat[4] even though they live in the cities, they still feel Australian, and that's part of them even though they might not even have set foot out here yet.
> *(LR95: male, 55–64, dairy farmer, European Australian)*

> LR111: Yes, yes it does [have meaning]. I think that it always brings you back to grassroots, it brings you back to where we started from and so it should give you a sense of pride to know that this country was started with something so hard and that we're very lucky with what we've got now, thanks to what people did originally.
> LR112: I mean the bush is the real Australia, but the cities aren't.
> LR111: [. . .], the cities aren't, well they are to extent . . . but, yeah, but they're off the sheep's back[5].
> *(LR111: female, 35–44, home duties, Australian; LR112: male, 45–54, contracting, Australian)*

These identity claims are also made in the context of a pervasive rural unease with and in the following example, active rejection of, Australian multicultural urban identities. In the following exchange between two visitors, multicultural Australia is disavowed as a 'real' representation of Australia:

> LR85: I just reckon that the majority of people take advantage of this [heritage] and it means something to people who have um, closer ties with the country. I look at what our urban city populations are today and unfortunately I feel that they really aren't what I call Australians.
> LR84: Yeah, but they come here to see where they came from and see what happened years ago.
> LR85: Yeah but Australia's not – we're getting political now! [*laughs*] A lot of Australians are now born overseas and the ones who were born in Australia, I believe yeah, they may be interested but when you have a large immigration policy that they're trying to introduce, will this place be of advantage to those new migrants 'cos they weren't born here and they don't understand what this is all about and a lot of them, as you know now, a lot of them make their own identities in Australia after their own traditions and beliefs that was in their countries.
> LR84: I don't agree with that.
> LR85: Well, I do. I reckon this is good for a certain number of people but only if you've got an Australian heritage background. If your parents have been here a long time to see what it was like or you, maybe, if you like the land

that much that you're thinking of going on it. This is a way to find out what it was all about but I don't think many Australians want to do that anymore. There you go, that'll do you, won't it?

LR84: Yeah, no, I don't agree. I think if you've got people coming from other countries and they like to, if they come to live in this country, they like to see what the people before went through to make this country what it is today and I think they appreciate um, what they've been through. That's my idea. Well, I like looking, if you go overseas, I like to look at what they did in their forming years just as people would like to see here I think.

(LR84: female, 55–64, housewife, Australian; LR85: male, 55–64, banking, Australian)

While LR84 disagrees with her husband, the inference is that she feels people will come to the Hall or places like it, and appreciate the history and thus assimilate into what LR85 would see as an acceptable Australian identity. In this interplay and the earlier responses, we can see a claim for recognition and redistribution occurring in the face of perceived urban threats to alter rural subsidies and an attempt to reassert the legitimacy of rural identities in the face of increasing recognition of urban multicultural Australia. According to the Australian Bureau of Statistics at the time of the interviews, 89% of Australians were living in urban areas, while 49% of the population were either migrants or had at least one parent born overseas.[6]

These claims for recognition were not ignored. Performances of *offering* recognition also occurred at this site. Visitors from urban areas often expressed deference and humility toward the achievements for past and present occupants of the outback, which often accompanied the naturalisation of Australian national identity as 'white/English/Anglo'. For example:

> Um, it makes me feel proud that I come from a country that has such, I guess, rich history and I know we all come from England, but this part of it is so interesting and yeah, I guess to get a greater understanding of where we come from and . . . yeah. [. . .] it gives you a greater appreciation of what you've got today.
>
> *(LR93: female, 25–34, accountant, Australian)*

> Um, it makes me fairly humble actually to see what these guys actually endured, you know, when they first came out here and squatted on the land [. . .] I mean they were the true, they were the true explorers of inland Australia which is something, you know, I just . . . it amazes me to see how they used to do it. It's amazing.
>
> *(LR7: male, 55–64, insurance broker, Protestant Australian)*

Cross-tabulations between postcodes from urban and rural areas comparing those demanding and offering recognition produced statistically significant results at this site. That is, on the whole, those from postcodes in the outback made demands for recognition while urban dwellers visiting the Hall offered expressions of humility. Indeed, this tied back to statements about the extent to which visiting this site was seen as a pilgrimage – the effort to get there embodying their respect for outback history and identity. This sense of embodying an offering of respect, while not talked about in terms of 'pilgrimage', was also prevalent at other sites where recognition was offered by visitors to Indigenous peoples, African Caribbean British, African Americans and migrant groups discussed in the next section.

Offering recognition

The offering of recognition was made in a variety of ways, from the complex and performative to simple expressions of acknowledgement and respect, as exemplified by these extracts:

> [The experience I value] I think respect, respect for the Aboriginal heritage. I think reaching a kind of understanding.
>
> *(U55: male, 55–64, company director, Australian)*

> I mean look, they [Australian society] are all bashing the Muslims left, right and centre but they were the Muslims, the Cameleers [nineteenth-century immigrant group]. Nobody knows about them, what good they did to the country.
>
> *(IMM19: female, over 65, shop assistant, British Australian)*

> [I like] just going back over the history and just reminding yourself of what the importance is of immigration to Australia and the wonderful influence that those immigrants have had to Australia's way of life and diversity.
>
> *(IMM91: male, 55–64, government policy advisor, English Irish Australian)*

> The determination of a people to maintain their identity, that's part of this, plus the fact that it's a way of taking the white man's money through the casinos, but I'm not agreeing to the casinos.
>
> *(PM52: female, over 65, education, Caucasian American)*

These straightforward statements of respect were sometimes identified as the messages that visitors reinforced or otherwise took away from their visit or the meaning the site had for them or they were spontaneously offered in response to the question about how an exhibition made them feel or the experiences they valued. In the last extract, from the Mashantucket Pequot Museum, run entirely, as was the nearby casino, by the Mashantucket Pequot community, the speaker acknowledges the struggle of Indigenous people, and while discomforted by gambling, acknowledges the need for reparations. A more active offering of recognition came from those who characterised their visit to sites and exhibitions as an embodied demonstration of their respect for diversity and/or the acknowledgement of past and continuing injustices. For example, one woman visiting the newly opened International Slavery Museum, Liverpool, used her visit to mark and acknowledge the British Bicentenary of its abolition of the slave trade, noting the message her visit reinforced for her was "it must never happen, we must never treat people like that again, which we did didn't we?", the 'we did' making a clear acknowledgement of British responsibility for this history and its legacies. In talking about the issue of a British apology, she notes that "we should apologise for what we did", but that this is beyond her capacity, going on to note that her visit to the museum was itself a "representative apology" (ISM223: female, 55–64, shift manager, Irish).

The act of visiting a heritage site that was not your own, or as one visitor to the Mashantucket Pequot Museum put it "It's not always about you" (PM82), can, when accompanied by active registers of self-reflection, be understood within the framework of recognition. Two visitors at this museum, PM82 and PM40, both had family histories of engaging with Indigenous Americans; for instance, PM40's father had worked for the "Bureau of Indian Affairs, and it destroyed him to see how they were being treated". PM40 used her visit explicitly to try "to figure out [. . .] where on the spectrum of responsibility" her family and the nation sat in the context of the history she was visiting (PM40: female, 35–44, self-employed, mixed-background American). PM82 was visiting because she had read a book about American Indigenous history and wanted to understand more "about why we were giving back their lands", using her affective and empathetic encounters with the museum to recognise the importance of land return and to "support the view that I've grown over the years to realise that, you know, the Native Americans were really treated unfairly and, I think, it just kind of [adds] support to all of that" (PM82: female, 55–64, teacher, European American).

Additionally, three separate female Caucasian American visitors to James Madison's Montpellier, Virginia, in talking about the development of the slave quarters, noted the importance of interpreting and visiting such locations. The importance of this lay not only in terms of ensuring that the history of slavery was not forgotten, as each was concerned about, but, as they all stated in various ways that "as Caucasian, I need to know more of that" and that visiting ensured that both they and wider society 'remembered' (JMM45: female, 55–64, accounting, Caucasian American). Visiting the history of enslavement in the context of the comforting and nationalising narratives of a house museum may dilute their visit as an act of recognition, but the sense to which all three noted not only the need to be aware of this history but that they needed to do so while acknowledging their privilege as Caucasian Americans renders their observance as a relatively active embodiment of recognition.

Not only could visiting itself be expressed as an act of attempted recognition but *how* a site was visited is also significant. This was particularly evident at the site of Uluṟu. To climb or not to climb Uluṟu had been a long-running debate in Australia (McGrath 2016). Some feel it important to climb to the top of this monolith, often characterised as the 'red heart of Australia's Outback', as an expression of Australian nationalism and pride. For example:

> Because it's the biggest rock in Australia, whatever, it's our heritage; it's a landmark. I mean it just – well, I was young when I [climbed it on a previous trip], and it's an achievement to say that you've climbed the rock, so, yeah.
>
> *(U51: female, 25–34, nurse, Australian)*

Or simply because it 'was there' and it was 'a thing to do' as exemplified here:

> U95: To see it properly.
> U96: Because he is a man [*laughs*].
> U95: I'd say because it's there as well.
> (U95: male, 35–44, scientist, Chinese Australian; U96: female, 25–34, accountant, Chinese Australian)

However, climbing the rock is considered not only unsafe but is an embodied act of disrespect for Anangu law and culture. At the time of the interviews, a page on the Parks Australia government website set out the reasons for not climbing,[7] with similar statements and information also available at the nearby cultural centre and at the foot of the climb. The decision not to climb for international visitors was often defined as simply respectful of Indigenous religious beliefs, for example:

> [We had decided not to climb] Oh ages ago, you know. We've read about it in a magazine and thought well, how would we feel if the Australian Indigenous people started swarming over St Paul's Cathedral.
>
> *(U22: male, over 65, air force, British)*

For domestic visitors, the context of the decision was more entangled, given the national significance some linked to the act of climbing, but also from simple peer pressure to climb, as young men in particular noted. Such pressure is wryly illustrated by one man, himself an Indigenous person (albeit from a different culture), who observed:

> I didn't, no, I left it. I heard just before I came that it's not looked upon kindly by the natives, and I do realise that – for me, I feel that the rain coming and closing the walk is a help to me to make the decision not to do it. I think that decision was taken away from me and I'm thankful for that because my ego says 'conquer', and my spirit side says 'don't do it', and so often I need help to follow the spirit side because my ego's pretty bloody noisy. So my partner [name], she wouldn't climb, and not because she couldn't do so, that she's not fit enough to do so, but out of respect. And being here with her helps me. Now if I'd have come with some mates, boofhead[8] mates, we would all be

challenging each other, and I dare say I would do it and I might feel regret afterwards, realising that I didn't listen to the proper voice.

(U114: male, 35–44, events manager, Australian born Māori)

Of the 114 people interviewed at the site in 2012, 96% of visitors resolved not to climb Uluṟu; of these, 69% had made that decision *before* they arrived at the site or before they had formed the intention of travelling to the National Park – it was something they would not do. Of those not climbing, 70% nominated that it was out of respect for Indigenous culture.

An example of a very complex embodied demonstration of recognition occurred at James Madison's Montpellier and illustrated how one middle-aged southern woman navigated and engaged with the ambiguity of her identity as a white patriotic citizen of the United States to offer a highly emotional recognition of herself, her family and that of ongoing racism. Almost all the visitors at Montpellier engaged in reinforcing performances that rehearsed patriotism and pride and, like many, this woman talked of how touring the inside of the house made her feel patriotic:

> Humbled, totally in awe of his [Madison's] great mind and how he compiled everything to come up with the words 'we the people'. Dolly, I mean, he was so very shy, and all and they were such a great blend and such a beautiful marriage because they brought so much to each other. It's just a really a great, wondrous, humbling thing to see.
>
> [. . .]
>
> *What does being here mean to you?*
>
> It's my life: it's who I am, of course, as an American. As I said, you must be here to know who you are, because the document [constitution] established who we are and therefore we must build on that every day that we live.
>
> *(JMM85: female, 55–64, teacher, American)*

She talks about the affective response she had sitting, with members of her tour group, in the room where Madison worked on the constitution. This is a performance of privilege that was prevalent at presidential houses and could be expected to be one that works to misrecognise or deny recognition – or to ignore wider contexts of American diversity and inequality. However, this was not entirely the case. Although particularly fond of Madison and his wife Dolly (she explained in some detail why she idolised Dolly), she also took time out of the normal tour route to visit the plantation's railway station illustrated in Figure 12.1.

This middle-aged white southerner informed me she had deliberately walked through the door marked 'colored' that led to the segregated waiting room so she could both remember, and experience prosthetically, what her black childhood school friend had experienced as a child growing up in the south. She outlined, through tears, how her experience walking through that door was intense and affective, and she used this to reflect on the racism in her family that had prevented

FIGURE 12.1 Montpelier train station, James Madison's Montpelier, restored to the period of segregation.

her from bringing her friend home after school, and what limitations being white, and from a racist family, placed on her friendship. That affective moment, a moment she actively sought, also reaffirmed her resolve to continue to question her racism:

> I'm a southerner [sighs]. We rebelled against our own nation to preserve state's rights. Slavery was a big part of my family's heritage and to see it abolished is a great joy. But to learn how it was conducted, you see very little of that in any other tour you get. This shows you the degrees of slavery and the Jim Crow Museum down there at the train station [sighs] I go through the coloured door. I lived that. My dearest friend in high school was a black girl, and my mother wouldn't let her come to my house [sobbing].
>
> *Sorry. I'm so sorry.*
> Well, but she does now.
> *She does now?*
>
> [yes] [name] has been my friend since we were fifteen years old. I've lived [the consequences of] slavery and I'll die to make sure nobody else has to live it. This isn't [...] This isn't [unclear, crying], you'd die to get rid of these feelings to people. I've got my family, some of them they still won't ... Civil

> War isn't . . . I'm only third generation on my mother's side from the war and believe me we were raised to know that we were different; and [I] fight that, coming here helps you do that.
>
> *(JMM85: female, 55–64, retired teacher, Caucasian American)*

In this interview, the visitor, who was always deeply engaged with the site, moved between investing in normative narratives of American nationhood, to explicit familial and self-examination of racism. This is a complex affective embodied expression of a very active sense of recognition that aims to reinforce and alter the visitor's behaviour. What is also significant about this example is the exercise of *choice*. This visitor chose to be affected, to have an emotional engagement with the site – in a number of different and competing ways. Visitors choose to visit certain sites and not others, and once at a site, people make choices to both feel and *not* feel. If, as Mercer (2010) argues, feeling is believing – how emotions are mobilised has consequences for how people engage in social debates and cultural practices. In this instance, strong affective responses to the site underpinned the visitor's resolve to behave in certain ways: as a patriotic citizen, but also as one on the alert for racism. The choices people make *not* to feel are explored in Chapter 13 alongside the consequences this can have for perpetuating misrecognition. However, the choices made by this particular individual also demonstrate her agency and that of visitors, in general, in their affective responses and how they use sites. Theoretical positions that essentialise the nature of material objects and attribute agency to them or that make claims that 'affect comes upon us unawares', cannot be sustained in the face of the powerful agency and choices expressed in this example (Chapter 2). Understanding the agency of individuals and the emotional features and choices people make in their interactions with heritage is crucial in understanding how the past informs and energises not only affirmations of self and belonging but also claims for recognition or indeed the perpetuation of misrecognition.

This Montpellier example also demonstrates that people may not only offer recognition to other groups and individuals but also sets of ideals, in this case, anti-racism. Some visitors talked about the meaning of their visits in terms that could be understood as offering recognition of the importance of social values, such as multiculturalism:

> There were a whole bunch of people in Australia before I was and they're all different.
>
> *(IMM103: male, 18–24, student, Australian)*

> The idea of that melting pot, and how well-meaning people tried to melt different cultures together, but I prefer the fruit salad, where we kind of mix together but you never melt it.
>
> *(TM64: female, 55–64, school counsellor, Black American)*

Look at [the] many different ethnicities, ancestry, how they all contributed to creating America, making it what it is today, so – and I like the fact that they're recognising that here.

(SJM19: female, 45–54, teacher, American)

These are explicit examples of recognitions of the idea of diversity and cosmopolitan multiculturalism. The role of museums in 'social inclusion' has been a concern of museological academic and policy debate for some time (e.g. Sandell 2007; Sandell and Nightingale 2012; Janes 2016; Bennett et al. 2017). While the concept 'social inclusion' is problematic for its tendency to require subaltern groups to assimilate into normative identities (Smith and Waterton 2009: 105), the desire of the museum sector to engage with and encourage the acceptance of diversity is very real and committed (Mason 2013). However, framing engagement with museum audiences within an overarching 'learning' context can lead to misunderstanding the utility of museums in reinforcing and validating people's identity and ideological positions and thus misconstruing the types of wider social impact that such institutions can have. The learning framework also facilitates the misidentification of how visitors actively use museums and authorised heritage sites to assess the extent to which wider society is offering recognition or maintaining misrecognition.

Museums and authorised heritage as 'social barometers' of recognition and misrecognition

A self-conscious and active way in which museums and heritage sites, particularly heritage sites recognisable within the AHD, were used in the politics of recognition was how some visitors engaged in critical assessments of exhibitions and interpretations. That is, museums and heritage sites as authoritative institutions were understood as representing wider social understandings of the identities of marginalised and traditionally misrecognised groups. Indigenous peoples, African American and African Caribbean British visitors, in particular, used museums as a form of 'social barometer' to test how they were being recognised or misrecognised. This use also illustrates how some visitors themselves perceived heritage sites and museums as playing an active role in the politics of recognition. The following examples come from the exhibition *Slavery at Jefferson's Monticello: Paradox of Liberty*, held at the NMAH in 2012, as a first exhibition of the then to be built National Museum of African American History and Culture. As African American visitors tended to observe, their history was often not well represented in American society:

Until I hit college, I learned very little about my own history and culture and all we had growing up was black history month in February, the shortest month of the year, where for 15 minutes each Friday we heard some story or history of a famous African American person, that was all.

(SJM29: male, 45–54, self-employed, African American)

Such visitors came to the exhibition to not necessarily 'learn' about their history, but rather to assess the version of it being told by the museum:

> Well, I didn't think that – it was good but it wasn't complete, and maybe because they're still building to complete everything. There wasn't enough information on the boats, on the slave ships and there should be. I think that gets to people and it teaches us a lesson that they see the inhumanity and the cruelty and the evilness of it all. And that was not, there was one single picture, and it was small. I just was disappointed in there.
>
> *(SJM50: female, 25–34, manager, African American)*

This is like a setback to me in relation to me, I think this is a setback.
Setback in what way?
Because it's just another thing saying 'oh, you were slaves. So you're still only expected to do certain things'. So instead of telling people about how they were slaves, how about telling them about how they can be doctors, can be lawyers or, you know, people like from the 1940s that went through a lot to be a doctor or be a lawyer. Because there were African American doctors and lawyers. So I think that's what I came to see. I didn't come to see about slavery.

(SJM20: male, 35–44, army officer, Native and African American)

These visitors feel, for different reasons, misrecognised. As one visitor noted, the fact that this was the first exhibition of the new African American Museum of History and Culture was particularly important, and many of those I interviewed who identified as African American were concerned that misrecognition of themselves had been continued. In England, the 2007 exhibitions on Britain's involvement in the slave trade, a history that up until 2009 had not been taught at schools (Gilroy 1987; Dresser 2009), was similarly assessed:

> *Whose history is being represented here?*
> I wonder. I mean somehow is it er, I think it too late for anger. I think it's too late for us to feel angry about this or to show it. [. . .]. Is it guilt that they believe that they feel that they must start making a token gesture by saying 'oh we do recognise that we had a part to play in slavery'?

> *Are you part of the history represented here?*
> Of course, of course, I am. I remember my great-grandmother she was born in 1872 and I remember the stories in my family.

> *Did you want these stories to be reflected?*
> Yes, I think there could be a lot more, I feel this is diluted it's a tokenism of England's involvement, Britain's involvement in slavery to me.

Heritage and the politics of recognition   281

What were the aspects of the exhibition that were of most interest to you?

Er, [pause] A lot of it I've seen, so to me, I don't know, I feel very disappointed, I'm very saddened, I feel like I'm crying inside, this is just a slap in the face really, if this is what the museum can present for our history.

(BECM140: female, 45–54, social worker,
Afro-Caribbean British)

In Australia, a similar and, in this case, a positive assessment was made between three Indigenous Australians who were together visiting the First Australians Gallery, National Museum of Australia:

NMA052: It makes me feel proud that we have uh, such information that's out there for, not just tourists but for the white Australians as well so yeah it's good to see that all this historical information is here.

NMA051: Well I'm actually quite happy seeing all the different people that are here and are, you know, interested in this as well.

NMA053: Yeah, I'm pretty surprised to see a lot of different people here, not just our backgrounds, but different ethnic groups and stuff, have come here to have a look and it's good to see the recognition and awareness shown here for our people.

(NMA51: male, 25–35, ranger, Aboriginal; NMA52:
female, 18–24, administration, Aboriginal; NMA53:
male, 25–35, ranger, Aboriginal)

The positive assessment of the content of the exhibition is implied in this exchange, but what this exchange reveals, and which is implicit in the examples from the United States and England, is that some degree of recognition is only achieved by the fact that other visitors, and visitors from a range of backgrounds, are engaging in the exhibition. This assumed collective performance of recognition is, of course, predicated on the assumption that visitors are indeed learning something new from the exhibition.

Collective performances of recognition and misrecognition

Wanting to see people like yourself is part of the performative process of reinforcing your sense of identity and social place in society and is part of the collective performance of visiting (Chapter 9). This desire, however, tended to be an explicit or implied position of those from dominant ethnic identities and was a feature at national sites. This was sometimes expressed as discomfort over the presence of ethnic minorities, but it is nonetheless evident in the fact that people from non-dominant ethnic backgrounds are significantly under-represented at sites of national narratives (Chapter 5). However, as noted in the introduction to the book, for the Black American postal worker and union president at the National Civil

Rights Museum, the presence of white people at that museum was an issue for her. In outlining her distress and anger on this issue, she talked about explaining the exhibits of painful and difficult histories of racism in the United States to her young son and having white visitors listening in. In the process of this private and sensitive intergenerational communication, she does not want the presence of white people to miscommunicate identity to her son. The presence of white people potentially signalled that injustice and marginalisation might become a part of his own identity. The inclusion of such harms within one's identity can be difficult for someone to leave behind when making claims for justice and parity (Butler and Athanasiou 2013: 87). The museum's story of the civil rights movement and its achievements made that mother and union activist "feel good to know that there was a history for us to move forward from" (NCRM53), which was jeopardised by the presence of people unlike herself and what they represented in terms of white privilege, continuing racism and social inequality.

As the assessment of the three Indigenous Australians indicated, the collective performance of visiting certain places, and of doing or not doing things at them – such as choosing not to climb Uluṟu – may also be read and understood as directly implicated in the politics of recognition or indeed of misrecognition. There are two intertwined implications of this collective performance. The first is that the collective aspect of visiting and seeing people like or unlike yourself at certain places is part of the processes of reinforcing and affirming self-recognition and self-esteem. Choosing to visit and support sites of marginalised sub-national groups may also be part of the process of claims for recognition or part of the offering of recognition. The second implication is that, as Falk (2009) argues, there is a social aspect to visiting. This is more than a sense of socialising with friends and family; there is also a sense in which, regardless of the individual meaning generated by the visit, it nonetheless has an overall meaning for society generated by the fact that so many visitors, or so few visitors, visit certain sites. The choices people make to visit or not visit is itself a performance of affirmation of wider social meanings – in the case of the three Indigenous Australian visitors, the fact that there were so many diverse visitors to the First Australians Gallery was taken as recognition of their history and culture, regardless of what each individual might in fact take away from the visit. Another visitor saw the presence of white visitors at the National Civil Rights Museum, regardless again of their motivation and any progressive or supportive message they might have taken from the museum, as potentially promoting collective misrecognition. The very fact of visitation authorises and justifies the wider social meaning a museum, an exhibition or a heritage site is presumed to have. For example, visiting the Australian War Memorial is taken to be an indication of Australia's commitment to the ANZAC story of sacrifice and nation-building (Roppola et al. 2019). Again, visiting *The Star-Spangled Banner*, or Harewood House in England, are collective statements about their wider meaning to ideas of, respectively, American Freedom or the romance and power of the English aristocracy – even if, for example, an individual walks away from Harewood House convinced of the historical and ongoing social and political evils of the aristocracy it represents.

That the collective practices of visiting have a wider social and political meaning is, of course, well understood in the museological literature. However, it is important to stress the consequence of that meaning. Understanding that museums and heritage sites are *directly* implicated in the politics of recognition allows a wider contextual understanding of the impact of museums. Further, it casts a different light on debates over social inclusion that aim to increase the diversity of museum and heritage site visitors.

The low representation of ethnic minorities and working-class people that visit national museums (Chapter 5) tells its own story about the representational inclusiveness of such places. The lack of visitor diversity at national museums is not only a finding of this study but is a consistent long-term finding of visitor research (e.g. Merriman 1991; Selwood 2006; Black 2012; Bounia et al. 2012). On the other hand, the high numbers of visitors from backgrounds other than white middle class at exhibitions or sites representing the histories of enslavement legacies, immigration and labour history are also telling. These may be understood as collective performances of recognition in that visitors chose to visit or not visit museums that represent themselves or others, and this choice understood through the framework of the politics of recognition, has wider social and political consequences. If the collective act of visiting is understood as authorising the narrative told at particular sites – *who* is doing (or not doing) the visiting matters. Thus, what is also telling in this process is the deep concern of museological policy and practice to widen the diversity of visitors to national museums, and yet is, on the whole, not equally energised by the relatively low numbers of 'traditional' museum visitors at museums representing non-nationalizing narratives and identities. The choices people make to go or not go to certain museums has a political consequence in signalling their support and esteem, or lack of support and esteem, for particular historical claims and identities and their place in contemporary society. The choices policymakers, museums and heritage professionals make to stress concern for increasing diversity at certain types of museums and not others say a lot not only about the assimilatory and nationalising tactics of museum practice but also a failure to either understand or commit to the politics of diversity. I want to stress I am not making grandiose claims that museums and heritage sites are entirely responsible for how the politics of recognition unfolds, just that they are implicated in this process and further, the understanding that this, as part of the context in which museums and heritage sites operate, requires heritage professionals and academics to consider the social and political responsibilities of heritage practices.

Conclusion

How visitors use heritage, and the institution of the museum more broadly, illustrates the commonplace and nuanced ways that the politics of recognition may occur at informal and vernacular levels. Moreover, understanding aspects of visitor engagement within the framework of the politics of recognition reveals how visitors can utilise sites to negotiate contemporary social and political issues and the wider consequences of these uses. While the mediation of wider political issues, particularly those over multiculturalism and diversity, outlined in this chapter tended to be politically progressive, it is important to note that claims to recognition do not always have such progressive outcomes. As was the case with the example of the new migrants at Rouse Hill and Ellis Island, where confirmation of normative national identities appeared to be the goal, diversity was effectively downplayed.

Moreover, appeals to recognition cannot be only understood as coming from subaltern groups; as the negotiations at the Stockman's Hall of Fame revealed, both privileged and politically conservative individuals and groups may also actively engage in struggles to maintain or reassert both recognition and their claims to resources. However, using the politics of recognition to inform and consider particular registers of engagement and performative practices of visiting allows for a greater assessment of what is at stake for visitors at certain sites and what informs their choices both to visit or not visit. The next chapter explores the far more common negotiations that visitors, particularly those from dominant ethnicities, engaged in over the maintenance of misrecognition.

Notes

1 Mount Vernon is a house museum and plantation associated with President George Washington.
2 A temporary exhibition on display at the time of the interview about the history of Afghan Cameleers in Australia.
3 'Afghan' refers to a range of ethnic groups and cultural identities whose members drove camels across the arid Australian interior and thus played an invaluable role in opening up the Australian 'frontier'. While some of these groups went back to their country of origins, others remained (Jones and Kenny 2010).
4 A 'driza-bone' is a brand of long waterproof coat worn by stockworkers in parts of rural Australia. The 'floppy hat' refers to the felted hats, often referred to by the brand 'Akubra'. Both garments are strongly associated with the outback image.
5 The idea that Australia 'rode on the sheep's back' references the historical importance of the agricultural sector to the Australian economy.
6 See Australian Bureau of Statistics, www.abs.gov.au/census; also E. Hunt, 2017, Barely half of population born in Australia to Australian-born parents, *The Guardian*. www.theguardian.com/australia-news/2017/jun/27/australia-reaches-tipping-point-with-quarter-of-population-born-overseas
7 See www.parksaustralia.gov.au/uluru/do/we-dont-climb.html. This includes statements by Traditional Owners and video footage explaining the significance of Uluru and a request to respect Anangu law and culture. These messages were also reiterated at the cultural centre (see Chapter 3).
8 Originally a newspaper comic character, 'boofhead' is an Australian term for someone who is a little slow on the uptake and does good-natured but silly things.

13
HERITAGE, PRIVILEGE AND THE POLITICS OF MISRECOGNTION

Heritage is a resource of power in struggles for recognition, but it is also a powerful resource for maintaining privilege and the status quo. Over the northern hemisphere summer of 2019, there was a spate of media articles in the United States about racist white visitor reactions to the interpretation of the history of slavery at heritage sites.[1] These responses essentially questioned the legitimacy of discussing dissonant histories at sites such as plantations and presidential house museums that were otherwise regarded as celebratory affirmations of nation and citizenship. Visitors will use heritage sites, either explicitly or implicitly, to help them mediate contemporary political and social issues. While 2019 marked the 400th anniversary of the first enslaved Africans being brought to what is now the state of Virginia, the apparent increase in negative visitor responses were reported to be part of longer-term white discomfort with the history of slavery. In the context of the Trump administration, a period that Parker et al. (2019) refer to as 'post-factualism', which has seen increasing racial tensions and legitimacy given to white racial resentment, it is not surprising to see an apparent increase in visitors expressing cognitive dissonance with interpretations of history they find ideologically uncomfortable. As Tully (2000: 476) points out, recognition will always have asymmetries of misrecognition.

This chapter explores how misrecognition can be maintained and propagated by how visitors use and engage with heritage sites and museums. Performances of misrecognition tend to be initiated by desires to negate negative emotions such as shame or guilt and, in turn, work to maintain or defend the more conservative performances of reinforcement discussed in Chapters 9 and 10. The process of disconnecting from negative emotions impacts an individual's ability to reflect on the experiences of others in the past and how those experiences may have implications for the present. This, in turn, has implications for debates over such issues as social justice, inclusion and diversity. Performances of misrecognition maintain privilege but also indifference to the situation of others. Performances of reinforcement can themselves be broadly understood as performances of misrecognition, in that they are predicated on the maintenance of the social and economic status quo. However, the performances elaborated on here generally mobilise more active registers of engagement than the ideologically conservative performances of reinforcement discussed in previous chapters. Understanding the mechanisms of how and why visitors recoil from curatorial and interpretive messages is vital for the development of interpretive strategies that aim to persuade visitors to debate or rethink their entrance narratives.

Heritage and misrecognition

For Fraser, misrecognition occurs when individuals or groups lack parity in participation due to their inequitable social and political standing, while for Honneth, misrecognition occurs when an individual's self-confidence is harmed by others' insensitivity to their needs, or when rights are inequitably experienced or when society ignores or dismisses a group's values (Thompson and Yar 2011: 8–9). As Thompson and Yar (2011: 9) point out, neither Honneth nor Fraser sees identity or difference as the direct object of misrecognition. For Fraser (2008: 24), the reduction of misrecognition to identity politics while providing insight into the psychological harm of issues like racism, colonisation, sexism, class-based prejudice and other forms of discrimination, nonetheless, dislocates struggles for redistribution. Rather, "misrecognition constitutes a form of institutionalised subordination, hence a serious violation of justice" that includes the maldistribution of resources (2008: 28). She goes on to note that recognition requires the deinstitutionalisation of "patterns of cultural value that impede parity of participation and to replace them with patterns that foster it" (2008: 28). The point to stress here is that heritage, tied up as it is with identity claims, does not just become entangled in misrecognition when respect for identity claims are withheld. More importantly, it occurs when the historical and contemporary experiences of exclusion that underpin and energise identity claims fail to be recognised. Such a failure will rest on particular social and ideological values that at best passively allow for, and at worst actively contribute to, the continuation of inequities. Museums and heritage sites as institutions that authorise and justify not only certain identity claims but also the social values that formulate the recognition and non- or misrecognition of such claims, and the historical and cultural narratives that contextualise them, are implicated in this process.

While misrecognition can come in many forms, it is often identified as the impetus for social action and struggles for recognition (Pilkington and Acik 2019). It can, however, also undermine and impede individual and group determination (Butler and Athanasiou 2013). In particular, as Thompson and Yar (2011) point out, misrecognition itself can be an ongoing state of affairs for which recognition is continually denied. Indeed, the existence of enduring state-sanctioned ontological misrecognition must be noted (Chen 2018: 946; see also Daigle 2016). Additionally, new forms of misrecognition can inadvertently occur in response to recognition claims (Butler and Athanasiou 2013: 87), while misrecognition can itself be a strategy for denying recognition claims and maintaining non-recognition and inequality (Tully 2000). In the following sections, different active registers of engagement that lead to misrecognition are identified. These are acts of misrecognition; predicated as they are on values that maintain injustices, they are institutionalised through the collective performative practices of museum and heritage site visiting.

Many of these instances are grounded in ideological inabilities to deal with the emotional ambiguities underlying national heritage. That is when cognitive dissonance was provoked by a desire, on the one hand, to affirm and experience positive valence in national identity, while on the other hand being tasked with acknowledging experiences of inequity and disenfranchisement of other groups with equal claims to citizenship and national identity. Emotional ambivalence, Thompson and Hoggett (2011) argue, is an important psychological reason for misrecognition and the withholding of esteem. They argue that respect and esteem can only be granted when narcissism and envy are overcome; however, their broader point that emotional ambivalence, or indeed ambiguity, stands in the way of recognition is important and supports Jost's (2019) arguments about fear of ambiguity and conservative ideologies. At issue for visitors maintaining misrecognition was often a desire not to feel the negative valence associated with guilt and shame, as they would rather concentrate on the celebration of the nation and national identity. The results of this was a simultaneous re/assertion of an affective state of indifference and a reinforcement of national celebration. In certain contexts, visiting museums and heritage sites may be understood as an affective practice of indifference. It is this embodying of indifference that informs and results from the performances of misrecognition discussed in the following. Before exploring these, however, it is useful to elaborate on the affective motivations for these performances.

Museums and heritage sites as unsafe places

Museum and heritage sites are often touted as 'safe places for unsafe ideas', places where visitors can explore difficult issues (Cameron 2005). As noted in previous chapters, the ubiquitous white middle-class visitor profile of national museums and heritage sites suggests that those whose social standing and identities' fall outside this profile may regard these sites as unsafe. However, museums and heritage sites can also be actively unsafe places for traditional white middle-class visitors who may be confronted with a curatorial message that they find cognitively dissonant. In this context, museums become emotionally unsafe.

When visitors meet with a narrative that they do not expect or do not agree with, visitors may engage positively in learning (Chapter 8), but they will far more frequently mobilise a range of emotional and discursive strategies to close down negative emotions such as shame and reinforce more positive emotions such as pride. Most commonly, these strategies come into play when a visitor is asked to re-assess an understanding of self as a member of a hegemonic group that has benefited from historical injustice. Some visitors may actively disagree with interpretive messages for a range of reasons; however, certain disagreements over dissonant history were not simply about maintaining celebratory narratives. They were also about denying the agency of negative emotions. The following example is from the Immigration Museum, Melbourne:

> *How does it make you feel to visit this museum?*
> Curious. That's all. I don't get any soft spots. I'm the sort of person who doesn't get affected easily. [. . .] [This museum is] a dead museum, this is just like a backyard museum.
> (IMM123: male, over 65, retired sales, **Russian Israeli Australian**)

The visitor, in rejecting the professionalism of the museum – it's a 'backyard' affair – rejects its content as relevant to Australia. The museum, he considered, only told the history of what he saw as "more to do with European [history] than anything to do with Australia" and goes on to note that "they could do so much more here, lots more on sporting history". This curiously irrelevant reference to sport is an allusion to the importance of sporting achievements to Australian national identity. This is invoked out of context here, as he was finding the central message of the museum about social diversity and equity too challenging to his sense of national pride.

Emotional instability not only occurs when dominant narratives are challenged but specifically when visitors experience emotional and cognitive ambiguity and, in particular, negative emotional valence. As this visitor at the First Australians Gallery at the National Museum of Australia notes in response to asking how the exhibition made him feel:

> Oh [pause] Very very proud but also somewhat, somewhat ashamed of some things that happened in the, in the past. Yes. But, but both, proud, and [pause] and a bit ashamed.
> *(NMA93: male, over 65, Australian)*

While this visitor was able to navigate these conflicting feelings and went on to undertake some critical reflection about Australian colonial history and culture, many others nominated shame and, in particular, guilt as emotions that were too difficult for them. It should be stressed that none of the exhibitions at which visitors identified guilt or shame aimed to elicit these emotions. In the following examples, there is an active disavowal of guilt, the first from the First Australians Gallery and the following from the English 1807 exhibitions:

> we can't be responsible for our ancestors' conduct, um and that therefore it's um, concepts, like some sort of collective guilt on the part of, of a state, or of, of a people are actually very dangerous. They're the sort of concepts that lead to wars, you know, like, like for people who still, for example, have um, feelings of animosity towards the Japanese [after WWII].
> *(NMA103: male, 45–54, solicitor, Irish/British Australian)*

How does the exhibition make you feel?
Okay, let's put the question in another way which I can answer it in a way that maybe you want. It *doesn't* make me feel guilty [laughs].
(BECM141: *male, 55–64, auctioneer, White British*)

I don't think we should have a great guilt trip about [the British slave trade] because it is 300, 350 or whatever it is years ago, we just need to learn at a macro and a micro-level.
(BECM22: *male, 35–44, company director, White British*)

In the first example, guilt is angrily identified as a dangerous, destructive emotion; the second is a simple repudiation in which 'it doesn't' may be read as 'it won't'. The third visitor is so unsettled by the emotion that they have exaggerated the temporal distance of the abolition of the slave trade (the exhibition was marking its bicentenary) to the present, and thus, the relevance of this history to contemporary society. While these visitors dismissed the legitimacy of the emotions that were for them elicited by the exhibitions, others while acknowledging negative feelings, searched for ways to dilute or occlude them. For example:

We happened to wipe these guys [Indigenous people] out of the way when we got here which was a bit of shame but, yeah, there's a balance there somewhere.
(LR160: *female, 55–64, arts administration, Australian*)

This visitor from the Stockman's Hall of Fame is discussing frontier violence, characterised and downplayed both as 'a bit of shame' and something that just 'happened'; the 'balance' this visitor seeks is not the considered assessment of NMA93. Rather, in softening the negativity of colonial dispossession and massacres, she is working to subjugate negative emotions. Another visitor to the Hall noted in a very lengthy discussion of how he believed Australia had a "continuing guilt problem" over colonisation in which Australians "are made to feel guilty because we stole their [Indigenous peoples] land and stole their people" (referencing the Stolen Generations). Such a discussion, he observed created:

a problem with my granddaughters who, as soon as this topic rises and I suggest that there [are two sides to this history] or there needs to be a balance in the debate of Aborigine [sic] problems, 'oh Grandpa you're a racist!' and so we all back off and who wants to be called a racist merely because we're saying there are [some positive aspects of history] even [for] our stolen generation.
(LR1: *male, over 65, public servant, Australian*)

While this is an extreme example, it bluntly illustrates both the fears underlying the hesitancy to deal with negative emotions and the degree to which misrecognition maintains the social values of racism and other forms of prejudice and discrimination.

290 Emotional heritage

Others who acknowledged negative feelings expressed an honest difficulty in engaging with that emotion, for example:

> I'm English, born in England I feel responsible yes, I feel guilty . . . I don't quite know how to sort of, sort it, you know.
>
> *(BMAG71: female, over 65, art historian, white Irish)*

> it's very emotive sometimes, it . . . you know you feel a bit guilty being here, you see a couple of Afro-Caribbeans and Nigerians, there you are staring, and you feel it's their place and you shouldn't be here at all. In the wrong kind of way, it's like you I don't know, it's like being a spectator in a kind of you know their history and I feel as if a bit it's their history and here we are instructing for education purposes and I feel it's a bit patronising.
>
> *(ISM103: female, 35–44, white European British)*

In the first example, the speaker cannot 'sort' her feelings out and unfortunately goes on to offer quite conservative readings of the exhibition. In the second example, the visitor, more sympathetic to the exhibition content, cannot mediate her feelings of shame and discomfort; she literally does not know where to look. As argued in Chapter 11, the idea that visiting national sites is meant to be celebratory is both learned and embodied in the practice of visiting. Not all visitors have the skills to navigate negative emotions that they may encounter – particularly, in the well-worn registers of positive valence routinely deployed at national sites. The following sections elaborate on the strategies visitors deployed to avoid or subdue negative valence.

Not seeing is not feeling

Dissonant aspects of national history as either special exhibits or as permanent correctives to dominant national narratives at national sites were often met with cognitive dissonance. Examples of these included exhibitions outlining enslavement at Harewood House, the Hermitage, James Madison's Montpellier or the 'Work and Play' exhibitions at English house museums or the inclusion of Indigenous history at the Stockman's Hall of Fame. This is not to say that dissonant sites themselves were not met with cognitive dissonance by some visitors. However, a uniquely dissonant response by visitors that edited out the dissonant information occurred at those sites that were both publicly defined as sites of national memory but that also included elements that attempted to disrupt normative templates.

Some visitors, once at an exhibition or site, did not 'see' anything that might challenge the dominant narrative template. Instances of not seeing were quite blatant; visitors having, for example, walked past very large banners at the entrance to Harewood House advertising the exhibition contained in the first two rooms through which visitors had to pass would ask, when questioned, "what exhibition?" Others would sincerely claim not to have seen, for example, the slave quarters being interpreted and excavated by archaeologists a very short distance from the Montpellier mansion (Figure 13.1) or to have not seen the exhibition

Heritage, privilege and politics   **291**

FIGURE 13.1 James Madison's Montpelier, with the wooden frames of the slave quarters. At the time of the interviews in 2011, the slave quarters were under reconstruction. An extensive open archaeological excavation was occurring around these wooden framed structures. Note their proximity to the Big House.

material on servants interspaced through the house museums participating in the 'Work and Play' project.

Not seeing was in some cases an unconscious factor of the power of the national narrative template. A strong example of this was recorded at the Stockman's Hall of Fame, which had undergone refurbishments in response to criticisms that the Hall's original content had neglected the histories and experiences of Indigenous people and of women 'settlers'. The first gallery encountered was the 'discovery' gallery that outlined both Aboriginal life prior to 'settlement' and the horrors of colonial contact. In the galleries that followed, panels and artefacts that attempted to draw attention to the life of rural women settlers and Aboriginal men and women stockworkers were interspaced with more traditional accounts of frontier and rural history. Additional questions at the end of the interview schedule requested by Hall staff asked visitors to comment on the new material and to ascertain if visitors thought that further information about these neglected histories – particularly, that of Indigenous Australians – should be increased. While most visitors replied that more information would be good, many where nonetheless bewildered by the question, noting that they had not seen information either about Indigenous people or women settlers in the exhibitions. Some noted that they had not thought about these histories at all until the question drew their attention to it. As one visitor stated:

> Yeah, 'cos that's sort of something you don't really ... I mean you're walking around here but you [are] not taking away the message that Aboriginal stockmen were involved, but I'm sort of thinking where were they, or not even thinking about them at all 'cos there's nothing really to cause me to think about them.
>
> *(LR151: male, 45–54, systems administrator, Caucasian Australian)*

Some visitors were reflexively aware that they were engaging in a performance of "white Australian history [and that Indigenous people] were the first outback Australians" (LR135; female, 18–24, sales, Australian). However, most were so deeply engaged in performing and reinforcing the narrative template the Hall represented that the histories and experiences of Indigenous people and female colonists went unnoticed, and thus, misrecognition was maintained. LR151's statement that there was "nothing really to cause me to think" about Indigenous people, rather than a reflection on the content of the Hall's displays, is revealing about the power of the narrative template to edit out conflicting information.

Visitors, such as LR89 discussed in Chapter 9, who noted that they did not 'see' certain aspects of an exhibition may have been offering a 'polite' way to hide their sense of dissonance from the interviewer. Nonetheless, material that was not 'seen', either consciously or unconsciously, was an attempt at negating cognitive engagement and maintaining pride in national identity. In not seeing, a visitor is thus not required to feel. Those who often asserted they felt 'nothing' when asked how a site made them feel (Chapter 5) were often engaging in a performance of conservative reinforcement that was working to negate curatorial attempts to challenge narrative templates and thus facilitate recognition.

Misreading exhibition content

National narrative templates not only facilitated the complete editing out of dissonant material at national sites, but they also framed visitors' readings of an exhibition and its interpretive content. Dissonant information, in the following example from *Slavery at Jefferson's Monticello: Paradox of Liberty* was read within the framework of celebratory national narratives, straining credulity, readings that resulted in new forms of misrecognition:

> Yes, he [Jefferson] gave the slaves a chance, and that is what this country is about, giving people a chance and creating equality.
> *(SJM68: female, 35–44, hospice nurse, American)*

The visitor is actively misreading the message of an exhibition that aimed to remember and explore the lives of those enslaved by President Jefferson. It offered a reflection on what the exhibition called the 'paradox' of Jefferson's role in the writing of the Declaration of Independence and his apparent abhorrence of slavery with the fact he not only owned over 600 enslaved people during his life, he also fathered children with the enslaved Sally Hemings, only two of whom were freed on his death (Gordon-Reed 2008).[2] The idea that Jefferson gave the enslaved a 'chance' and that he created 'equality' is not only an active misreading of the exhibition, it upholds both the received national narrative of Jefferson and American ideas of 'freedom' while reworking and affirming the social values of misrecognition of African American inequality. Although this issue is illustrated with one example, this is not an uncommon occurrence; for instance, celebratory national narratives similarly frame readings that develop the trope of the 'good master', discussed in Chapter 10.

Clichés: 'we must learn from the past'

The strategic use of thought-terminating clichés often signalled a relatively passive register of engagement. While clichés could be resorted to when a person was lost for words, on the whole, as the longer interviews revealed, once deployed, they tended to restrict visitor reflection:

> That's why history tends to repeat itself, so if we don't learn from the past...
> *(H97: male, 18–24, unemployed, Slovenian Hungarian American)*

> That we have to learn from our mistakes probably [laughs]
> *(WH60: female, 45–54, teacher, British)*

> It's our history, you always learn by your history.
> *(OMG80: Male, over 65, manger wildlife sanctuary, Australian)*

Clichés worked to deflect potential or actual ambiguous or negative affective responses, insulating reasoning from emotional uncertainty. A particular clichéd response, which may appear counterintuitive, centred on the idea that the museum or site was 'educational'. A frequent clichéd response to questions such as how an exhibition made people feel or the experiences they valued, was to note that the site was 'interesting' or 'educational'. These examples are from the First Australians Gallery:

> Um, . . . Feel. Ok, that's a hard one. Um, ah interested, ahm inquisitive.
> *(NMA92: male, 35–44, public servant, Australian)*

> Well, I like looking at the artwork and I quite like the Dreamtime histories. I don't know a lot about it but it's quite interesting to see what it is.
> *(NMA1: female, 18–24, graduate student, White British)*

> I think it's good for the general public to see the exhibition and appreciate their history. I mean it's a very young country with a very young history, but it's a very interesting history.
> *(NMA40: female, over 65, house furnisher, Scottish Australian)*

The banality and context of these responses reveal indifference – a history of colonisation and dispossession becomes banally 'interesting'. I feel 'interested' or 'educated' was sometimes a legitimate response; curiosity had been enlivened for some. However, it was often simply a socially accepted non-committal response a visitor gave because they thought they should and because it hides the fact that they did not care, found the topic confronting and challenging or were having a nice day out and did not want to engage too deeply. As noted in Chapters 5–7, the degree to which people nominated their visit as 'educational' appears to contradict the response to the question about changed views and the degree to which people talked about reinforcement (Chapter 9). The language of learning and education offered by some visitors was, in part, deployed to hide cognitive dissonance from the interviewer – some visitors did not like to appear to be too critical. It, in part, however, allowed a visitor to mask emotional discomfort from themselves. In masking that discomfort, the emotional intelligence and skills needed to convert the affective response into reflection, to allow the possibility of learning, was short-circuited. In short, talk of learning or education became, in certain contexts, a thought-terminating cliché.

Self-sufficient arguments and active indifference

Indifference, or a nonchalant lack of interest, may be considered a relatively passive emotion. However, it has strong consequences and was often actively maintained or re-created by visitors. This emotion facilitated the active rejection of exhibition messages, and the withholding of empathy, compassion and recognition. This section outlines a slightly more active register of engagement than that based on the use of clichés to close down cognitive and affective dissonance. The outcome of this register was more active maintenance or re/creation of indifference – an 'active indifference'. This may be seen as a form of 'disengagement'; however, that assumes that there was nothing taken from the performance of the visit, that the visitor disengaged with the curatorial message, and thus, there was no 'result' of that visit. Each visit constructs its own meaning for a visitor. Assuming 'disengagement' as the net result of the registers that lead to indifference and lack of recognition or misrecognition also assumes passivity and inconsequence. Rather, it is important to identify the modes of engagement that facilitate indifference in the service of maintaining exclusionary narrative templates and national identity.

The more active register of engagement that denied empathy or compassion to a greater extent than simple clichés was the deployment of certain discursive repertoires or 'self-sufficient' arguments (Augoustinos et al. 2002). As Augoustinos and Every (2010: 251–252) point out, there is now an extensive body of research within Western democracies that have identified a range of self-sufficient arguments or rhetorical devices that are covertly used to express prejudice as "justified, warranted and rational". While not inherently self-sufficient, coherent or defendable, these stock statements are perceived as 'common sense' (Augoustinos, Lecouter and Soyland 2002: 110). They are circular statements, similar to socially acceptable clichés, which brook no argument or need no elaboration (Wetherell and Potter 1992: 21; Augoustinos and Every 2007: 134). Additionally, they may be based on liberal egalitarian principles and include tropes such as ideas of freedom and equality, making them seem both harder to dispute and useful for justifying inequality (Augoustinos and Every 2007: 134; Hastie and Augoustinos 2012: 120). Defined as covert forms of racism that have increasingly replaced overt racist statements, and it is important to stress that whether a speaker consciously intends prejudice or not, the consequence of deploying self-sufficient arguments is the failure of recognition and the maintenance of misrecognition.

Although not confined to such exhibitions or sites, these statements most often surfaced at sites addressing histories that deal with racial inequality (particularly exhibitions on enslavement and Indigenous sites). In no particular order of frequency, the self-sufficient arguments recorded across this study can be summarised as: 1) 'you cannot turn back the hands of time'; 2) 'you can't judge the past from the present/morals were different in the past'; 3) 'other nations engaged in this behaviour as well'; 4) 'it was another social group (often identified based on class) who are responsible for this history'; 5) 'we need to move forward/not dwell in the past'; 6) 'everyone needs to be treated equally'; 7) 'you can succeed with hard work' and 8) Nobody is perfect/blaming the victim, which was often linked to paternalism (or ideas that the victim 'benefited' from their special treatment). These latter statements include the idea of the 'good master' of the enslaved person or the domestic worker at grand houses, discussed in Chapter 10. Many of the statements outlined here are identical or similar to those identified by Wetherell and Potter (1992: 177) in their analysis of White New Zealanders' discourse on issues of racial inequality.

The self-sufficient arguments identified were more actively deployed than simpler clichés. Clichés were simple single-sentence statements. Self-sufficient arguments were deployed in longer statements that sought to explain a visitors' viewpoint on, for instance, the messages being taken away, the meaning of the site to contemporary society or the site's link to their identity. In the following example, from an English slavery exhibition, a visitor nominates the issue of guilt when asked how the exhibition makes him feel. He denies such feeling while deploying two self-sufficient arguments (2 and 3):

> I don't feel guilty; unfortunately that's the way life was 200 or 300 years ago you can't judge it today . . . yeah . . . I think it's quite nice, nice is not the right word, to see that European countries have had just as much to do with it [slavery] as the English, the British, because it's often perceived that Britain was involved in slavery, but we joined it last which is quite interesting.
> *(BECM60: male, 25–34, computing, White British)*

This visitor is emotionally uncomfortable, as demonstrated by his reference to guilt. He was visiting an exhibition marking the British bicentenary of the abolition of the slave trade and found his sense of national identity threatened by the exhibition's request that he recognise the suffering caused by Britain. The use of the self-sufficient arguments defers negative valence. His use of 'nice' illustrates the relief he feels that Britain was not the only country involved in the trade, and thus, any sense of guilt he claims not to feel is negated by the idea that other European powers were just as involved. More than just deflecting challenges to his sense of national identity, the deployment of self-sufficient arguments creates indifference as his affective response to the exhibition. Recognition is withheld through indifference.

In the following examples, visitors actively left the past 'in the past', thus distancing its relevance to the present through the trope of either 'moving forward' or 'morals were different then' (arguments 2 and 5):

> Satisfied the curiosity as well as a bit of disgust that it – you know – shame that it [slavery] happened this way, but glad that we've moved on from it.
> *(SJM63: female, 35–44, homemaker, Caucasian American)*

> Just knowing that, you know, Jefferson's not a perfect human being. That he really had his flaws, but it's hard to judge him – you have to judge him by his time period.
> *(SJM56: male, 35–44, teacher, American)*

The 'moving forward' trope was particularly problematic and used in two contradictory ways. Visitors who engaged in the affirming reinforcement performance outlined in Chapter 9 often nominated that having their political values and self-esteem affirmed was important for them to 'move forward from'; however, in the contexts of the previous examples, it is about insulating negative emotions that challenge contemporary experiences of privilege to the past. This is forgetting as humiliated silence (Connerton 2008).

Within heritage studies, the trope of moving forward can both signal energised positive valance of remembering and garnering self-esteem or it can be part of a discursive repertoire of prejudice. The latter tends to signal the fear that underlies conservative ideologies (Jost et al. 2003). This duality presses the point made in Chapter 2 that acknowledging affective responses without also considering the social context of the affect is ultimately misleading.

In the following examples, argument 6, 'everyone needs to be treated equally', is invoked. Each invokes the idea of equal opportunity and in doing so negates the legitimacy of, in the first two instances, Indigenous, and the third, African American, experiences of historical and contemporary social and economic inequity:

> No, what we did was quite horrendous, but Aborigines weren't guilt-free either. Inequality exists because of government handouts. We should be equal and treated equal.
> *(NMA68: female, 45–54, grazier, Italian Australian)*

> I think that instead of saying that 'we are all American Indian' or we all 'American Germans' or 'American this or American that' I think it's time we can all say we are one. We are just Americans you know: that we are one.
> *(NCWHM21: female, 55–64, bookkeeper, American)*

> [my views have not changed] I was taught to accept people for who they are, not what their colour was or not what their race was, but just who they are. And it was – I was never taught to look down on anybody. And when all this – I just don't understand what all the hoopla is about [exhibition on slavery], because I didn't live it, and I think – like I said – it was wrong, but I think that's just one small part of our history. Not the entire focus.
> *(SJM100: male, 55–64, corporate executive, American)*

In the last example, the visitor is explicitly drawing links between his sense of equality and a deflection of any responsibility he may have as a United States citizen to ongoing inequity. The history of enslavement in the exhibition is explicitly and emotionally 'not his' history, and his exaggeration that a single temporary exhibition on slavery in the NMAH equates to an 'entire focus' further belittles the relevance of this history to his national self-esteem. In the previous examples, the requirement of recognising ongoing inequality and another group's moral worth in contemporary society is withheld through the trope of 'we need to treat everyone equally' (argument 6).

NMA68, in addition to invoking argument 6, also engages in 'blaming the victim' of colonisation (argument 8). In such statements, the idea that 'nobody is perfect' underpins statements visitors made that Indigenous peoples participated

298 Emotional heritage

in colonisation or Africans participated in the slave trade. While such statements, alongside other self-sufficient arguments, negated challenges to visitors' emotional investments and security in celebratory national narratives, these statements also went further. In the context of the motif of the 'good master' (see Chapter 10), these arguments do not just negate discomfort to facilitate particular forms of forgetting and remembering; they seemingly maintain liberal values of 'freedom' and 'unity' as part of the cultural values that obstruct parity of participation (Fraser 2008: 28).

Further, the motif of the 'good master' and 'nobody is perfect' arguments work to assimilate and transform experiences of injustice into celebratory justifications of contemporary notions of nationhood. This happens as injustice is consigned to the past, as we 'move forward' – the foibles of 'nobody is perfect' suggest we need to be 'forgiving' or 'tolerant', while victims of injustice are characterised as having 'benefited' from their servitude or colonisation, and thus, unambiguous celebration of contemporary 'freedom', 'unity' and 'nationhood' is facilitated. Celebratory justification is exemplified by returning to visitor SJM100 (aforementioned), who, early in the interview, expressed outrage, nominating that he felt "pretty lousy" when asked how *Slavery at Jefferson's Monticello* made him feel. He explains:

> Because when I went into the exhibit, I thought it was going to represent all of the things that Thomas Jefferson did for this country. But what happened was, when I walked in, everything in that entire exhibition is about slavery. Slavery is an abomination, and I believe that it's wrong, and I think he believed that it was wrong, but he said he couldn't get out of it. He endeavoured to free everybody in this country and to present liberty to everybody, but what we've done here [with the exhibition], we've focused it on one ethnic group, when there have been thousands of other ethnic groups that have been slaves. The white Caucasian has been a slave at one time, and I think – and when we move past that we should be focusing on what he did for this country as a statesman, as a true patriot, as a founder of this country, and as somebody to look up to, not tear down because he just happened to be trapped or did something that was not considered appropriate for this time.
>
> *(SJM100: male, 55–64, corporate executive, American)*

The national narrative template employed by this visitor having edited out the 'slavery' in the title of the exhibition, mobilises a range of self-sufficient arguments to negate any challenges to his emotional investment in Jefferson's relevance to his national identity. A variant on 'nobody is perfect' in reference to Jefferson suggests he should be forgiven or 'understood'. 'Everyone was doing it', in this instance experiencing injustice; you cannot single out a group, 'we should all be treated equal'; this is one nation that needs to 'move forward' leaving negativity in the past. He ends with 'morals were different then' to reinforce the contemporary importance of what Jefferson means to him and to underline the transmogrification of injustice into a celebration of 'patriotism' and contemporary narratives of 'freedom' and 'unity'.

Self-sufficient arguments were not only deployed to negate particular messages or meanings of exhibitions but were also themselves *reinforced* for individual visitors in the ways they read exhibitions. In the following example, a visitor at the National Cowboy and Western Heritage Museum observed that the museum made her feel:

> It makes me proud. It makes me sad, err, a degree of bittersweet because I think it was a time of more honesty [pause] . . . just a better portrayal of values [laughs].
>
> *(NCWHM8: female, 55–64, human resource manager, Caucasian American)*

She is enjoying the museum, wistful about what she saw as simpler or more honest times with values she admired. When asked what messages she took away, she observed:

> that we were once people that didn't ask for handouts, that we worked and knew what hard work was [. . .] Our forefathers were self-sufficient, and they didn't expect anybody to pay their way. I guess this is very apropos [interrupts her-self] But considering what is going on in Washington right now that 60% of our taxes and things go to entitlements for people that aren't ill, that aren't handicapped, they just don't want to get off their butts and work [. . .] You know, I guess [the exhibition] brings up all that sort of stuff for me.

The self-sufficient argument 'that you can succeed with hard work' is being reinforced and used to discredit welfare entitlements. Welfare was not at all discussed within the museum's exhibitions; rather, the visitor was reflecting on a contemporary issue discussed in the media. However, that this message was taken away in the context of a museum that presented the history of frontier expansion and referenced the Trail of Tears, reinforces the withholding of recognition to Indigenous claims for the redistribution of resources.

Appropriation as misrecognition

Another active register of engagement that resulted in misrecognition were acts of appropriation or assimilation of another group's cultural values and knowledge. This practice was particularly marked at Ulu<u>r</u>u, where visitors most frequently nominated that heritage is something 'Indigenous people have, but I don't' (Table 5.4). Ulu<u>r</u>u as both a site of dissonance and of nation-making was used in similar ways to Australian house museums to add a sense of time depth, or 'heritage', to Australian national identity. As a Rotary tour leader explained, she hoped the children she had brought to the site took away the message that "while Europe's got buildings that are, you know, a thousand years old, but this is – you know – we don't need a building. You know, it's thousands and thousands of years old [. . .] we've been here [a long time]" (U107: female, 45–54, Australian). The 'we' in this statement referencing both Indigenous and non-Indigenous Australia.

The values of cultural respect underpinning the debate about climbing Uluṟu were also taken up within some non-Indigenous Australian's sense of national pride, for example:

> You don't have to climb it. [. . .] some idiot climbed the rock and then hit a golf ball. Well, that's just a total disrespect, and I believe some French female got up there and stripped, and that's – she should have been thrown out of the country for that [. . .] it's just totally disrespectful of all Australians
> *(U25: male, 55–64, police, Caucasian Australian)*

The respect sought by the Traditional Owners has, within this example, been assimilated into expressions of national sentiment and identity. Such acts and that of the Rotary tour leader are not necessarily misrecognition in and of themselves; indeed, it could be argued that what is occurring here are indeed examples of the recognition and respect by society of another group's values that Honneth (2005: 122) identifies as important. However, such appreciation without equal recognition of the inequity of that group in social participation, as Fraser points out (2008: 28), only maintains or accentuates misrecognition and injustice. This is because recognition is simply reduced to a human need rather than specifically connected to redistribution. Uluṟu was a site marked by acts of respect for Indigenous culture (Chapter 12); however, when the assimilation of another's cultural values occurs without *concurrent* deep and critical reflection of the asymmetries of ongoing injustice and maldistribution of resources, then misrecognition has, however inadvertently, indeed occurred. There is a fine line that needs to be navigated here, both in assessing the impact of visitor meaning-making and in how site and museum interpretation is developed and conveyed. At one level, the idea of positive recognition identified in Chapter 12 may be extended to these examples. However, what needs to be identified and stressed here is that assimilative or fleeting expressions of recognition risk a moral relativism that, as Fraser argues in response to Honneth, lack sufficient determinacy in the arbitration of social disputes and the material equity granted to some groups (in Fraser and Honneth 2003: 225–6). In effect, the stress on social solidarity and cohesion illustrated in these examples may on the surface appear as recognition. However, like the self-sufficient arguments that suggest 'all should be treated equally' inequity is obscured in a feel-good moment of privileged 'solidarity'.

In the following example, a woman who identified her occupation as a finance analyst and meditation teacher talked about her 'spiritual' connection to Uluṟu, noting she brought her students to the site so that they too could learn respect and feel what she defined as the feminine "energy" of the site. She goes on to explain her "perception" of local cosmology noting that when she "touch[es] the energy [of the site], it feels like I almost want to almost bury myself within it, kind of thing, like a nurturing mother energy" (U72: 35–44, New Zealander and naturalised Australian). Being at the site for her felt like "coming home because it's a very special sort of big energy" that spoke to both her personal and national identity as a naturalised Australian. She talked a lot about the healing powers of the site and how "really

Heritage, privilege and politics **301**

lovely" visiting the National Park is "because it's something that hasn't been affected by time". When asked if being at the site had changed her views about the past or the present she identified, "Well, for one I've never liked snakes before I had a meditation with the rainbow centre, and now I actually like snakes".

Although U72 talked a lot about respect, it was respect for her 'perception' of Indigenous culture. An explicit appropriation of a non-Indigenous persons' idea of spirituality has occurred with her visit to Uluṟu, embodying and thus authorising both the appropriation and her bowdlerisation of Indigenous cosmology. This is a process that has explicitly worked to mask or ignore Indigenous dispossession and colonial injustice. While this example is extreme, it illustrates again the contextual importance of self-recognition discussed in Chapters 2 and 12. That is, any sincere form of recognition of other groups' values, cultural knowledge and social experiences must be based on self-awareness of differential power relations. Failure to do so will lead to an appropriation that maintains misrecognition and maldistribution.

Another form of misrecognition centres on the emotional appropriation of another's suffering or affirmation. Superficial forms of empathy can, alongside superficial forms of recognition, be an act of power where compassion is offered or withheld by the privileged, particularly in ways that reduce the 'other' to simply the object of empathy (Pedwell 2013: 19). Consequently, oppressive relations of power remain unacknowledged and uncontested. While sincere and deep forms of empathy were indeed important in acts of learning (Chapter 8), shallow forms of empathy expressed in certain registers of engagement were a far more frequent occurrence at sites where dissonant history was displayed. While there were extreme examples of visitors, such as the individual at the International Slavery Museum, Liverpool who wanted to "smell the blood" and experience vicariously "the horror" of "slavery [that] civilised" African people (ISM214: male, 45–54, accountant, White British), many more simply felt 'sad'. Visitors were 'sad' in many ways; expressing 'sadness' was not necessarily indicative of shallow empathy; however, when it was part of a shallow empathic response, it was used to understate the impacts of racism, colonisation or other forms of injustice and prejudice. It was used precisely in ways that Pedwell (2013) warns against, the exercising of power in which limited empathy is conferred while misrecognition remains. For example, being sad in this exchange between two visitors at *Slavery at Jefferson's Monticello* works to deflect feelings of guilt, but also having felt 'sad' the couple found the exhibition affirming of established national narratives:

> SJM12: I mean it's saddening, but I don't think – I think the exhibition did a really good job in that it wasn't about guilt. I think it was very affirming. It was very much about what people did to get away from that [slavery] and how people persevered. So like I think it's a bit of guilt, just because it's hard to get away from that, but I really liked the way the exhibit did it. I don't think it tried to make me feel guilty.
>
> SJM11: No. The exhibits did a good job of showing how the whole culture was founded on this way of life. The economy would not have developed

had they not had that, and it was just taken for granted that this was what you did to get ahead in the world.

SJM12: So it's nice that it didn't demonise Jefferson, but it's still recognised that he was part of that whole system.

(SJM11: female, 45–54, teacher, White American; SJM12: female, 18–24, student, White American)

SJM12 finds how the enslaved persevered affirming; her sadness quickly moves to a shallow empathetic affirmation, this more positive emotion facilitating – along with SJM11's deployment of the self-sufficient argument 'that it was the morals of the times' – misrecognition. Jefferson is not 'demonised'; they are not required to feel too negatively about or reflect too critically on the American 'system', which can be again celebrated; having felt momentarily 'sad' this couple can move on.

Conclusion

Performances of misrecognition, from the relatively passive response of 'not seeing' and the deployment of clichés to the more active deployment of self-sufficient arguments and cultural or emotional appropriation, are acts of defending the performances of reinforcement that maintain social and economic privilege. While certain forms of reinforcing performances discussed in Chapters 9 and 10 themselves maintain misrecognition, the performances discussed in this chapter more actively deny recognition. They do so through simultaneous maintenance or re/creation of the embodiment of ambivalence and a justification of the more celebratory embodiment of the nation and national identity. In this process, ideologically conservative narrative templates of the nation, and the underlying social values that facilitate misrecognition and maldistribution of resources, are actively retained. Heritage sites and museums thus become theatres of memory and justification utilised for the preservation of the status quo.

This utilisation can occur regardless of curatorial or interpretive intent, and some visitors, as this chapter demonstrates, will actively repel challenges to comforting narratives and defend the role museums and other heritage sites are put to in reinforcing a visitor's sense of the status quo. This does not mean that interventions that attempt to challenge consensus narratives and the social values that impede recognition should be abandoned. Rather, it emphasises the importance of the role heritage as an emotive (Reddy 2001: 104) plays in the justification of those narratives and values. It further emphasises the importance of understanding the affective consequences of the past for the present and that affect is imbricated with ideology. The strategies that visitors engaged in to apparently 'disengage' from cognitively dissonant curatorial messages should also not be read as a form of disengagement but as a form of visitor engagement with their entrance narratives. Understanding how to intercede in such engagement, to offer successful challenges to those entrance narratives that maintain misrecognition and other forms of inequity, is an area warranting further research.

Notes

1 See, for example, Mzezewa, T. June 26, 2019, 'Enslaved People Lived Here. These Museums Want You to Know', *The New York Times*; Knowles, H. September 8, 2019, As plantations talk more honestly about slavery, some visitors are pushing back, *Washington Post*; Brockwell, G. August 8, 2019, Some white people don't want to hear about slavery at plantations built by slaves, *Washington Post*; see also September 4, 2019, *The New York Times Magazine*.
2 See also *Slavery at Jefferson's Monticello: Paradox of Liberty* at www.monticello.org/slavery-at-monticello.

CONCLUSION

In the rather long period over which I have collected the data this book is based on, we have seen a wave of right-wing populist political successes across the world. Two things stand out from this, which are very relevant to heritage studies. The first is the extent to which right-wing populism is almost defined by its use of the 'past' in its political rhetoric. The second is that drawing on the past to energise contemporary anger and resentment allows those of us in heritage studies who have started to analyse the emotional and affective aspects of heritage a head start in analysing an important moment in politics. The emotions mobilised within populist rhetoric have way too many similarities with the comforting performance of reinforcing conservative narratives of the nation found at some sites as well as the vigorous defence of these comforting narratives to maintain misrecognition in the face of curatorial challenges and cognitive dissonance. Fear of change and ambiguity; the reliance on 'gut feelings' in the face of challenging information; the fear of feeling guilt, shame or other difficult emotions that are often placated by assertions of indifference are a feature of support for right-wing populism. Museums and heritage sites, and how their visitors use them, have, as the literature frequently acknowledges, a consequence for social and political debate. To have any impact on that debate, it is vital to both acknowledge the passions and emotions that energise them and understand both the positive and negative role museums and heritage sites have, through their visitors, on these debates.

Having personally interviewed more than half of the visitors for the projects the database draws on and having read all the transcripts during coding and recoding, it was all too easy to get lost in the individuality and diversity of responses. The statistical analysis facilitated the sorting of this data and the identification of the four heritage-making performances detailed in Part III. It also helped clarify and identify the performances of social and political privilege and exclusion that gave variation and nuance to each of the four heritage performances. It needs to be acknowledged, however, that the themes and performances cannot entirely account for all the diversity and nuance identified in Chapters 5–7, but they account for most, and they point to core themes in the social and political work that visiting museums and heritage sites does.

As theatres of memory, heritage sites and museums are arenas where the social and political status quo is reinforced through individual and collective acts of simultaneous reinforcing, privileged self-esteem and the maintenance of emotional indifference to inequality. Such acts of reinforcement were frequently defended when challenged; visitors often sought narrative closure while avoiding emotional ambiguity and uncertainty. Conversely, they were also used as arenas of progressive affirmation, where self-esteem was entwined with the validation of individual and collective memories of social and political experiences of struggle and achievement. Affirming performances worked to re-energise emotional and considered commitments to progressive social and political agendas and aspirations.

Sites are also used as props and prompts that facilitate intergenerational communication and connections. They were used not simply as aids to memory, to reminisce and engage in 'imagined conversations' with absent family members, but also facilitated the telescoping of time and the provision of space to stop and recall. They were also actively and passively used to transmit familial histories, knowledge and social and political values between generations. Not only were family histories transmitted, but the act of visiting was itself learned, and families used sites of national narratives to facilitate the inheritance of social privilege and associated social and political values. Central to this was familial enculturation of the feeling rules and emotional repertoires associated with particular types of national sites. Conversely, sites of dissonance, with different emotional repertoires and feeling rules, were themselves also actively used to pass on familial identity and social and political values.

As resources in the politics of recognition, individuals and groups asserted their self-esteem and validated their contemporary and historical experiences during visits. Recognising oneself as the inheritor of privilege or disadvantage and embodying this through the practice of visiting is foundational to supporting acts of recognition or claims for recognition and redistribution. The act of visiting groups other than the one to which you identified was, for some, a form of working through or offering acknowledgement and recognition. Others critically and actively used exhibitions and site interpretations to assess the degree to which wider society was recognising or misrecognising themselves, their families and their communities. This latter use is a powerful indication of how museums and authorised or official heritage sites are perceived as politically powerful and representational. It emphasises the degree to which those outside the dominant demography of visitors to museums and authorised heritage sites do not, as Hall (1999) observes, see themselves as reflected at sites of national history making. It also emphasises the degree to which the dominant demographic of visitors safely and comfortably sees itself at such sites. A range of groups used national museums and authorised heritage sites as tools for measuring the continuity or otherwise of wider social injustice and misrecognition. In doing so, they also point to the ethical and political urgency of museums and heritage sites to actively and explicitly consider and engage, as Kinsley (2016) also argues, in the political and social work that such sites do in society. This does not mean that it is simply important to understand the power of museums and authorised heritage sites but rather to also engage with and act on their material consequences for redistribution.

Central to this is also understanding how sites can be emotionally used by their visitors to facilitate and justify the continuation of misrecognition. Addressing how indifference is maintained and reasserted by some visitors to placate the fear of change and ambiguity is important to counter misrecognition and conservative reinforcement. This is not simply useful in furthering museological and critical heritage studies' aims of greater social inclusion and democratic representation but also in understanding the educational role of museums and heritage sites. It not only reveals the choices people make not to learn but points to some of the emotional factors that generate these choices. Choosing not to learn is not a form of 'disengagement'; it is simply a different use of the museum or heritage site by a visitor than the one staff may intend.

Dismissing the maintenance of misrecognition or the performance of reinforcement as failure on a visitor's part to engage with interpretive content, as treating it as disengagement, misunderstands the agency with which visitors use sites for their purposes and needs and overemphasises learning as an important consequence of visiting. Effective learning or countering of misrecognition or reinforcement of conservative and exclusionary national narratives may be more effective through strategies built on understanding and engaging with the uses visitors put sites to and the emotional investments that are made in the meaning of the past for the present. If feeling is believing (Mercer 2010), and if emotional veracity underpins and validates judgements and the meaning made through the imaginative process of remembering (Sayer 2005; Campbell 2006; Morton 2013), then understanding the emotional investments people make through their visits is central to the development of educational strategies and agendas. Acknowledging the feeling rules of visiting certain genres of sites is important not simply to a pedagogy of feeling (Witcomb 2015) but also to opening up museums and heritage sites as arenas that facilitate the working through of complex and dissonant emotions that encourage sincere empathy and compassion and facilitate the changing of views or the deepening of understanding. Nonetheless, as Pekarik and Schreiber (2012: 495) argued, the inclination for visitors to learn may only occur in contexts where visitors are inclined to make such choices. As they also note, this means that heritage and museum professionals and academics are tasked with extending their understanding of visitor use and engagement of heritage. To facilitate the development of not simply educational agendas but also to assist in understanding the differing ways that visitors use individual museums and heritage sites and to assess the consequences of that use, the idea of registers of engagement is offered.

Registers of engagement is not a set of defined factors, but rather, an acknowledgement that not only do people, as visitors, draw their varied meanings from sites but that they do so using different intensities and emotions in tension with ideology. This study has identified a range of factors that influenced different registers of engagement that underpinned the various heritage performances. These occurred in differing frequencies at different genres of sites, and entirely different registers and modes of engagement may occur in other contexts and at other sites. The point here is to offer a heuristic device that allows a deeper and more nuanced understanding of visiting beyond marketing concerns about motivation and assumptions framed by a language of learning or a passive dismissal of touristic recreation. The idea of registers of engagement is a useful device for assessing how and to what extent the practice of visiting has social and political performative consequences. The individual and collective validation of conservative or progressive readings of the past and its meanings for the present have material implications for redistribution and individual and collective wellbeing.

Besides, visitors are not simply people who pass through a museum or heritage site or a passive audience engaged in learning the interpretive message; they are partners or cocreators in the wider historical and contemporary meanings such sites have. Visitors made a range of personal and emotional connections to places and used the act of their visit to invest emotionally in those connections. The conceptualisations and definitions of heritage that visitors gave and which are outlined in Chapter 5 often made little reference to definitions framed by the AHD and drew on explicit understandings of the heritage they were visiting as linked to their sense of identity and notions of personal and familial wellbeing. The investments in the connections people have with heritage illustrate that visitors cannot be dismissed from debates about the social and political role of museums and heritage sites. While one response to these observations may be to engage dialogically, this is not my intention.

My path through critical heritage studies has been influenced by the work of Samuel, Hall, Gramsci, Ashworth, Tunbridge and Graham, with a focus on contestation and renegotiation of heritage rather than what has been described as a dialogic process between actors who are equal but may possess uneven resources. The idea of the dialogic unfolding of heritage is too much like bland pluralism and does not sufficiently engage with issues of power, privilege and exploitation. An alternative way to think about this is to draw on Laclau (2005) and Mouffe (2013, 2019) whose stress on what they call agonism emphasises contests over the hegemonic distribution of power and the passionate and emotional dimensions that inform them while grounding this in the material politics of recognition and redistribution. Thus, rather than a dialogic response, my suggestion is a more robust engagement with the social and political hegemonic demographics of visitors together with the persistent absence of visitors from politically non-dominant demographics to certain genres of sites. This is not a call for revamping social inclusion debates and practices, as these have tended to either fail or to result in an assimilationist leavening of diversity (Selwood 2006; Tlili 2008; Smith and Waterton 2009; Kinsley 2016). Rather, it is a request that the social and political uses to which many visitors put sites, and in particular, national museums and authorised heritage sites, be addressed, to understand that national museums and authorised heritage sites are used for maintaining social hegemony not only through *how* they are visited but also by *who* does the visiting. The professional and academic sector needs to own that many national museums and authorised heritage sites speak to 'people like ourselves', a socially and politically privileged demographic – and recognise all the implications that this observation entails. As Janes (2016) observes, museums (and other authorised heritage sites) tend to work to maintain the status quo, and consciously or not, many visitors are also invested in that work. To engage in social justice debates and redistribution, it will be important to understand and work with the passions and emotional dimensions that justify and facilitate that work and its material consequences.

Central to the work of maintaining the status quo is the act of visiting. Visiting certain museums and heritage sites, particularly those that speak to narratives of nation, are affective practices of asserting, maintaining and inheriting social privilege. If the politically and socially critical agendas of critical heritage studies and new museology are to be achieved – that is, if the aim is to foster equity and social justice – then addressing the role heritage plays in maintaining privilege must be central to these agendas. Specifically, this means addressing the justificatory emotions that maintain reinforcements of conservative entrance narratives. In turn, this means engaging not only with fear, and specifically the fear of ambiguity and change, but to unflinchingly address not just 'difficult knowledge' (Simon 2011) but also the difficult emotions including, but not limited to, guilt, shame, remorse, embarrassment and humiliation, that are associated with such knowledge and history. If we take the idea that politics and heritage are agonistic seriously, then the idea of 'safety' needs to be abandoned alongside the idea that knowledge and information will 'speak for itself' or convince through reasoned engagement. It is worth experimenting with the idea that museums are intentionally *un*safe places. It may be useful to create discomfort rather than comfort while simultaneously providing the emotional resources to help individuals and groups negotiate emotional discomfort and their implications.

Additionally, it means engaging with different registers of empathy and challenging the simple 'I feel sad'. It may be necessary to provide the resources to facilitate deeper and sincere empathy and compassion that can enable not just a working through of ambiguity, but importantly, facilitate a frank recognition of individual and group privilege. It means challenging indifference and fostering caring and alleviating the fear of diversity and change. I am not suggesting that all this will necessarily undermine performances of conservative reinforcement and misrecognition, but it is worth trying to challenge and reduce their occurrences and actively facilitate recognition and progressive affirmation. Heritage will, of course, always be used and have consequences for both politically conservative and progressive agendas. However, this does not mean abandoning professional agendas of facilitating diversity and social justice; rather, it is about candidly recognising and working with the diversity of ways individuals and groups use and engage with heritage. It is about having clear professional agendas and working with emotions as much as information, artefacts, collections and places.

It must be stressed that not all work that visiting does is politically conservative; museums and heritage sites that represented dissonant histories tended to have more critical memory and identity work undertaken at them than the national or authorised heritage sites. The performances of affirmation and recognition that, for example, tended to occur at dissonant sites highlight their social and political importance to agendas of social justice and redistribution. Additionally, and on occasion, national sites were also used for politically progressive memory and identity work. Mapping the tensions between sincere and imaginative empathy and compassion with that of fear of change and ambiguity is an area worthy of further research. Not only, as argued earlier, for the development of pedagogies of feeling and for refining educational and social justice agendas, but more specifically, for making heritage more broadly relevant. That is, in broadening the appeal of museums and heritage sites, in making them more relevant to under-represented demographics of visitors and potential visitors, it is useful to understand how they are visited and used by such groups. Such a consideration means treating visitors as cocreators of meaning and not patronising them as simply 'learners', of recognising their social and political experiences and their knowledge and facilitating affirming reinforcement and explicitly providing resources to assist in recognition and redistribution.

This study did not look in systematic detail at specific curatorial and interpretive strategies and how they did or did not influence visitor heritage-making; rather, it offers a broader analysis of the array of ways visitors use sites by paying attention to the adage that visitors do not always take away the intended curatorial or interpretive message. The differences in visitor uses and responses at the different genres of sites suggest curatorial and interpretive strategies are as equally important in the relationship as visitor agency and choice. Further targeted and specific qualitative research that digs deeper into the relationship between heritage staff and visitor meaning-making is important to contributing not only to the development of educational agendas and strategies but also to the broadening of how museum and heritage staff provide resources to support active and affirming progressive uses of heritage.

Heritage is emotional, and the emotions it engenders work to validate and define the individual and collective meanings and consequences it has for the present. These emotions are contextual and are influenced by social and political experience. Different forms of heritage – authorised or dissonant – are used in differing and varied ways and have different emotional registers and repertoires that validate and facilitate those uses. Museums and heritage sites are places where people go to feel, as one visitor to the National Civil Rights Museum observed, "I come for emotional reasons" (NCRM61). Emotional investments for the meanings that a site has for an individual's sense of identity and place are made and embodied in the act of visiting. Even when passively visiting, ostensibly to have a nice day out, people are agents in the heritage meaning they construct to help them make sense of the present and their sense of place.

Moreover, this is not to say that museums and heritage sites play no role in the development or validation of those meanings. Indeed they are important sites of authorisation and validation, only that the meaning and social impacts of museums and sites are made in concert with visitors. Any challenges or interventions to the heritage meanings taken away by visitors may more usefully be developed through a clearer understanding of how people use such sites and places and the social and political consequences this use has. The individual and collective acts of visiting are as much about heritage-making as are the professional practices of curation; collection management and acquisition and site interpretation, management and preservation. People, and how and why they use the past in the present, are central to understanding the phenomenon of heritage.

REFERENCES

Abercrombie, N. and B. Longhurst 1998. *Audiences*. London: Sage.
Abram, R. J. 2007. Kitchen conversations: Democracy in action at the lower east side tenement museum. *The Public Historian* 29(1): 59–76.
Ahmed, S. 2004a. *The Cultural Politics of Emotion*. London: Routledge.
Ahmed, S. 2004b. Affective economies. *Social Text* 22(2): 117–139.
Ahmed, S. 2008. Sociable happiness. *Emotion, Space and Society* 1: 10–13.
Aikawa, N. 2004. An historical overview of the preparation of the UNESCO international convention for the safeguarding of the intangible heritage. *Museum International* 56(1–2): 137–149.
Aikawa-Faure, N. 2009. From the proclamation of masterpieces to the convention for the safeguarding of ICH. *Intangible Heritage*. L. Smith and N. Akagawa (Eds.). London: Routledge.
Akagawa, N. 2014. *Heritage Conservation and Japan's Cultural Diplomacy: Heritage, National Identity and National Interest*. London: Routledge.
Albert, M.-T. 2013. Heritage studies – paradigmatic reflections. *Understanding Heritage: Perspectives in Heritage Studies*. M.-T. Albert, R. Bernecker and B. Rudolff (Eds.). Berlin: De Gruyter.
Alivizatou, M. 2012. *Intangible Heritage and the Museum: New Perspectives on Cultural Preservation*. Walnut Creek: Left Coast Press.
Ambrose, T. and C. Paine 2018. *Museum Basics: The International Handbook*. London: Routledge.
Anderson, B. 1991. *Imagined Communities*. London: Verso.
Anderson, B. 2009. Affective atmospheres. *Emotion, Space and Society* 2: 77–81.
Anderson, B. and P. Harrison Eds. 2010. *Taking Place: Non-Representational Theories and Geography*. London: Routledge.
Anderson, M. 2002. Oh what a tangled web . . . politics, history and museums. *Australian Historical Studies* 33(119): 179–185.
Anderson, P. 1983. *In the Tracks of Historical Materialism*. London: Verso.
Anderson, S. and E. H. Gurian 2018. *Museopunks Episode 31: Are Museums 'Safe Spaces for Unsafe Ideas?'* www.aam-us.org/2018/11/15/museopunks-episode-31-are-museums-safe-spaces-for-unsafe-ideas/.

Anon. 2010. *Our Story: The Australian Stockman's Hall of Fame and Outback Heritage Centre*. Longreach: Stockman's Hall of Fame.
Appleton, J. 2007. Museum for 'The People'? *Museums and their Communities*. S. Watson (Ed.). London: Routledge.
Archer, M. S. 1995. *Realist Social Theory: The Morphogenetic Approach*. Cambridge: Cambridge University Press.
Archer, M. S. 2000. *Being Human: The Problem of Agency*. Cambridge: Cambridge University Press.
Archer, M. S. 2007. *Making our Way Through the World: Human Reflexivity and Social Mobility*. Cambridge: Cambridge University Press.
Archer, M. S. 2012. *The Reflexive Imperative in Late Modernity*. Cambridge: Cambridge University Press.
Arnold-de Simine, S. 2019. The stories we tell: Uncanny encounters in Mr Straw's house. *International Journal of Heritage Studies* 25(1): 80–95.
Ashton, P. and P. Hamilton 2010. *History at the Crossroads: Australians and the Past*. Sydney: Halstead Press.
Ashworth, G. J. 2009. Do tourists destroy the heritage they have come to experience? *Tourism Recreation Research* 34(1): 79–83.
Ashworth, G. J., B. Graham and J. E. Tunbridge 2007. *Pluralizing pasts. Heritage, Identity and Place in Multicultural Societies*. London: Pluto.
Atkinson, W. 2016. *Beyond Bourdieu*. Cambridge: Polity.
Attwood, B. 2017. Denial in a settler society: The Australian case. *History Workshop Journal* 84: 24–43.
Augoustinos, M. and D. Every 2007. The language of 'race' and prejudice: A discourse of denial, reason, and liberal-practical politics. *Journal of Language and Social Psychology* 26(2): 132–141.
Augoustinos, M. and D. Every 2010. Accusations and denials of racism: Managing moral accountability in public discourse. *Discourse and Society* 21(3): 251–256.
Augoustinos, M., A. Lecouter and J. Soyland 2002. Self-sufficient arguments in political rhetoric: Constructing reconciliation and apologizing to the stolen generations. *Discourse and Society* 13(1): 105–142.
Autry, R. 2017. *Desegregating the Past: The Public Life of Memory in the United States and South Africa*. New York: Columbia University Press.
Azevedo, F., J. T. Jost and T. Rothmund 2017. 'Making America great again': System justification in the US presidential election of 2016. *Translational Issues in Psychological Science* 3(3): 231–240.
Bagnall, G. 2003. Performance and performativity at heritage sites. *Museum & Society* 1(2): 87–103.
Balloffet, P., F. H. Courvoisier and J. Lagier 2014. From museum to amusement park: The opportunities and risks of edutainment. *International Journal of Arts Management* 16(2): 4–18.
Banks, P. A. 2017. Ethnicity, class and trusteeship at African-American and mainstream museums. *Cultural Sociology* 11(1): 97–112.
Baird, M. F. 2017. *Critical Theory and the Anthropology of Heritage Landscapes*. Gainsville: University of Florida Press.
Barbalet, J. M. 2001. *Emotion, Social Theory, and Social Structure: A Macrosociological Approach*. Cambridge: Cambridge University Press.
Barnwell, A. 2019. Convict shame to convict chic: Intergenerational memory and family histories. *Memory Studies* 12(4): 398–411.
Batson, C. D. 2011. *Altruism in Humans*. Oxford: Oxford University Press.

Bauer, A. M. and S. Kosiba 2016. How things act: An archaeology of materials in political life. *Journal of Social Archaeology* 16(2): 115–141.
Bauman, Z. 2001. *Community: Seeking Safety in an Insecure World*. Cambridge: Polity.
Bayne, S. 2015. What's the matter with 'technology-enhanced learning'? *Learning, Media and Technology* 40(1): 5–20.
Beggs-Sunter, A. 2015. Contested memories of Eureka. *Ethos* 23(4): 8–10.
Belohlavek, J. M. 2016. *Andrew Jackson: Principle and Prejudice*. New York: Routledge.
Bendix, R., A. Eggert and A. Peselmann Eds. 2013. *Heritage Regimes and the State*. Göttingen Studies in Cultural Property. Göttingen: Universitätsverlag Göttingen.
Bennett, T. 1995. *The Birth of the Museum*. London: Routledge.
Bennett, T. 2015. Thinking (with) museums: From exhibitionary complex to governmental assemblage. *Museum Theory*. A. Witcomb and K. Message (Eds.). Chichester: Wiley Blackwell.
Bennett, T., F. Cameron, N. Dias, B. Dibley, R. Harrison, I. Jacknis and C. McCarthy 2017. *Collecting, Ordering, Governing: Anthropology, Museums, and Liberal Government*. Durham, NC: Duke University Press.
Bennett, T., S. Savage, E. Silva, A. Warde, M. Gayo-Cal and D. Wright 2010. *Culture, Class, Distinction*. London: Routledge.
Berger, S. Ed. 2020. *Industrial Heritage, Culture and Regional Identity in Regions/Cities Undergoing Structural Transformation*. Oxford: Berghahn Books.
Berlant, L. 2004. Introduction: Compassion (and withholding). *Compassion: The Culture and Politics of an Emotion*. L. Berlant (Ed.). New York: Routledge.
Berlant, L. 2008. Thinking about feeling historical. *Emotion, Space and Society* 1: 4–9.
Berlant, L. 2011. *Cruel Optimism*. Durham: Duke University Press.
Bhaskar, R. 1978. *A Realist Theory of Science*. Hassocks: Harvester Press.
Bhaskar, R. 1989. *Reclaiming Reality*. London: Verso.
Bickford, A. 2010. Identity and the museum visitor experience. *Curator: The Museum Journal* 53: 247–255.
Biesta, G. 2004. Education, accountability, and the ethical demand: Can the democratic potential of accountability be regained? *Educational Theory* 54(3): 233–250.
Biesta, G. 2009. Good education in an age of measurement: On the need to reconnect with the question of purpose in education. *Educational Assessment, Evaluation and Accountability* 21(1): 33–46.
Biesta, G. 2012. Giving teaching back to education: Responding to the disappearance of the teacher. *Phenomenology & Practice* 6(2): 35–49.
Biesta, G. 2013. Interrupting the politics of learning. *Power and Education* 5(1): 4–15.
Biesta, G. 2015. Freeing teaching from learning: Opening up existential possibilities in educational relationships. *Studies in Philosophy and Education* 34: 229–243.
Billig, M. 1995. *Banal Nationalism*. London: Sage.
Black, G. 2012. *Transforming Museums in the Twenty-First Century*. London: Routledge.
Bloom, P. 2016. *Against Empathy: The Case for Rational Compassion*. London: The Bodley Head.
Bojesen, E. 2018. Passive education. *Educational Philosophy and Theory* 50(10): 928–935.
Bonnell, A. and M. Crotty 2008. Australia's history under Howard 1996–2007. *The Annals of the American Academy of Political and Social Science* 617(1): 149–165.
Bonnett, A. 2010. *Left in the Past: Radicalism and the Politics of Nostalgia*. New York: Continuum.
Bonnett, A. and C. Alexander 2012. Mobile Nostalgias: Connecting visions of the urban past, present and future amongst ex-residents. *Transactions of the Institute of British Geographers* 38: 391–402.

Bounia, A., A. Nikiforidou, N. Nikonanou and A. D. Matossian 2012. *Voices from the Museum: Survey Research in Europe's National Museums*, EuNaMus Report No 5, Linköping: Linköping University Electronic Press.
Bourdieu, P. 1990. *The Logic of Practice*. Stanford: Stanford University Press.
Braidotti, R. 2013. *The Posthuman*. Cambridge: Polity.
Brannen, J. 2017. Combining qualitative and quantitative approaches: An overview. *Mixing Methods: Qualitative and Quantitative Research*. J. Brannen (Ed.). London: Routledge.
Brennan, T. 2004. *The Transmission of Affect*. Ithaca: Cornell University Press.
Bright, C. F., D. H. Alderman and D. L. Butler 2018. Tourist plantation owners and slavery: A complex relationship. *Current Issues in Tourism* 21(15): 1743–1760.
Bright, C. F. and P. Carter 2018. Social representational communities and the imagined Antebellum South. *Sociological Spectrum* 38(1): 24–38.
Brumann, C. 2014. Shifting tides of world-making in the UNESCO World Heritage Convention: Cosmopolitanisms colliding. *Ethnic and Racial Studies* 37(12): 2176–2192.
Bryman, A. 2012. *Social Research Methods*. Oxford: Oxford University Press.
Butler, D. L. 2001. Whitewashing plantations: The commodification of a slave-free Antebellum South. *International Journal of Hospitality and Tourism Administration* 2(3–4): 163–175.
Butler, J. 1990. Gender trouble, feminist theory, and psychoanalytic discourse. *Feministm/Postmodernism*. L. Nicholson (Ed.). London: Routledge.
Butler, J. 1996. Performativity's social magic. *The Social and Political Body*. T. R. Schatzki and W. Natter (Eds.). Guilford Press, 113–128.
Butler, J. 1997. *Excitable Speech: A Politics of the Performative*. New York: Routledge.
Butler, J. 2005. *Giving and Account of Oneself*. New York: Fordham University Press.
Butler, J. 2010. Performative agency. *Journal of Cultural Economy* 3(2): 147–161.
Butler, J. 2015. *Sense of the Subject*. New York: Fordham University Press.
Butler, J. and A. Athanasiou 2013. *Dispossession: The Performanative in the Political*. Cambridge: Polity.
Bygstad, B. and B. E. Munkvold 2011. *In Search of Mechanisms. Conducting a Critical Realist Data Analysis*. Proceedings of Thirty Second International Conference on Information Systems, Shanghai, December 4–7.
Cameron, C. M. and J. B. Gatewood 2012. The numen experience in heritage tourism. *The Cultural Moment in Tourism*. L. Smith, E. Waterton and S. Watson (Eds.). London: Routledge.
Cameron, F. 2005. Contentiousness and shifting knowledge paradigms: The roles of history and science museums in contemporary societies. *Museum Management and Curatorship* 20(3): 213–233.
Cameron, F. 2006. Beyond surface representations: Museum, edgy topics, civic responsibilities and modes of engagement. *Open Museum Journal* 8: Online.
Cameron, F. 2007. Moral lessons and reforming agendas: History Museums, science museums, contentious topics and contemporary societies. *Museum Revolutions: How Museums Change and are Changed*. S. J. Knell, S. Macleod and S. Watson (Eds.). Abingdon: Routledge.
Campbell, G. and L. Smith 2011. *Association of Critical Heritage Studies Manifesto*. www.criticalheritagestudies.org/history.
Campbell, S. 2006. Our faithfulness to the past: Reconstructing memory value. *Philosophical Psychology* 19(3): 361–380.
Carlson, M. 2017. *Performance: A Critical Introduction*. London: Routledge.
Carter, J. 2016. Out of the box and into the fold: Museums, human rights, and changing pedagogical practices. *Museums and the Past: Constructing Historical Consciousness*. V. Gosselin and P. Livingstone (Eds.). Vancouver: UBC Press.
Casey, D. 2001. Museums as agents for social and political change. *Curator* 44(3): 230–236.

Cashman, R. 2006. Critical nostalgia and material culture in northern Ireland. *Journal of American Folklore* 119(427): 137–160.
Castro, F. G., J. G. Kellison, S. J. Boyd and A. Kopak 2010. A methodology for conducting integrative mixed methods research and data analysis. *Journal of Mixed Methods Research* 4(4): 342–360.
Chase, M. and C. Shaw 1989. The dimensions of nostalgia. *The Imagined Past: History and Nostalgia*. C. Shaw and M. Chase (Eds.). Manchester: Manchester University Press.
Cheathem, M. R. 2011. Andrew Jackson, slavery, and historians. *History Compass* 9(4): 326–338.
Chen, C. 2018. Race and the politics of recognition. *The SAGE Handbook of Frankfurt School Critical Theory*. B. Best, W. Bonefeld and C. O'Kane (Eds.). London: Sage.
Chin, W.Y. 2015. The age of covert racism in the era of the Roberts Court during the waning of affirmative action. *Rutgers Race & the Law Review* 16(1): 1–38.
Chouliaraki, L. and N. Fairclough. 2004. The critical analysis of discourse. *Critical Strategies for Social Research*. W. K. Carroll (Ed.). Tronto: Canadian Scholars Press.
Chronis, A. 2005. Constructing heritage at the Gettysburg storyscape. *Annals of Tourism Research* 32(2): 386–406.
Clark, A. 2018. Friday essay: The 'great Australian silence' 50 years on. *The Conversation* August 3. https://theconversation.com/friday-essay-the-great-australian-silence-50-years-on-100737.
Clohesy, A. M. 2013. *Politics of Empathy: Ethics, Solidarity, Recognition*. London: Routledge.
Clough, P. T. 2007. Introduction. *The Affective Turn: Theorizing the Social*. P. T. Clough and J. Halley (Eds.). Durham: Duke University Press.
Coats, R. D. 2008. Covert racism in the USA and globally. *Sociology Compass* 2(1): 208–231.
Cobb, M. D. and J. H. Kuklinski 1997. Changing minds: Political arguments and political persuasion. *American Journal of Political Science* 41(1): 88–121.
Coghlan, R. 2017. *Imagined Conversations: The Powerful (and Power-Shifting) Potential of Museum Participation*. Unpublished PhD thesis, The Australian National University.
Coghlan, R. 2018. 'My voice counts because I'm handsome.' Democratising the museum: The power of museum participation. *International Journal of Heritage Studies* 24(7): 795–809.
Coles, A. 2016. Museums and freedom of speech. *A Cultural Cacophony: Museums Perspectives and Projects*. www.museumsaustralia.org.au/ma2015-sydney, 38–47.
Collingridge, D. S. 2013. A primer on quantitized data analysis and permutation testing. *Journal of Mixed Methods Research* 7(1): 81–97.
Conn, S. 2010. *Do Museums Still Need Objects?* Philadelphia: University of Pennsylvania Press.
Connerton, P. 1991. *How Societies Remember*. Cambridge: Cambridge University Press.
Connerton, P. 2008. Seven types of forgetting. *Memory Studies* 1(1): 59–71.
Conrad, M., K. Ercikan, G. Friesen, J. Létourneau, D. A. Muise, D. Northrup and P. Seixas 2013. *Canadians and their Pasts*. Toronto: University of Toronto Press.
Coole, D. and S. Frost 2010. Introducing the new materialisms. *New Materialisms: Ontology, Agency, and Politics*. D. Coole and S. Frost (Eds.). Durham: Duke University Press.
Cossarini, P. and F.Vallespin Eds. 2019. *Populism and Passions: Democratic Legitimacy after Austerity*. New York: Routledge.
Cresswell, J. W. 2014. *Research Design: Qualitative, Quantitative, and Mixed Methods Approaches*. Los Angles: Sage.
Cresswell, J. W. 2016. Reflection on the MMIRA *The Future of Mixed Methods* Task Force Report. *Journal of Mixed Methods Research* 10(3): 215–219.
Cresswell, T. 2012. Nonrepresentational theory and me: Notes of an interested sceptic. *Environment and Planning D: Society and Space* 30: 96–102.
Crooke, E., 2008. *Museums and Community: Ideas, Issues and Challenges*. London: Routledge.

Crouch, D. 2010. The perpetual performance and emergence of heritage. *Culture, Heritage and Representation*. E. Waterton and S. Watson (Eds.). Farnham: Ashgate.

Cubitt, G. 2009. Bringing it home: Making local meaning in 2007 Bicentenary exhibitions. *Slavery and Abolition* 30(2): 259–275.

Cubitt, G. 2010. Lines of resistance: Evoking and configuring the theme of resistance in museum displays in Britain around the bicentenary of 1807. *Museum & Society* 8(3): 143–164.

Cubitt, G. 2011. Atrocity materials and the representation of transatlantic slavery: Problems, strategies and reactions. *Representing Enslavement and Abolition in Museums: Ambiguous Engagements*. L. Smith, G. Cubitt, R. Wilson and K. Fouseki (Eds.). New York: Routledge.

Cubitt, G. 2015. Displacements and hidden histories: Museums, locality and the British memory of the transatlantic slave trade. *Local Memories in a Nationalizing and Globalizing World*. M. Beyen and B. Deseure (Eds.). London: Palgrave Macmillan.

Cusack, C. M. and J. Digance 2009. The Melbourne Cup: Australian identity and secular pilgrimage. *Sport in Society* 12(7): 876–889.

Daigle, M. 2016. Awawanenitakik: The spatial politics of recognition and relational geographies of Indigenous self-determination. *The Canadian Geographer* 60(2): 259–269.

Darian-Smith, K. and C. Pascoe Eds. 2013. *Children, Childhood and Cultural Heritage*. London: Routledge.

Dawson, E. and E. Jenson 2011. Towards a contextual turn in visitor studies: Evaluating visitor segmentation and identity-related motivations. *Visitor Studies* 14(2): 127–140.

Dean, D. and P. E. Rider 2005. Museums, nation and political history in the Australian national museum and the Canadian museum of civilization. *Museum & Society* 3(1): 35–50.

De Cesari, C. and A. Kaya Eds. 2020. *European Memory in Populism: Representations of Self and Other*. London: Routledge.

Deckha, N. 2004. Beyond the country house: Historic conservation as aesthetic politics. *European Journal of Cultural Studies* 7(4): 403–423.

Derickson, K. D. 2016. On the politics of recognition in critical urban scholarship. *Urban Geography* 37(6): 824–829.

Dicks, B. 2000. *Heritage, Place and Community*. Cardiff: University of Wales Press.

Dicks, B. 2003. Heritage, governance and marketization: A case study from Wales. *Museum and Society* 1(1): 30–44.

Doering, Z. D. and A. J. Pekarik 1996. Questioning the entrance narrative. *The Journal of Museum Education* 21(3): 20–23.

Dresser, M. 2009. Remembering slavery and abolition in Bristol. *Slavery and Abolition* 30(2): 223–246.

Dresser, M. and A. Hann 2013. Introduction. *Slavery and the British Country House*. M. Dresser and A. Hann (Eds.). Swindon: English Heritage.

Dubinsky, L. and D. Muise 2016. Museums as in-between institutions: Can they be trusted? *Museums and the Past: Constructing Historical Consciousness*. V. Gosselin and P. Livingstone (Eds.). Vancouver: UBC Press

Dudley, L. 2017. 'I think I know a little bit about that anyway, so it's okay': Museum visitor strategies for disengaging with confronting mental health material. *Museum & Society* 15(2): 193–216.

Dudley, L. 2019. *Mental Health in Museums: Exploring the Reactions of Visitors and Community Groups to Mental Health Exhibitions*. Unpublished PhD thesis, Australian National University.

Dudley, S. H. Ed. 2010. *Museum Materialities: Objects, Engagements, Interpretations*. London: Routledge.

Eddo-Lodge, R. 2018. *Why I'm No Longer Talking to White People About Race*. London: Bloomsbury Publishing.

Elder-Vass, D. 2010. *The Causal Power of Social Structures: Emergence, Structure and Agency*. Cambridge: Cambridge University Press.
Engelhardt, T. and E. T. Linethal Eds. 1996. *History Wars: The Enola Gay and Other Battles for the American Past*. New York: Holt Paperbacks.
Fairclough, I. and N. Fairclough 2013. *Political Discourse Analysis: A Method for Advanced Students*. London: Routledge.
Fairclough, N. 2003. *Analysing Discourse: Textual Analysis for Social Research*. London: Routledge.
Fairclough, N. 2005. Peripheral vision: Discourse analysis in organization studies: The case for critical realism. *Organization Studies* 26(6): 915–939.
Fairclough, N., P. Graham, J. Lemke and R. Wodak 2004. Introduction. *Critical Discourse Studies* 1(1): 1–7.
Fairclough, N., B. Jessop and A. Sayer 2002. Critical realism and semiosis. *Alethia* 5(1): 2–10.
Falk, H. and L. D. Dierking 1992. *The Museum Experience*. Washington, DC: Whalesback Books.
Falk, J. H. 2005. Free-choice environmental learning: Framing the discussion. *Environmental Education Research* 11(3): 265–280.
Falk, J. H. 2006. An identity-centred approach to understanding museum learning. *Curator: The Museums Journal* 49(2): 151–166.
Falk, J. H. 2009. *Identity and the Museum Visitor Experience*. Walnut Creek: Left Coast.
Falk, J. H. 2011. Contextualizing Falk's identity – related visitor motivation model. *Visitor Studies* 14(2): 141–157.
Falk, J. H. and L. D. Dierking 2000. *Learning from Museums: Visitor Experiences and the Making of Meaning*. Lanham: AltaMira.
Falk, J. H. and M. Storksdieck 2005. Using the contextual model of learning to understand visitor learning from a science center exhibition. *Science Education* 89: 744–788.
Fetters, M. D. 2018. Six equations to help conceptualise the field of mixed methods. *Journal of Mixed Methods Research* 12(3): 262–267.
Fetters, M. D. and J. F. Molina-Azorin 2017. The *Journal of Mixed Methods Research* starts a new decade: Perspectives of past editors on the current state of the field and future directions. *Journal of Mixed Methods Research* 11(4): 423–432.
Fleming, D. 2012. Human rights museums: An overview. *Curator: The Museum Journal* 55(3): 251–256.
Fletcher, A. J. 2017. Applying Critical Realism in Qualitative Research: Methodology Meets Method. *International Journal of Social Research Methodology* 20(2): 181–194.
Fortun, K. 2014. From Latour to late industrialism. *Journal of Ethnographic Theory* 4(1): 309–329.
Fouseki, K. 2010. Community voices, curatorial choices: Community consultation for the 1807 exhibitions. *Museum and Society* 8(3): 180–192.
Fraser, N. 1995. From redistribution to recognition? Dilemmas of justice in a 'Postsocialist' age. *New Left Review* (212, July): 68–93.
Fraser, N. 1999. Social justice in the age of identity politics: Redistribution, recognition, and participation. *Culture and Economy After the Cultural Turn*. L. Ray and A. Sayer (Eds.). London: Sage.
Fraser, N. 2000. Rethinking recognition. *New Left Review* 3(May/June): 107–120.
Fraser, N. 2001. Recognition without ethics? *Theory, Culture and Society* 18(2–3): 21–42.
Fraser, N. 2008. Rethinking recognition: Overcoming displacement and reification in cultural politics. *Adding Insult to Injury: Nancy Fraser Debates her Critics*. K. Olson (Ed.). London: Verso.
Fraser, N. 2010. *Scales of Justice: Reimagining Political Space in a Globalizing World*. New York: Columbia University Press.

Fraser, N. and A. Honneth 2003. *Redistribution or Recognition? A Political-Philosophical Exchange.* London: Verso.

Fraser, N. and N. A. Naples 2004. To interpret the world and to change it: An interview with Nancy Fraser. *Signs: Journal of Women in Culture and Society* 29(4): 1103–1124.

Frevert, U. 2011. *Emotions in History – Lost and Found.* Budapest: Central European University Press.

Fyfe, G. 2004. Reproductions, cultural capital and museums: Aspects of the culture of copies. *Museum & Society* 2(1): 47–67.

Gable, E. 2009. Labor and leisure at Monticello: Or representing race instead of class at an inadvertent white identity shrine. *Heritage and Identity: Engagement and Demission in the Contemporary World.* M. Anico and E. Peralta (Eds.). Abingdon: Routledge.

Gilroy, P. 1987. *There Ain't no Black in the Union Jack: The Cultural Politics of Race and Nation.* London: Routledge.

Golding, V. and W. Modest Eds. 2013. *Museums and Communities: Curators, Collections and Collaboration.* London: Bloomsbury.

Gordon-Reed, A. 2008. *The Hemingses of Monticello: An American Family.* New York: WW Norton and Company.

Gosselin, V. and P. Livingstone Eds. 2016. *Museums and the Past: Constructing Historical Consciousness.* Vancouver: UBC Press.

Goulding, C. 2001. Romancing the past: Heritage visiting and the nostalgic consumer. *Psychology and Marketing* 18(6): 565–592.

Graburn, N. H. H. and D. Barthel-Bouchier 2001. Relocating the tourist. *International Sociology* 16(2): 147–158.

Graham, B. J., G. J. Ashworth and J. E. Tunbridge 2000. *A Geography of Heritage: Power, Culture and Economy.* London: Arnold Publishers.

Graham, C. 2017. *Happiness for All? Unequal Hopes and Lives in Pursuit of the American Dream.* Princeton: Princeton University Press.

Grahn, W. and R. J. Wilson Eds. 2018. *Gender and Heritage: Performance, Place and Politics.* London: Routledge.

Gregory, J. 2015. Connecting with the past through social media: The 'Beautiful buildings and cool places Perth has lost' Facebook group. *International Journal of Heritage Studies* 21(1): 22–45.

Gregory, K. and A. Witcomb 2007. Beyond nostalgia: The role of affect in generating historical understanding at heritage sites. *Museum Revolutions: How Museums Change and are Changed.* S. J. Knell, S. Macleod and S. Watson (Eds.). Abingdon: Routledge.

Grewcock, D. 2014. Performing heritage (studies) at the Lord Mayor's show. *International Journal of Heritage Studies* 20(7–8): 760–781.

Hafer, C. L. and B. L. Choma 2010. Belief in a just world, perceived fairness, and justification of the status quo. *Social and Psychological Bases of Ideology and System Justification.* J. T. Jost, A. C. Kay and H. Thorisdottir (Eds.). Oxford: Oxford University Press.

Hafstein, T. V. 2009. Intangible heritage as a list: From masterpieces to representation. *Intangible Heritage.* L. Smith and N. Akagawa (Eds.). London: Routledge.

Hafstein, T. V. 2018. *Making Intangible Heritage: El Condor Pasa and Other Stories from UNESCO.* Bloomington: Indiana University Press.

Hage, G. 2012. *White Nation: Fantasies of White Supremacy in a Multicultural Society.* London: Routledge.

Hall, C. M. 2009. Tourists and heritage: All things must come to pass. *Tourism Recreation Research* 34(1): 88–90.

Hall, S. 1999. Whose heritage? Un-settling 'The Heritage', Re-imaging the post-nation. *Third Text* 13(49): 3–13.

Hanquinet, L. 2016. Place and cultural capital: Art museum visitors across space. *Museum and Society* 14(1): 65–81.
Harrison, R. 2010. The politics of heritage. *Understanding the Politics of Heritage*. R. Harrison (Ed.). Manchester: Manchester University Press.
Harrison, R. 2013. *Heritage: Critical Approaches*. London: Routledge.
Harrison, R. 2015. Beyond 'natural' and 'cultural' heritage: Toward an ontological politics of heritage in the age of Anthropocene. *Heritage & Society* 8(1): 24–42.
Harrison, R., N. Bartolini, C. DeSilvey, C. Holtorf, A. Lyons, S. Macdonald, S. May, J. Morgan and S. Penrose. 2016. Heritage futures. *Archaeology International* 19: 68–72.
Harrison, R., S. Byrne and A. Clarke 2013. *Reassembling the Collection: Ethnographic Museums and Indigenous Agency*. Santa Fe: SAR Press.
Harvey, D. C. 2001. Heritage pasts and heritage presents: Temporality, meaning and the scope of heritage studies. *International Journal of Heritage Studies* 7(4): 319–338.
Harvey, D. C. 2015. Heritage and scale: Settings, boundaries and relations. *International Journal of Heritage Studies* 21(6): 577–593.
Hastie, B. and M. Augoustinos 2012. Rudd's apology to the stolen generations: Challenging self-sufficient arguments in 'race' discourse. *Australian Psychologist* 47: 118–126.
Hathcoat, J. D. and C. Meixner 2015. Pragmatisim, factor analysis, and the conditional incompatibility thesis in mixed methods research. *Journal of Mixed Methods Research* 11(4): 433–449.
Haviland, M. L. D. 2016. *Side by Side?: Community Art and the Challenge of Co-creativity*. London: Routledge.
Hein, H. 2006. *Public Art: Thinking Museums Differently*. Lanham: Altamira.
Hewison, R. 1987. *The Heritage Industry: Britain in a Climate of Decline*. London: Methuen.
High, S. C. and D. W. Lewis 2007. *Corporate Wasteland: The Landscape and Memory of Deindustrialization*. Ithaca: ILR Press.
Hill, J. H. 2008. *The Everyday Language of White Racism*. Chichester: Wiley-Blackwell.
Hirsch, M. 2008. The generation of postmemory. *Poetics* 29(1): 103–128.
Hirsch, M. 2012. *The Generation of Postmemory: Writing and Visual Culture After the Holocaust*. New York: Columbia University Press.
Hochschild, A. R. 1979. Emotion work, feeling rules, and social structure. *American Journal of Sociology* 85(3): 551–575.
Hochschild, A. R. 1983. *The Managed Heart: Commercialization of Human Feeling*. Berkeley: California University Press.
Hodder, I. 2012. *Entangled: An Archaeology of the Relationships between Humans and Things*. Chichester: Wiley-Blackwell.
Hoggett, P. and S. Thompson 2012. Introduction. *Politics and the Emotions: The Affective Turn in Contemporary Political Studies*. S. Thompson and P. Hoggett (Eds.). New York: Continuum.
Holtorf, C. and A. Högberg 2015. Contemporary heritage and the future. *The Palgrave Handbook of Contemporary Heritage Research*. E. Waterton and S. Watson (Eds.). London: Palgrave Macmillan.
Honneth, A. 2005. *The Struggle for Recognition: The Moral Grammar of Social Conflicts*. Cambridge: Polity.
Honneth, A. 2008. *Disrespect: The Normative Foundations of Critical Theory*. Cambridge: Polity.
Honneth, A. 2012. *The I in We: Studies in the Theory of Recognition*. Cambridge: Polity.
Hooper-Greenhill, E. 2006. Studying visitors. *A Companion to Museum Studies*. S. Macdonald (Ed.). Chichester: Wiley.
Hooper-Greenhill, E. 2007a. **Museums and Education: Purpose, Pedagogy, Performance**. London: Routledge.

Hooper-Greenhill, E. 2007b. Interpretive communities, strategies and repertoires. *Museums and their Communities*. S. Watson (Ed.). London: Routledge.

Herzfeld, M. 2016. *Siege of the spirits: community and polity in Bangkok*. Chicago: University of Chicago Press.

Hutchinson, M. and A. Witcomb 2014. Migration exhibitions and the question of identity: Reflections on the history of the representation of migration in Australian museums, 1986–2011. *Museums and Migration: History, Memory and Politics*. L. Gourievidis (Ed.). London: Routledge.

Hutchison, E. and R. Bleiker 2008. Emotional reconciliation: Reconstituting identity and community after trauma. *European Journal of Social Theory* 11(3): 385–403.

Illouz, E. 2007. *Cold Intimacies: The Making of Emotional Capitalism*. Cambridge: Polity.

Iosifides, T. 2011. *Qualitative Methods in Migration Studies: A Critical Realist Perspective*. Farnham: Ashgate.

Jagger, G. 2008. *Judith Butler: Sexual Politics, Social Change and the Power of the Performative*. London: Routledge.

Janes, R. R. 2007. Museums, social responsibility and the future we desire. *Museum Revolutions: How Museums Change and are Changed*. S. J. Knell, S. Macleod and S. Watson (Eds.). Abingdon: Routledge.

Janes, R. R. 2009. *Museums in a Troubled World: Renewal, Irrelevance or Collapse?* London: Routledge.

Janes, R. R. 2016. Museums and the responsibility gap. *Museums and the Past: Constructing Historical Consciousness*. V. Gosselin and P. Livingstone (Eds.). Vancouver: UBC Press.

Janes, R. R. and R. Sandell Eds. 2019. *Museum Activism*. London: Routledge.

Jansen, H. 2010. The logic of qualitative survey research and its position in the field of social research methods. *Forum Qualitative Social Research* 11(2): Article 11, http://nbn-resolving.de/urn:nbn:de:0114-fqs1002110.

Jenkins, T. 2011. Lest we should ever be allowed to forget. *The Independent*, accessed 14/09/11.

Johnson, C. 2005. Narratives of identity: Denying empathy in conservative discourses on race, class, and sexuality. *Theory and Society* 34: 37–61.

Johnston, R. and K. Marwood 2017. Action heritage: Research, communities, social justice. *International Journal of Heritage Studies* 23(9): 816–831.

Jones, P. and A. Kenny 2010. *Australia's Muslim Cameleers: Pioneers of the Inland, 1860s-1930s*. Kent Town: Wakefield Press and the South Australian Museum.

Jost, J. T. 2006. The end of the end of ideology. *American Psychologist* 61(7): 651–670.

Jost, J. T. 2017. A theory of system justification: Is there a nonconscious tendency to defend, bolster and justify aspects of the societal status quo? *American Psychological Association*, www.apa.org/science/about/psa/2017/06/system-justification.

Jost, J. T. 2019. A quarter century of system justification theory: Questions, answers, criticisms, and societal applications. *British Journal of Social Psychology* 58(2): 263–314.

Jost, J. T., C. M. Federico and J. L. Napier 2009. Political ideology: Its structure, functions, and elective affinities. *Annual Review of Psychology* 60: 307–337.

Jost, J. T., J. Glaser, A. W. Kruglanski and F. J. Sulloway 2003. Political conservatism as motivated social cognition. *Psychological Bulletin* 129(3): 339–375.

Jost, J. T. and M. Krochik 2014. Ideological differences in epistemic motivation: Implications for attitude structure, depth of information processing, susceptibility to persuasion, and stereotyping. *Advances in Motivation Science* 1: 181–231.

Kadoyama, M. 2018. *Museums Involving Communities: Authentic Connections*. London: Routledge.

Kaidesoja, T. 2013. *Naturalizing Critical Realist Social Ontology*. London: Routledge.

Kalela, J. 2012. *Making History: The Historian and Uses of the Past*. Basingstoke: Palgrave Macmillan.

Keightley, E. and M. Pickering 2012. *The Mnemonic Imagination: Remembering as Creative Practice.* Basingstoke: Palgrave Macmillan.
Kelly, L. 2002. *What is Learning . . . and why do Museums need to do Something About it?* Unpublished paper presented at Why Learning? Seminar, Australian Museum/University of Technology Sydney, November 22.
Kern, F. G. 2018. The trials and tribulations of applied triangulation: Weighing different data sources. *Journal of Mixed Methods Research* 12(2): 166–181.
Kidd, J. 2011. Challenging history: Reviewing debate within the heritage sector on the 'challenge' of history. *Museum & Society* 9(3): 244–248.
Kidd, J., S. Cairns, A. Drago, A. Ryall and M. Stearn Eds. 2016. Challenging ourselves: Uncomfortable histories and current museum practices. *Challenging History in the Museum: International Perspectives.* London: Routledge.
Kiddey, R. 2018. From the ground up: Cultural heritage practices as tools for empowerment in the homeless heritage project. *International Journal of Heritage Studies* 24(7): 694–708.
Kidron, C. A. 2013. Being there together: Dark family tourism and the emotive experience of co-presence in the Holocaust past. *Annals of Tourism Research* 41: 175–194.
Kikumura-Yano, A., L. R. Hirabayashi and J. A. Hirabayashi Eds. 2005. *Common Ground: The Japanese American National Museum and the Culture of Collaborations.* Boulder: University Press of Colorado.
Kinsley, R. P. 2016. Inclusion in museums: A matter of social justice. *Museum Management and Curatorship* 31(5): 474–490.
Kirshenblatt-Gimblett, B. 1998. *Destination Culture: Tourism, Museums, and Heritage.* Berkeley: University of California Press.
Kirshenblatt-Gimblett, B. 2004. Intangible heritage as metacultural production. *Museum International* 56(1–2): 52–64.
Kohlstedt, S. G. 2005. 'Thoughts in Things' modernity, history, and North American museums. *Isis* 96(4): 586–601.
Kohn, R. H. 1995. History and the culture wars: The case of the Smithsonian institution's Enola Gay exhibition. *The Journal of American History* 82(3): 1036–1063.
Kolesch, D. and H. Knoblauch 2019. Audience emotions. *Affective Societies – Key Concepts.* J. Slaby and C. von Scheve (Eds.). London: Routledge.
Kreps, C. 2003. Curatorship as social practice. *Curator: The Museum Journal* 46(3): 311–323.
Kreps, C. 2009. Indigenous curation, museums, and intangible cultural heritage. *Intangible Heritage.* L. Smith and N. Akagawa (Eds.). London: Routledge.
Krishnamurthy, R. 2013. Ethnic, racial and tribal: The language of racism? *Texts and Practices.* C. R. Caldas-Coulthard and M. Coulthard (Eds.). London: Routledge.
Kryder-Reid, E., J. W. Foutz, E. Wood and L. J. Zimmerman 2018. 'I just don't ever use that word': Investigating stakeholders' understanding of heritage. *International Journal of Heritage Studies* 24(7): 743–763.
Kuutma, K. 2018. Inside the UNESCO apparatus: From intangible representations to tangible effects. *Safeguarding Intangible Heritage.* N. Akagawa and L. Smith (Eds.). London: Routledge.
Laclau, E. 2005. *On Populist Reason.* London: Verso.
Lähdesmäki, T., S. Thomas and Y. Zhu Eds. 2019. *Politics of Scale: New Directions in Critical Heritage Studies.* Oxford: Berghahn.
Landsberg, A. 2004. *Prosthetic Memory: The Transformation of American Remembrance in the Age of Mass Culture.* New York: Columbia University Press.
Landsberg, A. 2009. Memory, empathy, and the politics of identification. *International Journal of Politics, Culture and Society* 22: 221–229.
Latour, B. 2000. When things strike back: A possible contribution of 'Science Studies' to the social sciences. *British Journal of Sociology* 51(1): 107–123.

Latour, B. 2003. The promises of constructivism. *Chasing Technoscience: Matrix for Materiality*. D. Ihde and E. Selinger (Eds.). Indianapolis: Indiana University Press.

Latour, B. 2007. *Reassembling the Social: An Introduction to Actor Network Theory*. Oxford: Oxford University Press.

Lawson, T. 2012. Ontology and the study of social reality: Emergence, organisation, community, power, social relations, corporations, artefacts and money. *Cambridge Journal of Economics* 36(2): 345–385.

Lean, G., R. Staiff and E. Waterton 2016. Reimagining travel and imagination. *Travel and Imagination*. G. Lean and R. Staiff (Eds.). London: Routledge.

Levitt, P. 2015. *Artifacts and Allegiances: How Museums Put the Nation and the World on Display*. Berkeley: University of California Press.

Leys, R. 2011. The turn to affect: A critique. *Critical Inquiry* 37(3): 434–472.

Linkon, S. L. and J. Russo 2002. *Steeltown U.S.A.: Work and Memory in Youngstown*. Lawrence: University of Press of Kansas.

Little, B. J. 2019. Violence, silence and the four truths: Towards healing in U.S.-American historical memory. *International Journal of Heritage Studies* 25(7): 631–640.

Little, B. J. and Shackel, P. A., 2016. *Archaeology, Heritage, and Civic engagement: Working Toward the Public Good*. Abingdon: Routledge.

Littler, J. and R. Naidoo 2004. White past, multicultural present: Heritage and national stories. *History, Nationhood and the Question of Britain*. H. Brocklehurst and R. Phillips (Eds.). Basingstoke: Palgrave Macmillan.

Long, J., K. Hylton and K. Spracklen 2014. Whiteness, blackness and settlement: Leisure and the integration of new migrants. *Journal of Ethnic and Migration Studies* 40(11): 1779–1797.

Longhurst, B., G. Bagnall and M. Savage 2004. Audiences, museums and the English middle class. *Museum and Society* 2(2): 104–124.

Lorimer, H. 2005. Cultural geography: The busyness of being 'more-than-representational'. *Progress in Human Geography* 29(1): 83–94.

Loveday, V. 2014. 'Flat capping it': Memory, nostalgia and value in retroactive male working-class identification. *European Journal of Cultural Studies* 17(6): 721–735.

Lovell, T. 2000. Thinking feminism with and against Bourdieu. *Feminist theory* 1(1): 11–32.

Lowenthal, D. 1985. *The Past is a Foreign Country*. Cambridge: Cambridge University Press.

Lowenthal, D. 2006. Heritage wars. *Spiked*, www.spiked-online.com/articles/0000000CAF. htm accessed 1/06/11.

Lowenthal, D. 2009a. On arraigning ancestors: A critique of historical contrition. *North Carolina Law Review* 87: 901.

Lowenthal, D. 2009b. Patrons, populists, apologists: Crises in museum stewardship. *Valuing Historic Environments*. L. Gibson and J. Pendlebury (Eds.). Farnham: Ashgate.

Lowenthal, D. 2015. *The Past is a Foreign Country – Revisited*. Cambridge: CUP.

Macdonald, S. 2002. *Behind the Scenes at the Science Museum*. Oxford: Berg.

Macdonald, S. 2009. *Difficult Heritage: Negotiating the Nazi Past in Nuremberg and Beyond*. London: Routledge.

Macdonald, S. 2013. *Memorylands: Heritage and Identity in Europe Today*. London: Routledge.

Macintyre, S. and A. Clark 2013. *The History Wars*. Melbourne: Melbourne University Publishing.

Maddern, J. 2004. Huddled masses yearning to buy postcards: The politics of producing heritage at the Statue of Liberty-Ellis Island National Monument. *Current Issues in Tourism* 7(4&5): 303–314.

Mah, A. 2012. *Industrial Ruination, Community and Place: Landscapes and Legacies of Urban Decline*. Toronto: University of Toronto Press.

Mandler, P. 1997. *The Fall and Rise of the Stately Home*. New Haven: Yale University Press.

Markell, P. 2003. *Bound by Recognition*. Princeton: Princeton University Press.
Mason, R. 2013. National museums, globalization, and postnationalism: Imagining a cosmopolitan museology. *Museum Worlds* 1: 40–64.
Massumi, B. 2002. *Parables for the Virtual: Movement, Affect, Sensation*. Durham: Duke.
Massumi, B. 2015. *Politics of Affect*. Cambridge: Polity.
Mata-Codesal, D., E. Peperkamp and N. C. Tiesler 2015. Migration, migrants and leisure: Meaningful leisure? *Leisure Studies* 34(1): 1–4.
Mayer, J. D., P. Salovey and D. R. Caruso 2008. Emotional intelligence: New ability or eclectic traits? *American Psychologist* 63(6): 503–517.
McCall, V. and C. Gray 2014. Museums and the 'new museology': Theory, practice and organisational change. *Museum Management and Curatorship* 29(1): 19–35.
McCray, K. 2010. Review of identity and the museum visitor experience. *Visitor Studies* 13: 121–124.
McGill, A. E. 2018. Learning from cultural engagements in community-based heritage scholarship. *International Journal of Heritage Studies* 24(10): 1068–1083.
McGrath, A. 2016. Conquering sacred ground? Climbing Uluṟu and Devils Tower. *National Parks Beyond the Nation*. A. Howkins, J. Orsi and M. Fiege. Norman (Eds.). Norman: University of Oklahoma Press.
McNay, L. 2008. *Against Recognition*. Cambridge: Polity.
Menzies, I. 2019. Heritage icon or environmental pest? Brumbies in the Australian cultural imaginary. *Equestrian Cultures: Horses, Human Society, and the Discourse of Modernity*. K. Guest and M. Mattfeld (Eds.). Chicago University of Chicago Press.
Mercer, J. 2010. Emotional beliefs. *International Organization* 64: 1–31.
Merriman, N. 1989. Museum visiting as a cultural phenomenon. *The New Museology*. P. Vergo (Ed.). London: Reaktion Books.
Merriman, N. 1991. *Beyond the Glass Case: The Past, the Heritage and the Public*. Leicester: Leicester University Press.
Mertens, D. M. and S. Hesse-Biber 2012. Triangulation and mixed methods research: Provocative positions. *Journal of Mixed Methods Research* 6(2): 75–79.
Meskell, L. 2014. Protection, politics, and pacting within the UNESCO's world heritage committee. *Anthropology Quarterly* 87(1): 217–243.
Meskell, L. 2016. Heritage and cosmopolitanism. *A Companion to Heritage Studies*. W. Logan, M. Nic Craith and U. Kockel (Eds.). Chichester: Wiley-Blackwell.
Meskell, L., C. Liuzza, E. Bertacchini and D. Saccone 2015. Multilateralism and UNESCO world heritage: Decision-making, states parties and political processes. *International Journal of Heritage Studies* 21(5): 423–440.
Mesquita, B. and D. Albert 2007. The cultural regulation of emotions. *Handbook of Emotion Regulation*. J. J. Gross (Ed.). New York: The Guilford Press.
Message, K. 2014. *Museums and Social Activism: Engaged Protest*. London: Routledge.
Minges, P. 2001. Beneath the underdog: Race, religion, and the trail of tears. *The American Indian Quaterly* 25(3): 453–479.
Mishra, P. 2017. *Age of Anger: A History of the Present*. London: Allen Lane.
Morphy, H. 2006. Sites of persuasion: Yingapungapu at the national museum of Australia. *Museum Frictions: Public Cultures/Global Transformations*. I. Karp, C. A. Kratz, L. Szwaja and T. Ybarra-Frausto (Eds.). Durham: Duke University Press.
Morse, N., K. Lackoi and H. Chatterjee 2016. Museums learning and wellbeing. *Journal of Education in Museums* 37: 3–13.
Morton, A. 2002. Emotional accuracy. *Proceedings of the Aristotelian Society* 76: 265–275.
Morton, A. 2013. *Emotion and Imagination*. Cambridge: Polity.
Mouffe, C. 2013. *Agonistics: Thinking the World Politically*. London: Verso.

Mouffe, C. 2019. *For a Left Populism*. London: Verso.
Mulcahy, D. and A. Witcomb 2018. Affective practices of learning at the museum: Children's critical encounters with the past. In *Emotion, Affective Practices, and the Past in the Present*. L. Smith, M. Wetherell and G. Campbell (Eds.). London: Routledge.
Mydland, L. and W. Grahn 2012. Identifying heritage values in local communities. *International Journal of Heritage Studies* 18(6): 564–587.
Nam, H. H., J. T. Jost and J. J. Van Bavel 2013. 'Not for all the tea in China!' Political ideology and the avoidance of dissonance-arousing situations. *PloS One* 8(4): doi.org/10.1371/journal.pone.0059837.
Nyhan, B. and J. Reifler 2010. When corrections fail: The persistence of political misperceptions. *Political Behavior* 32(2): 303–330.
Ochs, E. and L. Capps 2009. *Living Narrative: Creating Lives in Everyday Storytelling*. Cambridge, MA: Harvard University Press.
Olsen, B. 2013. *In Defense of Things*. Lantham: AltaMira Press.
Onciul, B. 2015. *Museums, Heritage and Indigenous Voice: Decolonizing Engagement*. London: Routledge.
Palmer, C. 2008. Royalty, national identity, heritage and tourism. *Royal Tourism: Excursions around Monarchy*. P. Long and N. Foster (Eds.). Clevedon: Channel View Publications.
Parker, C. S., S. Mayer and N. Buckley 2019. Left, right, but no in-between: Explaining American polarisation and post-factualism under President Trump. *Trumping the Mainstream: The Conquest of Democratic Politics by the Populist Radical Right*. L. E. Herman and J. Muldoon (Eds.). London: Routledge.
Pearce, S. M. 1992. *Museums, Objects and Collections: A Cultural Study*. Leicester: Leicester University Press.
Pedwell, C. 2013. Affect at the margins: Alternative empathies. *A Small Place. Emotion, Space and Society* 8: 18–26.
Pekarik, A. J., Z. D. Doering and D. A. Karns 1999. Exploring satisfying experiences in museums. *Curator: The Museums Journal* 42(2): 152–173.
Pekarik, A. J. and J. B. Schreiber 2012. The power of expectation. *Curator: The Museums Journal* 55(4): 487–496.
Pétursdóttir, Þ. 2012. Concrete matters: Ruins of modernity and the things called heritage. *Journal of Social Archaeology* 13(1): 31–53.
Pétursdóttir, Þ. and B. Olsen 2018. Theory adrift: The matter of archaeological theorizing. *Journal of Social Archaeology* 18(1): 97–117.
Pickering, M. and E. Keightley 2013. Communities of memory and the problem of transmission. *European Journal of Cultural Studies* 16(1): 115–131.
Pilkington, H. and N. Acik 2019. Not entitled to talk: (Mis)recognition, inequality and social activism of young Muslims. *Sociology*: 1–18, doi.org/10.1177/0038038519867630.
Poria, Y., R. Butler and D. Airey 2003. The core of heritage tourism. *Annals of Tourism Research 30*(1): 238–254.
Porpora, D. V. 2015. *Reconstructing Sociology: The Critical Realist Approach*. Cambridge: Cambrige University Press.
Prinz, J. J. 2007. *The Emotional Construction of Morals*. Oxford: Oxford University Press.
Prinz, J. J. 2011. Is empathy necessary for morality? *Empathy: Philosophical and Psychological Perspective*. A. Coplan and P. Goldie (Eds.). Oxford: Oxford University Press.
Protevi, J. 2009. *Political Affect: Connecting the Social and the Somatic*. Minneapolis: University of Minnesota Press.
Read, P. 2014. Reflecting on *The Stolen Generations*. *Indigenous Law Bulletin* 8(13): 3–6.
Reddy, W. M. 2001. *The Navigation of Feeling: A Framework for the History of Emotions*. Cambridge: Cambridge University Press.

Reed, A. and M. Chowkwanyun 2012. Race, class, crisis: The discourse of racial disparity and its analytical discontents. *Socialist Register* 48: 149–175.

Rizzo, M. 2010. Hon-ouring the past: Play-publics and gender at Baltimore's HonFest. *International Journal of Heritage Studies* 16(4–5): 337–351.

Robinson, H. 2017. Is cultural democracy possible in a museum? Critical reflections on Indigenous engagement in the development of the exhibition Encounters: Revealing stories of aboriginal and Torres strait Islander objects from the British Museum. *International Journal of Heritage Studies* 23(9): 860–874.

Rojek, C. 2000. *Leisure and Culture*. London: Macmillan.

Roppola, T., J. Packer, D. Uzzell and R. Ballantyne 2019. Nested assemblages: Migrants, war heritage, informal learning and national identities. *International Journal of Heritage Studies* 25(11): 1205–1223.

Rosenzweig, R. and D. Thelen 1998. *The Presence of the Past: Popular Uses of History in American Life*. New York: Columbia University Press.

Rowe, S. M., J. V. Wertsch and T. Y. Kosyaeva 2002. Linking little narratives to big ones: Narrative and public memory in history museums. *Culture & Psychology* 8(1): 96–112.

Rudd, K. 2008. *Apology to Australia's Indigenous Peoples*. Hansard extract. www.unitcare.com.au/pdfs/Sorry_Transcript.pdf.

Russell-Ciardi, M. 2008. The museum as a democracy-building institution: Reflections on the shared journeys program at the Lower East Side Tenement Museum. *The Public Historian* 30(1): 39–52.

Saldaña, J. 2016. *The Coding Manual for Qualitative Researchers*. Los Angeles: Sage.

Samuel, L. R. 2012. *The American Dream: A Cultural History*. Syracuse, New York: Syracuse University Press.

Samuel, R. 1994. *Theatres of Memory: Past and Present in Contemporary Culture*. London: Verso Books.

Sandell, R. 2003. Social inclusion, the museum and the dynamics of sectorial change. *Museum & Society* 1(1): 45–62.

Sandell, R. 2007. *Museums, Prejudice and the Reframing of Difference*. London: Routledge.

Sandell, R. and E. Nightingale Eds. 2012. *Museums, Equality and Social Justice*. London: Routledge.

Sayer, A. 2000. *Realism and Social Science*. London: Sage.

Sayer, A. 2005. Class, moral worth and recognition. *Sociology* 39(5): 947–963.

Sayer, A. 2011. *Why Things Matter to People: Social Science, Values and Ethical Life*. Cambridge: Cambridge University Press.

Sayer, R. A., 1992. *Method in Social Science: A Realist Approach*. Second edition. London: Routledge.

Sayes, E. 2013. Actor-Network Theory and methodology: just what does it mean to say that nonhumans have agency? *Social Studies of Science* 44(1): 134–149.

Schatzki, T. R. 2002. *The Site of the Social*. Pennsylvania: Pennsylvania State University Press.

Schatzki, T. R. 2006. Introduction: Practice theory. *The Practice Turn in Contemporary Theory*. T. R. Schatzki, K. K. Cetina and E. von Savigny (Eds.). London: Routledge.

Schatzki, T. R. 2008. *Social Practices*. Cambridge: Cambridge University Press.

Schatzki, T. R. 2010. *The Timespace of Human Activity*. Lanham: Lexington Books.

Schmidt, P. and I. Pikirayi Eds. 2016. *Community Archaeology and Heritage in Africa: Decolonizing Practice*. London: Routledge.

Schoonenboom, J. 2017. A performative paradigm for mixed methods research. *Journal of Mixed Methods Research*, doi:10.1177/1558689817722889.

Schorch, P. 2015. Experiencing differences and negotiating prejudices at the immigration museum Melbourne. *International Journal of Heritage Studies* 21(1): 46–64.

Schrauf, W. W. 2018. Mixed methods designs for making cross-cultural comparisons. *Journal of Mixed Methods Research* 12(4): 477–494.

Seaton, A. V. 2001. Sources of Slavery – Destinations of Slavery: The silences and disclosures of slavery heritage in the UK and US. *International Journal of Hospitality and Tourism Administration* 2(2–3): 107–129.

Seltzer-Kelly, D., S. J. Westood and D. M. Peña-Guzman 2012. A methodological self-study of quantitizing: Negotiating meaning and revealing multiplicity. *Journal of Mixed Methods Research* 6(4): 258–274.

Selwood, S. 2006. Unreliable evidence: The rhetoric of data collection in the culture sector. *Culture Vultures: Is UK Arts Policy Damaging the Arts*. M. Mirza (Ed.). London: Policy Exchange.

Shackel, P. A. 2018. *Remembering Lattimer: Labor, Migration, and Race in Pennsylvania Anthracite Country*. Urbana: University of Illinois Press.

Shannon-Baker, P. 2016. Making paradigms meaningful in mixed methods research. *Journal of Mixed Methods Research* 10(4): 319–334.

Shove, E., M. Pantzar and M. Watson 2012. *The Dynamics of Social Practice: Everyday Life and How it Changes*. Los Angles: Sage.

Simon, R. I. 2011. A short to thought: Curatorial judgement and the public exhibition of 'Difficult Knowledge'. *Memory Studies* 4(4): 432–449.

Skrede, J. and H. Hølleland 2018. *Uses of heritage* and beyond: Heritage studies viewed through the lens of critical discourse analysis and critical realism. *Journal of Social Archaeology* 18(1): 77–96.

Skrede, J., H. Hølleland, O. Risbøl and G. Jerpåsen 2018. Views, use and reception of visualisations of development proposals impacting cultural heritage. *International Journal of Heritage Studies* 24(4): 390–405.

Slaby, J. and C. von Scheve Eds. 2019. *Affective Societies: Key Concepts*. London: Routledge.

Smith, L. 1994. Heritage as postprocessual archaeology? *Antiquity* 68: 300–309.

Smith, L. 2004. *Archaeological Theory and the Politics of Cultural Heritage*. London: Routledge.

Smith, L. 2006. *Uses of Heritage*. London: Routledge.

Smith, L. 2007. Empty gestures? Heritage and the politics of recognition. *Cultural Heritage and Human Rights*. H. Silberman and D. R. Fairchild (Eds.). New York: Springer.

Smith, L. 2010. 'Man's inhumanity to man' and other platitudes of avoidance and misrecognition: An analysis of visitor responses to exhibitions marking the 1807 bicentenary. *Museum & Society* 8(3): 193–214.

Smith, L. 2011. Affect and registers of engagement: Navigating emotional responses to dissonant heritage. *Representing Enslavement and Abolition in Museums: Ambiguous Engagements*. L. Smith, G. Cubitt, R. Wilson and K. Fouseki (Eds.). New York: Routledge.

Smith, L. 2012a. A pilgrimage of masculinity: The Stockman's hall of fame and outback heritage centre. *Australian Historical Studies* 43(3): 472–482.

Smith, L. 2012b. The cultural 'work' of tourism. *The Cultural Moment of Tourism*. L. Smith, E. Waterton and S. Watson (Eds.). London: Routledge.

Smith, L. 2013. Taking the children: Children, childhood and heritage making. *Children, Childhood and Cultural Heritage*. K. Darian-Smith and C. Pascoe (Eds.). London: Routledge.

Smith, L. 2014. Intangible heritage: A challenge to the authorised heritage discourse? *Revista d'etnologia de Catalunya* 40: 133–142.

Smith, L. 2015. Theorising museum and heritage visiting. *The International Handbooks of Museum Studies: Museum Theory*. A. Witcomb and K. Message (Eds.). Chichester: Wiley-Blackwell.

Smith, L. 2016. Changing views? Emotional intelligence, registers of engagement and the museum visit. *Museums and the Past – Constructing Historical Consciousness*. V. Gosselin and P. Livingstone (Eds.). Vancouver: UBC Press.

Smith, L. 2017a. Explorations in banality: Prison tourism at the Old Melbourne Goal. *The Palgrave Handbook of Prison Tourism*. J. Z. Wilson, S. Hodgkinson, J. Piche and K. Walby (Eds.). London: Palgrave Macmillan.
Smith, L. 2017b. 'We are … we are everything': The politics of recognition and misrecognition at immigration museums. *Museum & Society* 15(1): 69–86.
Smith, L. 2020. Industrial heritage and the remaking of class identity – are we all middle class now? *Industrial Heritage, Culture and Regional Identity in Regions/Cities Undergoing Structural Transformation*. S. Berger (Ed.). Oxford: Berghahn Books.
Smith, L. and G. Campbell 2016. The elephant in the room: Heritage, affect and emotion. *A Companion to Heritage Studies*. W. Logan, M. Nic Craith and U. Kockel (Eds.). Chichester: Wiley-Blackwell.
Smith, L. and G. Campbell 2017a. 'Nostalgia for the future': Memory, nostalgia and the politics of class. *International Journal of Heritage Studies* 23(7): 612–627.
Smith, L. and G. Campbell 2017b. The tautology of 'intangible values' and the misrecognition of intangible cultural heritage. *Heritage & Society* 10(1): 26–44.
Smith, L., G. Cubitt, R. Wilson and K. Fouseki Eds. 2011. *Representing Enslavement and Abolition in Museums: Ambiguous Engagements*. New York: Routledge.
Smith, L. and E. Waterton 2009. *Heritage, Communities and Archaeology*. London: Duckworth.
Smith, M. 2018. What is learning? Exploring theory, product and process. *The Encyclopaedia of Informal Education*, http://infed.org/mobi/learning-theory-models-product-and-process/.
SOC (Standard Occupational Classification) 2000. Standard occupational classification and NS-SEC on the labour force survey. Office for National Statistics. https://webarchive.nationalarchives.gov.uk/20160108030321/http://www.ons.gov.uk/ons/guide-method/method-quality/specific/labour-market/soc-2000-and-ns-sec-on-the-lfs/index.html
Solli, B. 2011. Some reflections on heritage and archaeology in the Anthropocene. *Norwegian Archaeological Review* 44(1): 40–54.
Song, M. and N. Hayashi 2016. Open-Air museums as mediators for intergenerational transmission: Taking as example two ethnographic open-Air museums in Georgia and Ukraine. *Museum International* 68(3–4): 157–163.
Sontag, S. 2004. *Regarding the Pain of Others*. London: Penguin.
Sørensen, M. L. S. and J. Carman Eds. 2009. *Heritage Studies: Methods and Approaches*. Abingdon: Routledge.
Spatz, B. 2015. *What a Body Can Do: Technique as Knowledge, Practice as Research*. London: Routledge.
Staiff, R. 2014. *Re-imagining Heritage Interpretation: Enchanting the Past-Future*. Farnham: Ashgate.
Staiff, R., R. Bushell and S. Watson Eds. 2013. *Heritage and Tourism: Place, Encounter, Engagement*. London: Routledge.
Storksdieck, M., K. Ellenbogen and J. E. Heimlick 2005. Changing minds? Reassessing outcomes in free-choice environmental education. *Environmental Education Research* 11(3): 353–369.
Sturgis, A. 2007. *The Trail of Tears and Indian Removal*. Westport, CT: Greenwood Press.
Taber, C. S. and M. Lodge 2006. Motivated skepticism in the evaluation of political beliefs. *American Journal of Political Science* 50(3): 755–769.
Taksa, L. 2019. Remembering and incorporating migrant workers in Australian industrial heritage. *Labor* 16(1): 81–105.
Taylor, C. 1992. *The Ethics of Authenticity*. Cambridge: Harvard University Press.
Taylor, C. 1994. The politics of recognition. *Multiculturalism*. A. Gutmann (Ed.). Princeton: Princeton University Press.
Taylor, D. 2003. *The Archive and the Repertoire: Performing Cultural Memory in the Americas*. Durham: Duke University Press.

Terry, A. 2015. *Family Ties: Living History in Canadian House Museums*. Montreal: McGill-Queen's University Press.
Thien, D. 2005. After or beyond feeling? A consideration of affect and emotion in geography. *Area* 37(3): 450–656.
Thompson, E. 1994. *Fair Enough: Egalitarianism in Australia*. Sydney: UNSW Press.
Thompson, S. 2006. *The Political Theory of Recognition: A Critical Introduction*. Cambridge: Polity.
Thompson, S. and P. Hoggett 2011. Recognition and ambivalence. *The Politics of Misrecognition*. S. Thompson and M. Yar (Eds.). London: Routledge.
Thompson, S. and P. Hoggett Eds. 2012. *Politics and the Emotions: The Affective Turn in Contemporary Political Studies*. New York: Continuum.
Thompson, S. and M. Yar 2011. Introduction. *The Politics of Misrecognition*. S. Thompson and M. Yar (Eds.). London: Routledge.
Thorisdottir, H., J. T. Jost and A. C. Kay 2010. On the social and psychological bases of ideology and system justification. *Social and Psychological Bases of Ideology and System Justification*. J. T. Jost, A. C. Kay and H. Thorisdottir (Eds.). Oxford: Oxford University Press.
Thrift, N. 2004. Intensities of feeling: Towards a spatial politics of affect. *Geografiska Annaler* 86(B): 57–78.
Thrift, N. 2008. *Non-Representational Theory: Space, Politics, Affect*. London: Routledge.
Till, C. 2015. Zizek's critique of new materialism: Can we theorise natural subjectivity? *Blog*, https://thisisnotasociology.blog/2015/03/12/zizeks-critique-of-new-materialism-can-we-theorise-natural-subjectivity/.
Tlili, A. 2008. Behind the policy mantra of the inclusive museum: receptions of social exclusion and inclusion in museums and science centres. *Cultural Sociology* 2(1): 123–147.
Tolia-Kelly, D., E. Waterton, S. Watson Eds. 2017. *Heritage, Affect and Emotion. Politics, Practices and Infrastructures*. London: Routledge.
Tranter, B. and J. Donoghue 2008. Bushrangers: Ned Kelly and Australian identity. *Journal of Sociology* 44(4): 373–390.
Trinca, M. 2003. Museums and the history wars. *History Australia* 1(1): 85–97.
Trofanenko, B. 2014. Affective emotions: The pedagogical challenges of knowing war. *Review of Education, Pedagogy, and Cultural Studies* 36(1): 22–39.
Tully, J. 2000. Struggles over recognition and distribution. *Constellations* 7(4): 469–482.
Tunbridge, J. and G. Ashworth 1996. *Dissonant Heritage: The Management of the Past as a Resource in Conflict*. Chichester: J. Wiley.
Tunbridge, J. E., G. J. Ashworth, B. J. Graham. 2012. Decennial reflections on *A Geography of Heritage* (2000). *International Journal of Heritage Studies* 19(4): 365–372.
Urry, J. and J. Larsen 2011. *The Tourist Gaze 3.0*. Los Angeles: Sage.
van der Toorn, J., P. R. Nail, I. Liviatan and J. T. Jost 2014. My country, right or wrong: Does activating system justification motivation eliminate the liberal-conservative gap in patriotism? *Journal of Experimental social Psychology* 54: 50–60.
Vergo, P Ed. 1989. *The New Museology*. London: Reaktion Books.
Walkerdine, V. 2010. Communal beings and affect. *Body & Society* 16(1): 91–116.
Walvin, J. 2005. The colonial origins of English wealth: The harewoods of Yorkshire. *The Journal of Caribbean History* 39(1): 38–53.
Waterton, E. 2010. *Politics, Policy and the Discourses of Heritage in Britain*. Basingstoke: Palgrave Macmillan.
Waterton, E. 2011. In the spirit of self-mockery? Labour heritage and identity in the potteries. *International Journal of Heritage Studies* 17(4): 344–363.
Waterton, E. 2014. A more-than-representational understanding of heritage? The 'past' and the politics of affect. *Geography Compass* 8(11): 823–833.

Waterton, E. and S. Watson 2013. Framing theory: Towards a critical imagination in heritage studies. *International Journal of Heritage Studies* 19(6): 546–561.
Waterton, E. and S. Watson 2014. *The Semiotics of Heritage Tourism, Tourism and Cultural Change.* Bristol: Channel View Publications.
Waterton, E. and R. J. Wilson 2009. Talking the talk: Policy, popular and media responses to the bicentenary of the abolition of the slave trade using the abolition discourse. *Discourse and Society* 20(3): 381–399.
Watson, S. 2010. Constructing Rhodes: Heritage tourism and visuality. *Culture, Heritage and Representation.* E. Waterton and S. Watson (Eds.). Farnham: Ashgate.
Wells, J. 2015. In stakeholders we trust: Changing the ontological and epistemological orientation of built heritage assessment through participatory action research. *How to Assess Built Heritage? Assumptions, Methodologies, Examples of Heritage Assessment Systems.* B. Szmygin (Ed.). Lubin: International Scientific Committee for Theory and Philosophy of Conservation and Restoration ICOMOS.
Wertsch, J. 2002. *Voices of Collective Remembering.* Cambridge: Cambridge University Press.
Wertsch, J. 2004. Specific narratives and schematic narrative templates. *Theorizing Historical Consciousness.* P. Seixas (Ed.). Toronto: University of Toronto Press.
Wertsch, J. 2007. National narratives and the conservative nature of collective memory. *Neohelicon* 34(1): 23–33.
Wertsch, J. 2008a. The narrative organization of collective memory. *Ethos* 36(1): 120–135.
Wertsch, J. 2008b. Blank spots in collective memory: A case study of Russia. *The Annals of the American Academy* 617: 58–71.
Wertsch, J. 2012. Deep memory and narrative templates: Conservative forces in collective memory. *Memory and Political Change.* A. Assmann and L. Shortt (Eds.). London: Palgrave Macmillan.
Wertsch, J. and D. M. Billingsley 2011. The role of narrative in commemoration: Remembering as mediated action. *Heritage, Memory and Identity.* H. Anheier and Y. R. Isar (Eds.). Los Angles: Sage.
Wetherell, M. 2012. *Affect and Emotion: A New Social Science Understanding.* London: Sage.
Wetherell, M. 2013a. Affect and discourse – what's the problem? From affect as excess to affective/discursive practice. *Subjectivity* 6(4): 349–368.
Wetherell, M. 2013b. Feeling Rules, atmospheres and affective practice: Some reflections on the analysis of emotional episodes. *Privilege, Agency and Affect: Understanding the Production and Effects of Action.* C. Maxwell and P. Aggleton (Eds.). Basingstoke: Palgrave Macmillan, 221–239.
Wetherell, M. 2015. Trends in the turn to affect: A social psychological critique. *Body & Society* 21(2): 139–166.
Wetherell, M. and J. Potter 1992. *Mapping the Language of Racism: Discourse and the Legitimization of Exploitation.* London: Harvester Wheatsheaf.
Wetherell, M., L. Smith and G. Campbell 2018. Affective heritage practices. *Emotion, Affective Heritage Practices, and the Past in the Present.* L. Smith, M. Wetherell and G. Campbell (Eds.). London: Routledge.
Wierzbicka, A. 1999. *Emotions Across Languages and Cultures: Diversity and Universals.* Cambridge: Cambridge University Press.
Wildt, A., 2018. The city museum as an empathic space. *Museum International* 70(3–4): 72–83.
Wilkie, M. 1997. *Bringing Them Home: Report of the National Inquiry into the Separation of Aboriginal and Torres Strait Islander Children from Their Families.* Sydney: Human Rights and Equal Opportunity Commission.
Williams, R., 1977. Structures of feeling. *Marxism and Literature* 1: 128–135.

Wilson, R. J. 2015. Playful heritage: Excavating ancient Greece in New York city. *International Journal of Heritage Studies* 21(5): 476–492.

Wingfield, A. H. 2010. Are some emotions marked 'whites only'? Racialized feeling rules in professional workplaces. *Social Problems* 57(2): 251–268.

Winter, T. 2013. Clarifying the critical in critical heritage studies. *International Journal of Heritage Studies* 19(6): 532–545.

Winter, T. 2014. Heritage studies and the privileging of theory. *International Journal of Heritage Studies* 20(5): 556–572.

Witcomb, A. 2003. *Re-imagining the Museum: Beyond the Mausoleum*. London: Routledge.

Witcomb, A. 2013. Understanding the role of affect in producing a critical pedagogy for history museums. *Museum Management and Curatorship* 28(3): 255–271.

Witcomb, A. 2015. Toward a pedagogy of feeling: Understating how museums create a space for cross-cultural encounters. *Museum Theory*. A. Witcomb and K. Message (Eds.). Chitchester: Wiley Blackwell, 321–344.

Witcomb, A. 2016. Cross-Cultural encounters and 'difficult heritage' on the Thai-Burma Railway: An ethics of cosmopolitanism rather than practices of exclusion. *A Companion to Heritage Studies*. W. Logan, M Nic Craith and U. Kockel (Eds.). Chichester: Wiley-Blackwell.

Witcomb, A. and K. Buckley 2013. Engaging with the future of 'critical heritage studies': Looking back in order to look forward. *International Journal of Heritage Studies* 19(6): 562–578.

Wright, P. 1985. *On Living in an Old Country*. London: Verso.

Yosef-Hassidim, D. 2016. Review of *The Beautiful Risk of Education* by Gert J. J. Biesta. *Philosophical Inquiry in Education* 23(2): 222–228.

Young, I. M. 2000. *Inclusion and Democracy*. Oxford: Oxford University Press.

Young, I. M. 2011. *Responsibility for Justice*. Oxford: Oxford University Press.

Zembylas, M. 2018. Understanding the emotional regimes of reconciliation in engagements with 'difficult' heritage. *Emotion, Affective Practices, and the Past in the Present*. L. Smith, M. Wetherell and G. Campbell (Eds.). London: Routledge.

Zhang, R. 2016. *'Value in Change': What do World Heritage Nominations bring to Chinese World Heritage Sites?* Unpublished PhD thesis, Australian National University.

Zhang, R. 2020. *Chinese Heritage Sites and their Audiences*: The Power of the Past. London: Routledge.

Zhang, R. and L. Smith 2019. Bonding and dissonance: Rethinking the interrelations among stakeholders in heritage tourism. *Tourism Management* 74: 212–223.

Zweig, Michael. 2000. *The Working Class Majority: America's Best Kept Secret*. Ithaca: Cornell University Press.

INDEX

Note: *Italicized* page numbers indicate a figure on the corresponding page. Page numbers in **bold** indicate a table on the corresponding page.

active indifference 294–299
Actor Network Theory (ANT) 33, 35
aesthetic engagement 145
affect: definitions of 51–54; affective turn 20, 50–51; politics of recognition 55; and ideology 53–54, 64, 71–74, 205, 302; see also affective practices/emotion
affective practices/responses: emotion and cognition connection 68–69, 201; of heritage 4, 39, 49–61, 68, 257; politics of recognition 276–277
affirmation 6, 9, 169, 209–214, 216, 251, 257–258, 261, 285, 308; as a performance 6, 9, 134, 172, 189, 197, 209–214, 260, 282, 305, 309; and self-recognition 49, 262, 264, 269, 278; and misrecognition 301
Afghan Cameleers 98, 267
Against Empathy (Bloom) 45
age variables in visitor responses 162–163
aide-mémoires 37, 257
aide to memory 133, 134, 167, 171, 226, 146–156, 167, 171, 226, 231, 233
American Dream 98, 219, 233–234, 253, 268
Amsterdam Museum 186
anthropocentric humanities 33–34, 36
anti-Semitism 252
appropriation of heritage 27, 121, 155, 299–302
archaeological museum 255
Archer, Margaret 21, 22–24, 37, 52, 54, 55, 66, 243

aristocratic country houses in England 222
artefacts 2, 15, 28–29, 94, 117, 127, 149, 184, 244, 257, 292, 308
Arts and Humanities Research Council (AHRC) Knowledge Transfer Grant 87
assimilationist leavening of diversity 307
Association of Critical Heritage Studies 24–25
Austin, J.L. 26
Australian Bureau of Statistics 272
Australian colonial history 231
Australian 'outback' identity 270–272
Australian sovereignty 227–228
Australian visitor correlations 112; *see also* visitor correlations between countries
Australian War Memorial 94–95, 149, 206, 253–254, 282
authorised heritage discourse (AHD): critical realist heritage studies 19–20, 22–23, 32, 34; educational attainment/occupation 171; ethnicity of visitors and 164, 169; genres of museums and heritage sites 144; heritage, defined 117–121, **118**; heritage representations and 48, 49; introduction to 7–8, 19–20; learning framework and 77–78, 80; meaning-making and 47; persuasive power of 31; as social barometers 279–280; visitor demographics and 196; visitor understandings of heritage 138

'being at' houses 148
Bhaskar, Roy 21

bicentenary data 87, 89, 100, 126, 127, 132–133
bicentenary of Britain's abolition of slave trade 87, 264, 274
Biesta, Gert 177, 178–181
Big House heritage 218, 234, 238, 242
Bourdieu's theory of *habitus* 22–23
British Empire and Commonwealth Museum 186
British Museum 263–264
British slave trade exhibit 87–89, **88**, 97, 207–208, 264, 296
Brodsworth Hall 87, 94, 222
Bureau of Indian Affairs 274
Burton Constable house 87, 94, 222, 223
Butler, Judith 11, 26–27

Campbell, Gary 100, 104, 105
causal powers of social structures/practices 22
celebratory narratives 89, 126, 144, 152, 159, 177, 254, 285, 288, 290, 293, 298, 302
children and intergenerational communication 10, 222, 241–242, 249, 253–254, 255–257, 299
children and learning/education 10, 12, 134, 137, 150, 153, 178, 241–242
Chi-square test 107
civil rights movement 9, 10, 11, 39, 97, 158, 183, 209, 282
claims for recognition 269–273
class 172, 198, 256; and AHD 196; and memory 153; and emotion 56; and heritage definition 121; and house museums 222–226, 229, 232; and learning 78; and new materialism/ANT 34, 35; privilege and exclusion 170, 215; and recognition 42, 44; and the 'safe' museum 200; *see also* white middle-class visitors; working-class history; demographics of visitors
clichés 66, 130, 293–6, 302; thought-terminating 130, 203, 293–294
clichés and misrecognition politics 293–294
Clinton, Hilary 72
coded open-ended responses 117–119
Code of the Woosters, The (Wodehouse) 218
coding in MMR 105–107
cognitive dissonance 126, 154–155, 304
cognitive engagement 130, 137, 148, 156, 292
collective agency of visitors 75, 77
collective performances of recognition/misrecognition 281–283
collective wellbeing 307
colonial assimilation history 155
commemorative data 105–106

Common Ground: the Heart of Community exhibit 240
communicative action 26; *see also* intergenerational communication and connection
community museums 114, 240
compassion: and empathy 45–46, 187–188; scale and scope 70
conciliatory politics 190
conservatism: conservative *vs*. progressive tensions 66, 81; ideological conservatism 66; political conservatism 53, 67, 71, 73, 79
constitutive nature of heritage 49, 86–87
Convention for the Safeguarding of the Intangible Cultural Heritage (2003) 29, 33
cool logic and reasoning 45
cosy community motif 225, 235–236
country house museums in England 87, 94, 135, 222–226, 227
Critical Discourse Analysis (CDA) 22
critical heritage studies 7, 13–15, 20, 24–25, 32, 74, 306–308
criticality emergence 14
critical performances 8–9
critical realism, defined 21, 90–91
critical realist heritage studies: critical heritage studies 24–25; heritage, as performance 25–31; introduction to 19–21; New Materialism and 31–36; overview of 21–24; Post Humanism and 31–36; summary of 36–37
cross-generational interactions 241–243
cross-tabulation 108, 109, 116
Cubitt, Geoffrey 45, 97
cultural capital 8, 197–198, 226
cultural self-understanding 40
cultural tools 10, 26, 28, 37, 38, 48–49, 138
curatorial professional practices 108–109

Davidson, Donald 27
Deferred Action for Childhood Arrivals (DACA) 214
democracy and recognition 42
demographics of visitors: age 162–163; coding and statistics 105–107; comparison between 162; educational attainment/occupation 169–172; ethnic background/identity of visitors 10, 118–120, 141–144, **143**; introduction to 6–7, 161–162; negotiation of justice 43; non-dominant backgrounds of visitors 165–168, 198; summary of 172, 305; travel from home/vacation 163–164, 181; white middle-class visitors 196–197, 199; *see also* ethnic/racial demographics of visitors

Dicks, Bella 241
difficult emotions 12, 177, 189–190, 192, 194, 304, 308
difficult knowledge 2, 12, 188–189, 192, 308
diffused audience 86
discrimination and affirmation 210
disembodied textualism 22
disengagement modes 295
dissonant histories: critical memory and identity work 309; empathy engagement over 144–145, 152; intergenerational communication and recognition at 6; legitimacy in discussions of 285; nationalising narratives and 91; national narratives of 257; negative emotions over 266; performance of reinforcement 211, 213; registers of engagement 301; sharing by parents 252–253; storytelling and 254
dissonant sites 96–98, 144–147, 152–158; defined 91–94

educational attainment of visitors 11–12, 87, 141–142, 153, 161, 169–172
educational role of museums: discourse on 137–138; emotion and learning 182–194, *190*, 306; introduction to 177–178; learning, defined 64, 76, 79, 178–182; politics of education 179; received knowledge 20; registers of engagement 74–81; summary of 194–195; *see also* learning
edutainment 80
Ellis Island 1, 2, 4, 93, 98, 203, 248, 267–268
embodiment, defined 67
emotion: accuracy of 58, 238, 243–244; authenticity of 58, 69, 182, 184, 222, 238, 243, 248, 250; cognition connection and 68–69, 201; difficult emotions 12, 177, 189–190, 192, 194, 304, 308; engagement with museums and heritage sites 1–15, 309; indifference 226–232; inherited trauma 254; investment in meaning-making 309–310; learning and 182–194, *190*, 306; non-celebratory emotions 212; overemotional empathising 45; passive emotion 70, 127, 130–131, 146–155, 164–167, 294–299, 302–309; pedagogy of feeling 12, 177, 182, 185, 189–190, 306; positive emotion 69, 73, 127, 262–263, 287, 302; sadness feelings of visitors 301–302; sense of belonging 120, 138, 204, 221; as unexplainable 248; visitor correlations between countries 123–127, **124**, **125**; *see also* modes of engagement

emotional ambivalence 287
emotional authenticity 182–183
emotional banality and heritage-making: class and house museums 222–226; house museums and memory 219–222; introduction to 218–219; memory and house museums 219–222; sense of place and depth of time 226–232; summary of 237–239
emotional intelligence 46–47, 68–70, 157, 266, 294
emotional repertoires 12, 14, 64, 68, 153, 194, 207, 215, 238, 305
emotional truth 58, 69, 182
emotion and learning 182–194, *190*
empathy experiences 12, 45–47; at dissonant sites 186; imaginative empathy 46, 73, 153, 184–186, 194, 309; learning and 183, 185–189, 192–194; overemotional empathising 45; scale and scope 70; superficial, insincere or shallow empathy 46, 73, 236, 238, 301
English country house museums 222–226, 227
English middle-class 230
English visitor correlations 112–114; *see also* visitor correlations between countries
enslavement legacy sites 97, 126, 155–158; defined 89, 97; house museums 226–232, 274, 277; misrecognition politics 285; slave trade exhibits 225–226
entrance narratives 3, 14, 302
environmental movements 39
epiphanies in learning 187–188
epistemic fallacy 21
ethical goals 40
ethnic background/identity of visitors 10, 118–120, 141–144, **143**, 266
ethnic paternalism 235
ethnic/racial demographics of visitors 114–115; background/identity 10, 118–120, 141–144, **143**, 266; collective performances of recognition/misrecognition 281–283; definition of 106–107; overview of 164–169
Eureka Rebellion (1854) exhibit 96, 215
European Association for Heritage Interpretation 75
exhorbitation of language 32

familial politics of recognition 242
Federation of International Human Rights Museums 33
feeling of belonging 119–120
feeling rules 56, 59, 68, 145, 201, 206–207, 215, 253–254, 257, 305, 306
female visitors 114–115

Index

First Australians Gallery, National Museum of Australia 85, 97, 101, 281–282, 288–289
Foucauldian governmentality 8, 198
Fouseki, Kalliopi 104, 105
Fraser, Nancy 40–43, 260, 270, 286, 300
free-choice learning 75
frontier history heritage sites 95, 149–151, 256, 270, 289, 292, 299
fundamental rights of individuals 40
future-making 29–30

gay marriage 251
gender differences among visitors 142, 161
genres of museums and heritage sites: defined 91–94, **92**; enslavement legacies 97, 126, 155–158; frontier history 95, 149–151; house museums 91, 93, 94, 147–148; immigration history 98, 152–154; Indigenous culture and history 97–98, 154–155; introduction to 141; labour history 96; making connections 158–159; in mixed methods research 91–98; museum details 94–98; national and dissonant sites 144–147; summary of 159; visitor demographics 141–144, **143**; war commemoration 94–95, 148–149
good citizen construction 179
governmentality 8, 198, 200
group memory 153
guilt 45, 73, 88, 145, 156, 189, 266, 280, 285, 287–290, 296, 301, 304, 308
gut feelings 53, 66, 71, 304

habitus theory 22–23, 27
Hall, Stuart 42, 168–169
Harewood House 282, 290–291
Harrison, Rodney 31–32, 36
Hemings, Sally 293
heritage/heritage-making: appropriation of heritage 27, 121, 155, 299–302; connection to 121–123, **122**; constitutive nature of 49, 86–87; critical heritage studies 7, 13–15, 20, 24–25, 32, 74, 306–308; critical realist heritage studies 25–31; defined 117–121, **118**; emotional engagement and 3–15, 309; introduction to 2; liberty heritage 226–232; management practices 76; material heritage, defined 26; memory complexes and 26; political power of heritage 20, 38, 39–47; representational power of 37, 38, 47; values of 29, 250–254; *see also* genres of museums and heritage sites; misrecognition politics; politics of recognition; recognition and heritage
heritage performances 5–6, 14, 25–31, 74

Hermitage plantation 62, 94, 185, 208, 232–237, 290
Hirsch, Marianne 254
historic preservation 120–121
history wars 76, 97, 227, 357
Honneth, Axel 40, 44, 260, 286, 300
house museums: class and 222–226; English country house museums 222–226, 227; enslavement legacy heritage sites 226–232, 274; freedom and liberty 226–232; methodology of studies 91, 93, 94; overview of 147–148; sense of place and depth of time 226–232; as theatre of memory 219–222
human agency 23, 24, 26, 60
humanism and critical realism 23–24

ICOMOS charters 32–33
identity: Australian 'outback' identity 270–272; ethnic background/identity of visitors 10, 118–120, 141–144, **143**, 266; in intergenerational communication 250–254; legitimacy of 265; nationalism/ national identity 75–76, 132, 148, 221, 230, 275, 287, 299; normative identities 27, 41, 268, 279; offers for recognition 273–279, *277*; racial identities/racism 42, 278; reassessment of 265–266; sub-national identity 75–76; *see also* recognition and heritage
identity-making performance 28, 212
identity politics 39, 41–42, 47, 64, 260, 286
ideological conservatism 66; *see also* political conservatism
ideology in modes of engagement 71–74
Illouz, Eva 44
imagination and playfulness 69–70
imaginative empathy 46, 73, 153, 184–186, 194, 309
imagined conversations 14, 172, 202, 243–247, 305
immigration history heritage sites 98, 152–154, 185–186
Immigration Museum 98 101, 132, 152–154; *190*, 190–194, 247–248, 250, 264, 266–267
Indian Removal Act (1830) 62
Indigenous culture and history: collective performance assessment 282; dislocation and disenfranchisement history 227–228; heritage sites 97–98, 146, 154–155; intergenerational communication and connection 254; land rights and sovereignty 32; misrecognition 256, 299–301; movements of 39; recognition 132, 146, 151, 155, 261; Stockman's Hall

of Fame 101, *204*, 204–205, 207, 284, 289, 290, 292; visitor perception of 301
individual agency of visitors 75
inherited privilege 10, 254, 257
inherited trauma 254
institutional authority of museums 48, 75–76, 247–248, 257, 259, 263–264
integration of research methods 90
intensity of engagement 66
intergenerational communication 10, 11, 13–14, 154
intergenerational communication and connection: children and 255–257; as imagined conversations 243–247; introduction to 240–241; quiet reflections 249–250; self-worth and familial recognition 247–249; summary of 257–258; transference of values and identity 250–254; visitor engagement 241–243
International Slavery Museum 97, 202, 274, 301
interviews: background to questions 101–103; conducting of 103–104; in mixed methods research 99–105; staff interviews 99; summary of 304–310; transcriptions of 104–105; visitor correlations between countries 111–116, **113**, **114**; visitor interviews 99–105; *see also* performing reinforcement and affirmation

Jackson, Andrew 62–63, 208, 232–237
James Madison's Montpellier 202, 232–237, 274, 276–279, *277*, 290–293, *292*
Japanese American National History Museum 98, 112, 115, 142, 240, 249, 263
Jefferson, Thomas 97, 293
Jost, John 53, 66, 71–73, 287

Labour and Industry Museum 186, 212
labour history heritage sites 96, 152–154
Lanyon Homestead 94, 220, 226, 249–250
learnification 178–182
learning: authorised heritage discourse and 77–78, 80; defined 64, 76, 79, 178–182; difficult knowledge 2, 12, 188–189, 192, 308; educational attainment of visitors 11–12, 87, 141–142, 153, 161, 169–172; educational role of museums 74–81; emotion and 182–194, *190*, 306; empathy experiences and 183, 185–189, 192–194; epiphanies in 187–188; free-choice learning 75; individualistic learning 179; misrecognition politics and 189–190; self-identified choice to learn 186–187; social cohesion and 179; tourists and 80–81; *see also* educational role of museums
legitimacy of embodied knowledge 29–30
liberal social tensions 66
liberal values 6, 66, 298
London Museum in Docklands 142
Lower East Side Tenement Museum 98, 185–186, 202, 213, 244–245

Macdonald, Sharon 4, 26, 48, 58, 65
Madison, Dolly 276
Madison, James 221, 232, 276
Mashantucket Pequot Museum 98, 154, 212, 263, 273
meaning-making: authorised heritage discourse and 47; emotional investment in 309–310; heritage staff and visitor relations 309; impact of 300; introduction to 3, 31
memory complexes 26, 65
memory/memory-making: *aide-mémoires* 37, 257; class memory 153; house museums and 219–222; identity and 2–3; personal memories of visitors 134, 153, 210–211; postmemory 254; prosthetic memory 46, 67, 69, 250; social memory 69, 153–154, 170; triggering of 244–245; by visitors 139
Merriman, Nick 198
misreading exhibition content 293
misrecognition politics: appropriation as 299–302; heritage and 286–287; introduction to 285–286; learning and 189–190; misreading exhibition content 293; museums and heritage sites as unsafe places 287–290; not seeing/feeling by visitors 290–293, *291*; politics of recognition 281–283; self-sufficient arguments and 294–299; summary of 302; thought-terminating clichés and 293–294
mixed methods research (MMR): aims of 86–87; coding in 105–107; genres of heritage sites 91–98; history of 87–89, **88**; interviews 99–105; introduction to 2–3, 85–86; limitations with 108–109; overview of 89–91; statistics in 107–108; summary of 109
modes of engagement: affect/emotion and cognition 68–69; embodiment, defined 67; ideology 71–74; imagination and playfulness 69–70; intensity of 66; in registers of engagement 67–74; scale and scope 70; social memory 69
Montpellier house (JMM) 94, 101, 202, 232–237, 274, 276–279, *277*, 290–293, *292*
moral self-worth 245–247

moral worth 44, 260–261, 263, 268, 297
motivated social cognition 53, 66, 68, 71, 74
'moving forward' trope 296–297
Mt Kembla Heritage Centre and festival 96, 115
Multiculturalism 39, 134, 278–279, 284; and identity 271–272
Museum Basics (Ambose, Pain) 78
Museum Experience, The (Falk, Dierking) 78
Museum of Australian Democracy 243
Museum of Australian Democracy at Eureka 96, 212–213
Museum of London Docklands 112
Museum of Work and Culture 96, 240
Museums, Libraries and Archives Council (MLA) 79
museums and heritage sites: community museums 114, 240; educational role of 74–81; emotional engagement with 1–15; immigration history heritage sites 98, 152–154, 185–186; labour history heritage sites 96, 152; regional museums 114; regulatory authority of 75–76; as safe places 11, 77, 199–200, 308; social history sites 2, 58, 66, 68, 98, 150, 267; as unsafe places 11, 77, 287–290, 308; war commemoration heritage sites 93, 94–95, 114, 142, 148–149, 153, 157, 207, 253; *see also* genres of museums and heritage sites; house museums; specific heritage sites; specific museums

narrative templates 14, 58, 64, 69, 71, 146, 170, 181, 196, 205, 238, 293, 295, 302
National Civil Rights Museum (NCRM) 9, 11, 77, 89, 97, 112, 115, 142, 158, 183–184, 209–210, 251–253, 262–263, 309
National Coal Mining Museum 96, 243–244
National Cowboy and Western Heritage Museum 95, 266, 299
nationalism/national identity 75–76, 132, 148, 221, 230, 275, 287, 299
National Maritime Museum 97, 207–208
National Museum of African American History and Culture 97, 279
National Museum of American History (NMAH) 94–95, 149
National Museum of Australia (NMA) 85, 97, 101, 281, 254, 288
National Museum of Immigration 1
national sites 94–96, 144–147; defined 91–94
New Materialism (NM) 24, 31–36
'no message' response 130, 132, 137, 145–148, 150, 153–154, 156, 166–167
non-celebratory emotions 212

non-Indigenous history in Australia 155, 219, 231, 238, 256, 299–301
Non-Representational Theory (NRT) 33, 50
Nordic Heritage Museum 98
normative identities 27, 41, 268, 279
North of England Open Air Museum 96
NSW National Parks and Wildlife Service 34

Obama, Barack 72, 210, 214
occupation: defined 106; as a variable 161, 169–172; in demographics 111–112, **113**, 142
offering recognition 273–279
Old Melbourne Gaol 93, 95, 151, 255
ownership, sense of 121, 123, 138–139

parity of participation 41–43, 45, 260, 268, 286, 298
passive emotion 70, 127, 130–131, 146–155, 164–167, 294–299, 302–309
past sensing 4, 26, 47
paternalism 225, 234–235, 237–238, 295
patriotism 118, 146–151, 201–203, 233–234, 253–256, 276, 298
pedagogical significance of heritage *see* educational role of museums
pedagogy of feeling 12, 177, 182, 185, 189–190, 306
performative nature of heritage: critical performances 8–9; critical realist heritage studies 20; heritage performances 5–6, 14, 25–31, 74; intergenerational communication and connection 257; politics of recognition 13; registers of engagement 63–64
performativity/performance of practice 27–28, 86–87
performing reinforcement and affirmation: affirmation overview 209–214; collective performances of recognition/misrecognition 281–283; house museum version of 219; introduction to 196–197; overview of 200–208, *204*; social insecurities and 219; summary of 215–217
personal memories of visitors 134, 153, 210–211
platitudes 66; 130, 132, 133–134, 137, 139, 140, 146, 148, 150, 154, 156–158, 167; examples of 146, 149, 203, 221, 255
pluralism 40, 307
political conservatism 53, 67, 71, 73, 79
political power of heritage 20, 38, 39–47
politics of difference 40, 42
politics of education 179
politics of recognition: authorised heritage used as social barometers 279 280;

claims for recognition 269–273; collective performances of recognition/misrecognition 281–283; identity politics 39, 41–42, 47, 64, 260, 286; introduction to 13, 39–47, 259–260; misrecognition politics 281–283; offering recognition 273–279, 277; recognition and heritage-making 260–262; self-recognition 262–269; self-worth and 247; summary of 283–284; *see also* misrecognition politics
positive emotion 69, 73, 127, 262–263, 287, 302
Post Humanism/Post Human (PH) 24, 31–36
postmemory 254
Price of Freedom: Americans at War, The exhibit 145, 149, 203, 206, 214
privileged groups recognition claims 270
progressive affirmation 9–10, 14, 214, 305, 308
progressive values 6, 53, 63, 66, 71–79, 85, 105, 168, 214
progressive *vs.* conservative tensions 66
prosthetic memory 46, 67, 69, 250

racism 42, 45, 97, 107, 157, 193, 211, 235–236, 264, 269, 276–278, 282, 295–296, 301
recognition and heritage: affective practices of heritage 49–61; claims for recognition 269–273; democracy and 42; familial politics of recognition 242; introduction to 38–39; politics of recognition 13, 39–47, 247, 260–262; self-recognition 11, 44–45, 49, 260, 262–269; subaltern groups recognition claims 48, 270, 279, 284; *see also* identity; misrecognition politics; politics of recognition
reflexivity 14, 23–24, 37, 243
regional museums 114
registers of engagement (RoE): 'being at' houses 148, 231; defined 64, 65–66; dissonant histories 301; at dissonant sites 145; educational attainment/occupation 170; educational role of museums 74–81; ethnicity and 164, 168; at halls of fame, 150; identity and 143–144, 164; at immigration museums 152–154; at Indigenous genre 154–155; introduction to 62–65; at labour history sites 152–154; at legacies of enslavement genre 155; modes of engagement 67–74; at national sites 144, 147, 151; nationalising narratives 149; overview of 74; at presidential houses 237; reflection and introspections 144; summary of 81–82, 307–308; underpinning heritage performances 144; at war commemoration sites 149
reinforcement discourse 137–138, 207
relativism 21, 24, 179, 300
repetitive practice of visiting 205–206, 220
representational power of heritage 37, 38, 47
restorative justice 41
right-wing populism 39, 304
Rivers of Steel National Heritage Area 96, 183–184
Rouse Hill House and Farm 231, 255, 267–268, 277, 231, 241, 284
Rudd, Kevin 85, 97

sadness feelings of visitors 301–302
'safe places for unsafe ideas' phrase 77, 199–200, 287
same-sex marriage 251
Samuel, Raphael 4, 26, 28, 67, 219, 242, 307
Sayer, Andrew 21, 32, 44, 260, 267
self-assurance 7, 11, 14, 253–254
self-awareness 58, 154, 189–190, 194, 257, 301
self-determination 41
self-esteem 44, 49, 72–74, 260–263, 287, 297, 305
self-identified choice to learn 186–187
self-narration 27
self-organisation 35
self-recognition 11, 44–45, 49, 260, 262–269
self-sufficient arguments 294–299
self-talk 24, 187, 243
self-worth 247–249, 261, 264–265
sense of belonging 120, 138, 204, 221
shame 44–45, 73, 88, 145, 156, 189, 212, 265–267, 285, 287–290, 296, 301, 304, 308
Simon, Roger 2, 188, 308
Slavery at Jefferson's Monticello: Paradox of Liberty exhibit 89, 97, 157–158, 188, 279–280, 293, 298
slave trade exhibits 225–226, 274
Smithsonian National Museum of American History (NMAH) 89, 94, 95, 97, 200, 214, 279, 297
social barometer 11, 79, 279–280
social cohesion and learning 179
social constructivism 21–22, 35, 56, 90
social deference performance 222
social exclusion 7, 172, 251
social hegemony 308
social history sites 2, 58, 66, 68, 98, 150, 267
social inclusion 41, 48, 251, 279, 283, 306–307
social justice/injustice 11–12, 33–34, 46, 60, 73, 209, 247, 257–259, 285, 306, 308–309
social memory 69, 153–154, 170

social morphogenesis/morphostasis 66
social power 27
social relations 23, 42, 54
socioeconomic background 10, 47
spirituality discussions 130, 300–301
staff interviews 99
Star-Spangled Banner: The Flag That Inspired the National Anthem, The exhibit 95–96, 127, 149, 200–203, 207, 215, 253, 256, 282
state-sanctioned ontological misrecognition 286–287
Statistical Package for the Social Sciences (SPSS) 107, 161
statistics in MMR 107–108
Stockman's Hall of Fame 94–96, 101, 181–182, *204*, 203–205, 207, 208, 270, 284, 289, 290, 292
storytelling connections 246, 254
'Strategies for Change' exhibit 9
subaltern groups recognition claims 48, 270, 279, 284
subjective knowledge 76
subjective wellbeing 66
sub-national collectives and movements 30, 39, 49
sub-national identity 75–76
superficial empathy 45, 50, 301
system justification theory 66, 71–74, 79

Taylor, Charles 28–30, 40, 41, 44, 260
Temple Newsam 87, 94, 222, 223
theatres of memory 2, 4, 26, 28, 67, 219, 257, 302, 305
thought-terminating clichés 293–294
Tolpuddle Martyrs Museum 96
tourists: criticality of 7, 14, 116, 143–144, 164–169; defined 64, 80; demographics of 112, 116, 143–144; education and 115; ethnicity of 64; learning and 80–81; as management problem 50; perceptions of 50, 163; *see also* visitors
traditional management practices 32
Traditional Owners 93, 98, 183, 256, 300
Trail of Tears 62, 232, 299
transference in intergenerational communication 250–254
travel from home/vacation 163–164, 181
Trump, Donald 72, 285

Uluṟu-Kata Tjuṯa National Park 93, 98, 142, 154, 155, 183, 184, 256–257, 274–275, 299–301
UNESCO 19, 26, 29, 32–33
unions, affirmation of 187, 213, 252, 282
United States visitor correlations 111–112; *see also* visitor correlations between countries

valence of engagement 66, 120, 141, 145–149, 155, 189, 197, 218, 243–244, 287–290
values in intergenerational communication 250–254
Vaucluse House 124, 226–227, 231–232
Victorian National Trust 95
visitor correlations between countries: Australia 112; changing views 135–137, **136**; connection to heritage 121–123, **122**; contemporary relevance of exhibitions 133–135, **135**; discussion on 137–139; England 112–114; feelings of 123–127, **124**, **125**; interview population 111–116, **113**, **114**; introduction to 111; meaning-making **129**, 129–130; meaning of heritage 117–121, **118**; reasons for visiting 116–117, **117**; responses and comparisons 116; summary of 139–140; take-away from visit 130–133, **131**; United States 111–112; valued experiences 127–129, **128**
visitors: collective agency of 75, 77; defined 64–65, 80; as diffused audience 86; educational attainment of 11–12, 87, 141–142, 153, 161, 169–172; female visitors 114–115; individual agency of 75, 242–245; interviews in MMR 99–105; learning and 80–81; maintaining the status quo 7–9, 43, 48, 53, 71–81, 158, 285–286, 302–308; non-dominant backgrounds of 156, 165–168, 198; personal memories of 134, 153, 210–211; repetitive practice of visiting 205–206, 220; *see also* demographics of visitors; performing reinforcement and affirmation; tourists

war commemoration heritage sites 93, 94–95, 114, 142, 148–149, 153, 157, 207, 253
Wentworth, William 227
Wertsch, James 26, 28, 58, 69, 71, 205
Wetherell, Margaret 4, 27, 38–39, 51–60, 296
white middle-class visitors 196–197, 199, 211, 282
white racial resentment 285
Wilson, Ross 104, 105
Witcomb, Andrea 12, 177, 182, 190, 194
Wodehouse, P.G. 218
woman's movement 39
working-class history 98, 152, 198
World Heritage list 30
World Trade Centre 192

Yellowstone National Park 93, 96, 142, 144, 146, 150, 151–152, 184

Zembylas, M. 177, 194